Not Quite World's End

JOHN SIMPSON

Not Quite World's End

A Traveller's Tales

MACMILLAN

First published 2007 by Macmillan
an imprint of Pan Macmillan Ltd
Pan Macmillan, 20 New Wharf Road, London N1 9RR
Basingstoke and Oxford
Associated companies throughout the world
www.panmacmillan.com

ISBN 978-1-4050-5000-5 HB
ISBN 978-0-230-70135-9 TPB

1 3 5 7 9 8 6 4 2

A CIP catalogue record for this book is available from
the British Library.

Typeset by SetSystems Ltd, Saffron Walden, Essex
Printed and bound in Great Britain by
Mackays of Chatham plc, Chatham, Kent

Visit www.panmacmillan.com to read more about all our books
and to buy them. You will also find features, author interviews and
news of any author events, and you can sign up for e-newsletters
so that you're always first to hear about our new releases.

To my son Rafe,

in the hope that the things you see in your life will be

as interesting as the things I have seen in mine,

and a lot more peaceful.

Contents

Introduction

This is a book of stories about a particular stage in our own lives, and the life of our world: the stage at which we have started to worry seriously about its future. It isn't a book about ecology or global warming, though these things certainly appear in the pages that follow. Instead, it's intended to be a collection of snapshots of life in different parts of the world, as I have observed it over the last few years.

Because I am a journalist, and because my work takes me rather often to Iraq, many of the snapshots come from there; but (you may be glad to know) by no means all. If you go through the album with me, we will come across at least one crooked extortioner, an elusive emperor and empress, a dictator facing execution, several film-stars, a group of Bushmen facing persecution by their government, a couple of Serbian contract killers, a child sorcerer in the Congo, a group of Chinese tomb-raiders, and a variety of other thoroughly dubious people including Robert Mugabe and Alastair Campbell.

I hope this book will help you to make up your mind finally about what has happened in Iraq. And perhaps I will be fortunate enough by the end – assuming I haven't bored you too much long before that point – to persuade you to look at the world in a way which, if it isn't necessarily all that optimistic, may at least be a little more accepting.

Henry Fielding gives a warning in the early pages of *Tom Jones* about his methods, which I should probably echo at this point:

> Reader, I think proper, before we proceed any farther together,
> to acquaint thee, that I intend to digress, through this whole
> History, as often as I see Occasion.

I'll try to stick to the point, but not too much; in the hope that if you find the point tedious, the digressions may be something of a relief.

About the time I began to gather the materials for this book, I came back with my wife Dee to live in London, after a number of very happy years in Ireland. We settled in a small house near World's End in Chelsea: a place which supposedly became famous when King Charles II's coach broke down there on a wintry afternoon as he was on his way to see one of his various mistresses.

'What's the name of that inn?' he is said to have asked his coachman.

'The World's End, your majesty.'

'Highly suitable,' shuddered the king, wrapping his cloak more tightly around himself.

To me, though, it has been very far from being the end of the world. During the time we have been there and this book has taken shape, we have scored a goal in extra time by having a child: an engaging and very jolly little boy called Rafe (short for Ranulph, in the hope that he, like the original owner of his name, Sir Ranulph Fiennes, will explore his world with courage and perception). Rafe has altered my entire outlook on the world, in a way I will explain in the pages that follow.

A lot of people have helped me, of course. Some knew they were doing so, others didn't. This is the fortieth anniversary of my arrival at the BBC as a humble trainee sub-editor in the radio newsroom, and I have stayed with the BBC ever since; a bit like still living with my parents ('It's very convenient, you see . . .'). By the way, I had to inform the BBC it was my fortieth anniversary with them, and the occasion, such as it was, went unmarked by any kind of celebration. Well, did the Man In The Iron Mask get a cake from his warders? I imagine not. But the great thing about the BBC isn't the way it treats you, it's that it offers the opportunity to work with a large number of talented and mostly very pleasant people at the BBC, a few of whom will appear in this book.

So it is dedicated to quite a few people. To the producers, editors, cameramen, technicians, security advisers, secretaries, receptionists, telephonists and others of the BBC whom I have worked alongside in the past and present – including the charming ladies of the tea-bar at Television Centre. To my bosses, more in number than the sands of the sea, I have also good reason to be grateful because of their tolerance of someone who has never really been very compliant. To Mark Nelthorpe-Cowne, who accompanied me on a couple of the adventures in this book, and has been both excellent company and a splendid manager. To his wife Gina, Dee's sister, who has been my unfailingly good-tempered and loving PA. To Julian Alexander, best, most imaginative and most amusing of agents. To George Morley, my editor at Macmillan, whose charm and enthusiasm and frequent kindness has always jollied me along when times were rough. To Philippa McEwan, whose company around the country makes the business of publicizing a book more enjoyable than I ever thought possible, and to all the others at Macmillan who have made my publishing life a genuine pleasure. To Joe Phua, cameraman and friend, who helped with the cover of this book in his usual generous fashion. To Tamsin Jaggers, who runs the World Affairs Unit at the BBC, and fields all sorts of unreasonable demands for me and from me. To Agnieszka Freeman, who was generous with her time and helpful when I needed the illustrations that follow. To the fixers and translators around the world whose work it celebrates. And finally, of course, to my wife, Dee, whose love and help and advice has sustained this whole book, and who has been obliged to give up travelling with me (which she unaccountably enjoyed), in order to tend to the superb little boy we almost thought we would never have.

London, June 2007

1

WORLD'S END

It may not entirely have escaped your attention that the world seems to be getting worse.

Most people would say that their lives were often more violent, usually more disturbed, and always less predictable than in the past. Nuclear weapons are spreading, violence is rampant, terrorism has become commonplace, the breakdown of conventional morality has weakened our relationships with one another.

Of course, anxiety has been a leading feature of every decade for the past century, and probably forever; people in the supposedly golden Edwardian years before the First World War were worried sick by the rise of German militarism, the decline of Britain's standing in the world, the growth of violence in Ireland and in the streets of Britain, and the sudden manifestation of free love, socialism, feminism and strange new art forms.

But there is one difference: nowadays we worry that the very existence of our world is threatened. Billions of people face shortages of water and food, and the increased danger of flooding. Climate change would (no, will – this isn't just some vague theory) be devastating for the world's poor. And therefore it will have a savage effect on the world's rich as well.

Since the end of the Second World War, what we vaguely call, with some geographical inaccuracy, 'the West', meaning the developed countries of the world, has experienced the most remarkable period of economic growth in human history. Yet it doesn't seem to have made us particularly happy or safe: at the start of the twenty-first century the chances of being robbed or violently attacked are approximately twice as great throughout 'the West' as they were in the early 1950s. (Nevertheless statistics of this sort aren't necessarily much of a guide to the nature of the life around us. It wasn't until

D-Day in 1944 that the fighting in the Second World War took over as the leading cause of premature death other than illness for the British people. From September 1939 to that point, despite all the bombs that had rained down on British cities, and despite the fighting on four continents, the chief cause of death had been the un-glamorous road accident.)

The great majority of us lead a far more comfortable existence than at any previous stage in history. Things that were beyond the reach of the super-rich sixty years ago are standard for most people now. Even our children have mobile phones. We are all constantly entertained in ways of our own choosing, we scarcely have to wait for anything we want, and we expect to have holidays in the warmest and most distant places.

In the world at large, more people live in abject poverty than ever before, yet the poor now form a noticeably smaller proportion of the human race. When, at any previous time in human existence, could anyone even have suggested staging a campaign to Make Poverty History? That has happened in our time; and, if we were only prepared to make some fairly basic sacrifices, we might actually achieve it.

But above all, we who live in the wealthy countries of the world have come to expect that our lives will be peaceful: something that no other generation in human history could have considered. There are fewer full-scale wars going on now than at any time since 1945. It is true that Tony Blair, during his ten years in office, involved Britain in more wars than any prime minister for forty years. But there were only four of them, and by the standards of the twentieth century they were mostly small affairs, in faraway countries of which most people knew little. By the start of 2007 the so-called War on Terror, supposedly the great issue of our time, had been quietly put to one side, and even George W. Bush's White House decided not to mention the phrase in public any more. The police and the intelli-gence services took the leading role in countering terrorism, and the soldiers concentrated on trying to shore up the governments which the Americans and British had created in Iraq and Afghanistan.

Altogether, living in Britain after the end of the Second World War was rather like living in Queen Victoria's reign: great and

growing wealth at home, small wars abroad, and occasional outbursts of terrorist violence which achieved nothing.

It is only human nature, of course, to assume that we can go on
like this indefinitely. British people thought, right up to the day in
July 1914 when the Archduke Franz Ferdinand was murdered by a
Serbian extremist, that life would simply continue as before. Five
years earlier, the leading political theorist Norman Angell – his full
name was Ralph Norman Angell Lane, and he was later knighted
and awarded the Nobel Peace prize – had published a huge best-
seller called *Europe's Optical Illusion*, later issued in the US as *The
Great Illusion*. The cineaste Jean Renoir borrowed the book's title
for his magnificent film. Angell argued that the international economy meant that war had become entirely futile, and was virtually
unthinkable between civilized nations. He didn't quite say that war
had become impossible, but that was the comfortable impression
most people drew from it; which is why they bought his book in
such numbers.

Nor was this the first time that it was possible to believe in the
inevitability of peace. Just over a century earlier, in 1792, William
Pitt the Younger, who was usually a remarkably sensible politician,
told the House of Commons, 'There never was a time when, from
the situation, we might more reasonably expect fifteen years of
peace.' The words were only just spoken when the execution of
King Louis XVI took place. The war which broke out with France
was to last, on and off, for twenty-three years.

Imagining anything radically different from our comfortable,
peaceful existence is really hard. It was well into the start of 1940
before people in Britain or France could be persuaded to take the
war with Nazi Germany seriously. Human beings have always had
a tendency to assume that everything will continue pretty much as
usual; we don't trouble to envision anything else. As I write this,
western Europe has experienced sixty-two years of unbroken peace
and prosperity. The only time such a thing has ever happened before
were the eighty-four years of peace and prosperity which the Roman
empire enjoyed from 96 to 180, under the emperors Nerva, Trajan,
Hadrian, Antoninus Pius and Marcus Aurelius. Edward Gibbon
famously wrote of this period,

If a man were called to fix the period in the history of the world during which the condition of the human race was most happy and prosperous, he would, without hesitation, name that which elapsed from the death of Domitian to the accession of Commodus.

Unfortunately, Commodus turned out to be a disgustingly bad ruler, a man constructed along the lines of Uday Hussein, Saddam's son. Rome's decline, once started in earnest as a result of his rule, never really stopped until the empire itself collapsed, more than two hundred years later. Contrary to popular belief, prosperity and good governance aren't inevitable: they have to be worked at.

§

In 2000 I wrote a book called *A Mad World, My Masters*, which was a series of traveller's tales. This new book of mine is slightly different; I think of it more as a book of tales by a traveller. You may think that a pretty pointless distinction to make, and I agree that it probably doesn't matter very much; but I didn't want the stories to be largely unrelated this time, as they were before. I wanted this to be a book with attitude.

So there is a kind of theme to it. Often it will be so faint that it will be hard, maybe even impossible, to detect; but to my mind it's there, all the same. I have tried to create a kind of mosaic of our strange world in recent years: wonderful, appalling, immensely sad, uplifting, depressing, optimistic, stupid, full of imagination and creativity and destructiveness, and heavily under threat. A continuing theme in the book is the war in Iraq, because for the past five years that has dominated my life. But other things have dominated it too: especially the birth in January 2006 of my son Rafe, which has changed me greatly.

Until a couple of decades ago, it was usual for authors to put a little tag from another writer on the title page of their books: the more highbrow the writer and the more obscure the tag, the better: *Bread was his lust, and pain his glory – Rilke*; you know the sort of thing. Graham Greene used to go in for it, perhaps because he found it funny. Now, though, the habit has gone out of fashion, just as hand-drawn illustrations have gone out of fashion and seem landed, then turned away because his mother rang his mobile phone to wish him a happy birthday and so saved his life. We praised the courage and firmness under fire of our security adviser, Craig Summers, who rescued all our luggage from our burning car. We talked in affectionate terms about Dragan Petrovic, who had come with us to northern Iraq even though his wife had been about to give birth, and who had staggered across after the bomb landed to pick me up and pull me to safety, because he thought another one might hit us at any moment. And we talked about the remarkable pictures our cameramen had got of it all.

Then, in the way of these things, we ordered three glasses of some fiery white spirit and a small dish of *dulce de leche* to share between us, and started talking about something else.

So it was understandable that I should have had my nightmare that night. Yet even so it came as a complete surprise. After four years, I thought I had come to terms with the bombing and its terrible aftermath, the bodies burning, the eviscerated man stumbling around, the brains lying on the ground. But I suppose you never do sort these things out entirely, and they attract other, unrelated memories, like the rail of a sunken ship attracts coral.

In my dream I lay in a gutter, sheltering from the bombs. The only time I have taken shelter in a gutter was in June 1989, during the massacre in Tiananmen Square. I could take you now to the place in Chang'an Avenue where I threw myself down that night; and I promise you, a kerbstone gives remarkably little cover from bullets. Perhaps that, rather than the bombing, was what disturbed my sleep.

But the apologizing was completely up to date. The fact that I have had a baby son at the advanced age of sixty-two is one that the professional busybodies of Fleet Street have discussed often and sometimes condemned roundly. Like the inquisitive neighbour who twitches the curtains and watches your comings and goings with disapproval, the columnists of Britain's wonderful newspapers have also criticized the fact that I continue to work in places like Iraq and Afghanistan; as though any of it is their business. I suppose this sort of thing must have found its way into the area of the mind at which dreams and nightmares are formed.

Much of my life is spent in the sordid places of the earth; the

Plaza Hotel in Buenos Aires being one of the rare and very welcome exceptions. Nowadays, usually with my two colleagues Oggy and Nick, I travel to Baghdad every six weeks or so, and to all sorts of other countries in between. Going there is interesting, it is worthwhile, and it means I can talk with some authority about Iraq when I have to. But what, of course, the newspaper columnists have spotted is that I enjoy it, in a masochistic sort of way; and as a result they condemn it. It's true that these are often the most interesting places to visit; what would there be to talk about, after all, if I just went backwards and forwards to Geneva, or Chicago, or Dubai? Or, God help us, if I stayed at the BBC's soulless offices at Shepherd's Bush?

So I carry on travelling; and because I travel for news, my journeys often take me to the rougher kind of place. But I suppose, if I were to be really honest (and what's the point of writing a book if you can't be honest in it?), I suppose I feel nowadays that it's a way of fending off the approach of old age. Maybe, too, I want to demonstrate that it's perfectly possible to be over sixty, with white hair and a lived-in face, and still be immensely active. Others of my kind of age, I can see, feel the same impulsion: Sir Robin Knox-Johnston, the yachtsman, for instance, or the explorer Sir Ranulph Fiennes, a friend after whom my wife and I named our newly arrived son. (Soon, though, we cut his name down to Rafe, because Ranulph seemed a little daunting for someone only eighteen inches long.)

This attitude to age is unquestionably something to do with our generation. We are the ones who reached adulthood in the 1960s, and we were taught then to regard ourselves as the pinnacle of human civilization. Now that we are moving from late middle age towards eventual old age, I suppose we find it hard to cede that position to others. And at the same time each of us seems to want to send out a message, not just about ourselves but about others: that it isn't necessary to start the long decline into inactivity and irrelevance just because you've notched up more than three-score.

§

Sometimes it seems there are so many threats to our life and prosperity that it's hard to choose which of them to concentrate on. Human existence is becoming a little like one of those video games where you are a soldier dodging down endless corridors with some ludicrously large weapon in your hands, while enemies of every conceivable description jump out at you from all sides. The proliferation of nuclear weapons, not always in the safest hands; the enormous weight of First World debt; the rise of China, the return of Russia, the lack of strength in Europe and the obvious decline of America; grotesque overpopulation; the terrifying consequences of global warming; each of these things can destroy the delicate balance of our lives. But perhaps our civilization won't be destroyed by bankruptcy or terrorism or vicious dictators, but by a simple sneeze. Disease is a greater threat to our civilization than anything else, including global warming.

If some particularly virulent disease were to attach itself to the influenza virus and mutate, then we could see an enormous death toll in our crowded cities. Over the centuries, nature does occasionally seem to feel the weight of humanity on its shoulders, and shrug – with the most terrible consequences. The loss of life across Europe during the Black Death, from 1348 to the early 1350s, may have been as high as half the entire population. The influenza pandemic which swept across the exhausted world in 1918 and 1919, apparently gaining its huge strength among the soldiers in the trenches, killed between twenty and forty million people – many times more than died in the First World War itself. Quick, concerted action stopped the spread of the SARS virus after it appeared in November 2002, and only 774 people died of it. But such viruses show a remarkable cunning, and another outbreak with different causes might be harder to stop. The British government regards the threat from disease as greater than that from any other cause, including terrorism; and it believes that if there were a major pandemic like the influenza of 1918–19, anything up to 700,000 people might die in Britain alone.

But even if we manage to avoid some catastrophic outbreak of disease, we may simply experience the kind of slow decline which destroyed the Roman empire: corruption and weak government at home, coupled with the immense pressure from the poor, huddled masses outside our boundaries, whose homes are threatened or destroyed by the ecological disaster which our own carelessness has created.

This must be a serious possibility. Thomas Malthus may have got it wrong back in 1798 when he wrote his *Essay on the Principle of Population*, arguing that there were simply too many people on the planet for the amount of food they could produce. But now that there are six billion of us, and our unchecked activities have threatened the amount of land available for the growing of food, maybe we should re-read Malthus with a bit more sympathy.

We have, of course, fouled our own nest pretty comprehensively. The time when it was possible for sensible, unbiased people to wonder whether global warming was really happening, or whether the obvious changes in the world's climate were just a passing phase, has passed. Even in 1997 the evidence was thoroughly convincing, but only a few governments wanted to know about it. Today you have to be a committed contrarian to deny that there is a serious threat – or else, like the governments of the United States, India, China and others, you have to have a very clear short-term vested interest in claiming that it doesn't really matter too much, and that other, more immediate concerns are more important.

Even now, the proof is still not total. The best report so far was issued in several parts in 2007 by the Intergovernmental Panel on Climate Change, which included officials from the United Nations and governments around the world, and a large gathering of independent scientists. The scientific work which the IPCC's scientists reviewed included nearly thirty thousand pieces of data on physical and biological changes in the natural world, and found that 89 per cent of them were consistent with the idea that the world was heating up. The rise was, the report said (after much haggling over the wording, as a result of the reluctance of the Americans, Indians and Chinese), at least 90 per cent likely to be due to man-made greenhouse gas emissions.

Perhaps some of the scientists' rhetoric about the dangers of global warming is exaggerated; you have to scare people thoroughly if you are going to make them ignore their short-term interests and change the way they behave. But it smacks of wilfulness nowadays to argue that the evidence is not compelling.

Some of the worst possibilities can be averted if the world takes action by about 2015. But even maximum intervention and change, if all governments embraced it here and now (which they won't), will not prevent some of the devastating effects of global warming. The glaciers and polar ice-caps will continue to melt, at a much faster rate than we originally thought, and the result will be higher sea-levels, more flooding, and even more pressure on the existing land.

Higher sea-levels will ensure that poverty increases, rather than decreases, and greater poverty will mean less population control; which, as Robert Malthus correctly noted, is the only way of preventing disaster. By 2035, on present trends, there will be 8.5 billion people in world, and 98 per cent of them will be in the less developed countries. Poverty and faster population growth, acting upon each other, will bring more instability and extremism. The population of the Middle East, already the most unstable part of the world, is expected to grow by 132 per cent by 2035. Saudi Arabia, once an under-populated, docile country, has seen its population grow from seven million in 1980 to twenty-seven million by 2005. There is a clear undercurrent there of violence and anger.

To protect itself from unrest and terrorism, the Western world could well find itself using its technological advantages in ways which would be completely unacceptable at present. Faced with an overwhelming threat to their existence, people might empower their governments to take all sorts of violent and aggressive steps. In thirty years' time, a multitude of new and devastating weapons will be available to the advanced governments of the world. Many will be based in space, and neutron technology can produce weapons which will destroy all human life in a city at the touch of a button, yet do no damage to its buildings or structures.

You could imagine that by 2048, a century after George Orwell wrote *1984*, three or more large national blocs might well live in a state of complete mutual hostility, each capable of destroying the others yet held back by fear of the consequences, just as his Oceania, Eurasia and Eastasia were. To guard against terrorist infiltration, the different blocs would bar their borders against travellers and infiltrators. Holidays or business visits outside the blocs would be a long-distant memory. So would be a liberal approach to human rights. Superstates like these would maintain themselves in power by whipping up nationalist scares, fear of foreigners, and hysteria.

Monster cities will have swallowed up much of the national

territory. Immense *favelas* and shanty towns, greater than anything on earth at present, will surround them. These supercities,
unpoliced, unprovided for, deprived of basic decency and self-
respect, will be an immense source of rage and violence. A new class
warfare will exist, along roughly Marxist lines, with the have-nots
terrorizing the haves and forcing them to adopt ever-nastier forms
of self-protection.

As for the natural world, it would be cleared of much of its
animal, bird, insect and plant life. Tigers, gorillas, orang-utans, the
black rhinoceros, the Amur leopard and more than a thousand
other species of mammals will have ceased to exist in the wild. One
in eight species of bird will have vanished. So will ten thousand
species of flora. The dawns will be largely silent, the forest floors
and meadows bare of everything except the most common plants.

Whatever is still rich and rare about our world will be gone,
and we will have to go to zoos and special parks to have any idea
of what we have driven out and destroyed. The earth is already in
the grip of a mass extinction. In the normal way, species come and
go all the time; but the present process is anything from a hundred
to a thousand times worse than the natural 'background' level of
disappearance.

Of course, a great deal of this could have been written twenty-
five years ago, and it would all have been true: not quite in the way
it looks on the printed page, perhaps, but in aggregate. Supercities
already exist. If you travel twenty or thirty miles out from the centre
of Lima, for instance, through the urban sprawl, you will come to
the newest slums of all, on the very edges of the city. They spring
up on the bare desert floor without water or sewerage or transport
or schools, filled with the violent and the ignorant and the vengeful.
The only thing these people possess apart from a few belongings is
the vote, and demagogues of the left and right depend upon them
for their sudden rise and angry policies.

Class war between the destitute and the moderately wealthy
already exists in South Africa today, and only the South African
government refuses to acknowledge it. In 2006 there were hundreds
of violent attacks each day, in which an average of fifty people were
killed. South Africa, a delightful country in so many ways, and an

example to the rest of the world in terms of political decency and reconciliation, is one of the three most violent nations on earth.

Colombia is another, with its political instability and its cocaine wars; Iraq, its balance and stability as a nation hopelessly compromised by the American and British invasion of 2003, is the third. But Colombia and Iraq are special cases; South Africa is not. Apartheid did terrible damage to its basic moral structure, and population growth along the lines of the Middle East and elsewhere has given birth to a new culture of total violence and an almost complete lack of compunction.

'He was looking into my eyes all the time,' said a Nigerian woman in Johannesburg, describing the moment when an armed robber broke into her house. 'He put his gun against my baby's head and watched my face as he pulled the trigger.'

This was murder for its own sake: murder that had nothing to do with stealing money, or getting revenge for the injustices of apartheid.

And what about the xenophobic states which Orwell predicted in *1984*, frightened and angry about the outside world, and determined to control the lives of their citizens? Well, we saw a little of that in the United States after the attacks of 11 September 2001. Orwell would have recognized the PATRIOT Act as a perfect example of Newspeak. A few brave journalists and writers stayed firm against the general hysteria in America and ran the risk of being branded as unpatriotic – 'traitors', more than one reporter on Rupert Murdoch's Fox News called them. Some of this awkward squad, whose members included Gore Vidal, Graydon Carter and Lewis Lapham, noted at the time that scarcely any of the members of Congress who voted for the PATRIOT Act, Democrats as well as President George W. Bush's Republicans, actually had the time or the inclination to read through the wording of the act before voting it into law.

So we are not heading towards this disturbing future from a clean start. We have already shown our capacity for mindless violence, and our vulnerability to the hysteria of resentment. We have done great damage to ourselves and our environment, and the chances are that this damage will grow worse.

Yet it is important to try to keep a sense of balance about it all. People in Peru and Saudi Arabia and South Africa can live perfectly decent, law-abiding, happy lives, without being touched by violence or extremism. We may well lose some of the most beautiful and interesting animals and birds on the planet, yet we have already lost a great deal and still find our natural world fascinating and complex. In spite of our fears, we travel more now than we have ever done before, and London has resumed its old place as the world's capital city because it has taken in more immigrants from every part of the globe, just as New York did before it.

Past generations would have been appalled by the crudity and brashness and violence of our times, but we take it all for granted and would simply like to damp down some of the less attractive consequences. We certainly wouldn't want to go back in time and re-experience Edwardian medicine, or 1930s class-consciousness, or 1950s holidays.

To our grandparents and great-grandparents we would seem unbearably aggressive, godless and uncultured. Yet we rather like our world, and compare it very favourably indeed with the past, about which we tend to be critical and patronizing. Despite our dreadful reality TV, our coarseness of language and action, our celebrity-worship, our tabloids and our violence, we feel ourselves to be more advanced than any of the generations of the past, and their snobbery and racism and dreariness are unbearable to us.

The lesson, I suppose, is that human beings can get used to anything, and quickly make themselves comfortable with it as a result. Our adaptability is one of the main reasons for the fact that we have come dangerously close to destroying our planet; but it also helps us, not just to keep going, but to enjoy ourselves.

At the end of this book of stories, if you manage to get that far, I will put a rather different case from the one I have so far outlined. Countries, it seems to me, find their own balance, and what might seem hellish and unlivable to one generation is natural and sensible and logical to another. There is no reason for us to slash our wrists quite yet. Just as the future will seem better in some respects, it will also be intolerably dreadful by our standards. And yet the people who inhabit it will look back on us – *us!* – as dull, rather absurd primitives.

In the meantime, although we have every reason to be anxious about the future, our basic common sense (another of our protective, highly successful qualities) will keep most of us from committing mass suicide. We will endure the changes ahead with remarkable calmness, continuing to adapt our lives to the changes around us. There will be a few who will become over-excited along headless-chicken lines. During the late 1970s a couple in Canada became convinced that all-out thermonuclear war was inevitable, and that North America would be incinerated. So they took their children, uprooted themselves from their comfortable home and fled to the farthest and safest part of the earth in order to escape the dreadful certainty of war.

At the end of 1981, they arrived in the Falkland Islands. Four months later, the Argentines invaded.

§

Recently my wife Dee and I came back to live in London after a long and highly enjoyable time in Ireland. Leaving our flat in the outskirts of Dublin was a sad business. Behind us, the electronic security gates (to which everyone in the village seemed to know the code) juddered and squeaked to a close. We looked at each other: after years of living beside the sea in the village of Dalkey, we were leaving. The last couple of suitcases, containing everything from a tasteless commemoration mug from the handover of Hong Kong to an odd volume of Thomas Moore's poems, filled the back seat.

I shoved the car into gear, and we swung off for the last time down the hill to Bullock Harbour, to Dun Laoghaire, to the airport and thence to London. We would never again sit on the rocks with a glass of champagne in our hands, looking out across the placid waters of Dublin Bay to Howth Head, or lie in bed at night listening to the wind howling round the eaves, or walk through the quiet village to get the papers on a Sunday morning, or sit drinking a pint of something warm and bitter in the bantering conversation and thick atmosphere of Finnegan's pub: still, I think, the finest pub I have ever come across.

Another chapter of my life had closed. It happened because of a meeting I had late one afternoon in a featureless office in Television Centre in London, when I realized from something one of my many, many bosses had just said that everyone was expecting me to fade out pretty soon.

'Presumably you'll be wanting to spend more time writing books now,' he said.

Having worked for the BBC for forty years, I spotted the danger signal at once. I knew, as he didn't, that I had a very good reason for not wanting to stop work. After some years and much disappointment, Dee was expecting a baby, and that would require me to have a proper full-time job for a long time to come.

Dublin had been wonderfully good to us, and we had had an unforgettable time; but there was no denying that living there had given a certain early retirement feel to our lives. Perhaps it was the fact that after a week or ten days there, we found it hard to remember anything we'd done.

'Was it last Tuesday or Wednesday that we saw that film about the man who gets shot? You know, the one with that girl in it.'

'What month is it?'

'Oh God, I think I was supposed to ring the office yesterday.'

Or perhaps it was the way I found myself looking out at the sea through the sitting-room window, and calling out to Dee that the ferry from Holyhead was just coming in: something it did twice a day.

Being in Dalkey was immensely restful, and after a difficult tour of duty somewhere like Afghanistan or Iraq it seemed like a brief foretaste of heaven. But heaven was something I wasn't really anticipating for some decades to come. Delightful though it was, I couldn't bear it if that was all there was to my life.

'I'm not thinking of giving up work, you know,' I said in the sudden quietness of the BBC office.

'Really?'

I detected a sudden alarm in his voice. BBC managers, even nice ones like him, have to do their choreography two or three years in advance. Someone would be moved up into my empty place, and someone else would be moved into theirs, and a third person into theirs; it was all planned out like a chess game. And now one of the

'No, really. I'm staying. Indefinitely.'

I made it sound as if I were a mildly unwelcome guest at an hotel, and the pleasant man sitting opposite me in the gathering dpieces on the board was arguing with the chess-player about the next move, like something out of *Alice's Adventures Through The Looking-Glass*.

arkness was duly obliged to make the comforting noises the hotel manager might make: we're absolutely delighted, of course, to hear that you're staying, and arrangements will be made at once to take account of it, and how would you like to settle the bill? He'd been a good friend of mine for decades; but it often occurs to me that if the BBC could arrange it so that you paid to work there, instead of the other way round, the managers would enjoy life a bit more.

And so I went back and told Dee that the BBC thought I was winding down to retirement, and she walked around the room a little, her hands under her stomach, and we agreed that we would have to come back to settle in London, otherwise the moment might come when the BBC would forget to pay me altogether.

And so eventually we found a house which no one else had wanted to buy, because the owner, a rather monstrous Spanish art dealer, had had the walls and ceilings painted with murals of a gruesomely rococo nature: there were naked cherubs and Roman emperors everywhere. It didn't worry either of us, though all that flesh on the ceilings and walls might have taken a bit of explaining to the baby at some point. They certainly took enough explaining to the decorator who had to paint them over.

There were worse problems: none of our furniture fitted, because it was large and rangy and leather-covered: the African explorer look. By contrast, this was a house that required spindly chairs and tiny, exquisite side-tables. I liked it very much. But what I liked best about it was the little garden, and the early sixteenth-century brick wall at the end of it.

I would sit out there, reflecting that this wall had stood here quietly while Columbus fumed about his latest voyage to the Americas, and my old school was starting to teach its second batch of pupils, and Sir Thomas More was worrying about whether Henry VIII was getting a bit too demanding. I didn't even mind the aircraft that flew low overhead. After a while you get used to having conversations that last around forty-five seconds. As I said, humans are amazingly adaptable, and the abominable noise of far too many overcrowded jetliners flying too low overhead has not the slightest effect on the price of property around here. It's as though we don't even hear it.

And so yet another phase in my life, which hadn't exactly been short of phases, began. Our house was close to World's End, whose name has a slightly unnerving ring to it for someone who does the kind of work that I do; and we were very happy. People would greet me in the King's Road as though we had been friends for years, but in a quiet, specifically British way that meant they just gave me a little smile and hurried on so as not to intrude. I only had a little trouble twice, once when someone screamed at me for revealing that Colonel Gaddafi had a problem with farting, and once when someone else accused me of being personally responsible for the revolution that overthrew the Shah of Iran.

'Oh, leave it out, dad,' shouted a man who was painting the house next door, and the infuriated little old Iranian wandered off in his shell-suit, still muttering.

As our good and much-missed friend and neighbour, the sculptor Eduardo Paolozzi, once said about some other minor drawback of daily life, it was a small price to pay for living in paradise. And after I've spent a few weeks in Baghdad or Kabul, wandering from World's End to Sloane Square can seem just as therapeutic, just as restorative, as sitting on the rocks at Bartra with a glass of something encouraging in my hand, peering down into the green waters of Dublin Bay to see if our resident seal was around.

§

There was a time, at the start of the 1990s, when in every country I visited – China, Argentina, Russia, South Africa, Japan, various parts of Europe, the United States – people told me how unusual the weather seemed to be. In hot countries it would be unseasonably cold; in cold countries, spring came earlier, and summer lasted longer. Temperate countries were sweltering, tropical countries were drenched with unexpected downpours or parched with drought. I thought of writing something about it at the time. If I had, I might have been able to claim some kind of credit for spotting the first clear signs of global warming. Characteristically, I never got round to it.

Perhaps, as with some wonderful, immensely complex machine that has developed a fault, something has gone fundamentally wrong with the world and its weather. It wouldn't be altogether surprising if it had, since for two hundred and fifty years mankind has been pumping the fiercest and most destructive gases into the earth's atmosphere. Our population has been doubling in size every few decades, and the richer we are, the more and faster we have trashed our surroundings.

We have of course had major scares before. In the 1970s we were certain that a new Great Freeze was about to begin; and scientists of great repute and experience seemed to put their weight behind it. In 1998 the scientific advisers to various Western governments became obsessed with the idea that all our computers were going to stop at midnight on 31 December 1999, aircraft would drop out of the sky, and civilized existence would collapse. One major international bank spent three-quarters of a billion pounds changing its entire equipment as a result. And, of course, nothing whatsoever happened. Advanced societies become prey to sudden fears like this, just as less developed societies do. The human animal prefers to hunt in packs, like chimpanzees or African wild dogs, and (contrary to the general opinion) scientists are almost as human as the rest of us.

These sudden mass fears are usually separated just enough in time from each other so that we have forgotten the previous one. The Great Freeze notion was highly popular at roughly the same time as the Great Oil Crisis of 1973, when several Arab countries cut off the supply of oil to the Netherlands, which supported Israel in the war of that year. The boycott spread, and only a fairly intensive act of grovelling by the Heath government in Britain, as well as by other European countries, got the oil flowing again.

My father, an instinctive, anarchic contrarian who was no great admirer of Edward Heath, Arabs, or the modern age, decided that oil was finished as the main fuel of choice for the Western world, and started negotiating with great enthusiasm for a pony and trap. The crisis finished before the negotiations did, or else my father would have got around Suffolk the slow way for the rest of his life.

He wasn't alone in his apocalyptic views. Economists played the role ecologists do now, and the newspapers were full of the greatest doom-saying. Europe was finished, and so was America, which was in the latter stages of the Watergate scandal. The region of the future, where the real wealth and its resulting political strength would come from, was – the Middle East. The huge rise in the price of oil seemed to confirm that. Arabs bought houses and great business concerns and a huge amount of political influence, and earned a good deal of unpopularity as a result.

And of course it didn't last; how could it? The theory that the Middle East was the future took its place in the recycle bin with the earlier theory, much in vogue in the United States, that Europe was finished and that – of all places – the Soviet bloc was going to dominate us all. There were various other whims and fashions after that, ending in the 1990s with the absolute certainty that the future lay with the Pacific Rim. After the collapse of the Thai baht in 1997, you scarcely ever heard the expression 'Pacific Rim' again – nor 'Asian tigers' either. All that is left of the idea is the occasional use, in Ireland, of the expression 'Celtic Tiger', left behind on the seashore of public discourse like the body of some strange fish, washed up from a completely different ocean.

So nowadays, when Americans tell us that Europe is old and exhausted, and Europeans tell themselves that America's day is over, and that India and China are the future, I sometimes allow myself a moment's scepticism. India is a wonderful country, vibrant and exciting, but it has a great many social and political problems. As for China, it has never managed to free itself intellectually from the bondage of Mao Zedong's brand of Marxism-Leninism, and still cannot work out how to let people think and act for themselves. Ever since 1945, long-term economic success has belonged virtually exclusively to countries with free and open systems. The one has depended on the other.

All the same, it is perfectly possible for countries to pick themselves up and turn their economies into a new wonder of the world. The Japanese did it, and they have remained the second largest economy in the world ever since. I remember how scathing people in Britain were during the early 1950s when the Japanese started to make simple gadgets. At that time, 'Made in Japan' simply meant 'shoddy'. But by the late fifties, all that had changed. The Japanese were starting to make motorbikes, and I remember reading an article in the British press – the old *News Chronicle*, perhaps, which was killed off in 1960 – which said, 'Heaven help us all if the Japanese ever decide to manufacture motor-cars.'

Half a century later, Britain, which was the world's leading exporter of motor vehicles in 1950, scarcely has a motor industry to call its own; though, curiously, it manufactures more cars than almost any other European country, many of them for the Japanese. 'Thus the whirligig of time brings in his revenges': another Shakespearean line, this time from *Twelfth Night*, which I might have put on the title page of this book.

Japan, Germany and France, which were all well ahead of Britain in terms of wealth and gross national product during the 1970s and 80s, all stumbled in the late 1990s, while Britain rebounded. Who nowadays thinks that Frankfurt is a serious rival to London, now that London is in the process of overtaking New York as the world's main financial centre? Its social centre too: London has the world's second biggest population of French people outside France, and when Nicolas Sarkozy was campaigning for the French presidency in 2007 he felt it worth his while to come to London and bid for their votes. London has the first or second largest external populations of many countries, among them Brazil, Russia, Poland, the Czech Republic, Japan, Algeria, Lebanon, Libya, Iraq, Iran, as well as America, South Africa and Australia. As you sit on a London bus, you are likely to hear people talking to each other in Japanese, Russian, Arabic, French, Spanish or German, and their telephone habits have affected the host nation as well. One of the many social changes that have happened in my lifetime is that the British, who once used to whisper for fear of disturbing everyone else, now shout the most intimate details of their lives down the phone.

'Yes, I told him I would sleep with him, but only that one night because I was going back to Gary the next day,' a rather nice-looking blonde girl yelled into her mobile on the 49 bus recently. Lucky old Gary, I thought; but her mother, and even more so her grandmother, would have been horrified.

Other changes are happening too quickly to take in. There are so many Poles in Britain that Catholicism is likely to become the country's leading religion in a few years. Yet for the first time in decades the Church of England has reversed the long decline in the numbers of people attending its services in London. This is partly because of the Anglicans from Africa who worship there, but only partly. My local church, which is mostly full of ethnic Britons, is packed out three times a day, and as with the cinema you have to be there early to get a decent seat.

Nothing stays the same; but things are changing, and the past is receding, faster than at any other period in my lifetime. Twenty years ago, no one would have believed that going to the pub could possibly fade as a pastime; it was the ambition of thousands of men and women to buy a pub and eventually retire on the proceeds. Now, hundreds of pubs close down every year, and those which are left are often scarcely recognizable as pubs at all: they are more like restaurants or coffee-houses, and the solitary old men in raincoats with dogs sitting at their feet seem to have been left over from a different era. As early as 1978 curry had replaced fish and chips as the British food of choice. Now curry itself has been replaced as the favourite by a mix of cooking styles, among them Thai and Italian.

Until about 1998 I used to congratulate myself on my good luck – it was nothing more than that – at having got the kind of job in the kind of organization in the kind of industry that would last me out. So many of my friends and colleagues in journalism had fallen by the wayside: they had gone to newspapers or television news organizations that were constantly culling their staff. Even within the BBC, the amount of documentary-making dropped sharply, and current affairs programmes were either cut back or disappeared altogether. Only BBC News, the area I worked in, seemed to hold its own, and even grow in size. News, we thought, would always be in demand.

Not so. Audiences continue to drop, and not because there are now so many news channels on television. With the exception of News 24 on the BBC, each of the others – Sky News, CNN, Al-Jazeera – has a minuscule audience in Britain. The various news websites have all shown sharp rises, but not enough to replace the missing audiences for television news and the readership of newspapers. All the signs are that British people are becoming less interested in the world around them.

Once upon a time we used to think that isolationism like this was something particularly American, just like high levels of crime, the possession of guns, wide-scale drug addiction and not turning out to vote at elections. Americans weren't interested much in anything that happened outside their city and their state, let alone outside their country, whereas Europeans had excellent newspapers and good television news – and the British more than any of them. Now we find that in all these areas – crime, drugs and isolationism – Europe was merely lagging behind America; it wasn't fundamentally different from it.

Once, watching the *Nine O'Clock News* on the BBC or the *News at Ten* on Independent Television was a kind of national duty for large numbers of people. In 1981 and 1982, I presented the *Nine O'Clock News*. When, from time to time, the audience dropped below ten million, this was felt to be my fault, and the fault of the other main presenter, John Humphrys. Yet ITN had an audience of approximately the same size, which was also inclined to slip below the ten-million mark. It took people some time to realize that the number watching the news, and even being interested in what was happening in the country and the world, was slowly dropping.

Nowadays, the thought that twenty million people – 40 per cent of the entire British population – would sit in front of their television sets each night to watch the news seems almost absurd. Nowadays the BBC thinks it's done well when it gets an audience of five million for the 10 p.m. bulletin.

So what should we in the business of television news do to increase our audiences? We have popularized our reporting and our agenda: that hasn't worked. We have tried a dozen facelifts and relaunches: no good. We have dropped some of our best presenters, and brought in young, attractive people, who have done nothing to increase the ratings. And now?

It seems to me we should first of all accept the situation, and then go back to basics. In an age where no one disapproves if you are ignorant about the world, and where reality seems less important to the programme makers than reality shows, television news shouldn't try so hard to attract an audience it will probably never see again. Instead, I feel, we should use the opportunity to return to Reithianism, the business of informing and educating people as well as entertaining them. It may not be fashionable, but it's what we know we ought to be doing. I personally believe the BBC should go back to its old Reithian principles, forget the focus groups and even, if necessary, the viewing figures, and tell people what we think they ought to know.

It's appallingly elitist, of course, and that alone is probably enough to ensure it won't happen. But expecting your audience to tell you what sort of news you should give them is like telling your doctor what sort of treatment you would like, or your garage mechanic how you would like him to mend your engine. We should be telling our audiences what we think is important for them to know, whether the focus groups say they're interested or not. Maybe the audience levels will drop even more; but we'll know we've done the job right, rather than turn ourselves into another branch of entertainment. If the BBC became a little more Reithian, and a little less inclined to chase audience numbers for their own sake, and made a virtue of what it was doing, it might weaken its position in the ratings but I think it would strengthen its moral position immensely.

Every single government during my forty years with the BBC has attacked it and threatened it, but the danger always faded or was seen off. At the height of her power in the 1980s, Margaret Thatcher used some fairly virulent language about the BBC and frequently encouraged the idea that it might have to be privatized; but she never thought seriously about doing it. By contrast Tony Blair, perhaps knowingly, perhaps not, began a process which, unless it is checked, seems in the end likely to destroy the BBC as the world's most powerful, free-standing, independent broadcaster, and one of Britain's principal world-class brands.

He understood that the key to the BBC's strength was the licence fee which funds it; and he allowed a process to start which is putting the BBC's future licence-fee income in doubt. This isn't necessarily the view of the BBC management, but it is my own. And if the management isn't worried, it ought to be. In 2006, possibly as a result of, or possibly before the BBC's own chairman, Michael Grade, suddenly resigned to go back to ITV, the BBC's income from the licence fee was sharply cut back by the Blair government. Was Tony Blair getting his own back on the BBC? Or was it merely because Gordon Brown, as Chancellor of the Exchequer, needed to clamp down on public spending and didn't see why the BBC should be an exception to his rule? Whatever the reason, the damage to the BBC is likely to be real and permanent. At the same time, the government encouraged talk that in future the licence fee might have to be shared with other broadcasters; in other words, future governments will, if they choose, be able to punish the BBC for broadcasting things they don't like, by cutting the BBC's share of the licence fee even more.

If you work for the BBC, you can expect a good deal of institutional hostility from the government and the press. Tony Blair, as prime minister, gave the appearance of doing everything he could to appease and propitiate the Murdoch group, which includes Sky and noisily anti-BBC newspapers like *The Times* and the *Sun*. In September 2005 he was unwise enough to confide to Murdoch that he was shocked at the BBC's coverage of hurricane Katrina, which did immense damage to the city of New Orleans. Murdoch could scarcely wait to break the news of this confidence to a conference of influential American media figures the following week. 'Tony Blair . . . told me yesterday that he was in Delhi last week and he turned on the BBC World Service to see what was happening in New Orleans, and he said it was just full of hate at America and gloating about our troubles,' Murdoch told the conference. (The reporting which seems to have upset Blair was about the evident failures of the Bush administration to act efficiently or quickly to come to the aid of one of America's major cities; some leading figures in America suggested that the president deserved to be impeached for his slowness in responding to the catastrophe.)

Britain's political parties always support the BBC when they are in opposition, because they know it offers them their best hope of getting their views across to the public. But when they get into government, they change. They regard the BBC as the voice of opposition and hostility, and they are frustrated by its unaccountable failure to act as the government's mouthpiece. During my career, the governments of Harold Wilson, Ted Heath, James Callaghan, Margaret Thatcher, John Major and Tony Blair have all gone through this metamorphosis.

Few prime ministers in my forty years, though, have done as much damage to the BBC as Tony Blair and his head of communications, Alastair Campbell. It is now clear that the evidence which Tony Blair presented to Parliament in 2002 about Saddam Hussein's weapons of mass destruction was exaggerated and misleading.

Strangely, though, no one from the Blair government had to resign over the clear misuse of intelligence and the misleading of Parliament. The only resignations came from the BBC: its chairman and director-general both went. The careers of most of the BBC people involved have been affected by it all in some way. The opinion polls showed that it wasn't the BBC that suffered in the public's mind; it was the government that lost public confidence and respect.

The relationship with the Blair government never recovered from all this. Tessa Jowell, the minister with responsibility for negotiating the BBC's new charter and setting the level of the licence fee, accepted the BBC's argument for a licence-fee increase to take account of inflation and the extra demands for technical change which the government was making of the BBC. Tony Blair and his then chancellor, Gordon Brown, turned this down.

Tessa Jowell had known they would. But she was a supporter of the BBC and approved of its plans, and she had prepared to play her trump card.

'You can't afford to refuse the BBC a full licence-fee rise,' she planned to tell Blair and Brown, 'because if they don't get it, Michael Grade will resign as the chairman of the BBC. And you simply can't afford to lose two BBC chairmen in a short space of time like this. It would do terrible damage to the BBC, and it would look bad for the government.'

But as it turned out, she wasn't able to say that. With dreadful timing, Michael Grade, who had taken over as chairman after the resignation of Gavyn Davies in 2004, announced at this critical moment that he was jumping ship and going back to Independent Television. So the BBC lost another chairman after all.

The BBC is just about the only broadcasting organization left which operates entirely by the licence fee. Every other broadcaster which followed the same system, and that meant those in just about every major Commonwealth country, and some minor ones, has been forced to shift away from it. And the result has been very damaging.

Take the example of CBC in Canada. In the 1980s it still got most of its income from the licence fee, and it produced programmes of outstanding quality. Then something in one of its news reports annoyed the then prime minister, Brian Mulroney. He came down on CBC very heavily, and rewrote the protocol under which it operated. As a result, the licence fee was cut and the government insisted that CBC should make up the difference from extra advertising. And the government assessed the amount of cash it would get from advertising at an unreasonably high level. So from that moment on, CBC was hobbled. The quality of its programmes declined, and so did its influence. Brian Mulroney was soon out of office, but CBC never regained its old position.

It's not impossible that something like this will happen to the BBC. At some stage a government, in a fit of anger such as affected Alastair Campbell over the Gilligan report into the government's actions prior to the invasion of Iraq in 2003, might decide that the licence fee should be shared with other broadcasters to make better programmes. Then the government would be faced with a choice: either to let the BBC decline through lack of money, or else force it to make up the difference by taking advertising.

Not taking advertising isn't merely some strange quirk, like not eating tomatoes. The idea behind it is that if you aren't beholden to anyone for the money you spend, you won't yourself be in anyone's pocket. For more than eighty years it has worked very well. But I now believe that the fury of the Blair government over an accusation which proved to be largely true will one day lead to the destruction of the BBC in the form we have always known it. Some people, mostly the ideologues among us, will be glad about that. The rest, who simply want decent reliable broadcasting to watch and listen to, will find it deeply depressing.

§

At a little after 7 a.m. on 1 September 2006 I woke up to the sound of a distant explosion. Somewhere in Baghdad, a car bomb had just gone off. I could imagine the dreadful scene, the blood, the screaming, the stink of explosive, the noise of sirens and alarms and car horns. It was an inauspicious but not totally unfitting way to start the fortieth anniversary of my joining the British Broadcasting Corporation.

After two decades of this kind of thing, you might think I'd have had enough. And indeed any sensible man of sixty-two, awakened by an explosion from his fitful sleep in a disgustingly uncomfortable bed which he had shared all night in a temperature of around forty degrees with some minuscule biting insect, would have had breakfast and then announced that he was going home as soon as possible.

Somehow, though, the thought didn't even occur to me. For reasons I shall explain later, I have come to loathe and despise the kind of violence that this latest explosion represented. Yet I didn't want to stop reporting on events in Iraq, or anywhere else for that matter.

And I had another reason for wanting to carry on working: Rafe, my baby son with cheeks as round and red as a Ribstone pippin, who will expect to be kept in some style for the next two decades; by which time I will be, God help me, eighty-two. And although everyone tries to reassure me by saying that eighty-two isn't what it was, and that it will be even less so by the 2020s, I haven't yet heard anyone suggest that eighty-two will be the new forty.

The author and playwright John Mortimer wrote with gentle humour about the day when his daughter, who was twelve, asked him with great tact if he would mind not taking her right up to the school entrance any more. He was in his late seventies at that stage. This is a moment I will have to prepare myself for, clearly: an unexpected rite of passage for the older father, standing on the corner and watching as the Ribstone pippin of his eye walks quickly away on his own, anxious not to be embarrassed by his aged parent.

But it may help if I'm still occasionally on television, perhaps wheeled out to reminisce interminably about some event that I have witnessed in the distant past. Being on television seems to confer an entirely illusory reality on people which nothing else, not even writing books, seems to do. It's a help in other ways, too. Sometimes an ancient character comes up and shakes my hand, and introduces himself as someone I last saw, fresh-faced and slim, at school or university, back in the days when people wore ties and suits. I have to hide my shock at what the years have done to him, while he has watched me decay slowly over the years and has become entirely used to the white hair, the wrinkled face and the clearly deficient memory which are now presented to him.

Forty years' hard labour is a very long business. Yet, like any other kind of addiction, the longer it is a part of your life, the harder it is to shake it. And although it does sometimes involve sleeping on a broken, lumpy bed in the same temperature as a medium sauna and being awoken each morning by bombs, it can also involve, say, staying at the nicest hotel in Buenos Aires and eating superbly every night before heading off to the leather shops in search of a jacket that will cost half as much as in London and be twice as well cut.

Like some elderly dating agency, the BBC provides me with ready-made companions. I nowadays tend to travel everywhere with the same two people – Nick and Oggy, with whom I sat in Buenos Aires, talking about the friendly fire experience in Iraq.

In the past, the BBC used to allocate your team, and if you suggested that someone else might be better suited to the job, you were made to regret it. Once, I remember, I had to spend three weeks in Germany, and although my German isn't too bad I knew there was a cameraman whose German was much better; he was also an excellent cameraman. I was told fiercely that he couldn't come with me under any circumstances. Then I was given one of our two worst cameramen as a punishment.

Some cameramen often seem to miss the key shot. They aren't lazy or stupid or unwilling, they're just unlucky.

'Were you running when that character pulled the gun and pointed it?'

'No, sorry, I was getting a shot of the crowd at the time.'

Nick Woolley isn't like that. While I'm still formulating the question in my mind, he has spotted what is happening out of the corner of his eye, swung round and got more of the incident than I have noticed. I've learned that I don't even need to ask him.

But the companionship matters a great deal too. The three of us spend almost as much time with each other as we do at home. We are widely separated in age, and we have very different backgrounds. In order to work properly we have to make an effort to get on, but it helps if you like each other to start with. I have, of course, told Oggy and Nick every one of my stories several times over, often with slightly different endings, and they both laugh dutifully in the right places. We each know what the others like for breakfast, and how they take their tea or coffee, and even what books to bring on a trip, in case the others run out of reading matter.

The kind of work we do is extraordinarily rewarding. Even if I didn't have to do it in order to keep Rafe in nappies and plastic toys, I would enjoy doing it for its own sake. And, besides, I'm too old now to start doing something different. Like some antiquated machine chugging away in the corner of the factory, everyone knows I'll need replacing at some stage; but until I break down irrevocably I'm determined to keep on running. And a little oil helps the process.

2

SADDAM

The last time I saw Saddam Hussein in the flesh, he had just been sentenced to death. And he was smiling.

He walked past me, just a couple of feet away from where I habitually sat in the press box: smaller, thinner, vaguer, weaker, more vulnerable than the pictures of him from the old days, but with a renewed sense of himself and his power to attack his enemies and rally his friends. The date was Sunday, 5 November 2006.

I had chosen that particular seat months earlier in order to have the occasional opportunity of looking him in the eyes. It had happened several times during the trial. His searching glance would take me in as he was brought onto the floor of the courtroom, or led out of it.

Sometimes he seemed angry, as though he felt I was like a visitor at a zoo staring at a caged animal. Sometimes he was neutral, distracted, as though only his body was captive and his mind was fixed elsewhere, on his old fantasies of power. Only once did I feel I had made personal contact with him. It lasted for just an instant, while those obsidian eyes caught mine and held them. The defensive, expressionless look faded, and was replaced by – what? Warmth? Scarcely. Interest? Not really. A kind of fellow feeling, as though he might think we were both prisoners of something much greater than a mere prison or a mere superpower?

Probably not, but there was definitely something there. Then the moment passed.

The final time, though, his eyes didn't seek out mine at all. Instead he looked down as he passed me. But I could clearly see the little grin of pleasure which crossed his face. He knew he had achieved everything he had wanted in court that day, when the judge sentenced him to hang.

Saddam Hussein must have decided long before that there was no hope of escaping the executioner. Now he was concerned solely with creating the kind of effect in the minds of people in Iraq and around the world which would act as his epitaph. This morning, he had achieved precisely that. Hence the secret smile.

I had attended a good deal of the trial since it began, a year earlier. Like all trials – even, someone who was at Nuremberg told me, those of Goering and Hess and the others there – it had included long periods of boredom, and some of absurdity. This, though, was the sole resemblance to the trial of Saddam Hussein. It did not, after all, turn out to be the Nuremberg Trial of our time. Instead, like so much else that was done after the invasion of 2003, it was ramshackle, ill thought out, full of big intentions but lacking any serious link to the reality of Iraqi existence: a memorial, in fact, to the grand pretensions and smallness of mind of the entire enterprise of overthrowing Saddam.

There is a sad memorial on the internet to all the good intentions of 2003 and 2004: a website called 'Grotian Moment', set up by a group of American lawyers and carrying this explanatory rubric:

> As arguably the most important war crimes proceedings since Nuremberg, the trials of Saddam Hussein are likely to constitute a 'Grotian Moment' – defined as a legal development that is so significant that it can create new customary international law or radically transform the interpretation of treaty-based law.

But there was no Grotian Moment, no transformation of treaty-based law. Worst of all, it was hard to see what significance his trial really had – except as a warning that if you set out to do something irrevocable on the world stage, you need considerable intelligence and the strength of character to achieve it. The men and women who planned and carried through the overthrow of Saddam Hussein often liked to compare themselves to Churchill's and Roosevelt's people who overthrew Hitler and put his henchmen on trial. But most of them simply weren't up to the job, either intellectually or morally.

Behind the actuality of the trial of Saddam Hussein lay the Régime Crimes Liaison Office in the vast American embassy which was based in Saddam Hussein's own former palace in Baghdad's Green Zone. It was staffed by dozens of American lawyers and security experts, plus a few mildly disaffected British ones who often found the mood of self-righteousness and lack of self-questioning difficult to stomach. The very title made the basic approach clear. The RCLO was created at a time when few of the Americans working for the Interim Authority had any doubts about the invasion of Iraq. The basic expectation was that, as with the proceedings at Nuremberg, all that would be required would be to make the crimes of Saddam Hussein and his colleagues public. Their very awfulness would convince all but the most bigoted that it was necessary to put Saddam on trial.

Given that so many of the crimes of Saddam Hussein's regime were indeed appalling, that might not have been impossible. But because the decision to invade Iraq was so contested, and so unpopular around the world, any rational assessment of the pluses and minuses of overthrowing Saddam Hussein became impossible. So the proceedings at the trials, instead of convincing international opinion that the invasion had been right, merely divided it more deeply.

Worse, the hand of the United States was often so evident in the business of putting Saddam and the others on trial that it scarcely seemed like an Iraqi process at all. The Americans controlled virtually everything except the moment-by-moment legal proceedings: setting up the court, staffing it with lawyers and judges, broadcasting its proceedings and maintaining its security. The Iraqi government, which wanted to see Saddam brought to trial and found guilty, nevertheless found it humiliating to have to depend so heavily on the Americans.

Immediately before he first appeared in court, we could hear the clink of his chains and handcuffs as the Americans delivered him to the Iraqi officials in the court. The chains were taken off outside the door to the courtroom, but when Saddam walked into the court he was still rubbing his wrists and already starting to complain. At first the American security officials wouldn't allow him to bring his copy of the Koran into court with him. He had never been a devout Muslim, and had dealt harshly with Islamists when he was in power, but he realized the value of presenting himself as an Islamic martyr, and the Americans made that possible by the way they treated him.

Saddam Hussein often complained to his lawyers and to the occasional visitors he saw about the way he was being treated; his lawyers described it as 'vindictive'. It seems likely that some of the US Marshals and others who were in charge of security believed, as many Americans did, that Saddam had been personally involved in the plot to attack America on 11 September 2001.

One morning during the trial he appeared in court breathing heavily and apparently exhausted. There had been a power cut, and the lifts weren't working. His American captors had insisted that he should climb the stairs in chains from the basement of the court building, where he had been brought at the absurd hour of two in the morning, to the fourth floor where the courtroom was. The Iraqi judge ordered that he should no longer be chained, and that he should be allowed to bring his Koran with him, together with the pads of paper and pencils which the Americans had previously barred him from taking out of his cell on security grounds.

The Régime Crimes Liaison Office drilled and advised the Iraqi judges and lawyers who took part in the trial, but it was always an uneasy relationship. The trial was televised, and there were half a dozen or so unmanned cameras set up in fixed positions around the courtroom. Many of the lawyers and judges and all of the junior court officials demanded that their faces should not be shown, especially after several defence lawyers were attacked and murdered. This meant that right from the start there had to be some kind of control over the pictures that were made public. Soon, though, it became clear that it wasn't just the shots of certain people's faces which were being cut. Whenever Saddam Hussein seemed to be issuing orders or morale-boosting lectures to the anti-American insurgents, or struggled with his guards on the way in and out of the dock, the American in the control room would censor the broadcast.

So it was clear early on that this was never going to be a Grotian Moment, and that the world would not regard it as setting some new standard for justice. Yet Judge Rizgar Mohammed Amin, who presided over the start of Saddam's first trial, seemed to understand what was required. He treated Saddam Hussein with politeness, and even when he became obstreperous in the dock, Rizgar always remained mild and calm. This was not what the Iraqi government, or most of the country's Shi'ites and Kurds, wanted to see. Throughout Saddam's dictatorship and for decades before that, the only justice that Iraqis had known was the kind where the judges and prosecution joined in screaming insults at the accused. Rizgar's show of calm was not something they were used to. Rather like the Americans, they wanted an emotional purging, an outburst of righteous revenge.

The great majority of government ministers were Shi'ite Muslims or Kurds, and most of them had lost relatives or friends to Saddam's policies or his death squads. They knew perfectly well that Saddam had not been behind the 11 September attacks, but they had their own personal reasons for wanting to see that he was humiliated.

One evening during the trial, as I was leaving the press centre in the Green Zone, I bumped into Laith Kubba, the government's spokesman. I had known Laith for fifteen years, and admired his sense of neutrality and honesty. This evening, though, he was overwrought and excited.

'The street is angry,' he shouted to me as he hurried through the empty lobby. 'They think the judge is being far too lenient.'

'The street' is a slightly irritating synecdoche, much used in Arab countries, which really just means 'people' or 'public opinion', though in a region where policy can sometimes be influenced by angry crowds it carries a certain force. In this case, of course, Laith Kubba meant that Iraq's Shi'ites felt that the presiding judge had allowed Saddam Hussein too much latitude in making his points and challenging the prosecution's case. They wanted him humiliated, laden down with accusations, and eventually dragged away weeping and praying to a coward's execution. The very notion of a fair trial meant nothing to them; it wasn't fairness they wanted, it was retribution.

And so the government replaced Rizgar Mohammed Amin as the presiding judge, first with Sayeed al-Hamashi and then, after a close relative of his was murdered, with Raouf Abdel Rahman, a Kurd. He too tried to maintain an atmosphere of fairness in the court, but although he often made the mistake of allowing Saddam Hussein to shout from the dock or intimidate the witnesses, the government was more prepared to accept his way of doing things.

Perhaps they realized, too, that they could not sack a third judge without allowing the trial to descend into complete and final absurdity. Yet people all around the world had already decided that the trial of Saddam Hussein was a farce, and in many ways they were right. Nuremberg had degenerated into the Big Brother House, and justice had become less important than the need for public satisfaction.

§

Usually, when I travelled to Iraq, I would fly to Kuwait and take the Royal Air Force flight up to Baghdad. It was reasonably safe, although one Hercules was shot down the day after I travelled in it, and the entire crew, charming, relaxed and hospitable, had been killed, together with their passengers. Sometimes, if we were lucky, my colleagues and I would then be given seats on the Air Bridge, an RAF helicopter linking Baghdad airport with the Green Zone. Although the BBC office wasn't in the Green Zone – it was on the other side of the river, in the centre of Baghdad – it was a great deal safer at that stage to fly across the city than to drive across it.

But the RAF flights became increasingly unpredictable. You could turn up at 7.30 for an 11 a.m. flight, only to find that the Hercules would not leave until five o'clock that evening. Sometimes the flight would be cancelled altogether, and everyone who had been booked on it the previous day would have to compete for a place on the new flight. The RAF were always very helpful to us, and to me in particular; but journalists were taken to and from Baghdad as a favour, not a right, and any government employee was given priority over an outsider like me.

At that stage, Route Irish, the road to and from Baghdad International Airport to the centre of the city, was the most danger-ous stretch of road in Iraq, and therefore probably in the world. There were ambushes and car bombs along its length virtually every day, and it was always a nerve-racking ride when you arrived in Baghdad or left it.

It was the inexperience of the American forces which had

allowed Route Irish to become so dangerous. They patrolled it at various times during the day in convoys of armoured vehicles, the targets for anything the insurgents might like to fire at them. Instead of controlling the road, therefore, they were its hostages. With their experience in Northern Ireland, the British would have put 'packets' of soldiers on foot along the road, dominating it and preventing any groups of insurgents from gathering or getting near enough to set up ambushes.

Two or three groups of a dozen or so highly trained and well-armed soldiers patrolling on foot pose a deadly threat to any guerrilla band. But patrolling requires a great deal of training and experience, which the Americans lacked in the early stages of the war. To them it seemed a good deal safer to drive up and down Route Irish in their armoured Humvees than to patrol the side of the road on foot; yet their tactic allowed the insurgents to control the road for most of the time.

After more than a year of this, the Americans decided to set up road-blocks along Route Irish, and found that it worked. After that they handed over the road-blocks to the Iraqi army, which worked even better because the Iraqis knew who and what to look for when they searched the passing cars. At long last, after a great waste of time and lives, Route Irish became relatively safe again, and the number of suicide bombings along its length dropped to around one a week.

By comparison, flying over the city in an RAF helicopter became more dangerous. In July 2006, as I was flying to the airport – the journey took ten minutes at the most – I sat beside the open door, with the ground only fifty feet below me. The RAF pilots took a delight in flying low across the city, believing it was much harder for anyone with a gun to know exactly which direction they were coming from; a helicopter would have vanished beyond the rooftops before it could be properly sighted. The RAF's reasoning convinced me, and although I was always nervous when I took the Air Bridge, at least it was over quickly.

On this particular flight, I felt more anxious than usual. I had struck up an impromptu friendship with a charming former Irish Guards officer, who was now in charge of one of the big security companies working in Iraq. He sat opposite me, staring out through the open door at the buildings as they flashed by just below us. Alongside him was the loadmaster, who manned the heavy machine-gun poking through the opening.

Suddenly the Irish Guardsman spotted something, and opened his mouth to yell. At that instant the helicopter heeled hard over, so that the rotors were almost ninety degrees to the ground. So were we, and our seatbelts strained accordingly. Then we seemed to roll and swoop all over the sky, and I could see that our accompanying helicopter (they always flew in pairs) was also being thrown around just as we were. There was a loud crack as the metallic chaff was thrown out, in order to fool the missile which had been fired at us. Another fifteen seconds of this, and then the helicopter settled down again and resumed its course to the airport.

I was shaken by it all, but also rather exhilarated. No doubt surviving a rocket attack always makes you feel pretty good. My friend the Irish Guards officer was furious, though, and he was shouting at the loadmaster, who was looking at the helicopter floor. A combination of my partial deafness (the result of an American 'friendly fire' attack) and the racket from the helicopter's rotors made it impossible for me to hear what was being said; but afterwards, as we climbed down out of the helicopter, I asked the Guardsman what had happened.

'I saw this bloody character stand up on top of a big block of flats, just about level with us, and aim his RPG [rocket-launcher] at us. I yelled at the loadmaster, but he was so bloody slow we were well past by the time he was ready to fire at him. He could certainly have got him.'

It was letting slip the chance to kill the man with the RPG that had irritated the Guardsman, not the incident itself. In future, I thought to myself, I shall drive down Route Irish. This helicopter business is a bit too disturbing.

I had already begun to prefer going to Baghdad via Amman rather than Kuwait. It had become increasingly hard to love Kuwait. Its climate was ferocious, hotter even than Baghdad, its city centre was run-down, and its 'dry' policy was much flouted by the Kuwaitis themselves but was imposed with some rigour on Western visitors. If they found a bottle of whisky in your luggage during Ramadan, you could end up in prison. And although the food was quite good at the hotel where we stayed, it had to be accompanied by interminable glasses of fruit juice. There was little pleasure in travelling through Kuwait, either in or out.

Amman, by contrast, is charming. Maybe it is a little dull by comparison with the great cities of the region, Cairo or Damascus or Baghdad itself before the 2003 invasion, but it is the dullness of stability and comfort and order. The whiteness of its limestone buildings gives it considerable beauty, and it has an antiquity which the Gulf entirely lacks. Its airport is good, and alcohol is readily available. I am only a moderate drinker, but I like to have a couple of glasses of red wine with my dinner and a glass of single malt before I sleep; and I feel that as long as I don't offend anyone else either with my behaviour or with the sight of what I am drinking, then it should be nobody else's business.

I arrived in Amman, the penultimate stage in the journey to Baghdad, on 3 November 2005. Saddam's trial was due to begin two days later, and a seat had been reserved for me in the press box. Everything seemed to be going reasonably well. I stayed that night in the InterContinental Hotel, where I had spent so much time over the years. The InterContinental was the press hotel during the Black September uprising by Palestinians against the young King Hussein, and it was some time before they got rid of all the bullet holes.

In the late 1990s Dee and I had come here to cover a visit by Tony Blair to the Middle East, and we had gone to his suite late at night to interview him. It seemed to me, as he patted his hand on the bed for her to sit beside him with the microphone, and addressed most of his answers to her rather than me, that he wasn't entirely immune to the attractions of a good-looking female producer. But maybe that is what a jealous husband always feels; and I suppose I would have thought it even odder if he had patted the bed for me to sit close beside him. Under the watchful eyes of his press adviser, Alastair Campbell, who was standing beside the bed, none of it felt natural anyway.

In the past I had spent a good deal of time in the Inter-Continental, waiting for visas to Saddam Hussein's Iraq, and when I travelled there in the dangerous period soon after the invasion of Kuwait I was treated by the management and my fellow journalists with a certain inquisitive respect, as though I was making my way to the gallows. It was on that trip that I met Robert Wiener, the CNN producer who wrote the best book on the first Gulf War, *Live From Baghdad*, which was made into a Hollywood film. As we checked in for the Baghdad flight at Amman airport I asked him why he was going. 'Because I left Saigon just before it fell,' he said, 'and I don't want to spend another sixteen years of my life trying to make up for it.' He not only made a first-class reputation for himself, he helped to put CNN on the map.

This time the plane to Baghdad would, I knew, be full. A lot of people wanted to be there for the first day of Saddam Hussein's trial. But I had a reservation for the flight, and assumed that all would be well. It was only after I had checked in and was sitting in the departure lounge café with a group of people from the American organization Human Rights Watch that I realized things were not going as planned. The time for us to board the plane came and went. We drank more coffee. Every now and then an official from Royal Jordanian Airlines would hurry past, and be surrounded by anxious would-be passengers shouting questions. There was, it seemed, a sandstorm over Baghdad. The outlook was uncertain.

And then, in the way of these things, everything was suddenly all right. We were urged through into the departure lounge and crammed onto an airport bus in a matter of minutes. It drove us far away from the main terminal building, with the smart jets of Royal Jordanian in their slate-grey, red and white paint clustered round it. Eventually, on the outskirts of the airfield, the bus stopped in front of our plane. It had no markings whatever, and I couldn't work out what the registration letters signified. (Swaziland, someone told me later.) It looked like the cheapest aircraft Royal Jordanian could find to charter, so that if it crashed or were shot down the loss would be relatively small. The plane was entirely superannuated, having been built in 1978, and it was a Fokker. You can imagine the jokes.

At the top of the steps, crammed into the tiny galley, were two women whose background I guessed immediately, even before I had heard them speak. Both were very attractive: a tall, slender blonde and a smaller, slighter black woman. Afrikaner and Zulu, I thought, and was proven right when they spoke to me. There were only two of them, plus a pilot and co-pilot, both Afrikaners.

South Africans, white and black, turn up nowadays in every difficult part of the world, doing the dangerous jobs most other people are scared to do. Sometimes I wonder if they understand quite how dangerous the jobs they are doing actually are. In this case, neither of the stewardesses seemed to have any great idea of what was going on in Iraq or why flying there might be a problem.

The seats were uncomfortable, tiny and inclined to collapse. Having had only three hours' sleep the night before, I quickly nodded off. The tones of the Afrikaans stewardess woke me:

'Ladies and gentlemen, we are now starting our descent before landing at Baghdad International Airport. We ask you to tighten your seatbelts and switch off any electronic equipment.'

'And kiss your ass goodbye,' said the American behind me.

We descended. It was the kind of thing passengers hate and pilots adore. I could see now the extent of the sandstorm, an angry reddish-yellow cloud which hung so thickly over the ground that it covered everything like liquid cement. Then, suddenly, we broke through and saw the ground, close below us: always a shock. We were only about a hundred feet above it.

And at that point there was a gut-wrenching jerk, and we started to climb as fiercely as we had dropped down out of the sky. A moment of two of that, and then the laconic voice of the Afrikaans pilot. 'Ladies and gentlemen, we are returning to Amman.' That was all. There was groaning and shouting from the passengers, but no one explained anything more to us until we made the ninety-minute flight back and landed at Amman once again.

It turned out that two planes, ours and another, had tried to land at Baghdad. The other plane went in first and its wheels actually touched the runway. But at that instant the pilot realized he couldn't see the end of the runway, and pulled up again into the open sky. We were flying just behind him, and had to pull up as well.

Now, it seemed, there was a real danger that we might not get to Baghdad in time for the start of the trial: a nuisance to many, and something of a humiliation for people like me. Most of us have a touch of Schadenfreude in us, no matter how we try to ignore it, and in a big organization like the BBC, full of highly competitive people, it exists in large quantities. If I failed to make the first day of Saddam's trial, it wouldn't be good.

Nowadays, having worked for the BBC for forty years, with relatively few failures that anyone else knows about (I know of thousands, of course), my career, or what is left of it, can probably survive a few high-profile foul-ups. Not many, but maybe four or just possibly five. The trouble lies not in the failures themselves, but in the pattern they seem to present. As English lawyers used to say in the Middle Ages, twice makes a custom. In my case, I suppose, people would look for any sign that I was slowing up, or losing my interest in the job, or getting even more forgetful than I already am.

And then, like astronomers examining a group of random, unrelated stars in the sky and deciding that they look like a ram, or a man with a belt and a sword, or a gigantic plough, they would make a pattern. 'Poor old Simpson,' they would say, 'he can't really hack it any more. It's cruel to let him wander round the world like this.'

As things stood, I was going to have a real problem getting to Baghdad in a sandstorm, and stopping the pattern from establishing itself. At Amman airport there were crowds of angry, gesticulating people standing at the Royal Jordanian ticket desk. I hung around for a little while to see if there was any point in joining in, but it seemed to me that the reaction of the would-be passengers was just a way of letting off steam. Much better, I thought, to get back to the InterContinental and get a bit of sleep. I suppose I also thought, with something of the rat-like cunning which the wonderful late Nick Tomalin once said was a requirement for a journalist, that the number of rooms at the InterContinental was limited, and that it might be a good idea to get there before the mob.

I had a quiet, restful evening and a decent sleep. Maybe that helped to give me the pleasant, easy feeling the next morning that things were going to be what they would be, and that a lot of screaming and shouting was unnecessary. Working for television news can turn you into a kind of Mussolini, using the full force of your willpower to make people do exactly what you want them to do. Plenty of television reporters and producers become distinctly fascistic, and eventually forget how to switch it off, remaining bullying and loud the whole time. I have certainly had my Mussolini moments: I once stood in front of a tall television headquarters building in Geneva, thinking 'Somewhere in this building is the video cassette I want, and although everyone says it is lost I am going to find it.' Fifteen minutes later, standing in a small group of angry, humiliated men and sniffly girls, I held the cassette triumphantly in my hand. But that was a long time ago. I doubt nowadays if the exercise of the will is ever really worth it. And to be honest the pictures on the cassette weren't that good.

So I have slowly mellowed. Other people do the yelling for me, while I stay quietly at the back watching what happens, or perhaps, like Jeeves, reading an improving book; not the noblest approach, of course, but one that puts less strain on the heart and nerves.

Now, though, there was no one to yell for me. I had joined up with a BBC engineer, Bobbie Adefope, a charming, resourceful, wonderfully reliable scion of a princely house in Nigeria, who was also trying to get to Baghdad. We went to the airport together. Predictably, it was dreadful. Large numbers of people were shouting and waving their tickets, and it soon became clear that a distinctly un-European system had been put in place. All the people booked on today's flight would get priority, and all those who had been on yesterday's flight would have to take their chances.

At one stage Bobbie and I had the idea of taking the much less reliable Iraqi Airlines flight, which apparently had some seats available, and poor Bobbie loaded up all his gear and headed out to the next terminal to catch it. I was going to join him, but at that moment I saw that a space had cleared in front of one of the check-in desks. A young, pleasant-looking man sat there, looking and though he had been gone over by a very large gang of possibly Albanian muggers.

'Excuse me,' I said.

He glanced up at me dully.

'I know you've had a really bad time, but I just wanted to ask you a favour. I work for the BBC, and I have to get to Baghdad for

Saddam Hussein's trial tomorrow. I understand, of course, that all the seats on this morning's flight are taken, but do you think you might be able to find room for me?'

I felt very calm and easy. If I didn't get on, I thought, there might be a bit of awkwardness at the BBC, but what else would happen? Would I die, or be badly injured? Would my marriage fall apart? Would I lose my collection of Laurence Sterne first editions? Would our (so far) unborn baby be taken from us?

Exactly.

'I watch the BBC,' he said, 'and I know you are Mr Simpson. But I can't do anything to help you.' He paused. 'I will look again, though,' he said, 'because you didn't shout at me. And if there is a chance, someone will call out your name in about fifteen minutes. So you should stay over there.'

I moved away, and the crowd settled round him again like rugby forwards on a loose ball. It only occurred to me then that I hadn't asked for a seat for Bobbie. Not very thoughtful of me, but I doubted if King Abdullah II himself could get two of us on the flight.

I read a little more. And then I heard someone call my name. I had a seat after all.

Bobbie's flight was much later, and he not only had to spend the night at the airport, but some of his equipment went missing. I didn't feel good about that; but I arrived on time at midday, and was driven down Route Irish in perfect safety and reached the BBC bureau an hour afterwards.

But my troubles still weren't over. The next morning I turned up at the conference centre in the Green Zone to meet up with the other journalists who were going to cover the first day of the trial; among them was a particular friend of mine, Christiane Amanpour of CNN. We stood outside in the chilly morning sunshine, talking about what we had done since we saw each other last, and we greeted other friends and acquaintances there. I saw, with some pleasure, that I was the only person from British television, or indeed from the British media in general; though Reuters news agency had an Iraqi journalist there.

There had been something of a scandal over the screening process to which we had all been subjected. A team of American officials had interrogated everyone who had been allocated a seat at the trial to see if they were suitable to report on the case. Twenty-six journalists were being allowed in, more than half of them Iraqis. The rest (apart from me) worked for American organizations.

The questions had apparently varied greatly. The Iraqis were asked if they supported the American-led invasion of Iraq, whether they or any of their relatives had belonged to the Ba'ath Party, what they thought of Saddam Hussein, and how they had voted in the recent Iraqi elections. They were also asked about their financial situation, and one said he had had to list the names and addresses of all of his relatives who lived outside the country.

With the journalists working for American organizations, who included at least one Canadian and one Briton, they wanted to know about their political opinions and, oddly, their financial situation. One American was asked why he had voted Democrat in the 2004 election. Another was asked to supply the addresses and approximate value of any property he owned outside the country.

The Canadian, Dana Lewis, worked for Fox News, but much to his credit (and perhaps Fox's, too) he wrote a long and angry account of his interrogation for the Fox website. It had caused a fuss, and the saner people at the State Department had managed to explain to the CIA, or the FBI, or whichever organization had supplied the interrogators, that this kind of thing did not go down well and would not make the trial of Saddam Hussein easier or more generally popular.

By the time I arrived the following day, everything was more relaxed. The pop-eyed patriots, the veins throbbing on their foreheads, had apparently been parked behind the screens, and a newer, calmer group of interrogators had been brought on. Mine was a good-looking blonde woman in her late thirties.

'Hi – I'm here to help you get accredited.'

'I thought you were here to investigate my politics.'

To be frank, I had been rather looking forward to having an argument.

'No, no, no. I don't know how that idea has gotten around.'

'Aren't you going to ask me how I voted, or whether I think the invasion was a good idea?'

'No, of course not. I want to make sure you understand what the ground rules are for covering the trial.'

She explained them.

'And what about property I own?'

'Unless you very much want to tell me about it, I'm not going to ask you.'

She looked remarkably attractive, like a character in a 1940s gangster film. There was, I felt, definitely space here for some heavily charged banter.

'No truth serum?'

'Definitely no truth serum.'

We went on a little longer, but I was baulked of becoming a martyr for my journalistic faith.

Now, as I chatted to Christiane and the others, I became aware of a faint disturbance in the atmosphere nearby. Dennis, the pleasant, witty, BBC-watching State Department man who was in charge of the press arrangements at the trial, was talking to the BBC bureau manager, Kate Peters, a little way from me.

'But he's got to be on the list,' I heard Kate say.

With a certain ominous feeling, I walked over. Dennis, greatly embarrassed, was explaining that someone else from the BBC was on his list, and not me. And if, as Kate pointed out, there was no time for the other person to get across from the BBC bureau to the Green Zone, then the BBC wouldn't have anyone at the trial.

'I must make this clear,' Dennis said. 'I'm not stopping John. I'm just saying that it's highly unlikely the Marshals will let him in.'

The US Marshals were the notoriously inflexible, mildly ludicrous set of people who controlled access to the court. I could see his point.

Kate stayed remarkably calm.

'But if you just explained to everyone that it was a mistake . . . ?'

'I'll try. I promise I'll try. But you've got to be prepared for a disappointment. I know and accept that it's our fault, and I'll do my best. But . . .'

I tuned out. It was such a pleasant morning, and I felt so good to be here, that I thought it would probably work out.

It did. No one stopped me getting on the bus with the rest, under Dennis's guidance. When we were all seated, a US Marshal climbed aboard, wearing an oversized cowboy hat and strange whiskers, like a bit-part player in *Deliverance*. He carried a shotgun, and two outsized handguns were jammed into his belt. This was his big moment. He started barking instructions at us. Do this, and we would be thrown out. Do that, and we would be thrown out. Fail to do the other, and we would be thrown out. And at that point, having alarmed and depressed us all, he came to an inadequate end.

'Gosh, folks, sorry if I sound a bit sore, but I haven't slept for two nights and there's been a heck of a lot of work to do.'

'Ah,' said Dennis, loud enough for everyone on the bus to hear, 'just what we needed: heavily armed men who haven't had enough sleep.'

Security was, as you might expect, everything. If the trial itself had been carried out with the same degree of care and obedience to orders, things might have been different in Iraq today. We hung around and waited in a long line, while the strange and often unexplained process worked itself through. We journalists were first in the queue, and behind them came the court officials, and then the judges. Immediately behind the judges came the defence and prosecution lawyers, and after that, chatting and smiling, came the witnesses. Everyone had to wait so long in the pleasant morning sunshine that we all got into conversation: in particular, the judges with the lawyers and the lawyers with the witnesses. At Nuremberg, I think it is safe to assume, the judges and lawyers and witnesses and foreign journalists did not stand around outside the courtroom and chat.

What was delaying us was the X-ray machine: a strange oval thing like the airlock in a science fiction film. You stood in it with your arms raised, while a tall scanner which acted rather like a camera shutter passed quickly across the glass in front of you. Then a disembodied voice would say 'OK'. The machine was the kind that peered through your clothes and showed you naked. I thought Christiane Amanpour reacted very well when I told her that.

We waited nearly an hour for our X-ray experience. Just as we began to shuffle forward I looked round and saw Ahmad Chalabi arriving to join the queue, right at the back with the witnesses. Chalabi was one of the most intriguing figures of the entire post-invasion period. His family were wealthy Shi'ites, and Ahmad had played a part in the political uprising against Saddam Hussein after the first Gulf War ended in 1991. At the time, President Bush had called on the Shi'ite and Kurdish peoples to rise up against Saddam, which would have saved a great deal of trouble later. But directly they did what he asked, seizing control of sixteen of Iraq's nineteen provinces, and coming close to capturing Baghdad, the president took the advice of General Colin Powell, the chairman of the joint chiefs of staff, and abandoned the Shi'ites and Kurds to Saddam Hussein's vengeance. Hundreds of thousands of people were put to death as a result.

There was guilt and sympathy in Washington afterwards, and when Ahmad Chalabi arrived there his views were treated with remarkable respect. The CIA debriefed him, and probably recruited him as an agent then and there. Slowly he got to know more and more of the relatively small number of men and women who, in the American political system, move easily between the big think-tanks and government. Some are scholars; others want to use their sudden political influence to change things.

Chalabi quickly learned how to operate smoothly in this environment. He was pleasant and plausible, and he used the information he received from inside Iraq to good use. During the eight years of Bill Clinton's presidency, the political opposition built up massively and swung farther and farther to the right. The radical neo-conservatives, many of whom had personal links with the Likud Party of Binyamin Netanyahu and Ariel Sharon in Israel, believed that Clinton was too weak and too unprepared to use the full force of American power against America's enemies; which they increasingly identified with Likud's enemies.

Chalabi saw all this, understood the growing power of the neo-conservatives and waited patiently for the chance to use the opportunities such power afforded him. He said the things about Saddam Hussein's Iraq that the neo-cons wanted to hear. Above all, he was the primary source of the theory that if the Americans invaded Iraq, the population would greet them as liberators. The neo-cons wanted to hear it, and they believed it all the more because a leading Iraqi politician told them it was true.

Few of the ideologues understood anything about the new and greatly damaged Iraq which had emerged from the first Gulf War;

certainly not the elderly British-born historian Bernard Lewis, who was the leading neo-con intellectual authority on the Middle East, and who had never written anything particularly insightful about Iraq anyway. But the neo-conservatives weren't really interested in facts; they merely wanted more arguments. Few of those who mattered once George W. Bush had become president – Donald Rumsfeld, Paul Wolfowitz, Douglas Feith and one or two others – seemed to have known anything about the deep division between Arab Sunnis and Shi'ites in Iraq, a division which had been forcibly hidden during Saddam Hussein's time as president. Two senior Iraqi politicians who met President Bush three months before his invasion of Iraq had the impression that he was hearing about the Sunni–Shi'ite split for the first time. When the CIA, which did understand the complex nature of Iraqi society very clearly, warned of the likely consequences of an invasion, their reports were ignored.

Ahmad Chalabi did nothing to explain the uncomfortable fact of the divisions between Sunnis, Shi'ites and Kurds to his neo-con friends. He had troubles of his own at this time, and was found guilty *in absentia* at a trial in Jordan on charges of corruption. Nor did he tell them how close he had become to the government in Iran during the years since the abortive Shi'ite uprising of 1991. This was wise. After Iraq, most neo-cons identified Iran as Israel's greatest enemy, and therefore as America's.

After 2003 it became commonplace to accuse Chalabi of having acted as a conscious agent for Iran, by persuading the American president to take out Iran's chief enemy, Saddam Hussein. Whether or not he really was an Iranian agent, the proposal to invade Iraq and overthrow Saddam was precisely what Iran's religious leaders wanted. At a stroke, Iran became the biggest power in the region. And as the world's great Shi'ite power, it began to have huge political influence among Iraq's Shi'ite majority.

When I caught sight of Ahmad Chalabi at the very tail-end of the queue for the courtroom, it was the first time I had seen him since the invasion. I had always had a soft spot for him: he seemed to me to be a charming rogue – an Iraqi Jeffrey Archer, perhaps, whom you couldn't possibly dislike but whose word it would be unwise to believe wholeheartedly about anything.

How it came about I couldn't say, but by the time I emerged

from having been displayed in all my nakedness to the American operators of the X-ray machine, Ahmad Chalabi had managed to worked his way to the front of the queue, speaking briefly to the judges as he passed, smiling politely at everyone else. Somehow, he must have shimmered past the supposedly mandatory security screening without having to stop for it. When I went into the hut to be X-rayed, he had been behind me in the queue. As I came out, I saw him heading for the building where the trial was to be held, talking briefly to people before politely easing his way past them.

And in the end, having arrived at the precincts of the court last, he was the first person into the building. By the time I arrived he was waiting to give us a self-serving briefing about the trial.

'This will be a quick trial, and a highly successful one,' he said. 'Saddam will of course be found guilty, and I suspect he will crack under the pressure of the evidence against him.'

Little of it turned out to be true, of course, but those journalists who didn't know him wrote it all down faithfully. I stood at the back of the group, my hands in my pockets, and when he had finished I gave him what I hope was a cynical smile. He smiled back, and rather engagingly raised his eyes to heaven.

It was the last public appearance Ahmad Chalabi made in Iraq. The man who had persuaded the United States to overthrow Saddam Hussein in the interests of Iran (for that was the result, whether Chalabi consciously set out to do it or not) finally slipped out of Iraq, having helped to turn it into appalling turmoil, and went to ground somewhere. He was not a poor man, so I'm sure it was somewhere comfortable. Maybe one day he'll write his memoirs.

§

The building where Saddam was to be tried was typical of Iraqi public architecture during the 1980s and 90s: large, pompous, and poorly constructed. International construction companies made fortunes out of cheating Saddam Hussein, and this one must have been a particular money-spinner. It had been designed as the headquarters of the International Ba'ath Party; but since the Iraqi Ba'ath Party had fallen out heavily with its sister parties in Syria, Egypt and Lebanon (though the Lebanese party was so exiguous that it may never have had a serious objective existence) the building's functions were pretty limited.

If you looked carefully at the marble, you could see that some of it was just cheap rock, ground down and artificially coloured. The lavatories began to stink the moment they were used. Skimping on the drainage and sewage systems was a particular trick of the various companies which tendered for contracts under Saddam Hussein, and presumably they were encouraged to do it again and again when it was obvious no one was going to complain. Every house and palace built for Saddam and his extended family which I visited in Iraq stank of sewage.

The courtroom was on the third floor, up several flights of unnecessarily pompous stairs. Yet as so often seems to happen, the courtroom itself was too small for the job, and the arrangements were unsatisfactory. The American journalist Martha Gellhorn, who reported on the Nuremberg trial, once told me that this was also true of the arrangements there. Certainly, when I filmed in the courtroom at Nuremberg, I was amazed by how small it was. Cameramen, using their wide-angled lenses, gave a very different impression of the size of the court, and the same was true of the automatic cameras in the Baghdad courtroom.

The arrangements were poorly thought out. At one point, early on in the first trial, it became necessary to hold everyone in the press box because Saddam was being escorted past the door to his temporary holding cell in the basement.

The press box itself was divided from the courtroom by large windows of armoured glass, so that we would not be able to shoot Saddam with the guns we could not have brought in. It quickly became stiflingly hot, and the long hours combined with extended testimony from a number of rambling witnesses made it hard to keep awake sometimes. For some reason, never properly explained, it was often impossible for us to have a proper translation of what was happening. On the first day it was absurdly bad, and long passages during which Saddam complained about his conditions and set out some part of his defence went completely untranslated.

But we could see clearly for ourselves most of what was going

on. It was far more satisfying than watching the sometimes heavily
edited television version, which concentrated on the faces of the
accused and of the presiding judge (the other four judges refused to
allow their faces to be shown). It also gave us a sense of the
courtroom as theatre. The judges sat facing us, the accused sat in
the dock, constructed rather like a child's play-pen, the prosecution
sat to our left and the defence to our right. Like some reach-me-
down Greek tragedy, their robes showed their functions: the
prosecution's gown were black with red facings, the defence had
green facings and the judges had white – presumably to show their
complete lack of bias.

On that day, 5 November 2005, when Saddam Hussein's trial
began, his reputation was very low, even among his former supporters. So we had not come expecting to watch a caged lion,
but a vanquished prisoner. Saddam challenged the authority of
the court to try him, given that it was set up as the result of an
invasion which did not have anything like full UN sanction. Yet
he seemed not to have thought through his approach properly.
And when the judge asked him to plead, he meekly called out,
'Not guilty'.

Sometimes, as the trial wore on, his half-brother Barzan (whose
head, when he was later hanged, a couple of weeks after Saddam
himself, was wrenched from his body by the force of the drop) put
up the best show of defiance from the dock. There was a particularly
telling moment when Barzan decided to attack one of the chief
figures on the prosecution bench.

> *Prosecutor:* Kindly tell the court whether you were present on this
>   occasion.
> *Barzan:* Well, Comrade Prosecutor . . .

The prosecutor put up with this for some time: all through one day.
But the following morning he had plainly had enough.

> *Prosecutor:* So you are saying you did not see the witness?
> *Barzan:* Yes, Comrade Prosecutor.
> *Prosecutor:* Don't call me 'Comrade'. I'm not your comrade.

He had walked right into the trap.

Barzan: But Comrade Prosecutor – we were comrades in the
   Ba'ath Party for nearly forty years. How can you forget so
   quickly?

Even the judges laughed.

Saddam Hussein, by contrast, often seemed plodding and uncertain. Sometimes he had good days, when he would challenge the evidence of the witnesses with remarkable effect. Then a day or so would pass, during which he failed to make any points at all.

Gradually, though, his confidence grew. He learned to extract the most from his use of the Koran, which he brought into court as soon as his American captors allowed, waving it at the judges and ostentatiously looking up references in it. The more outbursts he made, the more he realized he could get away with it. Slowly, people who had previously watched the proceedings on television in Iraq for the extraordinary novelty of seeing their former dictator paraded in front of their eyes, a broken man who would soon be executed, found themselves sympathizing with him. In the teahouses of Baghdad they would bang the tables when he made a good point. And when he merely sat there in the dock and growled they would watch him with a new respect, as though they were temporarily in his power again.

The fear of him had long faded. At first a fantasy had gone the rounds, to the effect that the Americans would eventually be forced to put him back in power, because they would recognize that he was the only man who could get Iraq under control once more. Soon, though, only Saddam Hussein himself and his closest supporters genuinely believed it. Yet even in 2005 most people in Iraq still assumed that the Americans would get their way there, because they were the world's only superpower. The extraordinary truth, that the United States was not as powerful as everyone had assumed, had not yet begun to sink in.

As for the trial, the natural sympathy that human beings have for an underdog, a loner, began to show itself in the cafés and teahouses of Sunni Baghdad. Far less in Shi'ite and Kurdish Baghdad, of course, and not much either in what remained of Christian Baghdad; but he had great rallying power among Sunnis once again. Putting Saddam Hussein on trial certainly didn't create the

Sunni insurgency in Iraq, but it did provide it with a martyr, an authority figure who was mocked and humiliated daily in front of everyone's eyes. By contrast, Shi'ite anger grew commensurately. It was at this time that defence lawyers and their relatives began to be murdered.

Slowly, Saddam Hussein's authority in the courtroom grew. Barzan, whose antics had entertained everyone, became quieter again. Saddam sat alone in the front of the dock, and was treated with respect by most of his fellow defendants. They stood up when he came in, and leaned forward politely on the few occasions when he spoke to them. Once or twice he even joked with them – on one occasion rubbing his beard sardonically and smiling when, after a long recess in the trial, another defendant turned up in court with a beard. Saddam was being rehabilitated in front of our eyes; and even for someone like myself, who had seen something of the terror he had created and the crimes he had committed over the years, it was hard not to feel a certain respect for him. For people around the world who knew little about his crimes, or suspected that they had largely been invented as a pretext for the invasion of 2003, Saddam began to be a hero.

The charges against him were strangely chosen. This was a man who had ordered the murders of hundreds of thousands of men and women as a matter of policy, just as his role model Stalin had. Some of these massacres were well known, even outside the country: Halabja, for instance, where I saw for myself the aftermath of the decision to drop poison gas onto the rebellious townspeople, or the systematic killings of Kurds and Shi'ites after the abortive uprisings of 1991.

Yet the Régime Crimes Liaison Office advised Saddam Hussein's prosecutors to select an incident about which most of us knew very little: the killing of 143 men and boys after an attempt to assassinate Saddam in the Shi'ite town of Dujayl in 1983. Saddam himself made the point that in any country an attempt to murder the head of state would bring some kind of retribution; and there was the expected confusion over who precisely had been responsible for which deaths. In at least one case it was suggested that someone who was supposed to have been executed was in fact still alive in Dujayl. No one tried to find out if this were true.

The trial rambled on for a year, and then came to its faltering end. Soon Saddam Hussein appeared in court again, this time charged with the murder of many thousands of Iraqi Kurds during the so-called Anfal campaign in the late 1980s. Saddam had sent his relative and co-defendant Ali Hassan al-Majid – 'Ali Chemical', as the Kurds nicknamed him after Halabja, reversed by Western journalists to 'Chemical Ali' – sweeping through the Kurdish areas, killing tens of thousands of people and destroying their towns and villages.

But Saddam Hussein would not live to see the end of this trial. The Iraqi constitution specified that any punishment had to be carried out within thirty days of the final appeal being rejected. Saddam was found guilty of the Dujayl killings on 5 November 2006, and his appeal was turned down on 26 December. By 30 December he was dead.

A sense of confusion always hung about the courtroom during his trials. Like a vapour created by the interaction of two different compounds in a laboratory, it started when the foggy idealism of the American lawyers in the Régime Crimes Liaison Office combined with the carelessness and lack of precision which was so depressingly characteristic of the Iraqi legal system. For thirty years, under the influence of Saddam Hussein, justice had mostly been the exercise of the Ba'ath Party's will. Exactitude was never required, as long as someone was found guilty. And although many Iraqi lawyers wanted to change the atmosphere, there was still an unmistakably slapdash air about the court proceedings.

Was Saddam Hussein's trial a fair one? Moderately so, in the strange circumstances of the time. He was allowed to defend himself and be defended, he could answer the allegations made against him, and so on. Did it match up to the standards of Nuremberg, or of international justice? Of course not. In many ways it was an embarrassment, and the best you could really say about it was that it was the first time a Middle Eastern country had put its former ruler on trial for crimes against human rights. Was Saddam Hussein lynched, as one or two of the more excitable commentators said? Not in any literal sense, of course; but it was always plain that he would eventually be found guilty and executed.

Saddam Hussein said as much in court:

> Everything that was done, was done under my orders. Saddam
> Hussein [he had the autocrat's unnerving habit of talking about
> himself in the third person] is the President of the Republic, and
> the President takes responsibility for what is done in his name
> . . . This is all a waste of time. You should take me out and
> shoot me now, since that is what you and your American
> backers want.

Saddam Hussein could have made a far better defence. He would
not have saved himself – he was right that the Americans and the
three successive Iraqi governments after 2004 all wanted him dead
– but he could have piled on the embarrassment for them if he had
insisted on challenging the authority of the court to a much greater
extent. He was only on trial because the Americans had invaded
Iraq, and that invasion had not had the unequivocal backing of the
United Nations. In those terms, the invasion and everything that
flowed from it was illegal.

But Saddam lacked all proper mental clarity and rigour by this
stage. The years of supreme power and constant flattery had sapped
his judgement, and the sudden overthrow had disoriented him. One
sympathizer, the former American attorney-general Ramsey Clarke,
described going to visit him in prison, to help him work out a
defence strategy for the trial.

> The prison authorities [i.e. the Americans] would only allow us
> to meet with him for one hour a week, which in itself represents
> a major infringement of his legal rights. We would go in there
> and sit down, and for the first half-hour he would read Arabic
> epic poetry to us.
>
> Now I like the sound of Arabic poetry, but since I don't
> speak a word of the language, it wasn't much use to me in
> practical terms. It meant that we only had Saddam Hussein's
> attention for thirty minutes a week.

The Americans and the Iraqis agreed on one thing: Saddam Hussein
was evil, and deserved to be hanged. When it became plain that
opinion around the world didn't necessarily agree, President Bush's
supporters were confused and resentful; partly, of course, because
so many of them believed that he had been behind the most serious
attack on American soil in history.

Yet the US forces and the White House realized before the Iraqis did that Saddam's execution would not, after all, be a particularly popular move, and they slowly began to distance themselves from the Iraqi government over it. But the Iraqi prime minister, Nouri al-Maliki, who was politically allied with some of the fiercer Shi'ites, didn't understand the difficulties he would create for himself by executing Saddam until it was too late.

3

VILLAINS

Because I lead a complicated life, and because I am out of the country so often, and because I am careless and forgetful, I employ a personal assistant; though she is more of a keeper, really. There was a time, since much of my work has to do with the BBC, that the Corporation would have taken care of this little matter for me, and given me a secretary. But not nowadays. As in so many other ways, the BBC has cut me loose, and everyone like me.

It used to give me an office and a car, and an allowance to buy the occasional suit, and money to take taxis and entertain important people to lunch. (Though it has never at any time paid me danger money for the places I go to.) I was allowed to have a free haircut every fortnight or so, from the BBC's make-up artists – some of the best in the world. I could even claim for a few cinema tickets each year, supposedly in order to help me catch up with the latest filming techniques and, hopefully, incorporate the better ones into the films I made for television news. And the Chancellor of the Exchequer looked on all this benignly, and even gave me a rebate on my taxes, because while I was abroad I wasn't using my fair share of the country's roads and hospitals and the attention of its police, its firemen and its street-sweepers.

All that has gone now, of course. These benefits and many more like them have simply evaporated. Instead, your employer and your government are in a competition to see which of them can provide you with least, at the greatest possible cost to yourself. I promise you I'm not complaining; in fact I prefer not to be kept by my employer, like some fat, lazy concubine. But it's a big change in a relatively short space of time, and it induces a lot of changes in the way you live. In my case, it meant I gave up having a car. Living near World's End, with buses shooting past the door and taxis notionally available all the time (except, somehow, at the moment you need one) I didn't want one any longer. Instead, I make my way to work on the Tube or the bus.

'If tickets cost a pound apiece,' Michael Flanders and Donald Swann sang in 1961, 'why should you make a fuss? / It's worth it just to ride inside / That thirty-feet-long by ten-feet-wide / Inside that monarch of the road, / Observer of the Highway Code, / That big six-wheeler, scarlet-painted, London Transport diesel-engined 97-horsepower omnibus.' In 1961 a pound was such a large amount of money that the idea of paying so much for a ticket was a joke, and the audience laughed aloud at it in the stalls; I know, because I went to the show with some school-friends, and laughed at it with the rest of them. In 2007, however, my bus fare costs two pounds, and because of the expense I'm thinking of shedding my pride and getting an old person's bus pass: just about the only thing on earth, as far as I can see, that I don't have to pay for now.

But having a personal assistant is worth it; or at any rate having Gina is worth it. She divides her time between me and Bob Geldof, a friend and near neighbour of mine, and both of us are inclined to ring her up and ask her where we are and what we're doing here. She is remarkably patient when we do, and everyone who deals with her tells me how pleasant she is. It helps that she is my sister-in-law.

So one day I was sitting in her office, trying to work out how to say no to the importunate organizer of a literary festival who wanted an immense amount of effort from me for her money, except that there was no money; and who would cut up very rough indeed when Gina explained to her that the BBC wanted me in Baghdad on the day of the festival. Just as Gina was about to pick up the phone to speak to her, the fax machine sprang into life. It was probably a relief to Gina to put the phone down again.

Fax machines are a slightly elderly concept nowadays. They remind me of seeing a fifty-year-old in a three-piece pin-striped suit selling phones in a high street shop: nothing whatever wrong with that, but slightly unusual. I bought my first fax machine in 1989, when the coated paper curled up and the writing on it faded quickly in the sunlight. It saved me, when I wrote an article for a newspaper or magazine, from having to get in my car and drive across the face of London to hand my work in, in person. It's not that long ago, yet the way it changed my life is extraordinary.

This particular fax machine began spewing out a rather nice-looking document with an impressive heading. I watched it develop in front of my eyes.

'The Spanish State Lottery,' I read upside down; and then, 'Congratulations!!!!'

Today, of course, everybody would instantly realize that this was just part of a rather obvious scam. Within a couple of years I was getting thirty or forty emails like this a day. Sometimes I had won a lottery in some foreign country. Mostly, though, some senior figure in an African bank (Burkina Faso was the most usual one; employees from BF's unsurprisingly small banking sector seemed remarkably active in their crookedness) would corruptly offer me a large slice of some blocked account which he or she happened to have access to. On one occasion the widow of the unpleasant Nigerian military dictator Sani Abacha emailed me to say she was prepared to give me 30 per cent of her late husband's fortune if I would send her my bank account number and allow her to pay it in.

I know you should never reply to this kind of thing, but it was late at night and I felt mischievous. 'This is a very kind offer,' I wrote back to her, 'but I would have had a little more confidence in it if you had spelled your late supposed husband's name correctly.'

I pressed 'send'. Three minutes later, from somewhere presumably in the depths of Nigeria, the reply pinged onto my computer screen.

'Fuck you,' said Mrs Abacha tersely. She still spelled it 'Abachu'.

Now, in Gina's office, the first page of the fax slipped out neatly onto the floor. Gina picked it up and read it out, mistakes and all.

'We happily congratulate you being one of the lucky winners of our yearly International Promotions Program.'

I had, it seemed, won a big prize on the Spanish State Lottery. And if this seemed slightly unusual, given that I had never bought a Spanish lottery ticket in my life and hadn't even been to Spain for some years, the fax explained that in order to encourage future investors and draw attention to the lottery, a computer randomly selected fax numbers, whose lucky owners would receive large amounts of money. Very large amounts of money.

'Seven hundred and five thousand, three hundred and sixty-six euros,' Gina read out, relishing every word.

We looked it up on a currency converter: it amounted to a little over £494,000.

I needed the money, of course; one always seems to. Even the £4,000 off the end would help.

'It could be genuine, couldn't it?' Gina said wistfully.

We had a bit of a laugh about that.

But the fax asked me to ring a Madrid phone number, and it seemed better than ringing the woman at the literary festival.

There was a brief moment between pressing the last number and hearing the ringing tone when I thought of hanging up. It was all, I knew perfectly well, just some kind of scam. Yet it was also amusing and interesting, and maybe I could turn it to some kind of profit, financial or intellectual.

'Hola?'

I knew then and there that it was a con. There are many ways of saying 'Hola?', but this one sounded big and pudgy and very un-Spanish. And if this really was the Spanish State Lottery Board answering, how come they didn't have a switchboard and someone Spanish to answer the phone?

'Hello – do you speak English?'

The pudgy voice admitted cagily that it did. And it sounded even less Spanish than before.

'I've just received your fax. It seems I'm a winner of your International Promotions Lottery.'

I was waiting for the voice to turn congratulatory, but it didn't. It stayed cagey.

'What is your name?' it asked.

I'd got the accent now: Nigeria.

Nigeria is a wonderful country, and my heart lifts every time I go there. It is full of life and enjoyment and noise and bustle. It is also full of crooks.

'My name is Simpson; John Simpson. And yours?'

'I am Mr Bobby Williams.'

With Gina sitting beside me, listening, I couldn't resist pushing him a bit.

'I'm intrigued that the Spanish State Lottery Board employs someone who isn't Spanish.'

There was a long silence at the other end. It seemed to me that Mr Bobby Williams was deciding how to play this. In the end, characteristically, he decided to be jolly.

'Hello, my dear friend,' he boomed, as though we were speaking for the first time. 'Many, many fine congratulations on winning your handsome prize.'

Nigerians are boisterous and expressive, and they like their adjectives. 'I am very happy and celebratory for you and your family. You have won a huge deal of money, you know.'

'How much?'

'Aha, that depends on the Promotional Draw, Mr John.'

'It says here I've won seven hundred thousand euros.'

'Wonderful, wonderful, yes. Now all we must to do is make the arrangement for you to receive your money and taking it away with you.'

'Sounds good to me. What do I have to do?'

There comes a moment in every developing confidence trick when the trickster has to put the hard word on the poor, unsuspecting mark. That moment had now come.

'We will be writing you a cheque. A big cheque, eh? Lots of figures on it! Ha, ha! We will send it to you immediately. You will be a very rich man. We will send it off to you directly we receive your facility fee.'

So there it was.

'How big will the facility fee have to be?'

'Oh, nothing, nothing. Very small. A proportion only.'

'But how big a proportion?'

'Just a little one. Maybe a thousand euros, maybe more. The more you win, the fee gets bigger! Ha, ha!'

An idea was forming in my mind. By chance, somewhere in Gina's superbly efficient files was an unused return ticket to Madrid. I could hop over there, go and see Mr Bobby Williams, and write an article for one of the newspapers about his scam.

'Can I come and pay my facility fee in person?'

The geniality froze, and suspicion took its place. I could imagine Mr Bobby Williams taking the handset from his ear and looking at it, frowning, like people do in comic American television soaps.

'It's highly unregular, but you could.'

'All right, I'll see you the day after tomorrow. What's the address of the State Lottery Board?'

'Ah, you see, I work in an out-office.'

He gave me the address. I knew the area slightly.

'I'll let you know exactly when I'm coming.'

Gina was worried.

'Don't you think they could get violent?' She thought a moment. 'Perhaps Mark should go with you and take the pictures.'

Mark is her husband, my brother-in-law: a property entrepreneur from South Africa who, before he settled in Britain, created game reserves. He transported lions and other ferocious animals from one place to another, so he's a good man to go into the jungle with: including the jungle of crooks and confidence tricksters. I asked him if he would go to Madrid with me, and he threw himself into the plan with his usual energy and enthusiasm.

I rang Bobby Williams again with the details of our flight.

'When you and your brother arrive,' said Bobby Williams, 'we will have a limousine to collect you and bring you to the office. Ring this number' (he gave it to me) 'and ask to speak to Mr Greg Williams, the head of our Protocol Department.'

'Another Williams, eh? Keeping it in the family, I suppose.'

'Ha, ha!' said Mr Bobby, but he didn't sound very amused.

We took a pleasant early-morning flight to Madrid, making jokes the whole way about the Williams brothers and what was going to happen. I suppose if I'm really honest I still hoped, in some innocent corner of my being, that it would suddenly all come right and I would be given half a million pounds. But I kept quiet about it, because the rest of me knew it wasn't going to happen.

I rang Mr Greg Williams from the Protocol Department the moment we got into the arrivals hall. Mr Greg sounded exactly like Mr Bobby.

'My name is Simpson, John Simpson. Mr Bobby Williams told me to ring you.'

Again, that non-committal silence.

'Am I speaking to Mr Bobby, or to Mr Greg?'

'Where are you now?'

We established where I was.

'The driver will meet you.'

It wasn't a limousine. It was a beaten-up Seat, and it was driven by a gloomy Spaniard who seemed to have no great affection for the Williamses, but couldn't be coaxed into talking about them either.

He drove us the short distance to the centre of Madrid. I had a particular affection for this road, because my team and I had once joined up with the official convoy of the Soviet foreign minister, Andrei Gromyko, and been waved through all the checkpoints with him. We followed him into the main conference centre in Madrid, where I interviewed him and got a world exclusive. Nowadays, of course, we would simply have been shot as potential terrorists.

At the back of the conference centre was a little street, and at one end of the street was a modern office building: not expensive, not cheap, not impressive, and yet not entirely unimpressive either. Well chosen for a scam, I thought. There was a board in the entrance hall with the names of all the companies based there. The Lottery Board wasn't mentioned, of course, but against the floor where Mr Greg had told us to go, it said simply, in English, 'Office Suites'. We got into the lift, and Mark pressed the button marked '14'.

The lift doors opened onto a large open space, rather pleasantly decorated. Two attractive young women sat at a desk in the middle of the room, talking to each other. I stood there for a while, waiting for a lull in the conversation. It came when one of them looked at her fingernails and picked up an emery board.

Where was the office of the Lottery Board, I asked, in my not very good Spanish. She looked through a list, then looked back at me.

'Mr Bobby Williams?' I ventured.

Recognition dawned. She pointed to an office down at the end of the suite. Mark and I looked at each other, and headed towards it.

Mr Bobby Williams, or possibly Mr Greg Williams of the Protocol Department, was standing in the doorway: a magnificent sight. He was big, and wearing a brown mohair suit with a very large gold-striped tie. Gold hung from him and clinked at every movement. He had several rings on his large though baby-like hands. His vast gold wristwatch was one of those brash, noisy brands advertised by film stars. Business was clearly booming in the confidence-trick industry.

He excavated an enormous white silk handkerchief from his trouser pocket as he sat there to greet us. He blew his nose with a sound like a fog-bound ship.

'Good morning, good morning, good morning,' he beamed, showing us some fine dental work and directing us to the seats opposite his large desk.

Mr Bobby Williams didn't stint on himself, I decided.

'This is my brother-in-law and business associate, Mr Mark Nelthorpe-Cowne,' I said.

'Glad to meet you, Mr Nel,' he said, and sank back into his chair.

I looked around. The place was pleasantly enough furnished, but it looked like a showroom; and the more I thought about it, the more I realized it *was* a showroom. There were no pictures on the wall, not even the meaningless ones people usually use to decorate their offices. There were no certificates, not even phoney ones announcing that Mr Bobby Williams held a degree from some ultra-dubious university; perhaps it hadn't occurred to him to buy one of those yet. My eyes wandered down to the neatly placed filing trays on his desk. Those little white rectangles on them: surely they were price tags? I leaned closer, as though just shifting my position. They *were* price tags.

Everything here had either been hired or bought for the occasion, just for our visit.

There is a short story by Sir Arthur Conan Doyle, 'The Red-Headed League', where one of Sherlock Holmes's clients, Jabez Wilson, a pawnbroker with a remarkable shock of bright red hair, is lured into a criminal scam. A crook advertises in *The Times* for people with red hair to come forward and be selected for a select club of red-headed men, paid for by an eccentric millionaire. All sorts of people turn up at the given address, an office which is hired out by the hour. In the end it turns out the criminal master-mind behind it all wants to rob the City and Suburban Bank, and needs to get Jabez Wilson out of his shop while he does it. It's an enjoyable story and well worth reading.

I looked at Mr Bobby. He didn't look like a reader of Sherlock Holmes stories, but you never knew.

'Where are you from?' I asked, sounding like an American trying to strike up a conversation.

It was a harmless enough question, but it seemed to catch Mr Bobby on the raw. He had been staring out of the window, but now looked around at me suspiciously, with a clink of gold as he moved.

'South Africa.'

Mark, who knows every part of South Africa, had already spotted that he certainly wasn't from there.

'Oh,' he asked, with apparent innocence. 'Whereabouts?'

Mr Bobby turned aggressive.

'I don't have to tell you that.'

There was an awkward pause. Even Mr Bobby seemed embarrassed.

I decided to distract him from these questions with a show of willingness.

'So, how much do I have to pay to get my money?'

Mr Bobby did a calculation with his brand-new pen on a brand-new pad of paper.

'Two thousand, eight hundred euros,' he said with a self-satisfied air.

'That's quite a lot of money,' I said. 'Can I pay you when I've got my winnings?'

He smiled apologetically, and spread his beringed hands in a 'What can I do?' way.

'It's the rules. You know.'

He reached into one of the brand-new trays and pulled out a receipt book in a rather marked kind of way, as though to let me know it was time to pay up. Then he started filling in one of the receipts. I could see his big, rather well-formed numerals, upside down: €2,800.

I hadn't actually got anything like that amount of money with me, but I didn't like to tell him so. There was a pause, as he looked at me expectantly.

I have to say, he looked pretty good. That tan suit of his wasn't bought off the rail, I was sure. And, when I looked more carefully, his shirt had clearly been hand-sewn: there's always something about the collar. If it hadn't been for the garish gold-striped tie, the kind you see on elderly Middle Eastern godfather politicians, he would have looked quite superb.

One last glance, down at his feet. Always, a long-dead colleague of mine, very charming, beautifully dressed, discreetly gay, had once told me, always look at their shoes: you can see from them whether there's real class there. His advice was enough to make me buy my shoes from Tricker's ever afterwards, even though the rest of my turn-out is distinctly on the careless side.

Mr Bobby's shoes let him down badly. They were imitation crocodile, with bits of gold on them, and two little leather tassels on top of each one. It's never been entirely clear to me why people would want to walk down the street with little leather tassels flip-flopping on their shoes.

I looked at his face again. He was still waiting for me to pay up.

'I wonder if you've got some card or certificate to show that you really are working for the Spanish Lottery Commission?'

More aggression.

'I don't hold them just at the moment. My business associate, he's got them.'

'Is that Mr Greg Williams?'

Too many questions, of course. I didn't want to frighten him off until we had some idea of the extent of the scam. He sat there sulking for a moment, then with a kind of monumental convulsion, his gold chains chinking, he reached for his mobile phone and dialled a number. Then he started shouting into it, in a language that had none of the flow or the pleasant clicks of any of South Africa's languages that I had heard.

He was making so much noise that I was able to ask Mark what he thought. No, nothing remotely South African.

Then Mark pulled out his own mobile phone. It was a brand-new type, the first mobile phone on the market with a camera in it. He had brought it because he didn't think he'd be able to get a shot of Mr Bobby in any other way.

Now he, too, started making a call; except that I could tell there was no one on the other end of the line. His voice paused for a moment, in an artificial question, and he took a photo of Mr Bobby on the phone. The trouble was, it was the first time Mark had taken a picture with it in earnest, and he forgot that an imitation shutter noise came with it as an optional extra. Mr Bobby had also stopped shouting at that moment, and the shutter noise sounded horribly loud.

Mr Bobby jumped up and walked across the room, shouting even louder and more nervously into the phone for a sentence or two.

'My business associate is coming,' he said, with a certain menace.

He pushed the receipt book over towards me. Deciding that we were getting close to being thrown out, or worse, I flicked through the pages ahead of the one he wanted me to fill in. There were five carbon copies there, all of them covered with his big writing. I suppose he had filled out the top copies and sent them off by post. And I assumed that in some way he had received the money from these five people, or else he would never have sent off the receipts.

All of them had British names, and all of them were for even larger amounts of money than the €2,800 he wanted from me. I totted up the figures in the carbon copies in my head: around €18,000, or £12,500, and all the payments had been made in the previous month. Not a king's ransom, but it was a nice little income; and presumably Mr Bobby had plenty of other scams going as well. No wonder he could afford so many gold rings.

Suddenly, I felt angry. Fraudsters like this don't inflict physical injuries on anyone, but they cause a lot of damage all the same. I was about to launch into a lecture when I caught sight of Mark's face. He realized, better than I, that it was time to go. Reinforcements were on the way, and Mr Bobby was blowing up into something of a state. His face had gone a very fierce colour indeed.

Nothing more was said about paying him. We shook hands, mumbling something about coming back soon, and headed for the door. The two girls were still sitting talking at the fourteenth-floor reception desk as we passed. They scarcely even looked at us.

I was still a bit worried that we might bump into Mr Bobby's friend. Even if we assumed that he and Mr Greg Williams were one and the same person, Mr Bobby had certainly been bellowing down the phone to someone: I could hear the answering bellow.

But there was no one in the lobby as we left. We jumped into a taxi and headed off. It was pouring with rain, but we soon found a highly convivial Peruvian restaurant, where we sat and ate *ceviche* and some interesting meat dish whose name I didn't catch, washed down with a fiery Rioja. We laughed a great deal during the meal, and did Mr Bobby imitations. And then we headed back to the airport for the late-afternoon flight.

The article looked very good in next Sunday's newspaper. But the best things were the photographs. Mr Bobby looked magnificent in his chair, the rings flashing, as he shouted into his phone. There was another picture of me, with my head over the receipt book. The editor told me later it had all provoked an unusually large number of letters and emails from people who had been the victims of scams like this.

When we checked with the real Spanish Lottery Board, which had a reputation for being well-run, efficient and honest, a press spokeswoman said they'd had many complaints that several Nigerians working out of Madrid were offering prizes in the Board's name, and demanding money.

It didn't take Sherlock Holmes to guess that when I called the number of the office suite, there would be no further record of a Mr Bobby Williams. He had moved out the same afternoon, soon after we left, having rented the office for no more than a day. A call to his mobile simply resulted in a recorded message saying the number was no longer in use.

There would always be another phone number, another fax machine (I forgot to check whether that was brand-new, like the document trays; my guess is it wasn't), and if necessary another rented office. There had to be. The trick was too good not to be turned again.

§

I had never been to China before the extraordinary month of May 1989, which resulted in the massacre in Tiananmen Square; what the Chinese government for years afterwards referred to, if it

absolutely had to mention it, as 'the incidents'. For some time
afterwards I was unwelcome in China. But in the end I was allowed
back, and even given a small banquet by a group of officials who
were remarkably polite to me, in the circumstances.

During the Tiananmen period we employed a translator whose
name was Mr T'ang. He was supplied by the government, and all
the students who worked for us thought he was a government spy.
He certainly jotted down everything everyone said in a little notebook, and when I asked him why he did so, he said he was going to
write a short story about his experiences with us. He probably did:
though whether the readership comprised the secret police, it is
impossible to say.

Things were pretty strange at that time. The secret police and
the judges actually joined the enormous demonstrations against the
government, standing on huge floats which drove slowly through
Tiananmen Square like the Lord Mayor's Show in London. The
secret policemen in their official uniforms (why do secret policemen
have uniforms?) and the judges in their robes waved happily to the
crowd, certain that they were on the winning side, which is where
every Chinese bureaucrat wants to be, and that Deng Xiaoping, the
country's leader, would be forced to resign.

The sequel, as Georges Brassens says in his cynical song 'La
Gorille', proved them wrong. Three weeks later, troops loyal to
Deng attacked the students in the square, and the entire rebellion
collapsed. I've never forgotten the strange experience of being
waved at in such a jolly way by so many secret policemen, though.
Mr T'ang vanished when things got difficult, of course, so he
probably was a spy, as the students suspected. But he introduced
me to Chinese poetry, and for that I am very grateful. His two
favourite poets were Li Bai and Du Fu, and he would talk to me for
hours on end about them, and about Chinese poetics in general;
and the result was that, with the help of a Chinese friend, I took to
translating some of Li's and Du's poems. Classical Chinese poetry
is exasperatingly difficult to render into English, because everything
is pared to an absolute minimum; and since large amounts of
grammar are simply left out, it is often very hard to work out what
on earth the poet is talking about. Not only that, but English is a
wholly different kind of language, not brief and understated at all,

but rambling and full of short words which provide the complexity and interest.

I struggled for a long time, for instance, with a poem by Du Fu, who lived from 712 to 770 and saw at first hand some of the appalling devastation which followed the rebellion of General An Lushan in 756. The rebellion smashed the wonderful artistic achievements of the T'ang Dynasty, which was one of the high points of Chinese civilization. The poem is in the *lü-shih* style, which is technically very demanding. Here is a literal rendering of the characters Du Fu uses in the first four lines:

> Empire broken mountains rivers remain
> City spring grass trees thick
> Feel time flowers sprinkle tears
> Resent separation birds shock heart

That's all; and like some complex puzzle the poor translator has to make sense of it all. When I look now at my efforts, I find them pretty empty. An awful lot of space, it seems, is taken up with trying to explain to the English-speaking reader, who's used to a much more expansive kind of poetry, what it's all about.

> The Empire has collapsed, yet the mountains and rivers remain.
> In the city it is springtime; the grass and leaves grow thick.
> Flowers drop tears for the troubled times.
> The sound of the birds is shocking, as if they resent leaving.

Oh dear. And yet someone actually published that. They even paid me for it. Looking at it now, I am reminded of something by the early twentieth-century humorous novelist Ernest Bramah, who went in for a gentle, witty form of chinoiserie. Someone in one of his stories wants a portrait of a particularly beautiful girl. 'After secretly observing the unstudied grace of her movements,' he writes, 'the most celebrated picture-maker of the province burned the implements of his craft, and began life anew as the trainer of performing elephants.' (He also wrote this about the literary tastes of different social classes: 'The prosperous and substantial find contentment in hearing of the unassuming virtues and frugal lives of the poor and unsuccessful. Those of humble origin, especially tea-house maidens and the like, are only really at home among

stories of the exalted and quick-moving, the profusion of their
robes, the magnificence of their palaces, and the general high-
minded depravity of their lives.') Like the celebrated picture-maker
with his brushes, I threw away my Chinese dictionaries. But I kept
my interest in the T'ang Dynasty. Who wouldn't? The emperor who
was overthrown in the An Lushan rebellion was an almost absurdly
romantic figure called Xuanzong, who ruled extremely effectively
until he fell in love with one of his concubines, Yang Guifei. She
bewitched him with her beauty, and he gave up the tedious business
of government in order to spend all his time with her.

She, meanwhile, intrigued so effectively that her relatives took
the most lucrative jobs in the administration, and began to bleed
the state dry. General An Lushan tried to become Yang Guifei's
lover; but he was an ugly bear of a man, not a Han Chinese at all,
and she dismissed him. In revenge, he staged a military *coup d'état*.

When General An captured the capital, Chang-an, the emperor
fled in the direction of Szechuan, taking the beautiful Yang Guifei
with him. But on the journey his guards mutinied, and said they
would continue the journey only if Yang Guifei were killed. Weeping tears of horror and despair, the emperor agreed; but he insisted
that she should be strangled with the finest silken cord. You can
still see the rest-house where all this happened, more than twelve
hundred years ago, on the road outside Chang-an.

To our eyes, Yang Guifei might not have been quite the beauty
Emperor Xuanzong felt she was. Like a film star, her looks were
celebrated and imitated everywhere. Nowadays, thousands of
images based on her have survived; but collectors and dealers know
them, prosaically, as 'the fat lady'.

During the month of the Tiananmen demonstrations, I spent
every free hour I could exploring the antiques quarter of Beijing,
which is known as Liulichang – the ceramic tile quarter. This
was where all the tiles for the Forbidden City were manufactured,
though it later became an upper-middle-class area, the Kensington
of Beijing. An entire neighbourhood of *hutongs*, little traditional
lanes, has been preserved there, keeping out the developers who
have ruined most of the rest of the city. Much of the stuff in the
shops is junk, and almost all the pieces which look good are copies.

In 1989, less than twenty years after the end of the Cultural

Revolution, it was pretty much impossible to find anything at all interesting in Liulichang which genuinely dated from the T'ang Dynasty. The shopkeepers used to shake their heads and look away when I asked, as though they expected an inspector to come and arrest them. You could find pleasant enough things from the Qing Dynasty, which ended in 1911 with the proclamation of the Republic, but they always had a fussy, Victorian look to them.

It was when I was allowed back into China, some time after the Tiananmen massacre, that I realized that things had changed. I walked into a shop in Liulichang, just the kind of grubby, cluttered, unattractive place I like, and started looking round. There were some lovely clay figures there, and some in a glorious multicoloured glaze known as *sancai*.

The man behind the counter watched me.

'You don't remember me, do you?' he said after a while.

He got up, shut the door, and turned the 'closed' sign round.

I looked at him carefully, but couldn't remember that I'd ever seen him before. He was in his late twenties, I suppose. I smiled as politely as I could. If you appear on television, you tend to forget the people you've interviewed; but for some of them it is often a once-in-a-lifetime experience, and they remember a great deal about it.

'In the Square. I was a student. I told you that this demonstration could never be defeated.'

He gave a light, bitter laugh. Over the next hour, as we sat over a pot of tea, he told me all about his life since then: going on the run in his native province, being hunted by the local police, and finally being captured and confessing and being gaoled. In prison he learned things – he didn't say what – and was able to get a job when he came out.

'Not in a factory, though. The only way now is to be a trader. I'm a trader in' – he waved his arm expansively round his shop – 'ancient art. And art that looks ancient.'

He laughed and laughed. And then he started to give me a master-class in the forgery and discovery of antiquities, using his stock as examples.

'This horse with its rider: yes, it's OK. It's not very good, and it's not worth much, but I can promise you it's genuine because I know who found it, and where. Look: if you wet your finger and rub it on the clay, the moisture sinks in immediately and the clay dries. That usually means it's old. Now look at this.'

He pulled out a rather attractive *sancai* figure of a fat lady with Yang Guifei looks, playing a stringed instrument that looked a bit like a guitar. He put another one alongside it. This one had a flute.

'Lick your finger, like I showed you.'

I did. The moisture took a long time to sink in.

'But these two still have clay on them,' I said artlessly. 'They haven't even been cleaned up properly. Doesn't that show they've just been dug up?'

He laughed. 'All it shows is that they've been buried recently. That's all part of the treatment.'

He explained that the moisture test wasn't anywhere near foolproof, and that new batches of figures were being made which would pass that particular trial. The only way to be absolutely certain was to send a piece off to a laboratory in Oxford for testing. And even then he could put a small piece of genuine T'ang work into a figure that was fake, and send a sample from that to Oxford.

'But I don't do that kind of thing: it's too complicated. I sell mostly fakes. But I do have some good pieces . . .'

He showed me; they were beautiful, but way beyond my means. And anyway, smuggling antiquities isn't my thing. I bought a couple of the phoney figures, because I liked them. To this day I haven't washed the clay off them.

I went back to Beijing several times after that, and saw him each time. He told me on my last visit that the Chinese government had set up a secret factory for manufacturing the highest grade of antiquities and selling them off to wealthy Chinese and Western collectors. Apparently they ground up real but poor-quality antiquities and reconstituted them from the original clay, so they always passed the wet-finger test.

But things had changed in other ways. All over China, he said, people were digging up ancient tombs and robbing them. The market was flooded, profits were down. The best pieces were still to be found in Hong Kong, from where they could legally be exported, and the tomb robbers simply made their way there, rather than coming to dealers like him in Beijing.

'I think I need to find another business,' he said, wrapping a rather charming tomb-figure of a general in cotton wool and putting it back in his 'high quality' drawer. 'Maybe computers.'

He didn't seem to understand when I laughed.

Five years passed, during which I didn't go to China at all. Nowadays I was no longer barred, though the government was annoyed when I interviewed a leading dissident at a time when China was assuring its friends abroad that their human rights policies were improving. The dissident told me how he was arrested and kept in the cells every time some big foreign leader paid a visit. The Western embassies weren't interested when he complained to them, he said.

'They just want to keep trading with our government.'

When he and I went out for a walk, we were followed by a black car; and then, as we left the road, a man with a briefcase got out and followed us at a distance.

'Who's that?'

'Oh, he keeps an eye on me.'

'What's he like?'

'Pleasant enough.'

With the dissident's agreement, the cameraman and producer and I went over to the secret policeman. He seemed entirely unfazed by the whole thing, and bowed to me most politely. If I hadn't been on camera, I would have bowed back.

I finally went back in 2006. Beijing was more crowded, more polluted, more jammed with cars than ever before. Many of the surviving *hutongs* I had come to love had vanished. Enormous palaces of glass, ugly and featureless and foreign, had reared up in their place.

Liulichang remained, though. I went straight to my friend's shop. A very pleasant girl who spoke excellent English was standing behind the counter.

'Is Mr Li here still?'

'No, sir, not Mr Li. Mr Hu works here, sir, but he has gone to his home for a short sleep. Can I help you?'

I didn't feel she could. The shelves were now full of figures which even from a distance I could see were entirely imitation.

I wandered round for a while. I bought a flute from one very charming shopkeeper, and photographed him as he played it, the shelves behind him crammed with the kind of stuff that was interesting enough to look at but contained nothing serious for a collector. I took tea, and bought a couple of Qing scrolls, and had decided to head for my hotel when I noticed a little side alley I had never spotted before.

There were one or two smaller, cheaper shops down here, and a sign in English that said 'Silk Caprets'. I wasn't in the market for a silk capret, or even a silk carpet, but I thought I'd take a look.

The alley stank of rotting vegetables, and there were feathers and blood on the earthen ground. I'm not in favour of dirt, but I do like things to be normal; and normal in China is not beautifully swept and shiny. Real life seemed to exist down this little lane, as compared with the sham in so much of the rest of Beijing. It felt good just to amble down it; as long, that is, as I watched where I was walking. It was narrow, and small noisome courtyards opened off it. I caught sight of a quick swirl of a skirt, a dog with its fangs bared, an old man splashing his naked torso from a tin bath.

And then there was a shout. My Mandarin is pretty rudimentary – I got it from a set of tapes in 1989, have never improved it since then, and have forgotten most of it anyway – but I can still tell when someone is inviting me indoors for a cup of tea. I spun round: there was a skinny little man in shorts and a dirty vest, making scooping signs in the air to encourage me inside.

Sensible people, of course, smile politely at such moments and move on, their heads tilted slightly upwards so as not to have to see anything more. But I've made a living for forty years out of not being very sensible, and anyway I felt I could do with another cup of tea. So I pushed my way through the curtain the skinny little man indicated, and found myself in a small and very smelly room.

It was plain that at least four people lived, cooked, ate, defecated and slept in this room. It was an easy enough deduction, since three of them were lying on some very provisional beds, and the fourth, the skinny one, was clearly at home here. They had seen me through the window as I passed. There were no curtains across it, just a thick, miasmic layer of dirt which did the job just as well. Someone put the kettle on, and the smell of gas from a bottle was suddenly strong.

Now that I was in, there was a silence. No one quite knew what to do or say. I sat there looking at them, and they sat there looking at me. The tea provided a brief respite, but not a very long one. Soon we were looking at each other and smiling again.

The skinny man I'd seen at first started talking at me very loudly, since it was clear that I was an idiot who couldn't speak decent Chinese. The problem was, it didn't sound to me as though he was speaking Mandarin; and my tapes didn't include any of the hundreds of other languages and dialects which are spoken in China. I smiled and looked into my cup, and there was more silence.

I was just about to get up and leave, when the curtain over the doorway twitched again, and a man pushed his way in. This time I recognized him; but I suppose he was so surprised to see me that he couldn't think for a moment who I was. He was larger and better dressed than when I had seen him last. He had an air of authority, too.

'Hello, Mr Li.'

'Oh, it's Mr John from the BBC! Welcome, welcome! I didn't expect to see you again.'

'You've given up the shop?'

'Too much controls.'

I said nothing more.

The inhabitants of the room all started talking to him at once. He raised his hand, and they went quiet. Clearly, they regarded him with some respect.

'They want to show you some things they've found,' said Mr Li. 'They should have waited for me to come. Maybe they weren't going to pay me.'

He smiled a slightly pained smile.

'But who are they?'

'Oh, they are just peasants from the north-west. They dig things up, you see, and bring them to me. I let them use this house.'

'What sort of things?'

'Tomb goods. *Sancai* figures. Sometimes gold and silver. I sell them to collectors from Europe and America.'

'They're tomb raiders?'

He laughed.

'Just local farmers, working with a few simple tools.'

'They're tomb raiders.'

'Whatever you like.'

At this point the skinny one pulled a bundle wrapped in a large and very dirty sheet out from under one of the beds, and started to open it up. A lot of wrapping had gone on, in blankets, small cloths, toilet-paper and newspaper. Finally the last layer remained: and when that was taken off I had to stop myself from saying something out loud. It was a sensational ewer with a light green glaze, and a beautiful craquelure. I'd seen things like this in museums and catalogues, but never wrapped up in toilet paper and the *People's Daily*. A faint amount of dark red clay was stuck to it, but I had the feeling no one had added it on in this case.

'Northern Sung,' said Mr Li.

'From 950 to 1200,' I said, showing off my knowledge of Chinese dynasties.

Actually, I got both dates slightly wrong, but it was a reasonable effort and Mr Li acknowledged it.

'First Crusade, Battle of Hastings, Third Crusade,' I added, to put it into context for myself.

Nowhere in Europe could something as well crafted and delicate as this have been made at that time. It must have been worth ten thousand pounds, at least; and although the four vest-wearers had no idea of that, Mr Li did. That ruled me out as a buyer.

Another sheet, another pile of rags, another wonderful revelation: a tall, pale porcelain construction which must have been intended to hold some kind of juice or wine. The delicacy of the colour and the beautiful way the tiny cracks ran in the glaze showed me that this too belonged in a museum.

Mr Li, to do him credit, was too tactful even to suggest a price for these things. Clay horses and riders were one thing; two triumphs of Northern Sung art were something else. He knew I wasn't in the market.

'How did they find them?'

He rattled off an instruction in a harsh dialect that contained no word I could understand. The youngest man, only around twenty, went into the corner and brought out a series of implements. He piled them up in the middle of the room, and looked expectantly at Mr Li. Mr Li nodded.

The young man, so thin in his vest and shorts that you could see his emaciated chest when he bent down, picked up the first implement. It was a heavy wooden mallet, with a handle four feet long. In dumb show, he demonstrated walking round the rolling hills of north-western China, the mallet over his left shoulder, looking for likely places where a tomb might be.

Then he freezes, staring intently at an area just beyond the bits of toilet-paper which had been wound round the porcelain wonder. It is a Chinese opera, though he looks more as though he is acting in a silent film. He inches forward, stamping his right foot on the ground; then he stops to listen, hand cupped round his ear. He looks round to check that no one is looking. Then he bangs the mallet down, quite gently, on his chosen spot.

The mallet is laid aside. Now he picks up a nasty-looking spear of iron, six feet long, with a sharpened point. He mimics sticking it into the ground and pressing down with all his strength, until suddenly and rather dangerously he finds a cavity in the ground, and the spear moves downward fast. Then he puts it down and creeps away, still looking to see he hasn't been observed.

The others enter into the spirit of the thing. They move forward off their beds, and each takes up a short-handled spade from the bunch of tools. They mimic digging, until one of them, the eldest of course, finds some imaginary object of value. They all gather round, looking at it and taking it in their hands one by one; I have the impression it is very large.

'Gold,' says Mr Li complacently. He doesn't play any part in the digging, acted out or real.

They put the imaginary object into an imaginary sack, and then all four of them mime their way across the tiny room on tiptoe, having looted even more from China's heritage. Then they lie down on their smelly beds and pretend to sleep.

'You make good money doing this?'

Mr Li looks at me as though I'm crazy.

'Good money, yes,' he says.

'And you will get a lot for these lovely pieces?'

I found it hard to take my eyes off them.

'Especially these.'

It was a long way from being a rebellious student in Tiananmen

Square. Then, as I recall, he and all the others wanted peace, democracy and freedom. What they got was a government that watched them carefully but gave then freedom of a sort: the freedom to loot China's hidden goods and sell them round the world.

§

It was October 2000, and in the Balkans the winter was coming on fast. NATO had bombed Serbia and Kosovo the previous year, in a campaign which lasted eleven weeks and showed up all sorts of embarrassing disagreements among NATO members. It turned out that some of Serbia's friends inside NATO were quietly slipping information to the unpleasant regime of Slobodan Milosevic.

I spent the whole period in Belgrade, and drew down on myself the wrath of Tony Blair and some members of his government as a result. Politicians who advocate bombing often dislike it if you tell people what happens when the bombs land. Dee joined me there, a month or so into the campaign, and then I slipped over on the steps of the swimming-pool in my luxurious but deserted hotel, did something absolutely horrible to my knee, had an operation in a hospital which NATO managed to hit more than once and spent the rest of the war in plaster from my ankle to my hip. I didn't tell the BBC what had happened, because I was afraid they would call me home.

So my good friend and producer Dragan Petrovic would wheel me downstairs to the front of the hotel and prop me up against one of the pillars, while Dee arranged my hair and tie, and I would do my piece to camera standing there. Afterwards, when I looked at some of the tapes, you could see I was leaning at a strange angle, as though on the deck of a ship that was slowly sinking.

As in a sense it was. Eventually, after more than ten weeks of not very effective bombing, a heavy-duty Russian businessman persuaded Slobodan Milosevic to agree to pull his soldiers out of Kosovo, where they had been planning to drive out and perhaps massacre large numbers of people of Albanian origin, and the bombing stopped. As a result, the ethnic Albanians started to drive out and massacre the Serbs in Kosovo. That is the Balkans for you; and to the amazement of the US and British governments, it turned out in the end that there were no real good guys or bad guys after all; just a collection of mutually hostile tribes with a millennium-long history of killing each other.

In the autumn of the following year, 2000, Milosevic had to hold a presidential election. He had been clinging on to power with the fingernails of one hand since the end of the bombing, but was hoping to be able to cook the books sufficiently to get himself re-elected. He didn't want the world's press hanging around and observing the process; so there were no visas, and Serbia's borders were firmly closed.

There was only one place to be, if you couldn't get to Belgrade, and that was Podgorica, the minuscule capital of the semi-independent state of Montenegro. Notionally, after the final break-up of the former Yugoslavia, Montenegro and Serbia formed one country. But Montenegro, though smaller, poorer and much more remote, was a more sensible place than Milosevic's absurdly overheated republic, and it kept its distance from him. That didn't stop NATO dropping a bomb or two on Montenegro, just to show it didn't care about such distinctions, but even then Montenegro stayed out of the war.

Now, Montenegro's relations with Milosevic were worse than ever, and the world's press were welcomed to Podgorica. There were only a couple of half-way decent hotels, and very few cafés and restaurants. Soon, every room and every table was permanently taken, and small, earnest groups of men and some women in their thirties and forties gathered everywhere in the centre of town. Most seemed to have television equipment on the floor beside them.

I have to say, I hate occasions like these. To have to be pleasant and make polite conversation with people whose professional throats you are being paid to cut is not my kind of thing. I much prefer to be out on my own somewhere with my colleagues, and not have to see any other journalists. But in Podgorica, there was no getting away from them.

Many of the journalists were from small organizations, or maybe freelances, only too anxious to find others to link up with: especially a big organization like the BBC. I felt like some large, predatory shark with the scars of battle on my hide, surrounded by smaller fish who often performed very useful tasks. I might want to get away from them all, but a shake of the tail wasn't enough to do it, somehow.

The other journalists all seemed to be from the world's big television news companies, and it was with something of a shock that I realized the BBC was now the biggest television news organization of the lot. Twenty years earlier the Americans had dominated the reporting of foreign news around the world. Now they had largely evaporated, with the exception of CNN International, which anyway had a rather British feel to it. But it was the BBC that dominated everything.

That can be a problem. Size may matter, but on these big set-piece occasions it can get horribly in the way. The year before, when NATO troops invaded Kosovo, the BBC was comprehensively beaten by its smaller competitors because of its unwieldiness. Sky News, a small organization with a smallish audience, deservedly won much praise for its reporting deep into Kosovo, while the BBC got stuck on the border with its large numbers and out-of-date satellite equipment. And even when one of our teams headed for the capital, Pristina, things went unpleasantly wrong. It's the kind of thing people tell stories about for years afterwards, but with a kind of *absit omen* feeling. I happened to be in the clear, because I was lurking in Belgrade with my leg in several hundredweight of plaster, but I knew perfectly well that there, but for the grace of Lord Reith, I might also have gone.

So there was a score or so to be settled in Podgorica. This was the next big television battlefield, and I was determined not to let us be defeated a second time. The big beasts from the television news jungle had gathered there. You passed them in the revolving doors of the hotel, you stood beside them to ask for your room key at the concierge's desk, you found yourself in the lift with them or sitting next to them at breakfast. Some of them were extremely pleasant people, with whom, under different circumstances, I would like to have a long, alcoholic lunch. But not now. This was war, and I didn't want to take any prisoners.

Most of all, of course, I didn't want to be taken prisoner myself. You can, as the South Africans say, come short very easily on a story like this. A piece of wrong or misunderstood information can lead you to take decisions which afterwards seem disastrous and wholly indefensible: leaving the capital for some distant border-crossing, for instance, on the half-understanding that you might be allowed through there – and while you are stuck, or arrested, or run out of petrol, your competitors simply stream across the border at the normal place, cover the story, and garner all the awards and all the glory. At such moments, you don't find that your colleagues are particularly understanding. They tend to point the finger, and rightly. Our debacle in Kosovo brought at least one famous BBC career to a full stop. I didn't want the same thing happening to mine.

But, on the plus side, I had an important secret weapon. In our business, as in so many others, contacts are everything. Dragan Petrovic, the Serbian television producer I had learned to trust with everything I had, was a Belgrade man. But he had a sensationally beautiful girlfriend, Daniella, whom he was about to marry and who came from Podgorica. And Daniella's father had not only been President Tito's personal bodyguard, he had been the head of public security in Montenegro. And even though he was now retired, he still knew everything that was worth knowing.

The Serbs had sealed the border on their side; but might it be possible for us at least to slip across at some point, and head to Belgrade on the day of Milosevic's presidential election?

'I'll see if it's possible, John,' Dragan rumbled in his deep bass voice, which always reminds me a little of Paul Robeson's. 'I can't be sure. You understand, don't you?'

I did, of course.

Dragan is a wonderful human being. He took care of me when I injured my knee the previous year with remarkable thought and tenderness. In 2003 I asked him to come with me to northern Iraq for the American invasion (the idea, which was derailed by the Turkish parliament's vote to refuse to allow the Americans and British to move into Iraq from Turkish soil, was to link up with the coalition forces and head down to Baghdad with them.) Dragan agreed, even though his wife gave birth to their little daughter on the night we reached northern Iraq. When the Americans bombed us he was hit in the leg by a piece of shrapnel, and received the same ear injuries I did. Yet even though he had been hit, he came back for me where I was lying dazed on the ground, knocked over by the closeness of the explosion, and pulled me to safety in case another bomb fell on us. For which my thanks were to shout at him, 'Stop pulling me so fucking fast.' At that stage, I should say, I still hadn't quite worked out what the situation was.

Dragan is a big, fine-looking man, as tall as I am, with a shaven head which makes him look remarkably tough: a bit like a tall Vin Diesel. When I walked down the street with Dragan during the bombing of Belgrade, no one messed with us. His political advice was always remarkably good; and when, as is often the BBC's way with people who have served it well, it cast him off, he got an excellent job as bureau chief with Fox News in Baghdad; not because he shared Fox's right-wing views, but because it was work, at a time when he needed it.

But in October 2000 that all lay in the future. Now, as the date of the Serbian election drew closer, we had to decide what to do. The safe thing, of course, was to stay in Podgorica and report on events from there. After all, it was only an election; we would get agency pictures of the voting, and I could put my commentary on them, while making it clear that we weren't allowed into Serbia. That would be perfectly acceptable. But suppose the opposition staged some big demonstration, and Milosevic was overthrown? Not to be there at such a moment would be appalling. And although of course you can't act entirely on the basis of what you believe your opponents will do, it is as well to assume that they will be sharper, cleverer and braver than you; if only because that will improve your own performance a little.

'I think they [I meant our opposition] will try to make it to Belgrade,' I said.

Dragan nodded. Not everyone else agreed, and we talked it over at enormous length, without reaching a consensus.

The day before the election, Dragan came to see me in my room. When he has something important to say, he keeps very quiet and looks down at the ground. That's what he did then.

'Someone has put me in touch with a couple of people who'll get us across.'

'Get me across, you mean.'

'No, John, I can't let you go on your own. But I have to tell you, these are not good men. They are smugglers.'

'People smugglers?'

'No, cigarette smugglers. But they're crooks.'

'Can we trust them, then?'

Dragan, who had been reared on the strange loyalties of the Balkans, where the code of conduct is as fierce and strongly held as it is on the North-West Frontier or in Somalia or the mafia villages of Sicily, looked mildly annoyed.

'Yes, of course we can trust them. But I thought the BBC might not like it. You're always telling me what we can't do.'

'In this case,' I said, 'I've got a feeling the BBC isn't going to find out.'

But it did: to a certain degree, anyway. We had another long debate about the safety and wisdom and rectitude of crossing the border illegally, and as part of that I had to explain a little more about the people who would take us across.

'I think we got hold of them through Dragan's intelligence contacts,' I said truthfully, 'though he hasn't told me. His father-in-law-to-be was the head of intelligence here, you know.'

Shall I tell them what is the case, I thought – that I'm going anyway, whatever they decide? In the end I didn't need to. The foreign editor consulted the boss, who knew me very well and may have guessed that I wouldn't allow myself to be held back. If the world affairs editor thinks it's OK, he said, then that's good enough for me. I'm not sure I've ever had a better endorsement.

I went out with Dragan and bought a black leather jacket, of the kind every Serb seems to wear. It would keep me warm, and it would keep me anonymous. I packed a few things in a rucksack – a razor, a change of shirt and underwear, a charger for my phone, several books to read, a toothbrush – and went to bed. The election would take place the next day, and Dragan and I would meet the cigarette smugglers at six in the morning. Once again, Dragan, turned down my suggestion that I should go to Belgrade alone.

'And what happens if we get arrested?'

'We pray,' Dragan rumbled in his fine bass voice.

I couldn't quite work out what I would do, apart from praying,

if Milosevic won the election. I would be in Serbia illegally, without
a visa, and I would be laying myself open to a prison sentence; or
at the least a humiliating deportation. But my motto has always
been 'leap before you look', from W. H. Auden's poem. Since you
can rarely foresee the consequences of anything you do, you might
as well do it.

I woke up early on the morning of 5 October 2000 with the
first 'ping' of my alarm, having dreamed in a disorganized way of
journeys and policemen and gaols. Looking around my room, I
wondered when or even if I would see my familiar travelling objects
again. My friend Nick Springate, who was the producer in charge
of the BBC's operation in Podgorica, had promised to pack my stuff
up and take it back to London if my plans changed. That was a
polite way of saying, if something bad happened to me.

I crept out of my room. The big beasts of the news jungle were
probably still asleep, but it would never do to bump into any of
them now. Dragan was waiting downstairs, and had of course
organized a pot of coffee. It tasted good. These moments, when you
are about to head off into the unknown, are immensely liberating.
All the worrying, all the uncertainty, is over. As I say, you just have
to leap.

Nick appeared, still looking worried. I could see only the
exciting possibility that I might reach Belgrade and beat the bejaysus
out of all our competitors, but Nick's concerns were much more
serious: he was worried that something would happen to us, and
that we would get into serious trouble.

'You're sure you still . . . ?'

I was sure. We shook hands – these moments bring out the
Victorian in one – and slipped quietly through the side door of
the hotel. The darkness was just starting to lift a little, and there
was a pleasant agricultural smell in the air.

'They're waiting for us in the car park.'

And there they were, standing by their car: two tallish, dark-
featured men, in identical black leather jackets. That made four of
us. We looked like followers of Radovan Karadzic, out for a day's
ethnic cleansing.

I shook their hands. They showed no great interest in me, and I
didn't want to look too closely at them. They got in the front, while

Dragan and I sat in the back. It was a small east-European car, and there wasn't much room.

Neither of them spoke English, apparently. We drove straight for the main border crossing. The driver was going far too fast, and insisted on driving down the middle of the road. When an ancient tractor pulled out in front of us, I thought we were all going to die.

'Slow down, slow down,' I said, making flapping motions with my hand. If I was paying, I wanted a little more safety than this.

Both men laughed. Dragan stayed quiet.

We reached the area of the border at around seven. There was a café by the side of the road, one of those attractive old Yugoslav places where you can get disgustingly but deliciously greasy things to eat, like *burek*, and a cup or three of fierce Turkish coffee. The smugglers dropped us off there, while they went ahead to scout out the border.

The *burek* was particularly greasy, and particularly good. We sat there companionably, looking out at the road. Dragan is good to be with on these occasions: quietly confident, and sensitive enough to know when to talk and when to stay quiet. He was pretty quiet now.

There was a certain flow of traffic, but it was all coming away from the border. There was none going in our direction. That didn't look good for us.

After an hour, one of the smugglers arrived back.

'He says there are ninety-five extra guards on the border crossing. They've been brought in to make sure there's no trouble.'

The fiction was that some anti-Milosevic dissidents had threatened to get into Serbia and disrupt the election. The reality was that the Serbian authorities wanted to keep out the foreign journalists based in Podgorica.

'Well, that's it, isn't it?' I said. 'I mean, we'll never get across if they're taking it this seriously. Maybe we should think about trying to walk round the border?'

Dragan is very tactful, but even he finds it hard to take too much stupidity sometimes. He simply looked at the landscape around us. The road went through a narrow pass between two vertiginous mountains. It would take us all day to scramble a way round; and by that stage the election would be over.

'So there's not much point in staying here, anyway,' I continued.

'Well, Jarko has gone to talk to the officer in charge.'

Jarko was the chief smuggler.

The other one drove off again. We had another coffee and another mineral water which tasted faintly of sodium. Then we had some more. It was getting on for ten, and I had started to despair. How humiliating, to have all these discussions about safety and then not be able get through the border.

'Maybe—', I started to say, but at that point the car came back.

'OK, we go,' Jarko grinned.

The border turned out to be just around the next turn in the mountainous road. There were only a couple of guards on duty, and they waved us through without looking inside the car.

'But I thought—'

Jarko said something in Serbian. The others laughed.

'Jarko spoke privately to the officer,' Dragan explained. 'He knows him, from the times he crosses here.'

With cigarettes, I assumed.

'The officer suddenly announced that he'd been told over the radio that a big group of dissidents were planning to cross the border a few miles away. He got up on a chair and said, "Ninety-two of you come with me, and the rest stay here to guard this crossing point."'

We all laughed then.

'And the guards who were left?'

'They were cheap.'

So we had done the impossible: we had crossed into Serbia, in defiance of the government. Now all we had to do was make the three-hour drive to Belgrade.

As we headed down the road, still far too fast, it did occur to me to wonder what the BBC's news guidelines said about bribing border guards and disregarding the orders of a lawfully established government. Nothing, probably, but there would certainly be some ambiguous formulation which covered it. And there would always be some monomaniac viewer or listener who would write in to complain about the misuse of licence-payers' money. There always is.

But we certainly weren't out of trouble yet. Fifteen minutes down the road, at the entrance to a little town, the smugglers slowed down. The driver said something in Serbian.

'There's a new guard on duty here,' Dragan translated. 'Jarko is going to deal with him.'

It was skilfully done. The rest of us sat in the car and watched as Jarko monopolized the attention of the two guards, handing them each a packet of cigarettes and always managing, skilfully and unobtrusively, to block the guards' view of us as we sat in the back seat. Sometimes he draped his arm over the rear window, sometimes he just leant against the side. Perhaps the guards got the message, and decided not to look.

'The next road-block will be the most difficult one,' Dragan explained after another torrent of Serbian. 'The two guys back there said there's only one man on the next one, but you can't get round him.'

In other words, he couldn't be bribed. I felt thoroughly on his side . . . except that I didn't want to be stopped and arrested.

'You mustn't show him your *podpis*, whatever you do.'

Podpis was a silly joke, which had now passed into common usage between Dragan and me, so he wasn't even saying it to be funny. The word actually means 'signature', but I used it to mean 'passport'.

It was pretty clear, as we drove up, that our friends in the front of the car had no real idea what to do. A straight border guard, anxious to carry out his duty, was clearly something of a novelty for the smugglers. We stopped. The border-guard called to us.

'He wants us to get out,' Dragan whispered.

I was very much a passenger on this trip, being told what to do and what not to do, without having any initiative of my own. But at this instant I knew what I had to do, and it got me to Belgrade and helped us beat the opposition.

I hunched down in my corner and pretended to be asleep.

Dragan immediately understood; so did the others. I might be wearing a black leather jacket, but I didn't look at all like a Serb. Nor, of course, did I have a Serbian identity card. When the guard asked to see my ID I would either have to pretend I didn't have any, or else I would be obliged to show my *podpis*. Either way, I would end up in gaol. Pretending to be asleep gave us half a chance of getting through.

Through my closed eyelids I could sense the guard peering at me through the side window of the car. He said something in Serbian, and the others laughed. I kept my eyes shut. Then the doors opened, and the three Serbs got back in.

As we drove off, I asked Dragan what the guard had said.

'Oh, he just said "never mind".'

I know Dragan and his tactfulness; and he knows me, and my dislike of being treated patronizingly because of my age.

'No he didn't.'

'All right. What he said was, "We'll let the old man in the back go on sleeping."'

I laughed for pure pleasure at having got us through an awkward spot. Dragan laughed, realizing I wasn't offended. The two smugglers laughed because we were laughing, and because they would get the money Dragan had promised them. (For the benefit of any monomaniac reader, the deal was that Dragan, who was a locally hired freelance, would take care of the payments to the smugglers, and we would then reimburse him. I know it's dishonest, but it got us round the immediate ethical difficulty. My gamble was that if it all worked, none of my meticulous bosses would think to question it too much.) To celebrate, the driver turned the radio on and started playing some almost unbearably loud Serbian folk music. The car was filled with it: you could scarcely even hear the occasional screech of brakes.

We came across one more road-block, but the occasional news reports which interspersed the music told us that the attempt to cut off Serbia, and particularly Belgrade, had failed. In the town of Cacak, about halfway between the border and Belgrade, we could see from the water on the ground and the crumpled steel crowd barriers lying around, that there had been a confrontation with the police. It was also clear who had won. The road leading to Belgrade was thick with mud from the treads of farm vehicles.

The mayor of Cacak was called Ilic. He was a tough character who was determined to see the end of Milosevic once and for all, and he had worked out his tactics for this important moment very carefully. He had gathered together a group of experts in karate and other forms of unarmed combat, and had arranged a sizeable number of bulldozers and tractors to carry them to the capital. The police had simply vanished.

'How long ago did this happen?'

We stopped and asked a group of people standing by the roadside.

'Three hours ago,' Dragan said. 'We'd better hurry.'

By the time we reached the outskirts of Belgrade, the car radio was telling us that fires had been started outside the main parliament building. The radio seemed unwilling to tell us why people were protesting.

I fished out my mobile phone and found I'd got a signal. We drove on, and I dialled the number for what the BBC calls 'Traffic'. Traffic is the department which takes in phone calls and dispatches, and routes them through to the right programme or studio. The people who work there are famous in the BBC for their calmness and common sense.

'Traffic.'

It was the pleasant voice of a woman. When you're in some horrible place, a voice like that on the other end of the line makes you feel better immediately. You know you're in safe hands. Things may be exploding all round you, you may fear for your life, but somewhere, hundreds or perhaps thousands of miles away, there is a decent, normal, honest, calm person to remind you of the real world.

The traffic operator put me though to the foreign desk, and I explained where I was and what I could do. It was only then, when I heard the voice at the other end, that I realized no one else had expected my plan to succeed. Clearly, the message hadn't been passed round that I was even trying to get to Belgrade; it wouldn't work, so there was no point in telling anyone what I was doing.

'Where are you, again?'

'On the outskirts of Belgrade.'

'Any chance of getting into the centre?'

'I'll be there in half an hour.'

The smugglers dropped us off by the side of the road, at a prearranged spot. I saw the quick flash of an envelope – Dragan was, I could see, anxious to shield me from the precise details of the arrangement – and then, just as we were shaking hands, another small car drove up. I recognized the driver as one of Dragan's Belgrade friends.

On our way into town, the driver told Dragan everything that had been happening, and Dragan told me. A vast crowd had gathered outside the parliament building, and the efforts of the police to hold them back seemed to be fading. We had to hurry, Dragan said; the crowd could get into the parliament building at any moment.

It seemed to take a long time, but we finally arrived at the Hotel Moscow, several hundred yards from the parliament. The crowd seemed enormous, and we had to force our way through. There was the insidious, pricking smell of tear gas in the air, and I found myself coughing and spluttering as I smelled it. I had once inhaled a good deal of the stuff in Northern Ireland, and ever since I seem to be particularly sensitive to it.

As I got on the phone again to London and started describing what I could see, I soon started coughing: distinctly embarrassing when you're live on air. I walked through the crowd, describing what I saw, and as I did so a line of uniformed men filed out of the parliament building and the roaring became louder and more ominous. It wasn't clear to me what was going on, but after I ended my report Dragan explained it to me.

'Those are the guards at the parliament building, and they've just surrendered to the crowd. Now they're going to get inside.'

They were indeed. As we came closer I could see a determined group pushing and shoving their way up the main steps and in through the grand entrance. Soon, a few minutes later, windows on the upper floor were broken or thrown open, and box upon box of papers was thrown out. The papers fell from the boxes as they came down, falling like heavy snowflakes. The crowd on the ground rushed forward, and the papers flew up again as they were grabbed and tossed around.

Dragan and I ran forward too. I could see pencilled markings on crudely printed papers, but couldn't make out what they were. Dragan knew.

'These are voting papers. The Party must have filled them in already, before the election happened.'

I kept several as a kind of evidence. Now it was obvious what they were.

A number of trustworthy Party members must have spent an immense amount of time filling in these phoney ballots, preparing them for the count. This was clear evidence that the voting was fixed.

Soon fires were burning, great flames licking up into the air. The smoke lay heavy over the entire area. Dragan and I fought our way into the parliament building. There were no guards; only the weight of numbers made it hard to get through the door. People were seizing everything they could lay their hands on: chairs, filing cabinets, pictures. It was scarcely a noble sight. Perhaps their behaviour stemmed from a sense of victory over an oppressive government whose arrogance had taken the country into a series of wholly unnecessary and destructive wars.

The downfall of such regimes is rarely very uplifting. A decade earlier in Romania, Nicolae Ceausescu's overthrow had been accompanied by mindless violence. Three years later, after Saddam Hussein's fall, the crowds attacked every conceivable symbol of the state, including schools and hospitals. It was the response of people who had felt themselves to be weak and powerless in the face of an overwhelmingly strong government; and in the moment of that government's overthrow, the reaction was savage and inexplicably damaging. It was a little like a funeral in some poor and primitive place, when the widow and children beat themselves, striking their heads and faces savagely because of the loss they've sustained.

Still, the overthrow of Slobodan Milosevic was a pretty mild business. No one was killed, and only a few people were injured. It wasn't even the last we would see of Milosevic. When he was eventually handed over for trial in The Hague his self-defeating cleverness rendered the whole process pointless; and he died of a heart attack, perhaps self-induced, before the trial could be completed. He had beaten his opponents, yet the victory was without meaning or value.

Serbia, meanwhile, was held back by more than a decade.

Croatia, which had had an equally distasteful government and whose soldiers had carried out almost as many atrocities, swiftly made its peace with the European Union and gained all the benefits of membership. Serbia remained glowering in its corner.

A year or so later, while we were watching a football match on television between Serbia and Slovenia, Dragan said to me, 'You are watching the national characters of these countries.'

He was right. At a key moment in the match, when Serbia was losing 3–0, a Serbian player punched a Slovenian in the face, right in front of the referee, and was sent off. A Croat, Dragan (who is half-Croatian himself) maintained, would have waited for a quiet moment to nobble one of the other side's players out of the referee's sight. Only a Serb would be stupid enough to do it when the referee was looking. Yet the sending-off galvanized the Serbian team. They came storming back in their anger, and eventually won the game 4–3.

'So the guy who punched the other guy will now be a hero,' Dragan said.

Back in Podgorica, our exploit caused a satisfying amount of rage, and one of the big beasts of the jungle complained that our behaviour had been outrageous. Well, maybe it was. But having endured bullets and bombs and cold and hunger because of Milosevic, it was extremely satisfying to have been on hand when he was overthrown.

As for my leaving the country, there was no longer any problem about it. The next day, Dragan and I went round to the Foreign Ministry and announced that I had entered Serbia illegally from Montenegro. That was the point at which the slivovitz bottle came out, and we toasted Day One of the post-Milosevic era. I flew out later that afternoon, with my *podpis* in proper order.

As I was about to go through *podpis* control, Dragan put his hand on my shoulder.

'I should have told you something, John,' he said, sounding more like Paul Robeson than ever.

I looked at him. 'If it's about money, don't worry. I've—'

'It's not about money. It's about the two guys that got us over the border. I told you they were cigarette smugglers.'

'And?'

'Well, they probably did smuggle cigarettes. But afterwards I found out who they really were. They were contract killers.'

'Maybe we didn't need to know that,' I said.

'No. I just thought I'd tell you.'

He was still waving when my *podpis* was handed back to me and I headed off to the departure lounge.

§

What follows is the story of how something valuable – a gold ring – was stolen from me, and then restored. I don't altogether expect you to believe it, and there are times when I find it hard to believe myself. Yet this is precisely what happened, and all I can do is think that the mind sometimes operates in strange and unmapped territories, unsuspected by its owner; like some quiet household pet which, at night, makes a habit of escaping from the house and goes hunting.

I don't expect you to believe this, either, but I was once caught short in a New York office block which I happened to be visiting on a Saturday, when it was empty of people. I had never been there before, and had no idea what the four-digit number on the lavatory door-pad might be; but I concentrated on it pretty hard, and tapped in the right combination, first time. It was, I remember, 5398. To say I was relieved, in more ways than one, scarcely expresses it.

Back to the missing gold ring. In 1990 I spent a lot of time in Baghdad, reporting on the build-up to the first Gulf War. Saddam Hussein's spies and secret policemen were everywhere, of course, but after a while they got used to me and followed me around a little less often. I got to know the spooks who operated in the hotel, and grinned at them each morning as they sat in their leatherette armchairs, drinking an occasional glass of tea and reading the newspaper. That was, I thought, one of the cushiest jobs a spy could have.

I would go to the front of the hotel and find the BBC driver, Mr Hattem. He was a spook too, of course, but once you realized that and were careful not to let him know who you were meeting or what they might say, there was no real problem. And since in those days scarcely anyone in Baghdad was prepared to talk openly anyway, there were no great secrets to reveal.

Mr Hattem was a small, sharp-featured, sharp-witted man, with thinning slicked-back hair like Jacques Chirac's. He drove rather well, and was always on hand ten minutes before we needed him; so I approved of him. He also came to know my interests. I like books, and I like antiquities, and Mr Hattem sought out booksellers and antiquarian shops to take me to.

I had very little time to myself, of course. I was often the only BBC correspondent in Baghdad, having established a friendly relationship with the head of the Information Ministry, who was a great Anglophile. But when, after the invasion of Iraq in 2003, he was accused of being a secret agent, it turned out not to be the British he worked for, but the French. They passed him on to the Americans. I broadcast virtually every day from Baghdad, yet there were occasional times when there was nothing to do and then I would ask Mr Hattem to drive me to the copper-market for an hour or so's wander round.

The copper-market was the oldest section of the bazaar, down by the left bank of the Tigris. No buildings in Baghdad are very old, because the traditional building material of grey mud-brick tends to crumble after fifty years or so. But in the bazaar they simply rebuilt everything as it had previously been; and this part of it survived the otherwise almost total destruction of Baghdad by the Mongols in 1258.

The Mongols had a violent hatred of cities, especially those which tried to withstand them, and they destroyed this one so comprehensively that some parts of it have never been rebuilt. It's a great shame: for much of the five hundred years before the Mongols came, Baghdad was the most advanced city on earth. It was built on a circular plan, and contained the world's biggest and most expensive library at the time. The Mongols, of course, especially hated books – barbarians of all kinds do – and they spent a lot of time burning the ones in the Baghdad library.

Nevertheless plenty of books survived, and they were dumped in the Tigris. Since the mud of the Tigris is famously thick and glutinous, it seems possible that at least some of the books may have survived in its smelly black bosom; but while there's a civil war there, it's impossible even to think about getting a diving team together to search for them. But one day, maybe . . .

In the copper-market I got to know several of the shopkeepers quite well. Often, as things got worse in Baghdad before the war started in January 1991, I was the only person buying anything. Iraqis had no money, and only a few Westerners, almost all of the journalists, even went there. One antiques dealer, Hamid, became quite a good source of information for me. It was thanks to him that I began to realize how hated Saddam Hussein really was.

It was so easy to be deceived by the exaggerated displays of loyalty which we saw almost every day. Hamid, who was a thoughtful man, explained to me how the Mukhabarat, or secret intelligence, would come round to schools and factories and announce that the people there would be expected to provide the support for a demonstration on such and such a day. Anyone who was ill, or failed to show the proper degree of loyalty and enthusiasm, would be in trouble. And under Saddam Hussein, trouble was something you didn't want to be in.

One day in late October, 1990, I walked into Hamid's shop. It was still hot, and he always gave me a cold drink when I dropped in. Over the weeks I bought several nice things from him, most of which I still have: a tribal carpet from Iran, an ornamental knife, several silver *dirhams* from the time of the original Abbasid city of Baghdad.

'I have something to show you,' he said. 'You will like.'

That was what he always said. Sometimes I liked, sometimes I didn't. And sometimes I liked but couldn't afford.

This time he pulled out a drawer, with a little square brown envelope in it. He held the envelope upside down over his open palm, and something very yellow fell out and lay there, as he held his hand out to me.

It was a particularly fine Roman ring, made of the kind of warm buttery-yellow gold you never find nowadays. Set in it was the most beautiful figure of a Roman god I had ever seen. Usually the figures on Roman gems are pretty rudimentary. This one was a minuscule work of art: a figure of Mercury on a piece of cornelian the colour of a good red Bordeaux.

It took us an hour to settle the price. Unexpectedly, late in life, I had discovered a pleasure in haggling – previously I had only felt a great sense of truly English embarrassment – and looked forward to a session like this. I ate several of his biscuits, had another two soft drinks, and drank seven glasses of *noumi basra*, the tea Iraqis make from dried limes; they come from India and farther east, but have always been offloaded at Basra. We only finished when he agreed to throw in a cup and saucer marked with the head of the young Iraqi king Feisal II, murdered in the savage nationalist coup of 1958.

Where had the ring come from? With his rudimentary English and my virtually non-existent Arabic, I couldn't work it out. He had plenty of things from Iran in his shop, so I assume he was a Shi'ite Muslim. A lot of Iranian pilgrims came to visit the holy Shi'ite cities of Najaf and Kerbala in Iraq, bringing objects of value to sell. Maybe it came from Iran, then.

But maybe it came from somewhere else. The Roman emperor Julian, who tried to turn the state religion back from Christianity to the worship of the old gods, invaded Iran and Iraq and his army had come short at Ctesiphon, not far from Baghdad, in 363. Could one of Julian's officers have been stripped of the ring after the battle? It was pointless to speculate, and the shopkeeper himself wouldn't have known anything about its provenance.

I'm not much given to wearing rings, especially not flashy ones, but it fitted my finger perfectly. I started to think of it as a kind of talisman. Somehow I kept it with me all through the Gulf War, when cruise missiles flew past our hotel and turned left at the traffic lights. It was with me in Peru, when we sought out the military officers responsible for murdering the local peasantry. It was with me in Brazil, when our boat sank in a tributary of the Amazon and I had to swim for my life. It was with me throughout the daily and nightly dangers of the siege of Sarajevo.

It was also with me when I trekked with a television crew across the wildest part of Afghanistan, the fierce north-east, to the mountain from which true gem-quality lapis lazuli comes. Our guides eyed my ring continually during our three-day journey through the Hindu Kush mountains. In the end, when they delivered us close to the Pakistan border at seven o'clock one particularly dark evening, they stole all sorts of things from us (though not the ring).

I am embarrassed to say I went completely crazy. Maybe it was the altitude, maybe it was the total absence of food that day, or maybe it was the fact that only half an hour earlier we had found one of our own people eating the last tin of corned beef, which we had planned to share among us. He gulped the last of it down before starting to defend himself against accusations of greed and selfishness.

Then it became clear that the guides had stolen various things from us, including my notebook and my wonderful little Psion computer (now, sadly, no longer made). I grabbed one of the guides, almost throttling him, and ordered our translator to go and find a Kalashnikov. I would, I shouted, use it to kill the man I was holding round the neck. He was squirming and smelled very strongly of horses and not washing.

I assume I didn't mean it; I certainly hope I didn't. Yet in the darkness of the Hindu Kush strange passions can come over you. Fortunately the other guides thought I did mean it, and suddenly they discovered the things we had lost after all. By the time the translator got back with the Kalashnikov, we were all friends again.

I carried on wearing the ring after that; it seemed churlish not to. And then I went to Algiers in 1998, and stayed at a huge Soviet-type hotel. We filmed in the Casbah, which seemed rather alarming, and I saw enough of Algeria to realize that it was a stunningly beautiful country to which I must return for a holiday, if ever it calmed down. (I don't necessarily object to risking my life for the BBC, as long as it continues to pay me, but the petit bourgeois streak in me rebels against paying my own way to dangerous places, just to enjoy myself.)

When I finally checked out of the hotel, I stupidly left the ring lying on the bed in my room. I realized in the taxi that I had lost it, and rang the hotel as quickly as I could. The housekeeper went and found it, and said she would give it to the manager. It was more than a year before I returned, but I rang the hotel several times and was always assured that it was in the manager's safe.

'No problem,' said a pleasant-voiced, stout-sounding man. 'Whenever you come, it will be here for you.'

Finally, I went back. The first thing I did, after inspecting my large but uncomfortable room, was to go and see the manager. The manager turned out to be thin, and there was nothing pleasant about his voice or his appearance. In fact, he seemed to think I was intruding. He had no memory of the affair, he said. Neither did the housekeeper, when she arrived. I raged, and they promised to investigate further. That was the last I heard. The El Aurassi Hotel in Algiers. I'd avoid it, if I were you.

Strangely, it's the only valuable object I've ever had stolen from me. I don't even care all that much about the ring itself, but I do hate being ripped off and lied to. It's rankled with me greatly over the years.

Anyway, one night at the end of 2006 I was sitting at my computer, writing a dull speech about the Middle East which I had to deliver the following day. My mind soon wandered, of course, and I found myself thinking of the ring. Were things like that ever offered for sale on eBay, I wondered. I went to the eBay site, typed in the words 'Roman gold ring', and pressed 'enter'.

My ring appeared. Not something similar, not a copy, but the ring itself. I recognized it instantly from the enlarged photograph: I could even see the familiar slight fault in the cornelian intaglio, with its carved figure of Mercury. I had owned the ring for eight years, and lost it for seven; and now, by the most fantastic of chances, it had turned up again. The auction on eBay was due to end the next evening. I put a bid in, and won. It felt quite extraordinary: magical, almost.

The ring had been cut down, and rather spoiled. It was now far too small for me to wear, though Dee could do so. No matter: I've got it back. I don't believe in magic, and I don't have much faith in the concept of telepathy, though I suppose it exists. Something, after all, made me check the eBay site, and now my ring has mysteriously come back to me. I don't think I'm going to wear it any more, though. It's all become a bit too weird.

4

STARS

Television interviewing in Britain tends to be an adversarial business. The interviewers find out what their guests believe, take an opposing view, and put them through their paces. It can, I agree, be rather tedious, and sometimes downright rude. But it can also be very revealing, and sometimes it adds definitely to the public's understanding. And at least it doesn't give you the feeling that interviewer and interviewee are both members of the same comfortable, self-perpetuating club, which their viewers will never be allowed to join. Watch an interview with Larry King on CNN, or one of the big French or German talk shows, and you will see what I mean.

But there is one important exception to this pattern of tough interviewing. If you listen to a British chat-show host interviewing a Hollywood star, the result can be positively creepy. There is a reason for this, of course. Partly, it is the result of that forelock-tugging, provincial tendency in contemporary Britain, which leads people to be astonished and flattered to find that actors and actresses from Hollywood might deign to come and spend a bit of time in our small-time, out-of-the-way capital.

'Ladies and gentlemen,' said Jonathan Ross on one of his programmes not long ago, 'I can hardly believe it, but this is Bruce Willis actually sitting in the studio.'

As it happens, Jonathan Ross is one of the better show-business interviewers on television. But aside from him and Michael Parkinson, it seems that chat-show hosts aren't interested in extracting anything new and interesting out of a studio guest. All that matters to the host and to the programme's producer is that there should be a famous star sitting on the couch, smiling and answering questions. A few anecdotes, some laughter, a few seconds spent on some slightly more serious subject, and that's it. Finding something different isn't the purpose at all. The purpose is to show us what we already knew. The closer this interview is to all the others the star has given, the better the producer will like it.

The presenters of television talk shows, like the predators of the jungle, hunt to live. If they fail to bring in the necessary number and quality of guests, they will be taken off the air. They have to maintain themselves on those lists that agents and publicists all keep, of programmes on which their clients will look good. You have to be a very big and important chat-show host indeed, some-one of the stature of Michael Parkinson, to start asking your guests probing questions. The managers and image-consultants and life-style gurus they take around with them don't like that kind of thing.

So what happens on these programmes is that during the weeks before the interview a researcher will examine the videos or tran-scripts of each major appearance the potential guest has made on television, searching for the kind of question which will produce the best answers. As a result, those will be the questions you will hear when you switch on the show. In other words, all you get is what you got before.

Much the same thing (this is a longstanding complaint of mine) happens when you are interviewed by a newspaper journalist: he or she will usually only have read the newspaper cuttings on you, because they are short and easy to digest. As a result the same small number of subjects comes up again and again. It's no use trying to break out of the stockade the programme makers want to corral you into. And if you insist on talking about other things, you will find when the article appears that the new subjects have failed to make it.

§

Because my line of business is international politics and hard news, I'm not often called on to interview Hollywood stars. It has hap-pened occasionally, though, and when it does I am usually struck by two things: how short they are, and how nervous they seem to be. (I prefer to differentiate between actors and actresses rather than using the modish 'actor' for both sexes. The distinction does have value. When, at the start of 2007, the Italian film producer

Carlo Ponti died, his obituary in the *Guardian* said he had had a couple of affairs with actors over the years. Eyebrows were raised, and people mused on the nature of his long marriage to Sophia Loren, until the paper's excellent Corrections column made it clear that these actors had in fact been actresses, and that the *Guardian*'s politically correct house style had confused the issue.)

When we see them on the screen, actors and actresses are buffed and controlled and made up and advised and directed to the limit. They are speaking other people's well-honed, much rewritten words, and they have taken on other people's personae. So when they are released into the real world, and have to deal with real people, they are often jumpy, embarrassed and uncertain.

At the Edinburgh G8 summit in 2005, for instance, Bob Geldof and Bono gave a press conference about their meetings with Tony Blair, George W. Bush and various other leaders. Both men are experienced, articulate and intelligent, and their press conference went well. I have been friendly with Geldof for years – we frequent the same café in Chelsea, apart from anything else – but at the press conference I asked him a sharp, difficult question, because that was what was required of me. He answered it swiftly and well, avoiding the possible man-traps which were strewn around the subject.

And then, late and sweating slightly, the actor George Clooney slipped in at the back of the stage, just behind Geldof and the others. Clooney is one of my favourite actors: clever, versatile and with a mature approach to his famous good looks which means he often disguises them or mocks them. But he isn't used to speaking to a hundred international journalists in a hot room, and when his turn came to say something about Third World debt, which was one of the summit's main subjects, he stumbled, sweated, apologized and showed that he felt thoroughly inadequate. I certainly didn't think any the less of him for it; I felt he had a pretty clear sense of the film actor's place in the world.

Yet the distance between the self-assurance of the figure on the screen and the real-life human being without the costumes, the make-up and the script can be immense. In 2002, with the 11 September attacks of the previous year still powerfully in the minds of most Americans, the US embassy in London had a private preview of a new Hollywood film about the Cuban missile crisis of

1962, *Thirteen Days*. I was invited, together with several dozen other people.

It was a good, well-acted film, and Kevin Costner, in particular, was thoroughly convincing as Kenneth O'Donnell, one of President John F. Kennedy's close advisers. It was he who steered the president successfully through the confrontation with Nikita Khrushchev's Soviet Union. Thanks in part to his coolness and wisdom, the world survived. Of course, some part of you knew all the way through that it was Kevin Costner, and not O'Donnell, but the suspension of disbelief was agreeable while the film lasted, and you were left with the feeling, rightly or wrongly, that what you had seen must have been very like the real thing.

And then, in the embassy cinema, the lights went up. The ambassador spoke for a few moments, and introduced Costner. As he came into the room where we were sitting, it was plain that he was an utterly different person from the man we had just been watching on the screen. The assurance, the courage, the weight of moral judgement had all somehow evaporated. He was smaller than he had seemed on screen, and not nearly so well dressed.

But all that might have been acceptable if he hadn't made the mistake of talking to us. This made it finally obvious that the self-contained, understated, cool figure he had played was just a persona he had assumed in front of the camera.

'I'm just so grateful for American embassies all round the world,' he gushed. 'Just now, as I was driving up, I realized I'd be safe if I could only just get inside that door, and nobody could threaten me here. We all owe a great debt to our wonderful United States embassies.'

I suppose it was meant as a graceful compliment to his hosts. But the rest of us, the British politicians and writers and journalists who were sitting listening to him, found ourselves contrasting his courage and toughness on the screen with this nervous performance by a man who seemed to think he was dicing with death by getting out of his limousine with its blacked-out windows and crossing the five yards of pavement to the steps of the embassy building in Grosvenor Square. Even the American diplomats there, sophisticated and worldly, seemed to be embarrassed.

Kevin Costner is an easy target, and in a way I'm sorry to have selected him to make my point. In his own sphere of operation, the film business, he is no doubt a bold and decisive figure; you have to be, to sell the idea of making a film to the savage studio bosses of Hollywood. Believe me, I would be ten times happier facing an angry crowd in Mogadishu or Baghdad than making a pitch to the people Costner has to win over to make a film.

But my point is that we willingly accept the on-screen performance in its own terms, and badly want to believe that it is true. Even I, jaundiced as I am, would have preferred to discover that Kevin Costner was as cool, tough and self-confident in real life as he had been in the movie. But Costner himself knew, as actors always do, that his screen personality was just a fiction, while the reality was that he felt as nervous and anxious as many Americans when they find themselves on foreign soil. That being the case, venturing out of his safety cocoon and coming to London at a time when Americans felt themselves to be targets may well have been one of the more difficult roles he had ever had to perform.

§

When I first got to know the American comic actress Ruby Wax, she introduced me to a whole new world of British actors and comedians. They were invariably charming, but usually had a little more bite to them, I found, than the Hollywood version: they were sharper, more acidic, less gushing. Yet they showed the same acknowledgement that they were 'only' actors, and many of them tried to impress me by insisting on talking about politics. I, on the other hand, wanted to impress them with my (largely non-existent) wit; so we talked past each other constantly. They would go on about Saddam Hussein and George W. Bush, and I would insist on making my rather amateur jokes. If you are a comedy actor, I suppose you want to show your more serious side. If, by contrast, people only know you for your serious side, you want to make it clear that in reality you are easy-going and funny.

Yet comedy is as serious as any other subject, and the distance between the professionals and those of us who like to make jokes with our friends is as great as it is between a Premiership footballer and you or me kicking a ball around with our young sons. In the company of Rory Bremner, I have learned to stay quiet and be the audience. And once, when I had dinner with a group that included Ruby Wax, Alan Rickman and John Sessions, I stayed uncharacteristically quiet all evening. Well, perhaps not quiet, because I laughed noisily and embarrassingly for most of the time, but I realized that no one was there to listen to me.

Towards the end of the meal, over coffee, Sessions, who has the talent to act out the most far-reaching fantasies, taking all the parts himself as he improvises, had asked me where I was going next. I told him Nigeria. He then began a one-man duologue between me and an identikit African dictator, loosely based on Idi Amin, who mixed up my name with that of Michael Jackson. He went on and on relentlessly, driving us to ever greater depths of helpless laughter, while the bill was paid and we found ourselves out on the pavement. I longed for him to stop: the muscles of my jaws ached and my eyes were weeping from near-hysteria. But he didn't stop; and every time I pass that part of Kensington High Street I look at the place where Ruby Wax and I, no longer able to stand, lay down on the pavement crying with laughter while John Sessions' voice boomed around us in the darkness.

§

Nowadays you occasionally see it in the 'for sale' bins at DVD stores or marked down especially cheaply in video rental shops. It has a garish, typically 1970s cover, with the uniformed figures of the main stars on it, a gun or two, and a baobab tree to show that it's set in Africa. *The Wild Geese* is the kind of thing you might rent if you've had enough of *Zulu* or *The Guns of Navarone*. Contrary to what you might expect, it isn't based on a Wilbur Smith novel, though there is the same hormone-heavy masculinity, the same degree of awkward armchair violence and the same pretence of being connected to some kind of African reality. The bodies of enemy soldiers go flying through the air or lie in uncounted heaps without differentiation, while the very occasional casualties among the good guys really matter. You know the kind of thing. Actually, it is perfectly watchable, and by comparison with some of the films that were made in later decades it is pretty harmless.

I was the BBC's radio correspondent in Johannesburg at the time when the African scenes in *The Wild Geese* were filmed. I first heard about it from a headline in the excellent, much-lamented *Rand Daily Mail* in September 1977: 'Never Have So Many International Stars Appeared In SA At The Same Time'. Perhaps it was true; but at a time when South Africa was the subject of a general, often unspoken boycott by the outside world as a result of the policy of apartheid and the brutal response to the Soweto uprising, white South Africans welcomed any sign of international interest in their country.

It scarcely made a news story, but my television colleague was keen to visit the Lowveld, where *The Wild Geese* was going to be filmed. I felt restless, and was happy to go with him. And the prospect of meeting Roger Moore, Richard Burton, Richard Harris and Hardy Kruger was, of course, an attractive one, though I probably didn't mention that side of it. It would scarcely have sounded sophisticated.

In those days we often used to get around southern Africa by chartering small planes. It was cheap, relatively safe and hugely enjoyable. Our King Air, rather larger and more expensive than the plane we had intended to hire, touched down on the grass surface at Messina, bounced a few times, and came to a halt in front of the hut which represented the terminal building. A man wearing rather new-looking bush clothes was there to meet us.

He was part of the publicity crew; not, I imagine, a very important part, since we weren't particularly important ourselves. Somehow you can always sense these things. I recently found the tape, right there in the 'special clearance' box of my local video rental shop, and when I watched it I paid particular attention to the credits at the end. I tried to remember who he was. But thirty years is a long time to remember a ten-second greeting and an exchange of names, and nothing registered.

We bumped and rattled through the bush in an open Land Rover, the television equipment banging around alarmingly at our feet. The Lowveld is Africa at its strangest, most primitive, and most attractive. As far as the eye could see, baobab trees rose up around us, not in a forest, because the ground is too inhospitable, but at intervals of fifty feet or so, the optimum distance for each tree to get the best out of the surrounding soil. Baobabs are wonderful, strange things, with great thick trunks and sometimes absurdly small branches, like the victims of some terrible mutation. They can grow to an enormous height and width, but not here in the steamy Lowveld of South Africa. They play host to many birds, including sociable weavers, noisy builders of small nests that hang from the branches like coconuts. Baobab pods contain a white substance which can quench your thirst for an hour at a time when you are walking through the bundu.

Not far away lay the waters of the Limpopo river, the boundary between South Africa and what was still at that stage known as Rhodesia. 'The great, green, greasy Limpopo', I quoted as we lurched along the track. The others, not having been brought up on Kipling's *Just So Stories*, stared at me curiously, then looked away. All round us the red earth which stretches for much of the entire length of eastern Africa forced itself through the feeble ground cover, and the road itself was the reddest of all, a sharp brick colour in the dull green. It was very hot and humid, like having a steaming wet blanket thrown over you. The sky was heavy and grey, but there was no sign of recent rain. Small clouds of insects gathered round our heads, and the progress of the vehicle wasn't fast enough to outpace them.

It was half an hour before our guide pointed out the camp we were heading for: a four-sided, single-storey construction of red brick. There was an outer perimeter fence of barbed wire, with wooden watchtowers along it at intervals. It could have been anything from a school to a small concentration camp; in fact it was an army barracks.

We drove through the Auschwitz-like wooden gate and saw the confusion inside. People who make a film are usually well disciplined and know exactly what they are doing, but it rarely looks like it. There is an immense amount of running around and shouting and hammering and drilling, which only stops when a scene is being filmed; and that is less often than you might think, especially in the early stages. Now there was more running around and hammering than ever, because one of the main scenes was about to be shot. The director stood in the middle of the compound wearing a large cap, and nothing seemed to be done without asking his opinion. People showed him guns and hats and pieces of material, and explained why the things they had been asked to do were impossible.

'*If* you want to shoot the scene from the west, we'll have to wait till at least five o'clock because the sun won't be right. And that means we won't finish it in daylight today.'

'I know what it means. But the west is where we're shooting it from.'

'All right, but don't say I didn't . . .'

'You see, this is a Czech-made pistol and the script makes it pretty clear their equipment is American.'

'Who's going to know?'

'Who's going to *know*???'

'The berets all seem to be on the small side, and they can't send out any more from Jo'burg till Friday.'

'Do you want their insides to come out? Because the butcher's sent in some pretty good steak. But it might not be quite what you're looking for.'

François Truffaut says two good things about directors in his delightful film-about-a-film, *Day For Night*:

'What is a film director? Someone who is asked questions about everything. Sometimes he knows the answers. Not always.' And, 'Shooting a movie is like a stagecoach ride in the Old West. At first you hope for a nice trip. Soon you just hope to get to your destination.'

The only people who weren't there, asking questions about their words or their motivation, were the stars. The great advantage of working with good, experienced older actors is that they just do what they know they ought to do, without any nervousness or uncertainty.

A whistle went.

'Lunch, everybody,' shouted someone through a megaphone. Directors need a great deal of self-control on set. They know very well how easy it is for a film to slip behind schedule, first by a couple of hours, then by a day, and then by weeks; and they know that this, more than anything else, is how the producers and the studio will judge them. But people have to eat, and if you insist too often on cutting down on their lunch breaks you will find that somehow, mysteriously, the schedule will slip even more. No one will blame the extras, the carpenters, the drivers if the film goes over time and over budget, yet they and the rest of the crews can ruin the entire schedule if they feel they aren't being treated properly.

We walked over in the heat to the mess hall: it seemed somehow natural, on the set of a film about mercenaries, to use military expressions. As we passed the area where the male make-up artists worked, one of them, perched on the roof, poured a bucket of water over our notably attractive sound-recordist. She took it very well, gasping with the unexpected cold and embarrassed by the sudden wetness of her T-shirt. She pretended to be glad that it kept her cool in the heat. But it hadn't been an accident; the high-pitched laughter from the roof as the water was falling showed that. We were angry on her behalf, but there was nothing to be done about it.

Inside the mess hall the overhead fans did nothing to cool the place down or disperse the basic smell of old cooking. Flies gathered on the tables, and sometimes dropped down with perfect timing on the food on your fork as you brought it up to your mouth. The food was institutional and heavy: pork chops, tough steaks, not much in the way of vegetables. Afterwards, big cups of coffee which the flies also managed to land in.

The PR man hurried away, returning a couple of minutes later.

'If you'd like to meet Richard and the others, now might be a good . . .'

We gathered up our coffees and followed him over to a separate part of the mess hall, which we hadn't previously noticed. Who had he meant by 'Richard', I wondered: Harris or Burton?

The moment I turned the corner and saw the stars' table, I understood. Richard Burton was a bit too grand, or at least a bit too remote, to have his lunch with the others. It was Richard Harris who was holding court at the top of the table. There was a lot of laughter.

'So I told him, "My dear fellow, I wouldn't be seen dead wearing that shroud."'

More laughter.

'Ah, yes, here are our inquisitors from the BBC. Come to discover that we really are planning a mercenary takeover of Africa, I suppose.'

We all shook hands. Each of them – Harris, Roger Moore, Hardy Kruger – was a little louder, a little more exaggeratedly polite, a little more deliberately funny because of the presence of our sound recordist. Her T-shirt was almost dry now, but her hair was still fetchingly damp. We explained what had happened.

'Typical,' Harris declared.

He was at his courtly best, with the optional Irish accent louder than ever. Roger Moore was at the height of his good looks, yet seemed rather charmingly to be unaware of it. I got to know him quite well in later years, and realized that his relaxed, amused, entirely detached screen persona was a precise reflection of his own character and behaviour. Hardy Kruger was more withdrawn, and seemed mildly in awe of the others.

But it was Harris who dominated the table, with his grandeur, his humour and the atmosphere of scarcely restrained hell-raising which hung around him. Even here, out in the depths of the African bundu, and even now, during the general lunch break, you felt he was capable of proposing and carrying through some extraordinarily destructive debauch, which very few of the actors or crew would be able to resist. He seemed (though perhaps it was nothing more than a pretence, a role he assumed) to be always on the brink of cutting loose. It added a tension and an anxiety to every scene, every moment he was on the set or off it. But had he gone off the rails at any point in this production? Everyone denied it. The threat was always potential, never realized.

Unwillingly, after the coffee had been drunk and the dishes cleared, the actors went back to the set and my colleagues followed them. Because I worked for radio, I had a different set of priorities from them.

'If you remember, I asked for an interview with Richard Burton.'

'Yes, well, not everything is . . .'

'But is he involved in shooting this next scene?'

'Well, not as such, actually, no.'

'So would you mind . . . ?'

This aposiopesis business was easy to get into. It meant that you never had to put the hard word on someone. Letting your voice drift away meant that the little line of dots could do the work.

The PR man went off to see if it was possible. I wasn't expecting anything. If Richard Burton was too grand to have lunch with the others, he would certainly be too grand to be interviewed by me. The PR man came back looking apologetic. I was ready with a sharp reply, assuming I would be given a crisp turn-down.

'He says if you don't mind the mess in his caravan . . .'

'But he'll do it?'

'Yeah, of course. He likes, you know . . .'

'But I thought he kept to himself.'

'Oh no, he's just going through it a bit. That's all.'

He certainly was. Richard Burton's ravaged, pockmarked face looked even harsher in reality than it did with all the care of the make-up artists. And despite the fierce sun outside he looked pale and unhealthy.

But nothing could affect the voice.

'Come in, come in, my dear boy,' he said, gripping my hand and pulling me up the steps. The warmth of his tone outdid the afternoon heat. I was enveloped in it, charmed by it, entirely won over by it. I have remained that way ever since.

'Will you be needing . . . ?' asked the PR man.

'No, no, of course we won't,' said Burton.

The PR man went off to follow my colleagues.

'Really sorry not to be down there with the others for lunch,' said Burton. 'The fact is, you see, I'm on the wagon at the moment, and it doesn't feel all that good, I have to confess. You drink much?'

'No,' I said.

'Very wise. Wish I'd been teetotal, like my old schoolmaster told me. But the stage, you know. And the company I've kept.'

He gave a huge laugh, which seemed to make the entire caravan shake. It was a big one, with room enough for a sizeable (unmade) bed and a table covered with books, make-up bottles and photographs in silver frames. The biggest photograph was of Elizabeth Taylor. I had wondered how to broach the subject, after their divorce. But with Burton, whether it was because of the influence of the bundu or his free, open nature, there was no trouble at all.

He saw the direction of my eyes.

'Ah, Elizabeth. Isn't she the most beautiful animal you've ever set eyes on?'

It's hard to remember, in the blowsy, embarrassing reality of today, how beautiful she once was. And how well she could act, with a good script. I nodded, and felt emboldened.

'So you don't feel bitter towards her?'

'Bitter?'

The caravan shook again.

'Look, if she'd have me back I'd leave this shitty film and this ghastly heat right now, and charter a plane to go wherever she was. Actually I know where she is. She's in Malibu. I kind of keep in touch, you know.'

'So why . . . ?'

'It's the old thing: can't live with her, can't live without her. But I adore Elizabeth, and I always will.'

There was a catch in his voice, and he looked out of the window at the baobab trees.

'I don't drink now, you know. I'm not pretending it's not painful, but I've given it up for good. It was what Elizabeth hated most in me, I think, even though she's pretty partial to it herself. It was like pouring petrol over our marriage. And now I don't do it any more. I hate it, in fact.'

If you are a radio or a television journalist, there is always an awkward moment when you have to tell your interviewee you want to start the proceedings. It usually seems to break the atmosphere, and the more emotional and frank someone has been up to that point, the more wooden you can expect them to become after you have pressed the 'Record' button.

'Do you think I could turn my tape-recorder on?'

I had my heavy, awkward old Uher with me in its leather case: outmoded now, but much more reliable and easy to edit from than the cassette recorders we were issued with later.

Burton scarcely seemed to notice, but he waved his hand all the same, still staring out at the baobabs. It seemed to me that a tear was glittering in his eye. I realized, with a shiver of professional excitement, that I hadn't broken the atmosphere after all. And perhaps it wasn't just professional: I felt somehow bound to this man by his frankness and the rawness of his emotions. And of course by the glory of his voice. Ever since I was a schoolboy I had listened to his recording of *Under Milk Wood* again and again, with immense pleasure. And I had an illicit recording of his famous version of *Doctor Faustus*, which he performed at Oxford with Elizabeth Taylor as Helen, launching a thousand ships. I remembered, too, the line by the famously unexcitable drama critic of the *Sunday Times*, Harold Hobson, who covered the play in which Burton first appeared on the West End stage. 'Watch out', he said, 'for the young man who sweeps the room but has no lines to say. While he is on stage you can't take your eyes off him.'

I dispensed with the usual banalities, and headed straight back to the central question.

'What is it about her that you love so much?'

'Ahhh,' he said expansively, waving his arms at the baobabs, 'where does one start? "Age cannot wither her . . ."'

'She's a magnificent actress, you know, if only they will let her be. Ever see *Night of the Iguana*?'

'Yes, and *Who's Afraid of Virginia Woolf?*, too.'

'Ah well, you have seen a rare—'

'And I've seen *Antony and Cleopatra* as well, you know.'

He laughed.

'She's lazy, they say, and they also say she's not very bright, though that happens to be an outright, damned lie. It's just that her brightness is a natural brightness, not necessarily a college brightness. She may not know all about Shakespeare or Marlowe or Albee, but she understands the emotional truth, and that is what she projects.'

Surreptitiously, I checked the recording meter. This was wonderful stuff, and I would hate to think that some technical hitch might ruin it. I could hear the reels hissing round happily, though. I only had twenty minutes' recording time, but that would be enough.

He leant back in his chair. At that moment there was a knock on the door.

'Director wants to know if you're all right, Mr Burton.' The voice was muffled by the door.

'Tell the director to go and fuck himself. I'm reminiscing here about the divine Elizabeth, and mustn't be disturbed.'

'You were telling me about her understanding of the emotional truth of a part.'

'Was I?'

He turned and looked at me as though he was seeing me properly for the first time.

'Was I? But you see, what I should have said was that she was a lass unparalleled. A woman of the most charming but also the most natural kind. She could take care of a man, you know.'

He glanced at me.

'No, I don't mean that. What I mean is that she could be so normal, so natural, so caring.

'Listen. Once I took my brother and my business manager to Twickenham for the Wales–England match. Wales won; they always did in those days. And of course we had too much to drink, even my little runt of a manager. Much too much. And we came back on the Tube, and fetched up for some reason at Tottenham Court Road station. I must have said I knew a bar near there. It was late, you see, about midnight.'

He paused, and laughed.

'So we made our way up to the street, and my little manager still had his briefcase with him. And of course we were shouting and singing about beating the English. Pretty loudly, actually. And I looked up to the top of the steps, and there was a gang of about a dozen skinheads at the top, all tattooed with England flags on their chests and faces and arms; a rather fearsome sight.

'Well, it was too late to turn back, so we decided to take them head on. When I say we, I mean my brother and me. The last I saw of my manager, he was shouting, "You can't hit me, I've got a briefcase."

'They gave us both a pretty good going-over. I think they were worse to me, though I don't think they'd seen me on the screen. Maybe I was just bigger and uglier than my brother.

'And then they left us lying there at the entrance to the Tube. My brother said he thought he could manage to get home by himself, and he hailed a taxi for me. He had to do quite a lot of persuading, because my entire head was a mass of blood. But at least I didn't seem to have any bones broken. I told the driver to take me to the Dorchester, and gave him a tenner. Which was pretty good money in those days.

'They wouldn't let me in at the Dorchester, of course, till I told them who I was and demanded to see the manager. Then they were niceness itself, and two of them helped me to the door of our suite, though I told them to leave before I banged on the door for Elizabeth.

'But, you see, she was magnificent. Utterly magnificent. She didn't have a fit of the vapours, she didn't get excited, she didn't even tick me off for being drunk and getting beaten up.

' "Oh, you poor thing," was all she said, and she rang down for bowls of water and towels and bandages and God knows what. And when they sent up some kind of quack to look after me, she shooed him away.

'She sponged the blood off my face, and found that my left eye was halfway out of its socket, so she carefully put it back in. Would you ever imagine that someone like her would be able to do any of that? But she was tough, you see, and brave too. And she tucked me up in bed with the bandages over my head, and at nine o'clock the next morning, when I was starting to feel a bit better, she ordered up a magnum of Bollinger to cheer me up. And then she sat on the side of the bed and toasted me and Wales's victory.'

He paused, and looked away from me and the microphone.

'Magnificent woman, in every way. Magnificent. If I'm honest, my life is a little empty without her.'

He thought for a moment.

'No, if I'm honest, my life is horribly empty without her.'

I said goodbye not long afterwards, and shut the door of the caravan on him. He waved me out in the most courtly fashion, but I think he was probably glad to be left alone with Elizabeth Taylor's picture.

I sent the edited version of the tape over to London when we got back to Johannesburg, but it was never used.

'A bit personal for us, a bit showbizzy,' the programme editor said. 'Maybe you ought to have asked him more about the politics of filming in South Africa.'

I played the unedited version to myself several times afterwards, and always meant to get it transcribed and scripted. I never did, of course. When Richard Burton died in 1984, at the age of fifty-eight, I dug down in my boxes of scripts and recordings to see if I could find the tape. Somehow, though, in all my moves and clear-outs, it

Rafe in his Moroccan coat with Dee and me in the market at Fez.
Frequent journeys have made him a calm and experienced traveller.

In mid-flow near the square in Baghdad where Saddam Hussein's statue once stood.
We have a strict rule not to film for more than fifteen minutes in any one place.

Saddam in court, making a point. His half-brother and fellow-accused, Barzan al-Tikrit, is sitting at the back; he, like Saddam, would later be the victim of a botched execution. I am in the press box at the back, on the far left.

The BBC's heavily defended office in a side street in central Baghdad.

Above Driving to Adhamiya, a Sunni stronghold in Baghdad: not the safest thing I've ever done. Craig Summers, our security adviser, is in the front seat, adjusting the little camera so we could film the journey.

Above, right The interior of the vehicle. Our protection lies not in heavy armour-plating, but in being inconspicuous.

Right Flying low over Baghdad in an RAF helicopter. The man who normally controls the machine gun has briefly moved aside.

Left Oggy Boytchev, the producer who works with me, seated on the throne that Yasser Arafat gave to Saddam Hussein. Wisely, Saddam parked it in a distant corner of his palace.

Below, left Nick Woolley, the cameraman, keeping remarkably cool in a temperature of fifty-six degrees centigrade.

Below Gina, Dee's sister, and her husband Mark Nelthorpe-Cowne. Gina is my PA; Mark has accompanied me as photographer on some memorable trips.

Above Photographed surreptitiously by Mark, a Nigerian fraudster who calls himself Bobby (or possibly Greg) Williams is summoning reinforcements. He has informed me that I have won the Spanish state lottery, but says I must first pay him a large facility fee.

Right I check his receipt book: many other people have, it seems, paid up.

A street in Liulichang, the antiquities quarter of Beijing.

A Liulichang shopkeeper demonstrates the musical qualities of a flute
he wants to sell me.

Dragan Petrovic, who took me to Belgrade in 2000 to cover the overthrow of Slobodan Milosevic.

On stage in New York with the actor Tim Robbins, author of a rather good play about the invasion of Iraq.

Richard Burton during the filming of *The Wild Geese* in South Africa; not one of his greatest roles.

The two-headed monster of the seventh arrondissement.
No wonder people looked at us strangely.

had vanished. Fortunately I made notes from it at some stage, and they survived. Now, if I want to hear his voice as it was at that time, I have to play the DVD of a second-rate film which he made only for the money. And which he would have walked out on in an instant, if Elizabeth Taylor had asked him to.

§

There was always something about Tim Robbins I liked. He wasn't a top-flight movie star, and he never would be; he was too tall, too odd-looking, too rumpled, perhaps a bit too humourless for that. But you could see that he had integrity, both as an actor and as a person. He would only appear in films that were good, or at least interesting, and on the few occasions when he spoke about his approach to the world I thought he sounded impressive and honourable. I rather liked it, too, that he was married to Susan Sarandon, a woman quite a bit older than himself, who also had character and integrity. If either of them was in a film, it might not be a guarantee that it was excellent, but you knew it wouldn't be cheap or bad or gratuitous.

It was in the autumn of 2003, a few months after I had been blown up by the Americans in a so-called 'friendly fire' incident during the American and British invasion of Iraq, that I first became aware that Tim Robbins was trying to get hold of me. I couldn't think why, and it seemed impossible to find out. Hollywood is different, clearly, from the kind of world I inhabit. In journalism, if you want to contact somebody, you keep on ringing and sending messages until they answer. Being chased by Tim Robbins wasn't like that. He had a personal assistant called Summer, and Summer was as vague and unspecific as her name. Sometimes she would call late at night – the notion that the world was divided into different time zones seemed to come as something of a surprise to her – and the quality of the phone line would always be extraordinarily bad, like calling the Congo. And somehow, even when we did speak, we never seemed to be able to make a hard and fast arrangement for Tim Robbins to call me. This to-ing and fro-ing went on for three weeks, and at the end of it I decided that even if he wanted me to star alongside him in some major epic, it wouldn't be worth it.

And that was when, finally, he got through to me. I was writing something against the clock at the time, and wasn't inclined to spend too much time talking to someone who seemed to find it so difficult to make contact. I was as crisp and irritable as he was rambling and apologetic. Perhaps, too, I was on my guard against being patronized. I do my utmost not to patronize the people I ask to take part in my programmes, as though I think it's some sort of honour for them that I should approach them, when I am the *demandeur*, and I don't want to be patronized myself. Perhaps, too, I felt Robbins might believe, like Lena Lamont in *Singin' in the Rain*, that 'If we bring a little joy into your humdrum lives, it makes us feel as though our hard work ain't been in vain for nothing.'

'Yes?' I said.

'Oh, ah, this is Tim Robbins here. I wanted to speak to you about something.'

'Well, now seems a good moment to do it.'

'Huh? Oh, yes. Well, I wanted to ask you about something.'

'Ask away.'

There was a moment's silence. This probably wasn't a phrase he understood.

'You see, I have a play off-Broadway. It's about the war in Iraq.'

He pronounced the name properly, to rhyme with 'bark', which pleased me. If you invade a country, overthrow its government (no matter how bad and corrupt), kill large numbers of its inhabitants and destroy its equilibrium for years to come, it seems to me that the least you can do is to call it by its proper name. From that point I warmed to him a little, and the crispness faded from my voice.

'And the thing is, I wanted to quote something of yours in it.'

'What was that?' I asked. Now I was thoroughly mollified.

'It's the broadcast you made when the American plane dropped a bomb on you and killed your translator and all those other people, and burst your eardrum and stuck you full of shrapnel.'

Now I was putty in his hands. Some of my own bosses at the BBC knew less about the incident than he did.

'And how do you want to use it?'

He went into a long and interesting explanation. In his new play, *Embedded*, there was a part for a woman journalist who, it seemed, stood for honesty and truth and honourable reporting, and my words, together with the words of other journalists who had seen the reality of what happened in Iraq, formed part of a speech she made. Tim Robbins hoped I didn't mind.

I thought about it. It was clearly an anti-war play, and my contract with the BBC forbade me to venture into areas of controversy. On the other hand, the words I spoke on camera immediately after the 1,000-lb bomb had landed in the middle of our group, killing eighteen people, were in the public domain. Maybe the BBC might want to make an issue of it, since they controlled the copyright, but it didn't worry me. And of course I was flattered; who wouldn't be?

'Assuming the BBC agrees, and I can't see why it shouldn't, then I've got no problem with it.'

'Well, thanks, John, that's good of you.'

'When does the play open?'

There was a pause, and I suddenly began to understand what lay behind all this.

'Well, to be honest with you, it opened last week.'

Now I understood the meekness of tone, the gratitude, the openness. All I had to do was to hire a fierce New York lawyer, slavering at the jaws, to sue Tim Robbins for using my words without permission, and I could probably win myself tens of thousands of dollars to assuage the hurt and humiliation and anguish I would naturally have suffered. If a Los Angeles agent could sue the Hyde Park Hotel for $7 million after being bitten by bedbugs there, I should certainly be able to garner a hundred thousand or two from Tim Robbins. The only problem was that I have real contempt for that kind of behaviour, and couldn't imagine doing it myself.

All the same, I wanted him to sweat a little.

'Last week?'

'Summer found it hard to contact you.'

Summer would find it hard to contact herself, I thought.

'You know, Summer is probably the only person on earth who can't contact me. I get calls from undesirables right across the globe, every day. Why not from her as well?'

There was a silence at the other end. He knew, and I knew, that this was just a case of carelessness and disorganization.

'Oh, what the hell,' I said, after extending the silence a little more. 'How about a couple of tickets to see the show, and then we're all square?'

Relief gushed down the three thousand miles of phone line towards me.

'Better than that, why don't Susan and I take you out to dinner beforehand? And maybe I could ask you some questions about the war on stage afterwards.'

It sounded very pleasant. Dee and I had been talking about spending a few days in New York, shopping and hanging out with some particular friends of ours, and this would give us a focus for the whole thing.

'I'd like to bring two other couples as well.'

'It's a deal.'

And it was. We arranged to meet a few days later, at a rather pleasant-sounding restaurant. Summer booked the table – but since it was just opposite the theatre, I suppose that was just about within her geographical capability.

What do you wear to an off-Broadway show, and dinner with a couple of movie stars beforehand? I just wore a black suit and a white open-necked shirt; the women in our party dressed up, and so did the other men: an instinctively conservative American banker, and a Dutchman who was something important in Microsoft (not, though, as important in it as Dee's South African friend, who brought him with her). I felt distinctly underdressed when we found our way to the restaurant and sat down at our table.

I needn't have. The door opened, and in shambled a very tall man with a familiar face. He was on his own. I rose and shook his hand. He glanced round the table and smiled a boyish smile.

'Susan couldn't come,' he said.

I suddenly realized that I hadn't expected that she would. In fact, if I were honest with myself, I was a bit surprised that Tim Robbins had shown up himself. You know those sudden moments when you understand everything; you get a view of yourself as others see you. Of course Susan Sarandon wouldn't have come. She would have thought we were just out-of-town hicks, our mouths hanging open at the thought that we might have dinner with some real movie stars.

And yet, I thought furiously, I was on first-name terms with some of the most famous people on earth, and had interviewed hundreds upon hundreds of the great, the good and the wicked in countries right around the world. And then I reflected that this was the most hick-like way anyone could possibly react.

So I merely said I was sorry she couldn't be there. And I was.

The American writer Elmore Leonard, who fought in the Second World War and was still turning out state-of-the-art crime novels at the beginning of the twenty-first century, had a very shrewd eye for Hollywood. He was plainly burned by some of his experiences, and turned them into good books: *Get Shorty*, for instance, in which an outsider tries to break into screenwriting. The book itself was made into a not very good film, which managed to lose much of the anti-Hollywood edge, but in the original there is a gentle, innocent, heartfelt liberal star whose inability to make up his mind and do the right thing creates chaos and almost wrecks the fictional film. And you know it's going to be like this when someone warns the hero that in a restaurant big stars always look at the menu and ask for something complicated that isn't on it.

'Could I get just an egg-white omelette with, like, asparagus tips and white crab-meat?'

Actually, I can't remember exactly what Tim Robbins ordered, but it was very much along Elmore Leonard lines. The waiter beamed and nodded obsequiously. The rest of us, not being Hollywood stars, ordered from the menu. It was some kind of fusion, which means you can have spring rolls and sushi with your Italian or French dishes, and it was very good.

As he picked at his egg-white omelette, and before he pushed the plate away, largely untouched, Tim Robbins directed most of his conversation at me. He was trying to work out what I really felt about the invasion of Iraq. Decades of doing my best to repress my personal feelings about the great issues of the day have made me very cagey about revealing what I think; but in Iraq, even at this early stage, it was absolutely clear that the enterprise was not going as President Bush, Donald Rumsfeld, Paul Wolfowitz and their friends in the American press and radio and television had assured everyone it would.

At that stage I was visiting Baghdad every six weeks or so, and each time the situation was markedly worse than before; though the absurd figures whom Paul Bremer, Bush's proconsul, had gathered around himself in the Green Zone, young men fresh out of American universities who wore a uniform of white chinos and dark blazers, maintained loyally that the only problem was the negative way in which news organizations like the BBC reported the successes that were being achieved. This much, and more, I explained to Tim Robbins.

'But you must feel pretty outraged when you have to report on all this.'

'I'm used to reporting on disasters. I've made a lifetime study of them.'

'Yeah, but in this case you've suffered yourself. You lost your hearing, you were hit by shrapnel, your friend was killed . . .'

This, though, I couldn't allow. How pathetic would it be of me to remain balanced and objective for more than thirty years of my career, and then to swing into campaigning anti-war mode simply because my inner ear had been damaged and I had a piece of America's finest-quality shrapnel lodged in my leg?

I have a tendency to dislike all wars and invasions on principle, and I knew enough about Iraq to be certain that there would ultimately be a major insurrection against the presence of British and American troops there, much as there had been against the British in 1920. But I had assumed President Bush's allies would turn out to be right in the early stages when they said the coalition forces would in the main be welcomed as liberators. Yet that wasn't entirely true by any means, and as the invasion wore on I wrote an apologia in one of the British newspapers about it. I'm still proud of that. Not many other journalists or politicians seemed willing to admit they had got it wrong.

I tried to explain these things to Tim Robbins, but he found the concept hard to grasp.

'I still don't understand. Are you for the war or against it?'

'It's not my job to preach about these things. I have my own views, but I keep them to myself. When I'm there I just try to give as clear a view as I can about what's going on, and then let the viewers make up their own minds.'

That probably sounds pretty feeble, of course, especially when you find yourself saying it to someone who feels intensely about the subject. Yet I feel strongly that someone has to try to present a balanced, unbiased account of what is going on.

But on some subjects, only campaigning journalism is acceptable for many people.

'That's fine for most things,' Robbins said, 'but some things are so important that you've got to stand up and be counted.'

I made some reply, but it was only afterwards, bolstered with a big helping of *l'esprit de l'escalier*, that I realized I should have told him that the really important things need calm, unbiased, honest judgement even more than the less important things.

Perhaps all this was too British for Tim Robbins. He saw Iraq entirely in black and white, just as Paul Bremer and his chinoed acolytes did. For all of them, it was good against evil; just a different good and a different evil. I thought he must be wondering whether I was really quite the right person to be answering the audience's questions after his show; but then he might have reflected that there was no one else off-Broadway that night who had been to Iraq as often as I had. And maybe, too, there was the memory that my words were about to be spoken again by one of his actresses, without any proper permission.

The bill came. The waiter waved it faintly in the air, but Tim Robbins looked away. There may have been too many people for him to pay for. I reached over and took it.

I liked his play. It had a Brechtian touch to it, I thought – savage political satire with a series of knockabout routines that had the audience rolling around with laughter. The lead actors, playing the parts of George W. Bush and his allies, wore rather clever masks to show who they were. A lot of the action, and the best part of the humour, was provided by a series of wonderful scenes in which a group of American journalists were knocked into shape and then leant on heavily by the US army, typified by a ferocious sergeant, brilliantly acted. As the play came to an end, and I prepared to go onstage, I felt that even though *Embedded* had been noisy and exaggerated and over-excited, it had a great deal of strength to it; and some at least of its points were entirely correct.

Our banker friend felt differently. He had been sitting next to

me, and I could see he wasn't at all happy with the mocking of the
president, or with some of the more savage anti-war points, though
he had laughed as loudly as anyone else at the burlesque scenes.

'I must say, I'm a little shocked,' he whispered to me.

'Presumably that's the intention.'

'I suppose you must be right.' He said it in a way that showed
he couldn't quite understand why anyone would want to criticize
the president of the United States.

Most of the audience, though, were very clear about what they
felt. Questioner after questioner tried to get me to say the invasion
was wrong – no, not just wrong, evil. I explained again and again
that these were not the kind of terms I dealt in. Was the invasion of
Iraq likely to succeed? No, for the reason that the British League
of Nations Mandate over Iraq in 1920 failed. Were the US military
using the wrong tactics?

They were, in many ways, I told them. Patrolling the streets in
armoured vehicles didn't work. Shooting at the traffic that came too
close didn't work. Kicking doors down unnecessarily didn't work.
Treating every Iraqi as an enemy certainly didn't work. Iraq wasn't
a war, it was – or it should be – a police action in support of the
elected government. And the US forces themselves had to obey the
law. Beating, half-drowning freezing prisoners or threatening them
with dogs was as foolish and counter-productive as it was wicked.
The audience liked the word 'wicked'. But it was a long-term affair,
I stressed.

'Hearts and minds,' I pontificated from the stage, 'aren't just
things you decide that morning to win. It's got to be a long, long
process, starting now and going on until the day the soldiers leave.
And there's no room for any other approach. You just have to put
up with all the stones and rockets and bullets they fire at you, and
you still have to go the rounds asking people what their problems
are, and trying to fix things. It worked in Northern Ireland. It won't
work in Iraq because it hasn't been systematically tried.'

There was a little pro-forma applause; Americans, no matter
what their political views, aren't attracted by talk of the long term.
As a nation, they like quick, clear-cut answers to problems. It's one
of the reasons they have been so successful. It's also the reason they

failed to win in Vietnam, and why they replicated the entire failure in Iraq, thirty years later. And I don't suppose any of them knew that Northern Ireland had really been sorted out.

But now, emboldened, I decided to try something else out on them.

'You see, I belong to the generation that marched and shouted about Vietnam.'

I gazed around for white heads like mine in the audience, and failed to see any.

'For us, the top US generals summed up everything we hated. We thought they were stupid, ignorant warmongers. Well, maybe they were; it's hard to be certain now.'

'But in Iraq, the top generals – men like Abizaid and Shinseki and Casey – all understand that they're being asked to do something that isn't working and won't work, and they're putting their careers on the line by saying so publicly.

'It's usually in coded form, sure, but you can tell they don't like it, they know it's not going to work, and they'll be blamed. In Vietnam, it was the grunts who realized that. In Iraq, the grunts think George W. Bush is great; it's the generals who know he's got them into a mess.'

It was a mildly sophisticated argument, perhaps, but this was a sophisticated audience, I told myself. Still, they didn't seem to get it. Was I for or against the war? That was the question they kept wanting me to answer.

Tim Robbins pointed out the next questioner, who was sitting right at the back of the packed audience. I got ready for more moral ambiguity.

'Tim, many congratulations on getting your Oscar for *Mystic River*. Can you tell us what it's like to work with Clint Eastwood as a director?'

Maybe it was my imagination, but I thought I detected a definite sense of relief. Robbins launched into his answer, and I was free.

Afterwards we partied briefly with the cast, who were delightful: the girls flirtatious, the men charming, the atmosphere happy and full of a real sense of achievement. They knew the audience had loved them.

Why not, I thought, get Tim Robbins to be a guest on my *Simpson's World* programme the next day? We could walk up and down the off-Broadway streets, and he could tell me what he thought about Iraq, the theatre, *Mystic River*, whatever.

I told him that its audience was 200 million or more, and that it gets seen right across the globe (though, I had to admit, not much in the US). He agreed happily enough, and some of the girls clapped.

'So we'll see you tomorrow, around two, outside the theatre?'

'Sure, great.'

Our party pulled itself reluctantly away. We had to meet some other people for drinks, then we were all going on to a restaurant in the meat-packing district called the Spice Market. It was the latest thing, apparently.

The couple we met up with were a little older than the rest of our party, though not as old as me. As the night wore on they let us know proudly that they were swingers. That worried me a little, but the dinner was excellent. At two in the morning someone organized a stretch limo for us all, and we forced ourselves into it in positions the swingers were probably familiar with. They suggested a little swinging that night, but we all made our excuses. Being tired, prudish, and a long way past that kind of thing, I was relieved.

The next morning Dee and I had breakfast at a nearby diner. The waitresses were in their fifties, walked on the sides of their shoes, and cultivated an air of some ferocity, like the appallingly ugly woman in the Coen brothers' film *Intolerable Cruelty* who is asked by one of the main characters if she has a green salad.

'What the fuck colour *would* it be?' she answers.

We had made the arrangements for a cameraman to film our *Simpson's World* with Tim Robbins, and we sat there over our corned-beef hash and our sunny-side-up eggs, working out the line of questions, the route we should take, and where we should end up. Planning out a *Simpson's World* is, I have always found, the most enjoyable part of it. The rest involves too much effort to be altogether pleasurable.

We went back to our hotel and got ready. Then my mobile phone rang.

Once again, Tim Robbins' voice seemed to come from an immense distance, as though he was making a call from the Antarctic.

'Hi, John,' he said.

There was a pause.

'Looking forward to seeing you at two o'clock,' I said, to help him along.

'Well, yeah, that's the thing,' he said.

Another pause.

'See, I'm so disorganized, and Summer says I've got to buy a Palm Pilot to help me get organized.'

'OK,' I said, letting him do the hard work.

'So that's why I won't be able to make it.'

'Because you're going to buy a Palm Pilot.'

'Yeah.'

And that was pretty much the end of the conversation. He was too laid back to yell at, and anyway it's often a bit of a battle to get a *Simpson's World* on air, unless the guest is someone really important, so in a way it was a relief not to have to make the effort selling it to the programme's overall editor.

Dee and I went shopping instead.

Tim Robbins said vaguely at some point that if he brought *Embedded* to London, he would take me out to dinner. He did; but he didn't.

Why wasn't I surprised?

5

RAFE

I suppose, looking back on it all, I felt we were certain to succeed because – well, because ultimately things always did go more or less right. And it was such a simple thing we were hoping for. Women get pregnant every day, often without wanting to; surely it would happen to Dee, who wanted to be pregnant very much indeed?

It did, easily and quickly. It was the first day of January, 2001: the dawn of the new millennium. Ignorantly, we at the BBC had celebrated the start of the twenty-first century a year before, on 1 January 2000, largely because everyone else was doing so. Dee and I and a small team of pleasant people had travelled to the far distant Pacific to mark the non-occasion on the desert island where, notionally, the first rays of the new millennium would shine. Well, if you were prepared to overlook a little jiggery-pokery in terms of the International Date Line, and didn't mind that it was all a year early, then we were indeed the first people to see the sun rise on a new epoch in human history; though as it happened we weren't, because it was cloudy that morning.

But 1 January 2001 was incontestably the real start to the new century, and the new millennium; and Dee and I were in Jerusalem, which seemed a particularly significant place – the navel of the world, it was called in the Middle Ages. We were staying at one of my favourite hotels, the American Colony (named after a group of American Protestant missionaries who established themselves at the end of the nineteenth century), and we had one of the grandest and oldest rooms. So things felt good that morning. We walked down to the Old City and found a pleasant place near the sixteenth-century battlements to have a coffee and a croissant. We were killing time until the shops and offices opened.

And then we headed for a small laboratory in West Jerusalem, where Dee could be tested. There was a pause for more coffee, and after that we went back.

'Congratulations! Your test was positive.'

Of course it was, I thought, but it was good to be certain, all the same.

Our baby would be due in late August or early September, so we started making some of the arrangements. Things would have to change, we knew, and for the time being at least Dee wouldn't do any travelling.

So when, at the start of March, I went to Belgrade to report on the political developments a year after the events which led to the seventy-seven days of NATO bombing I was on my own. She accepted that she would have to go to her twelve-week scan without me, but that is the kind of thing that happens rather often in our lives.

I was staying at the InterContinental; not a favourite of mine, but convenient enough. The Serbian warlord Zeljko Raznatovic, better known as Arkan, had been shot dead there some months before, and the bloodstained armchair he had been sitting in at the time was still in the lobby, though now pushed towards the back, where the bloodstains on the purple leather were less noticeable. The holes from a couple of stray bullets were still there in the wooden panelling behind the reception desk, I noticed. Belgrade was still a strange, uneasy, violent place, and many scores were being settled.

My team from the period of the bombing the previous year turned up to greet me: Dragan Petrovic, the producer, as gentle and funny as he was tough-looking; Bata, the picture-editor, a particular favourite of mine; and Balsa, the cameraman, brooding and easily offended, but brave and usually reliable.

It had been many months since I had seen them last, but we quickly slipped back into the old, easy, jokey way. I had a lot of catching up to do, so I asked plenty of questions which began, 'And whatever happened to . . . ?'

The waiter had just come in with a tray of coffee, and we were getting down to a discussion of what interviews we could get and where we could film, when the phone rang. I picked it up.

For a moment, I couldn't work out who it could be. There

seemed to be nothing but a series of deep intakes of breath at the other end. I was about to get irritable, when I realized it was someone crying. And then the words began to come.

'It's the baby.'

I guessed immediately, of course: the scan, the time of day, the crying. Dragan, with his quick understanding, also knew something was wrong, and signed to the other two to stop laughing and joking. I sat down, trying to come to terms with the sudden change. Only half a minute before I had made some comment about being a father again at my age. Now, in the blinking of an eye, it wasn't going to happen. This kind of change takes a little getting used to.

'I'll come home straight away,' I told Dee.

She had had some kind of feeling that things might not be altogether well, but I had laughed it off as nerves. That day, though, there was no sign of any problem, and she had gone to the clinic to be scanned, assuming things would be fine.

It was the look on the nurse's face that told her: the sudden change from brisk, impersonal efficiency to a sense that this was an individual woman who was about to suffer one of the cruellest of blows.

'I'm sorry,' she said. 'I can't detect a heartbeat.'

But there must be one, Dee thought, though she didn't say anything. Look again – it must be your scanner that's faulty. It's been so strong, so positive. The little heart can't just have stopped like that.

But it was pointless to look again. There was no longer a growing embryo, a child in waiting. Just something to be got rid of as quickly as possible.

I scarcely spoke to the others. There was no need to; Dragan fixed everything for me. There was a plane leaving for London in less than a couple of hours. He drove me to the airport at frighten-ing speed, taking a little country lane to save a few minutes, and got me there just in time. Dragan is half my age, but when I had a bad accident in Belgrade he carried me around and looked after me as gently and affectionately as a father. Now he put his arm round my shoulder, knowing that this time the injury was much worse. We didn't speak to each other, except to say goodbye.

On the plane, as bad luck would have it, a fellow passenger

insisted on talking to me about some failing of the BBC's news coverage. Usually when this happens I try to be polite. Now all I could think of was getting home, and I scarcely listened. At one point I realized I had said the wrong thing, and the man looked offended.

I explained that I was having to go home because I had had some bad news.

'Sorry to hear that,' said the man, scarcely listening himself. 'But, you see, the important thing is . . .'

I got up, anxious to make some sort of change. As I did so, an unpleasant pain shot through me – a pain I recognized. I had had several kidney stones before, and knew what I was in for. The shock of the news must have brought it on, though I couldn't understand how. Even now the man wouldn't stop talking to me. I just sat down and ignored him.

All I needed, I knew from past experience, was a medic to give me a big painkilling shot. Then I could get on my way home and be with Dee. The kidney stone could wait till later. I made the mistake of asking the crew if they would radio ahead for someone to meet me when we arrived at Gatwick Airport.

In many ways everyone was wonderful. Yet I could not have done anything worse. Instead of a medic with a needle there was an ambulance, and the ambulance team told me in the nicest possible way that I couldn't be allowed to make my own diagnosis or suggest the remedy. Only a hospital would do. And because I was in a certain amount of pain by this stage, I agreed.

We drove for a long time through the Sussex countryside. Dee needed me to be with her, but I was locked into this absurd journey instead. Literally, I discovered: when the ambulance stopped at some traffic lights, I tried to jump out. But the National Health Service had thought of this one, and the door was locked from the outside.

Nor could I escape from the hospital when we finally arrived. My bags were taken from me and put in storage, and I didn't want to leave them behind. By this time, too, the pain was getting pretty bad and I needed someone to take it away. So I filled in a long form about where I had been born, and whether I had had appendicitis, hepatitis, or coughed up phlegm when I awoke in the morning. All valuable information, no doubt, but not much related to my kidneys, I said. A big nurse smiled and told me this wasn't for me to decide. The only person who could do that was dealing with someone who had been in a road accident and was in a much worse state than I was.

'Surely that's not for you to decide,' I said nastily. She was entirely immune to the spiteful comments of patients.

'You just lie there and wait, darling,' she said, and then, 'You're the man on the news, aren't you?'

I nodded, and closed my eyes. I lay there waiting for what seemed like a very long time: any time at all seems long when you're in pain, of course. It was dark before an attractive young doctor came and looked at me. She explained to me with immense patience, as though talking to someone with Alzheimer's, that I had a kidney stone.

'Oh,' I said with renewed nastiness. 'Fancy that.'

She ignored me. She told me where my kidney was and how stones formed, and how you got rid of them. She also explained that they were very painful. What was needed, she went on, was a painkilling injection. Then, at long last, she gave it to me.

It took a couple of hours to get home by taxi. Dee was showing signs of some quiet, well controlled and fairly well masked despair when I finally arrived. Of pain, too, just as bad as mine had been. She had already been through a procedure to get rid of the baby which was called a D&C. We came to know it well in the years that followed. What the letters stand for, I have no idea, and no interest in finding out. The reality is the scraping out of the womb to get rid of every trace of the dead child. It's intrusive and painful, and afterwards this sense of pain and intrusion is all you are left with: no baby, no joy, no hope.

Well, we tried again, and again we were successful. And then, around the twelfth week, the same thing: the sudden quiet in the room, the sympathy replacing the efficiency in the voice, the inevitable, unpleasant D&C, the silent journey home. There was a coffee shop near the rooms of Dee's gynaecologist where she sat and tried to come to terms with the change that had come in her life. It would all happen, in much the same way, on two more occasions.

Four and a half years, four pregnancies, four D&Cs: the statistics weren't good. By the time of the third pregnancy, a sense of dread had started to creep in. We would be overwhelmingly relieved when the early scans showed that the little homunculus was still growing. Then came the moment of stillness and the sympathetic voice again. Worse still, I always seemed to be away when the bad news came. On three out of four occasions when Dee found her child was dead, she was alone. My job can be difficult in many ways, but I don't think I've ever found it harder than during the years when Dee suffered her miscarriages, or felt more inadequate.

After the fourth time, we pretty much decided that it wasn't going to work and that we should come to terms with the fact that we weren't going to have a child. It eased our minds, but there were always moments when we would feel the twinge of what might have been, like a brief jab of pain.

One of the most enjoyable things about being a father the first time around was reading stories to my two daughters. It has remained as a bond between us ever since, and we often talk about other people in terms of characters in books: 'He had a voice like Reepicheep,' or 'She was as patronizing as that girl in *Northanger Abbey.*'

So when Dee first became pregnant, I started collecting together the books I would one day read to our child. It was quite unnecessary, of course, but it was my equivalent, I suppose, of flying around and looking for the right kind of twig to build a nest with. After the fourth miscarriage I put the books away, somewhere I wouldn't see them. But whenever I came across one of them, or thought about reading to my child, the pain would come back. I have five attractive, intelligent grandchildren, but my constant travels mean that I don't see them nearly enough.

Now I found myself avoiding toy shops, walking past quickly so as not to think about what they might have represented in my life. I tried not to notice couples with their children in the streets. When I reported from abroad I tended to avoid including pictures of children in my reports – until I realized what I was doing, and told myself I couldn't work like this. It was stupid and wrong and mawkish of me. I must pull myself together.

Yet I couldn't help thinking occasionally of the possibilities I had once outlined to myself: family outings, playing with the baby in the morning before getting up, a pleasant baptism which would bring my friends and family together. The thought that my grandchildren might play with my child had been, for some reason, a particularly attractive one. Once, sitting quietly at the back of my local church, I saw a father in front of me with his little son standing beside him on the pew listening to the sermon, his arm round his father's shoulders. I didn't feel envious, or even more than usually self-pitying; I just felt the full painful realization that this would never happen to me, and that I would have to get used to it.

Jokingly, I had once bought a beautiful little Ibo fertility figure of a woman, painted dark red, as a present for Dee when we first decided we would like to have a baby. That certainly didn't work, I told myself now, and I put it in a dark corner in the basement, as though it were somehow the figure's fault.

But in the end, we just came to accept that there would only be the two of us, after all. I ought to have been relieved; at the age of sixty-one, I should probably be thinking more of my library, my slippers and my occasional cigar than checking to see whether the baby had a dirty nappy, or getting up at three in the morning when he or she had a nightmare. But when you marry someone, you marry their dreams as well, and although Dee had chosen a man twenty years older than herself for her husband, she had always wanted a child of her own. Slowly, Dee's wish became mine, and her pain was my pain when it didn't come about.

Afterwards, a newspaper columnist of the 'Glenda Slagg' persuasion attacked me for trying to father a child at my advanced age. She listed the many disadvantages to a child of having an elderly father, but seemed to forget that there were some definite advantages too. An older father is likely to be calmer and more fulfilled, aware of his shortcomings and more experienced at making sure his child will not suffer from them. Better off, too, so that anxiety about money won't poison the family life.

But ultimately it doesn't seem like anyone else's business. As long as I am an active, loving, lively minded father, and can survive long enough to see my child at least into adulthood, then I will have performed my proper function as a parent better than an uncaring, irreflective thirty-year-old who spends most of his time in the pub or watching television. That, at any rate, is what I tell myself.

But it seemed clear that none of this was going to happen now. Life would be easier and less expensive we were childless, we told ourselves, and I wouldn't be saddled in my old age with some noisy, aggressive kid who played incomprehensible music at unthinkable volumes, bought expensive drugs from the kind of violent dealer whose activities I have often reported on in Colombia or Peru, and stole my books or paintings to buy more of them.

That kind of child is endurable only until the age of twelve or thirteen; and by then I would be (I had to add it up on my fingers) seventy-three. So instead of drifting off into a peaceful dotage, looking out over the sea or wondering which wine to recommend to the committee at the Garrick Club, I would be raising my blood pressure with arguments about the time my child had to be home and the films he or she could see.

By the beginning of 2005 I had come regard with ever greater admiration both Dee and her ability to cope with the hammer-blows which the four miscarriages represented. After surviving the 'friendly-fire' attack in Iraq in 2003, I felt even gladder to be alive, and even more determined to enjoy it.

We sold our pleasant, light, modern flat overlooking the sea, near Dublin, gathered up our books and belongings, and moved to London to a narrow early Victorian house on four levels where the armchairs and sofas could scarcely fit through the doorways, and the paintings were too big for the walls. I had written a couple more books of interminable reminiscence, and we had decided we needed neither a car nor a dog. Instead, we had a charming little garden in which I always meant to hang my Amazonian hammock, but never got round to it.

And then came a lovely mild day in late spring, Sunday 8 May, when the sun shone obliquely down between the buildings in central London, the leaves on the trees had that lovely light yellow-green colour and the softness that only lasts a short while, and I took Dee to a celebration brunch at the Lanesborough Hotel. It was our ninth wedding anniversary, and life seemed pretty good. That was the day when it suddenly changed for us, and became even better.

Fourteen days later we were in our flat in Paris, taking advantage of the fact that nothing much was going on in the world. Arielle Dombasle was singing 'Quizas, quizas, quizas' in the background and I was reading *Tristram Shandy*. The windows were open to the noise of the street outside, but I still heard a shout of triumph from the bathroom which overtopped it all. I ran in.

'Look at this – I'm pregnant! And see how strong it is!'

Even I could see that the blue marker was pretty decisive: not at all the kind of thing you would need a second opinion on.

'Chattawak Junior,' I said triumphantly.

Chattawak Junior was the name of a kids' clothes shop near our flat, and we had adopted it as a kind of John Doe/Mary Roe name for the baby when Dee became pregnant for the first time. After that the joke had faded, and didn't seem worth repeating.

Until now.

We went out, passing Chattawak Junior on the way (though in the years we had been waiting for our baby it had grown into a clothes shop for adults), and had a celebration coffee and a Kir royale near the Eiffel Tower. We told ourselves a hundred times that we had been through this before, and it was probably nothing, and we mustn't get excited, and how awful it would be to go through another disappointment. Somehow, though, both of us knew it was different this time, even though the clock which regulated our lives was ticking louder than ever.

'It'll be like scoring a try in injury time,' I said. 'If it's a boy we'll have to call him Justin.'

'Why Justin?'

'Because he'll have come just in time.'

I always find my jokes killingly funny.

'But it won't be a boy.'

I had had two daughters by my first marriage, and each one of Dee's unsuccessful foetuses had been a little girl. The chances that we would have a boy were pretty small.

'Well, Justine then.'

Somehow Justine didn't sound quite right, and the joke was lost.

There was a shop for expectant mothers near our flat, and this time we felt justified in stopping and looking in the window.

'I'm coming back here this time to buy baby clothes,' Dee said with decision.

On one of the previous pregnancies the girl behind the counter had been rude and dismissive, as though she didn't believe Dee really was pregnant.

I peered in.

'That awful cow seems to have gone.'

Neither of us said anything, but we each knew what the other was thinking. It was a sign. When you go through troubles you start to see signs everywhere. It's a very bad habit, it's ludicrously superstitious, and it is totally misleading, but it can help you get through. And especially when your luck begins to turn, you can't stop seeing signs wherever you look. Merely because an unpleasant shop girl happened not to be standing behind the counter of a mother-to-be shop, we felt certain that Dee would carry her baby to term. Neither of us could sleep that night, and casting our anxieties aside, we talked about nothing else until two or three o'clock.

In the morning, while Dee made us some tea, I tiptoed into the bathroom and opened the doors of the cupboard as quietly as I could. It wasn't a secret; I was just a little embarrassed about my sentimentality. In 2001, when Dee was pregnant for the first time, we bought some duvets at the Samaritaine department store. As a promotional offer they threw in a couple of soft toys, two white polar bears. In 1950 my father had given me something like that, after a polar bear cub called Brumas had been born at London Zoo – its first – and there was a sudden short-lived flurry of Brumas enthusiasm across the nation; I suppose I liked them for that reason. But after Dee's first miscarriage I hid them away. I didn't like to throw them out, because that felt like bad karma. Now I had to stand on tiptoes and reach my hand up blindly. My fingers found fake fur, and I pulled them out. Suddenly, there seemed to be no reason to be afraid of toys any longer.

The specialist who looked after Dee was Marcus Setchell, who (according to the newspapers) was in charge of all sorts of famous women, young and old, but infuriatingly would never tell us anything about any of them. In our case, his years of observing pregnancies may have given him some insight into the likely outcome; he had certainly warned us at an early stage in our efforts to produce a child that the time might come when we would feel we should have done with the whole thing – and, he might have added, decide to live on together in peace and childless contentment, without worrying about what might have been.

I may be wrong, but it seemed to me that when Dee and I went to tell him that she was pregnant for the fifth time he reacted differently – almost as though he knew he wouldn't have to draw on his resources of compassion this time. Or maybe that was just another of my imagined signs. But we felt a little different too: less gloomy, more inclined to think of a future that stretched longer than a few months in front of us. Even so, we didn't buy anything new for the baby: no clothes, no toys, and nothing for the nursery. The signs weren't that good yet.

The morning when Dee went for her twelve-week test was a tense one. For once, thank God, I was at home and could go with her. We had coffee at the usual place in Marylebone High Street, and as we walked to the clinic I allowed myself a brief glance into a toy shop along the way. Just on the off-chance, you understand, but it was something new for me.

The doctor who was going to carry out the test was jolly and sympathetic, and knew a little of Dee's troubled history; I suppose it was spread out all over her file when he looked at it. He got the equipment ready, and there was a sudden silence in the room. This time, though, it didn't seem like those other silences, while the person doing the scan worked out how to break the bad news. This time, it was just that we were too nervous to talk.

The scanning process started.

'Well, this baby isn't going anywhere.'

For an instant I thought he meant that it wasn't viable, that it was another disaster. Then I could see he was grinning. What he meant was that the baby was going to be staying in place for the whole nine months. I started to grin, and tears came to my eyes as I saw the little heart beating away valiantly on the scanner. I was already holding Dee's hand, but now I squeezed it with sheer delight.

'Yes, he's good and strong.'

He? Perhaps, I thought, he's speaking generically: a better and more personable alternative to saying 'it'. Of course it must be a girl. I was marked out to be the father of daughters.

The doctor pointed to the screen. There was no question about it: we were certainly going to have a son.

Dee said, 'Oh.'

I knew how much she'd been looking forward to having a girl to dress up and play with. Her sister Gina, who had two sons, had been hoping it would be a girl too. As for me, I was so used to being the only male in the household it had never occurred to me that I might father a son at this late stage in my life.

And then, as the whole idea began to seep into our minds, it dawned on me how strange and unexpected and delightful it would be. A son. A boy. One day a man. Cricket. Rugby. Chelsea Football Club.

We sat in the coffee shop again, but this time it was with a sense of real triumph.

'I'd never have thought it,' I said, and laughed out loud, so that a couple of people in the corner looked across at me.

Dee was talking excitedly, but suddenly my mind wandered off in a different direction altogether. This was the place where we had come in order to digest such bad news in the past; the place where, for all I knew, everyone who'd been handed out a death sentence by some eminent specialist in nearby Harley Street came, in order to make sense of it all. Six months, a year, eighteen months: put your affairs in order, break the news to your nearest and dearest, try not to show what you think. There was a very effective poem by John Betjeman about it: 'No hope. And the X-ray photographs under his arm / Confirm the message.' And the quote from *The Winter's Tale*: 'Thou met'st with things dying, I with things new born.'

I smiled at Dee as she talked about names and clothes and prams, but I was thinking about things that were very different, and quite unsuitable. Perhaps one day, not too far in the future, I might find myself here, trying to make sense of some death sentence I had just received, round the corner in Devonshire Street. The one thing was just as much a part of human existence as the other. But not right at this moment. For now I had been given the best news imaginable, and I must get back into the spirit of it.

'How about Edward for a name?' I asked.

'*Edward?*'

'Just a suggestion.'

It would be the first of many.

§

At two minutes past four on the morning of Monday, 16 January 2006, Dee jumped out of bed.

'It's happening,' she said, and ran into the bathroom.

I calculated groggily that the baby was three days early; three days in which we had been hoping to get some real rest before the big moment. Dee was booked into hospital for a Caesarean section on Thursday.

We stayed quite calm and very jokey, though I started to dial for a cab by pressing the buttons on the remote control for the television set, rather than the portable phone. It was a moment or two before Dee noticed and started laughing. Fifteen minutes later, though we had had to pack from scratch, we were in the taxi and on our way to the Portland Hospital in Great Portland Street. We chatted away nervously, reflecting mostly on the pregnancy. It had mainly been pleasant, though the first three months had not been easy, and her spirits were very good.

Pregnancy and childbirth are two of a very short list of life's events which virtually everyone feels are positive. Not even getting engaged or married always matches up to them. I suppose giving birth represents some deep-lodged atavistic approval of the process of extending the life of the race; though you might think that since that process has happened more than six billion times within our lifetimes, the approval would have faded just a little.

Not so. Crabbed old men smiled at Dee in the street. Gangs of nasty-looking youths opened up politely to allow her to pass. People even offered her a seat in the bus, or offered to carry her shopping bag. We still obey our genetic orders, even though there is hardly much doubt now that the human race will continue, probably to the point where it wipes itself out.

Even the taxi driver smiled, looking at us in his rear-view mirror at 4.31 in the morning; and it wasn't just because he probably thought I would be so confused I would give him a fat tip. As for us, we sat in the back grinning in the darkness, because we knew that Dee would very soon be released from the increasingly heavy burden she had been carrying round for nine months.

'If Thursday is the nineteenth, what's the date today?'

I worked it out on my fingers.

'The sixteenth.'

'I thought so. It's my father's birthday.'

What a boy, I thought. Even before he had appeared in the world, our little unnamed son was behaving with the greatest tact. He had chosen the date of his birth in such a way as to please his only surviving grandfather, a charming, idiosyncratic newspaper commentator living in Johannesburg.

Dee was nervous, of course: the next few hours would hold all sorts of frightening unknowns for her, and her life would change permanently and drastically as a result. These were the last moments of her old life, and the start of something entirely new. For me too, of course, but to a far lesser extent. I know what it's like to have children, I told myself, though I didn't have the slightest idea how different the process was nowadays, and how much more would be expected of me as a father now.

We arrived at the hospital shortly before five, excited and apprehensive in roughly equal measure. Dee was brave and stoical as they prepared her for the Caesarean, but I could see how tense she was as they helped her change and gave her the necessary injections. The atmosphere was relaxed and intimate, and when Marcus Setchell arrived to carry out the operation he made me a cup of coffee as I sat there feeling more than usually useless.

'I may be a bit dislocated now,' I told him, 'but I promise you I won't faint when it happens.'

I could see he didn't altogether believe me.

Then his team put up a green curtain to shield Dee's lower half from our eyes, and they got to work.

Soon afterwards, at nine minutes past seven by the theatre clock, I watched the baby's head emerging, and Marcus gripping it firmly and pulling him out. It felt very strange indeed to see my wife's body opened up like a car bonnet, and stranger still to see Marcus holding up the wriggling, naked, empurpled little body of my son like a trophy. He had advised us to have a Caesarean for other reasons, but I saw how fortunate it had been: the umbilical cord was wound twice around the baby's neck.

A midwife called, delightfully, Mercy Darko took the baby with practised care, did the necessary tests on him and put him on the scales: 7.8 pounds. He yelled his protests in a scratchy, insistent voice. I looked at him covertly for any signs of deficiency, but could see none. He seemed fine.

'As right as a Ribstone pippin,' I said to myself, quietly.

The anaesthetist carried him round so that Dee could see him. She was calm and happy and relieved, and seemingly less emotional than I was.

When he was put into my arms he was still making his scratchy sounds and wriggling, as though his first experience of life in this strange, conflicted world of ours showed him it was something to be resisted. But I stroked his perfect little ear, which was purplish red in colour like a strange new orchid in a flower show, and it seemed to calm him down. He stopped crying immediately and lay still. Looking for a sign, as usual, I thought this was a particularly good one.

It took us several days to settle on a name. That was, I think, because of a wider lack of preparation. We were so worried something might go wrong at the last moment that we had scarcely provided anything for him beyond a Moses basket and a few clothes and blankets. We hadn't even furnished his room, in case we had to go home alone and get rid of it all. Better to go out and get everything for him later, we thought, than to have to face all the things we had bought for him if we went home alone.

But we wouldn't have to go home alone; not now. His colour became more human, as he lay in the cradle beside Dee's hospital bed, and the little snuffling sounds he made showed that he was breathing easily. I had to keep looking at him, to be certain he was really there and still alive.

'What do you think about "Guy"? No, OK, it probably isn't a very good idea. "Charles"? Yes, I rather agree. No, no, I really hate the name "John". I wish I wasn't called it. It would have been much easier and more descriptive if I'd been called by a number: 49, 68, or 108, say, rather than a name which every third person has.' I rattled on like this for some time, talking out of nervousness.

By Thursday the baby still had no name, and it was getting harder and harder to fend off friends and relatives who wanted to know what he would be called. The ideas became more and more wild.

'Since he may have been the one that tipped the British population over the sixty million mark, why don't we call him Mark?'

But there were too many Marks among our relatives and friends already.

'Frederick? With a "k"?'

But we each knew Fredericks we didn't like, just as we each knew people of just about every other name, and didn't like them.

My favourites were Laurence, after Laurence Sterne (*Tristram Shandy* is full of the comedy of fatherhood, birth and the naming of sons), Jasper (Dee's suggestion, put to me as I paced around on the balcony at the BBC office in Baghdad; a bomb went off in the distance while I was considering it), and Ralph or Rafe.

That was my favourite. I thought a Laurence would never survive his first term at school with his name intact, and he would be Larry or Laurie for the rest of his life. Jasper sounded militantly upper middle class, and was anyway linked forever in my mind, and the minds of hundreds of thousands of people of my age, with the lines: 'O, Sir Jasper, do not touch me [repeated twice] / As she lay between the lily-white sheets with nothing on at all.'

Calling my son after a fictional eighteenth-century rapist definitely seemed a bad thing. Ralph was fine by me, though because I am a stuck-in-the-mud traditionalist where these things are concerned I wanted it pronounced 'Rafe', as in Ralph Vaughan Williams. No one would ever do that, Dee rightly said, and she couldn't bear Ralph (pronounced as spelt) because she had had a boyfriend of that name. That was the first time I had heard of him.

'Why not "Rafe" with an "f"?' she asked, changing the subject fast.

I thought 'Rafe' looked wrong on the page – sloppy and illiterate and lazy, like 'w8 4 me' in a text message. What sort of people gave their son a name like an SMS?

Dee's mother, Adele, as calm as ever, provided the necessary compromise. She had just been listening to Sir Ranulph Fiennes, the explorer, talking on Radio 4. Why not call the boy Ranulph as his official name, and Rafe for short: thus neatly getting round my objection, since 'Rafe' wouldn't be his real name, just a nickname. I agreed at once. Dee agreed. Ranulph Fiennes, when appealed to, agreed too – on condition that we kept the Norman 'ph' and were careful not to spell it with a final 'f', like the Saxons.

If your surname is Fiennes, I suppose you are likely to be quite keen on the Normans; if it is Simpson, you are a Saxon (or in my case, an Angle) and your family was therefore dispossessed and quite probably enslaved by the Normans. On the other hand, 'Ranulph' looks nicer when it is written than 'Ranulf', which has a definite Lord of the Rings look to it, so Ranulph it was. The registrar at the nearby births, marriages and deaths office, a delightful lady from, I think, St Vincent, liked it. She had written 'Ranulph' on the certificate before I even had a chance to go into the question of the spelling. And she knew exactly who we were naming him after, too.

§

There is absolutely nothing in any way special about having a child; in fact it is one of the most dangerously common things we humans do, and we are wrecking our entire world as a result. Yet in the lives of each of us as individuals, the birth of a child is an epoch-making, life-changing event.

The sheer number of human beings is frightening. My response to the problem has scarcely been very helpful: I have produced another to add to the number. At the precise moment I write these words, the world's population is 6,598,417,161 and increasing at the rate of around three per second. When my son Rafe was born, the world's population stood at a mere 6,581,169,467.

The extraordinary thing is that each child is different, both in appearance and in mind. The genetic possibilities are so immense that even though we seem to be descended from one small mito-chondrial set of ancestors, we have mostly been able to bring in such new blood as was available. And now more than ever. My first wife is American, the descendant of English, Scottish, German and perhaps indigenous Indian ancestors; my second wife is South African, with French, German, Dutch and perhaps indigenous African forebears. I myself am the result of another cocktail shaker of ancestry: Angles, Saxons, Celts, Iberians, and no doubt other strains which are even more exotic. And my two daughters and my son have combined these varied streams and have already passed or will pass them on to their own children.

Now, as I write this, Rafe is sixteen months old, healthy, jolly, self-contained, and remarkably well behaved, apart from an interest in grabbing things off the tops of tables and desks. I have already lost a small, probably boring and almost certainly repetitious paragraph or two from this book because he pressed the wrong button, reaching over his head to do it. He stands up and roars his pride at the achievement, and then has to sit down again fast. He climbs up the stairs, but hasn't yet discovered how to climb down. Having spent a lot of time in South Africa with his Afrikaans relatives, his first words were not a conventional 'Dadda' or 'Mamma' but '*kyk da*', meaning 'look at that', and accompanied by a pointing finger. The word '*kyk*' is pronounced like 'cake', so people in England tend to thing he's begging for something to eat.

For some months after he was born, it was my job to look after him in the morning so that Dee could sleep after the interrupted nights, and while I wrote my weekly column for BBC Online he would rest in the crook of my arm, his little bottom on the desktop, looking into my face as I tapped away awkwardly with my right hand. At first, he didn't even smile. Recalling the shreds of a classical education, now incredibly distant, and wishing to show off to Dee, I quote from Vergil's fourth Eclogue: '*Incipe, parve puer, risu cognoscere matrem*,' – 'Come on, little boy, greet your mother with a smile.' That moment would have to wait for many weeks yet.

There were times when he looked deeply into my eyes, as though he understood something of our relationship. It was like looking into the eyes of a mountain gorilla: the closeness, the understanding, perhaps even the affection all seemed to be there, but the mechanics of communication weren't. Not quite, at any rate. The pressure of his little fingers was probably nothing more than his fear of falling backwards; but I liked to read it as a sign of love and trust.

Would he be clever or a fool? Would he come to dislike his old father, or treat him like a friend? You hope for so many contradictory things for your son – that he'll be easy and obedient yet a bit of a daredevil, an independent-minded thinker, not a tame consumer who will obey every whim of the advertisers and manufacturers. If an occasional element of wildness accompanies this independence, so be it; but I also long for him to be kind and honourable and courteous. And above everything, of course, I want him to like his mother and me, and to put up with us.

For months, our quiet, harmonious nights were shattered by that particularly insinuating, ear-piercing cry that babies have: genetically engineered, I suppose, to make sure their needs are addressed quickly. There was a time when I actively looked forward to my regular trips to Baghdad, since they were the only time I could get a decent night's sleep. Things have got to be a bit extreme if you have to go to a war zone for a rest. The heavy, indefinable smell of nappies filled the house. There were – there still are – food and faecal sights that a sensitive-minded old boy like myself shouldn't be expected to see.

We have become obsessed by our child. I have made his picture the screen-saver on my laptop, and have been tempted to make his cry the ring for my mobile phone. I have tried not to bore my friends by showing them his photographs, but without success. I have reacted irritably on the relatively few occasions when people have stopped me in the street to ask if he is my grandson. And I am even more irritable when they say, 'What a pretty girl!'

Was I like this in 1969 and 1971, when my daughters, Julia and Eleanor, were born? No, because the world was different then. I never mastered the business of folding and pinning a terry-towel nappy, but in those days I wasn't expected to. I had to make a fuss in order to be present at the birth, and my friends regarded it as unusual behaviour. Now everything is different. My daughter Eleanor was the one who demonstrated for me the speed, ease and odourlessness of modern nappy-changing. As a result, the mildly unreconstructed father of 1969 now actively looks forward to changing his new son's nappies, feeding him, putting him to bed.

And I have been gratified and relieved by my daughters' response to the fact that their half-brother is younger than their own children. I was very much afraid that they would feel there was something faintly disgusting about a 61-year-old fathering a baby. But we have always been close, despite the break-up of my first marriage, and they seemed to be delighted by the whole thing, plying Dee (who isn't much older than they are) with gifts and advice.

There are, of course, fashions in child-rearing as in everything else. In the Sixties kids were given what they wanted, when they wanted it: hence, you might think, everything that's happened since. But my American first wife brought over with her a book which ran counter to all that; contented children, it said, knew where the boundaries of their behaviour should lie. Julia and Eleanor were remarkably contented, and have remained so. Now, I find, this disciplined approach has become the fashion of our own time: tough-egg writers like Gina Ford advise you to be firm about feeding and everything else. Like my friend John Humphrys, another elderly father, my instinct with the child of my sixties is to let the kid do more or less what he wants; but since I have seen with my own daughters how successful the disciplined approach can be, that is the route we have taken. And it works.

Like most younger parents, I took my daughters for granted, not sufficiently appreciating their charm and beauty, and allowing the pressures of my everyday life to come between us. I shan't do that this time. I'm far more laid back and easy-going now than I was then.

§

Rafe has a clear-cut schedule, and he has slept through the night for many months as a result. Thirty or more years ago, my two daughters demonstrated the value of a regular pattern for eating and sleeping, and Rafe has already benefited from it. He has, of course, spread his toys throughout the house; and although I thought I might react with the irritability of a man to treading on a plastic toy in my bare feet, I have found it a charming pleasure: when the pain has worn off, that is. It reminds me of that delight-ful time when you start living with a girl, and come across her underwear or tights or make-up in all sorts of unexpected places. The message is one of intimacy, and Rafe's toys, even the pain-ful ones, provide a message which speaks of a new and almost despaired-of fatherhood.

The best part of any day is the morning. He lifts up his arms to

me when I go into his little room, and I carry him up into our
bedroom and put him down in the middle of the bed. He gurgles
with enjoyment and grabs his bottle of milk and jams it in his
mouth, while we lie on either side of him and enthuse to each other
about his qualities. Earlier in his babyhood he used to look up at
me with his brown eyes, the same colour as his mother's, as though
he could understand everything but couldn't speak. Now, though,
the communication is, if not quite verbal, then certainly vocal.

And what he loves best is to be hoisted on my shoulders so that
he can look at the top of my bookshelves, where the Russian dolls
and the small literary and political busts stand. Then I swing him
around and sing

> I'm an airman, I'm an airman,
> And I fly, fly, fly, fly, fly,
> Up in the sky, ever so high.
> The birdies cannot catch me,
> No matter how they try,
> I'm an airman, I'm an airman,
> And I fly, fly, fly, fly, fly.

He gurgles with joy, making sounds like a Frenchman saying the
letter 'r'. And, to be absolutely honest, I feel like doing the same.

When he was born I promised myself never to get maudlin over
him, just as I promised never to push his pram aggressively like all
those mothers who think they are in charge of the future of the
race, nor have a sign on my car that said 'Baby On Board'. Well, I
don't own a car nowadays – that's our ecological trade-off for
having a baby – but I have probably broken both of the other two
promises.

Still, I've kept another one: looking back over my diary of his
six months of independent existence I can honestly say I'm still a
hands-on father, changing even the most disgusting of his nappies,
feeding him at unpropitious times of the night, wiping his sick off
the shoulder of the suit I'll be wearing when I appear on that
evening's news, and (uncharacteristically) not complaining about
any of it. I honestly didn't know I had it in me.

§

One afternoon, a month after he was born, I went to Television Centre to edit a report for the *Ten O'Clock News*. The producer and picture editor were friends of mine, intelligent and sensitive, yet distinctly blokeish. As we sat in the darkness of the cutting-room, the producer mentioned that he had seen a newspaper picture of Dee and me pushing the baby. In the way of these things nowadays, the picture had been snatched without our knowledge or agreement. What type of baby buggy did we have, the producer asked? Mamas and Papas, I said, feeling strangely awkward, as though I were talking about underwear or my favoured suppository. Ah, said the producer, we have a Maclaren. The picture editor had another type. We each seemed to prefer our own. Once we might have been talking cars, or football; now we were talking prams.

Then the conversation turned to nappies, and thence to bum creams. What type did I use? Apparently there was a better type, in a tube not a tub. I made a note of it. Even blokeish blokes change nappies now, it seems.

Men have changed. In 1969 and 1971, when my first wife had Julia and Eleanor, I regarded myself as a new man. But because I was clumsy I found the business of folding the thick towelling nappies very awkward, I jabbed the safety-pins into the babies or myself, and all my attempts leaked. I was soon taken off that particular duty. Now nappy-changing is unrecognizably easy, and there are places everywhere to do it. And no one even looks when I feed Rafe in public.

§

By the summer he was two feet four inches long, distinctly pudgy, and still spoke no known language. Because he was teething, he had an alarming habit of grabbing his bare feet, stuffing them into his mouth, and sucking his toes. He had also demonstrated some sterling qualities as a companion on the road. And Dee and I had found, to our surprise and pleasure, that we got distinctly better treatment when he travelled with us.

This was not the first time in his short life that Rafe had been abroad: he flew to Monte Carlo in April, and to Sharm el-Shaikh, in Egypt, in June. My wife and I have always led a wandering life, and Rafe is to some extent condemned to share it. But we compensate by ensuring that we keep to his clear-cut routine wherever we are; and even when he was hurtling towards Paris on a train at 150 miles per hour he slept and had a nappy change and ate his meals at the correct times. As a result, he was immensely jolly, grinning at everyone around him with his moon face, and chewing his disreputable rubber elephant.

One day we were walking along the avenue Montaigne in the pouring rain, when we realized we wouldn't be able to get back to our flat in time to feed him and change his nappy. So we turned into the Hotel Plaza Athenée, soaked and refugee-like under the critical gaze of the doorman, and dripped our way across the lobby to the lounge.

A beautiful young woman in a severe uniform took a half-step forward, but her face softened when she saw Rafe. She showed us to a good and rather prominent table, peeled our wet coats off us, and wheeled his muddy pushchair into position for his feed. The *maître d'hôtel*, dressed like the archbishop of Paris, frowned slightly at the sight of us, but relented when Rafe grinned back at him and waved. The atmosphere was distinctly improved when I ordered a couple of glasses of rosé champagne; I suppose it made us seem a little less like Kosovans.

Rafe's little tub of spinach and fish, unutterably disgusting to look at, was heated to precisely the right temperature by the hotel kitchen. Someone brought a tiny silver spoon to feed him with. Waiters cooed around us. The archbishop beamed, even when Rafe's mouth was covered in greenish slime. People asked us how old he was, and what his name was, and if that was the same as 'Raphael'. He grinned at them all and kicked his fat little legs and gurgled, and as a result they treated us like film stars.

Late that afternoon, after his nap, I took Rafe out to buy a bottle of wine for dinner. In the past Dee and I would have gone to a restaurant, but now we have to stay in and watch a video instead. It was still raining heavily. This time he was in his little baby-carrier; or, as Dee and I called it, his pod. (Carrying him in it was known as pod-casting.) He was getting too big and elderly to be taken round like this, but it was such a pleasure to have him positioned in front of me, where I could hold him and talk to him, that I couldn't resist it.

The rain lashed us as we walked through the big front door into the street, so I fastened my coat around him, leaving a couple of buttons open for his little head to stick out, directly below my own head. It wasn't until I saw our reflection in a shop window that I realized how weird we looked: like a two-headed giant. Until then I assumed the people who stopped and stared at us were simply taken with Rafe's charm.

Our local wine merchant's is a grand place, and the man who runs it is even grander. It was at that point that I realized I scarcely had any money with me. 'What's the best bottle of Bordeaux you can give me for twelve euros?' I asked. He wasn't the slightest bit fazed, either by the question or by the strange two-headed creature it came from. He pulled out an excellent bottle of Haut-Medoc. 'I think you will enjoy this,' he said. 'And so will the young gentleman.'

§

The trouble is, I see Rafe everywhere now. At the risk of sounding unbearably pious, our earlier problems have made me understand what a miracle life is. And to take it away seems suddenly to be not just a crime but a disgusting, wasteful blasphemy.

Just being in Baghdad is dangerous. Ever since the invasion in 2003 I have gone back there again and again and each day I am there I do my best to get out onto the streets to film. When I walk along the pavement, the people I pass appear to me in an altogether different light from the way they once did. It must sound horribly corny, but each of them seems to me to have a quality, a value I have never appreciated before. Life itself is what matters – not who owns it. Fatherhood has changed me completely.

My son is surrounded by love, and will have all the advantages a wealthy country can give. Yet the most wretched urchins in the slums of Baghdad are no less human, no less alive than he is. And the old men, dragging themselves around and trying keep body and soul together, once shared the same exuberance, the same freshness, the same energy. And, perhaps, the same innocence.

I once heard an Anglican bishop, who was captured in the Far East by the Japanese during the Second World War, talking about his experiences in a concentration camp. For some reason the fact that he was a Christian bishop aroused the greatest hatred among his captors, and they tortured him cruelly and often. As his tormentors gathered round him, he tried to envisage what each of them must have been like as a child. It helped take his fear and anger away, he said, though it couldn't do anything to stop the pain. I now find myself looking at the people I pass in the streets of Baghdad, trying to imagine them as young children.

So Rafe has unquestionably sensitized me. I have at last understood how fragile, how delicate, how endangered life is, and how very valuable. A gerontologist would probably say I was suffering from emotional lability, the senescent condition which makes the elderly choke up at words like 'beauty', 'honour', or 'generosity'. But during every visit to Baghdad since Rafe was born I have become more and more enraged by the effects of violence and aggression, whether from an American soldier or a suicide bomber. This dead teenager, this dismembered woman, this old man groaning in the gutter could be my own child. Who could do such violence to the most precious thing there is: life itself?

6

APPROACHES TO BAGHDAD

In the years that followed the overthrow of Saddam Hussein, few things annoyed the small bunch of Western journalists and cameramen who went regularly to Baghdad to report more than the assumption by people who didn't go there that it was all pretty easy.

'They live in the safety of the Green Zone,' wrote one former journalist in 2006, with all the assurance that comes from a total absence of personal experience, 'and only venture out under military escort.' He had covered a couple of wars in the 1970s and 80s, so that made him an expert.

But the main burden of his complaint was that television correspondents had taken to appearing on camera in war zones *without wearing a tie*. The underlying sense was that, in his day (which was my day too), he had covered real wars for television news, nothing like this sanitized business in Iraq, with its safe living quarters and its heavy protection, and he had still managed to wear a tie.

I felt as I read this as if I had been approached in a West End club by the oldest member and told I was incorrectly dressed.

That has actually happened to me several times, of course, because I belong to a couple of West End clubs and only rarely seem to be able to wear the right clothes for any given occasion. I love my clubs for their ancient charm, for their largely unchanged routine, and for the pleasurable company of festive old boys like myself. But if you have the audacity to take your tie or jacket off at the height of summer, when the mahogany furniture and the thick carpets throb with the heat and the vodka-martinis are slow in arriving, you have committed a major solecism.

I have tended to keep quiet about the dangers of reporting from

Baghdad, because it sounds like a convoluted form of self-praise: Baghdad is dangerous, I go to Baghdad, *ergo* I must be amazingly brave. But of course I know, better than anyone, how nervous I get when I'm there, and how I constantly imagine that the worst is likely to happen at any minute; so we can, I assure you, discount any notion of bravery on my part. And although I don't have a military escort when I venture out, I do have some of the best security people in the business to look after me.

The brave ones, in my considered opinion, are not the tourists who turn up from time to time, like me, but the full-time correspondents who have stayed in Baghdad over the years since Saddam Hussein's fall. The BBC's first correspondent was Caroline Hawley, who was in the job for three long years, was involved in one of the explosions carried out by al-Qaeda in Amman, and saw her then boyfriend spattered with someone else's brains and blood.

It takes a particular form of determined, long-term courage to live in such places, to see so much death and destruction at first hand, and to carry on reporting it, day after frightening day. In my case, I would stay for only a couple of weeks and then head home; for Caroline, the nerve-racking conditions of Baghdad *were* her home.

For the slightly obsessive record, the insurgency against the American and British forces in Iraq is the thirty-sixth war I have reported on in my career. It has been by far the most dangerous of all of them: much worse even than the Israeli invasion of Lebanon in 1982. No other war I have reported has come anywhere near the daily perils of Baghdad.

By contrast, reporting from the southern city of Basra, which the British held from 2003 to 2007, was a good deal safer. The Sunni resistance, with the daily suicide bombings it carried out, didn't operate in Basra, and although it wasn't exactly safe to be there, life was a great deal easier than in Baghdad.

I had no complaint whatsoever against any journalist who didn't want to go to Iraq because of the danger. That seemed to me to be an entirely honest and perfectly reasonable position. But it was annoying to find some people declaring that because it was difficult to work in Baghdad, it wasn't worth going there. Reporting from Baghdad was, sniffed one journalist who hadn't been near the place since Saddam was overthrown, 'perpetrating a kind of fraud' on the public, because the journalists who did it gave the impression that they could report from there in the usual way, when in fact they couldn't. Another journalist wrote, 'Since I cannot get around and do a proper job of reporting, I regard it as dishonest to go there at all.'

Hmm. It's a good job that Vassily Grossman and the other correspondents who reported from Stalingrad in 1942–3 didn't feel it was dishonest, or a kind of fraud, to be there because it was so hard to get around and see the other side of the story. For my part, whenever I hear journalists talking about the morality of their craft, I always reach for the off switch.

So here it is, for the record. It won't do any good, of course, and historians will no doubt pick up the fiction and make it fact, but no journalists are based in the Green Zone, the vast area of southern central Baghdad on the western bank of Tigris which is controlled by the Americans and the Iraqi army. All of them, even those who are closest in spirit to the US military like Fox News, are based in Baghdad itself.

True, most of us want to be within striking distance of the Green Zone, because that is the seat of government and the place where the Americans are based. And, of course, one day we may be attacked and will need to take refuge there. But every news organization still in Baghdad (and there are very few of them now, which may explain the widespread misunderstandings) operates in the city centre. We are given no protection at all by the Americans or the Iraqi army, and if we were to appeal to them for help they would ignore us. We live either in rented houses or in hotels.

And because it's dangerous, and because maintaining proper security is expensive – much too expensive for smaller organizations like Sky News and ITV News, who only rarely send their people there – many of us huddle together for safety and convenience. The BBC, Reuters and the *New York Times*, for instance, are all based in a side-street in an area of Baghdad which is still more or less mixed. We cooperate with each other in terms of security.

Our street is patrolled by armed men, day and night, and there are chicanes made of concrete blocks twelve feet high. Steel doors protect the houses where we live and work. To attack us would certainly not be impossible, but it would take a certain amount of determination and effort, and so far no side in what is effectively the civil war in Iraq has thought it worthwhile to take us on. Whether the insurgents actually want to have international news organizations in Baghdad is a matter for conjecture. We bring their activities to the world's attention, of course; yet an attack on, say, the BBC, or the kidnapping of one of its employees, would gain some pretty big headlines.

The BBC employs security consultants, usually ex-SAS or other former military men, who come out with us when we go filming in the city. We have a rule that we never stop in the same place for more than fifteen minutes, that being the time which, it's reasonable to assume, it would take someone to spot us, get on the phone to someone else with a gun, and come and shoot us. Our security people are highly trained, and several of them have done close protection work in the past. They are armed, and I have learned to trust them implicitly whenever I go out.

This, then, is the pattern of one of my trips to Baghdad, even though some of the details have inevitably varied over the years. Every few weeks the cameraman, the producer and I gather our gear together and meet at Terminal Four at Heathrow. Apart from camera equipment, clothes, books, DVDs and so on, this gear consists of flak jackets and helmets. I am very attached to my flak jacket, because it saved my life in northern Iraq in 2003, and still has the hole in the material where a large chunk of shrapnel buried itself in the rear panel of laminated plastic protecting my back; the hole is directly over my spine.

The flak jacket didn't protect me from the other large piece which hit me, because it was near my hip. But it did me no real harm. Nowadays the doctors prefer to leave stray bits of metal like this inside you, as long as they aren't endangering any vital organ, because taking it out would do more damage to the network of nerves around it than leaving it where it is. It becomes an integral part of you.

And so, like poor old limping Dr Watson, who took a bullet from an Afghan *jezail* during the war of 1878–80, I complain about my shrapnel a bit when the weather is bad or I have to sit or stand for a long time, but I have actually grown quite fond of it. (I was once quoted in a newspaper as saying I had christened it 'George W. Bush', because it was a pain in the arse. Afterwards, I was rebuked by one of my various bosses at the BBC and I would never of course make such a joke again.)

If you are trying to get to Baghdad, there are some places, Dubai for instance, where they get excited by the sight of a flak jacket and helmet at Customs, on the grounds that they are part of the equipment of war. They take them off you for safe-keeping, then hand them back as you leave the country; as though a flak jacket were something you could kill people with.

So I prefer not to travel through Dubai. The choice of a staging-point to fly to Baghdad is therefore restricted to Amman and Kuwait; and although Amman is a far nicer and more relaxed place to be, Kuwait was more convenient for getting to Baghdad for the first couple of years after the invasion of Iraq.

I am not a fan of Kuwait, as I say. In fact, I'm not sure I have ever met anyone who *was* a fan of Kuwait, including quite a number of Kuwaitis. When you discover that they are regarded as arrogant by the Saudis, who are themselves often said to be the most arrogant people on earth, you realize that something fairly extreme is going on there. By some accident of overbooking I once had to fly first class on Kuwait Airlines. It was dreadful, because the cabin staff treated me like dirt. And the strongest thing they could offer me to drink was orange-juice.

Kuwait City feels like a building site. The summer heat is ferocious, the officials are rude (though not quite uniformly, since one or two in my experience have been quite helpful; but they are certainly in a tiny minority), and there is nothing to do or see there except to shop. The biggest traffic jams are at night, as people head out to the shopping malls to buy from the same big-name shops you find everywhere else.

I am a great admirer of Islam. I appreciate its good qualities as a religion, I like the societies it has created, I appreciate its history and its architecture and its customs, and I honour its laws. But since I am a Christian, alcohol is not forbidden to me. Far from it: a sip of wine is actually a part of my religion at the Communion rail. And outside church, I greatly enjoy a good bottle of wine with my dinner, and a *digestif* with my occasional cigar. As long as I take these pleasures sparingly and discreetly, I see no reason why they should be denied to me.

The hotel where we used to stay was annoying in all sorts of petty ways – these big international chains so often are – but the food was quite good, and a well-prepared dinner with your friends and colleagues the night before one left for Baghdad called for more than a glass of water to do it proper justice. I always went to bed afterwards with a mild sense of having been wronged.

Kuwaiti officialdom could be annoying in other ways. Once, going to one of Saddam Hussein's old haunts to film (it was the grandstand in Baghdad where he used to take the salute while his tanks and rocket-launchers rumbled by underneath the two sets of gigantic crossed swords, with hands and wrists modelled on his own), I saw that the Iraqi lieutenant in charge of the place had set out a number of Saddam-era objects, presumably for sale to passers-by. One was a statue of Saddam in some kind of gold-coloured resin, three feet in height, and I bought it on the spot. The problem was, his right arm was extended in Saddam's familiar and rather irritating gesture of greeting, so it needed careful packing. A Baghdad carpenter made a very wide coffin for it, and I took it to Kuwait with me when I left.

I suppose I thought the coffin would give it some degree of anonymity when it went through the X-ray machine at the airport, one of several checks you have to endure there, but there was a shout of anger from the security man, a Kuwaiti soldier, as he stared at his screen. I walked round. There was Saddam's statue, almost as large and certainly as colourful as in real life. You could see the general's flashes on his shoulders, the outsize revolver at his waist, and even the individual bristles of his moustache. Not much chance of trying to persuade anyone it was the unknown warrior.

In an instant I appeared to be under arrest. A sergeant, standing a little too close to me, shouted in my face in heavily accented English that I had insulted the dignity of the state of Kuwait. Although there were various possible answers to that, it didn't seem to be a good idea to make any of them.

There was a pause while we waited for someone senior to come along. It took some time. A queue built up behind me, and the sergeant hustled me rudely away from the X-ray screen, where I could still admire the detail on Saddam's face and figure. The more unlikely it seemed that I would be allowed to take it home, the finer it seemed to me to be.

Naturally, I could understand that Kuwaitis might not look favourably upon images of the man who had invaded their country, trashed it and allowed his men to kill and kidnap whomever they liked. My sympathies were entirely with the Kuwaitis on all that. But historical artefacts linked to political dictators are a particular interest of mine, and since I clearly hadn't collected it in any spirit of reverence it seemed pretty stupid for anyone to get upset about it.

In the end, as the queue grew longer and more vocal, an officer came swaggering up. He obviously didn't like the look of me, and it was mutual. But at least he understood what the limits of his power were. He gave me and Saddam a dismissive wave of his hand that might not have been complimentary, but at least made it clear we could both leave.

The coffin had now been thoroughly smashed up, so I had to get Saddam swathed in that clear plastic they put round suitcases at some airports, to protect them from theft and damage. Saddam's body was fine, but it took a bit of careful work on the part of the mummifier to get the plastic sheeting round the arm. Afterwards, as I stood in the check-in queue with a number of Kuwaitis, holding Saddam or letting him stand beside me, it was hard to conceal who he was. I didn't feel very popular.

Until, that is, the British Airways station manager heard about it. He came and pulled me out of the queue with a big smile, and shepherded me to another desk where he checked me in, together with Saddam. I walked onto the plane half an hour later, with Saddam under my arm. People talked and pointed a bit, but there was a seat for him in business class, and when the meal trolley came round, Saddam had his own tray. His lunch, suitably enough, consisted of red meat.

Nowadays he stands in our study, gesturing grandly towards the bookcases. I used to hang scarves round his neck, and put a hat on his head; but since the original was executed, I have stopped doing that. Somehow it no longer seems appropriate.

§

The RAF flights to Baghdad were liable to all sorts of delays.
Sometimes it was the weather, sometimes it was a shortage of
aircraft, since the RAF had another heavy commitment in Afghanistan, and sometimes it was technical. You never knew. It was like
flying from Sarajevo to Split with the UN during the Sarajevo siege
in the early 1990s, except that the UN treated non-UN passengers
rudely and carelessly and were hopelessly unreliable. (They admitted
as much, by stamping your passport 'Maybe Airlines'.) By contrast
the RAF were pleasant, friendly and much more dependable, but
delays could always happen. In the roasting heat of summer you
would sit out in the open, under a camouflage net, waiting for
news of your plane. Sometimes you had to sit with contingents
of American soldiers in a vast tent as they lay around listlessly,
watching excessively violent films on a huge screen, or just trying to
get some sleep. There were frequent, improbably noisy announce-
ments over the loudspeakers about the requirement to wear body
armour at all times. Occasionally some appalling Jack-in-office (or
Jill-in-office, since women were either given the role of vigilante
more often than men, or else volunteered for it more often) would
come round and threaten to throw you out unless you put your flak
jacket and helmet on. This in temperatures of up to fifty degrees
centigrade.

'But I'm not in the American military. I'm not in any military.
I'm a journalist.'

'That doesn't matter, sir. You are under US military jurisdiction
while you're in here, and I am instructing you to put on your
personal protection.'

Which made it sound like a condom, though I discovered that it
was unwise to make that or any other joke. Officialdom's sense of
humour, if it ever had one, has long since been surgically removed.

'And I am also instructing you not to take it off after I leave this
facility.'

Every structure the US military creates is called a facility, from
the gigantic tents that serve as departure lounges to the narrow,
smelly confines of a plastic toilet, with a tank which is always
three-quarters full and walls covered with writing, most of it either
obscene or the product of a seriously disturbed mind; though what

does that say about me, since I try to distract myself from the smell and the flies by reading what the others have written?

To move to the far smaller RAF corner of the Kuwait military airport was to get the faintest but most enjoyable flavour of home. Pleasant Midland accents prevailed, no one shouted unless it was to be heard over the sound of aircraft engines, and no one gave you orders for the sake of it, whether it was to sit somewhere or to wear your body armour. No one, round in the RAF section, was forced to do anything very much, except of course to wait. Sometimes the ground staff would let my team use the air-conditioned trailer which served as a VIP lounge. There were wonderful scrolls and citations on the walls there, one of which expressed the thanks of an American general to a US forces facility called the Royal Air Force. I thought there was a certain irony involved in displaying that.

The RAF usually seemed to like the Americans they worked alongside, but they often found them heavy-handed and inflexible. Perhaps smaller forces always feel that about larger ones. No one, however, felt that way about the US Marine who looked after the needs of the people travelling on the RAF flights. He scurried about in the hottest weather, handing out sandwiches and soft drinks and a particularly fierce brew of coffee. He made the whole experience a lot easier.

When the time came to get on the aircraft, everyone's bag was searched with a speed, an effectiveness and a lightness of touch which I always admired. Once, apologetically, someone dug out a large and very handy clasp-knife which I had mistakenly put in my carry-on bag rather than my suitcase.

'I can be certain, can't I, sir, that you won't be taking this out during the flight?'

He put it back in the bag. Someone had encouraged these people to employ their initiative; not a quality you often find in our security-obsessed world.

Often, I would be invited into the cockpit of the Hercules to spend the flight with the aircrew. It was much more comfortable than sitting in the back of the plane on little webbing seats, sideways-on to the direction of the flight. On the flight deck you were free, too, from the necessity – a real one as you flew into Baghdad – to wear body armour, since the plane's cockpit was itself armoured. In the heat of the summer, it became almost unbearable to sit in the body of the plane encased in Kevlar and wearing an intolerably heavy helmet; but you couldn't get on board the aircraft without them. One unfortunate passenger, at some stage fairly early on in the Iraqi insurgency, was killed by a stray round from an AK-47 as the Hercules was close to the ground. After that, it became mandatory to wear body armour.

Up front, though, with the enormous array of instruments winking and warning their way through the flight, I found a pleasant sense of freedom. The pilots were good company, and in the first years of the war they were pretty relaxed. They would always explain the plane's controls, though since most of the key expressions seemed to be acronyms it wouldn't have helped us much if the pilots had been shot and I had had to handle the plane myself.

The only things I could ever really understand, apart from the occasional insistent recording of a woman's voice warning the pilot that the plane was too low, or too high, or too close to another aircraft, were the electronic maps of the ground below us. There, through the heat haze, would be the marshes or the exact curve of the Tigris, or the glitter of the Euphrates far below; and there they were, clearly marked on the map as we flew over them.

At first, after the invasion, we would drive the whole way from Kuwait City to Baghdad. It took between seven and ten hours, and as the situation in Iraq deteriorated during 2004, it became increasingly dangerous. Sometimes we would be stopped at highly questionable road-blocks, by men who might be policemen but were just as likely to be gangsters or insurgents. Trouble might suddenly flare up as we passed through a town or village, and it was always possible that we might be spotted as foreigners and attacked. This kind of travel was always a strain on the body and the mind, so to be able to fly to Baghdad in an hour, with a styrofoam cup of strong RAF tea and a digestive biscuit, was an immense pleasure.

Because I made the journey so often, I lost track of the individual pilots and aircrew who took us, and I only once flew with the same team. But I do remember one particular pilot and co-pilot. They talked about their families, and how glad they were that their spell of duty was coming to an end soon. They were highly competent, unexcitable, sane men; reliable, inclined to make jokes about everything and good to be with. When we landed at Baghdad, one of them wanted to get a photograph of all of us together. We stood there for an instant, smiling in the bright sunshine; then we shook hands and I lugged my body armour over to the racks where our luggage would be delivered.

The next day, as I was about to leave for an interview, we heard that an RAF Hercules had been shot down on a flight out of Baghdad to the north. Everyone on board, including a number of SAS men, had been killed. I checked the names; it was the crew I had flown in with. For a while I could imagine the atmosphere in that cockpit as the plane went into its final dive. Then I stopped myself. It was too painful, too real.

§

I came to love Baghdad with a kind of angry possessiveness. It enraged me to hear American officials warning Iraqis that the patience of the United States could wear thin unless they did something to help themselves. Suggestions that America had sacrificed a great deal to help Iraq, and that everything would be fine if only Iraqis would stop their incomprehensible violence, made me boil with anger. I had not the slightest sympathy with the vicious criminals who blew up others in the name of religion. But if you invade a complex, finely balanced society and destroy all the constraints which stop people going for each other's throats in the name of politics and religion, the primary blame is scarcely theirs.

However much I love it, though, even I can't maintain that Baghdad is a beautiful city. There are moments when it does have a certain attraction, but they are brief. At sunrise and sunset, as the light plays on the crumbling buildings overlooking the River Tigris, and the little ferryboats ply backwards and forwards across the reddening water, it can seem as lovely as anywhere on earth. But the magic fades very quickly, and Baghdad is its workaday self again.

Not that I know too much about it nowadays. The last time I was able to explore on my own, as I used to do, the *souks* and alleyways of the oldest part of the city, was in April 2004. At that time US Marines attacked the small town of Fallujah, on the western outskirts of Baghdad. The intention was, apparently, to avenge the savage murders of four American security men who were dragged through the streets by a lynch mob and hanged from a bridge like slaughtered animals. It was appalling, and it seems that President George W. Bush himself gave orders that the people of Fallujah should be taught a lesson.

Until that moment, the insurgency against the coalition forces had been relatively mild. There were a few attacks every day, but it was still possible for Westerners to walk around alone, and drive from Baghdad to other parts of the country. I went to places as different as Tikrit, aggressively Sunni and strongly supportive of Saddam Hussein, whose pictures were still displayed in the main street, and the Shi'ite holy city of Kerbala, where the influence of the fierce young cleric Moqtada al-Sadr was strong.

At the moment when the Americans attacked Fallujah, they also decided to take on Moqtada al-Sadr. By voluntarily deciding to fight a war on two fronts, they put themselves in the position of the British in 1920, fighting the nationwide uprising which demonstrated to them that Iraq would never be fitted neatly into the British Empire, as Britain and the League of Nations had decided it should. The insurgency which followed the attack on Fallujah in 2004 showed everyone who had an understanding of Iraq and its history that it would be neither a loyal American ally nor a beacon of democracy in the Middle East.

And so I could no longer visit the Mustansiriya University or the little shops around it. And if I went to the book market, or drank tea in the intellectuals' teahouse nearby, it would be for only ten or fifteen minutes at a time, and I would need to have a couple of armed bodyguards to watch over me.

The assault on Fallujah, which was repeated more than once afterwards, was thoroughly questionable. The Americans warned everyone beforehand to leave the town (it is only the size of Brighton), and announced that they would regard everyone who remained there as an enemy combatant. But of course large numbers of the poorest, the weakest and the oldest were unable or unwilling to move, and there is no clear idea how many of them were killed by ground fire and aerial bombardment.

The Geneva Convention has a good deal to say about armies which attack cities from which the weakest, the oldest and the poorest have not effectively been evacuated. But the Bush administration decided that the Geneva Convention didn't apply to this kind of war, which was essentially (it considered) one of retribution and self-defence after the attacks of 11 September 2001. Except, of course, that President Bush later admitted that Saddam Hussein's Iraq had not been responsible for aiding and abetting those attackers.

Still, this was a distinction which went unnoticed by large numbers in the United States. In 2003 one in five Americans polled thought Saddam Hussein and Osama bin Laden, the real instigator of the 9/11 attacks, were one and the same person; among American servicemen, especially those fighting in Iraq, the proportion was even higher. No wonder so many civilians were killed.

So Fallujah was the turning point. After the spring of 2004, no one except for people like the rather engaging innocents who worked for Paul Bremer in the Coalition Provisional Authority can really have thought that the invasion of Iraq was going to end up a success. You could spot them at once in their navy blue blazers and white chinos, and they tended to wear ties at the height of summer. No doubt they believed that they would reap massive career benefits for having followed Bremer's star to Baghdad; and of course they had the comfortable knowledge right from the start that he, and therefore they, would be there for no longer than a year. I found it easy to make them feel uncomfortable.

'So how's it going?'

'Well, sir,' (it being one of the chief signs of their expensive education that they would address a desiccated old white-poll like myself with a certain politeness) 'the indications for the parties are pretty good.'

This was the period when the Americans were trying to stimulate the creation of new political parties, which didn't just follow sectarian lines.

'And how are the non-denominational parties doing?'

They were, it seemed, doing remarkably well.

'But you're not saying they'll do better than the big Shi'ite parties?'

It turned out that this was exactly what the young chap in the blazer and chinos was saying.

'But look at the demographics. The Shi'ites are the big majority of the population. Their parties are bound to walk all over everyone else.'

'That's not how we see it, sir.'

And he was right – it wasn't how they saw it. The young, enthusiastic, conservative politicos of the Green Zone always reminded me of Mormons. Their faith might seem to outsiders to be on the weird side, and they might find it hard to point to any evidence which could win over the sceptics, yet they stuck to their beliefs with a bland certainty. They believed in the leadership qualities of a former CIA informant, Iyad Allawi (the British, who should have known better, did too), and they shoehorned him into the prime minister's job when the Provisional Authority headed by Paul Bremer dissolved itself. Bremer left Iraq with unseemly haste a day or two before his mandate evaporated, but some of the blazered, chinoed tribe he had gathered round him remained for a little longer.

Perhaps it isn't altogether surprising that these young enthusiasts tended to discount the effect of sectarianism on the politics of Iraq. There were some American officials who understood the complexity of Iraq's political and religious make-up. The CIA and the State Department both tried hard to explain the unwelcome realities of Iraqi life to the true believers in the White House and the Department of Defense. The State Department, indeed, put together a 900-page document about how Iraq should be run after the overthrow of Saddam Hussein. Part of it dealt with the difficult business of maintaining a balance between Sunnis and Shi'ites. Donald Rumsfeld, the Secretary of Defense, whose arrogance marked the entire Iraq operation, threw it in the waste-bin with the words (according to one story) 'Well, we won't be needing that.'

Not long after the invasion I went to see an Iraqi friend of mine, a leading politician with an impressive record of non-sectarianism. He wore, as ever, a beautifully cut suit, and his manners were as fine as his clothes. I drank a little of the tea which Iraqis make out of dried limes, and asked him about his trip to Washington three months before the invasion to brief President Bush on the situation in Iraq.

'He was very charming, you know,' said my friend loyally. 'I think sometimes people' (he probably meant me) 'underestimate his charm and intelligence.'

'And what about his level of information about Iraq?'

'Ah well, he has access to some of the best information in the world, you know.'

'He may have access to it, but does he take any notice of it?'

My friend laughed.

'I'm sure he takes notice of everything he feels he should.'

'All right,' I said, 'how much did he know about the division between Shi'ites and Sunnis?'

It was, I suppose, a bit brutal. This was a man with a long and honourable history, whom I should not be trying to trap in my aggressive fashion.

There was a silence; a longish one. My friend knew I would use whatever information he gave me.

'I have to say,' he answered eventually, 'that he seemed not to know very much about it.'

'Not very much? How much did he know, then?'

Another silence, though not quite so long.

'Actually, I think he was hearing about it for the first time.'

Even I was shocked.

'He didn't know that 60 per cent of the Iraqi population were Shi'ites?'

It was a mistake. My friend, though determinedly non-sectarian, is himself a Sunni and likes to believe that there is a rough numerical balance between Sunnis and Shi'ites; or at least that there are more Sunnis than the 20 per cent which is probably the correct figure. We talked about that for a moment.

'But did Bush know about the religious divide here?'

'No.'

'So he invaded a country that was divided, while thinking it was united?'

My friend changed the subject.

At first, both the American and British governments (though not the diplomats of either country, who knew better) played down the sectarian divisions in Iraq. There was a tendency to talk about 'Iraqis' as though they were all pretty much the same, much as you might talk about 'Swedes' or 'Iranians'. Soldiers who had served in Iraq would write letters to the British or American newspapers complaining about the usually pessimistic coverage and saying that all the Iraqis where they had been stationed were delighted to have the coalition forces in their country. It usually became clear that they were either talking about the Kurdish areas, where people were overwhelmingly in favour of the invasion, or the Shi'ite ones, where the pleasure at seeing Saddam Hussein overthrown hadn't yet worn off. But since the main hatred and violence towards the coalition came from the Sunni areas, this was all pretty meaningless. After the invasion, talking about 'Iraqis' (as in 'Are the Iraqis happier now than they were under Saddam?') no longer had any real meaning.

Sometimes we ourselves added to the confusion. In April 2004, just as the assault on Fallujah was going on and it was becoming dangerous to wander round the streets alone, the BBC and various other international news organizations commissioned an opinion poll across Iraq. It may sound strange to think that pollsters could travel the country, knocking on people's doors and asking about their state of mind, when there was violence and death in the streets; yet even in 2007, when the violence reached an unprecedented level, it was still possible to hold an effective nationwide opinion poll.

The results, as we received them first, were very interesting. People were asked whether the invasion of 2003 had been a liberation or an occupation, and only a single percentage point separated the 'yes' and the 'no' votes: 49 per cent said it was a liberation, 48 per cent said it had been an occupation. 'Iraqis are finely divided between enthusiasm for the invasion and criticism of it,' said one BBC headline.

It was only the following day, when we were able to see some more of the basic data of the opinion poll, that it became clear how misleading this and other findings had been. Virtually every Sunni who had replied to the question had said the invasion was an occupation; a surprising number of Shi'ites, and even a small percentage of Kurds (the group with the most to gain from the invasion) agreed with them. Those who said it was a liberation contained scarcely any Sunnis at all; they were overwhelmingly Kurdish and Shi'ite. In other words, the country was already deeply divided along sectarian and national lines. Because we still regarded Iraqis as a single community, we misunderstood the nature of the answers we had received.

As the election of January 2005 came closer, there was immense pressure from both governments on the Western journalists in Baghdad to provide 'balanced' coverage of it. 'Balance' in this case meant ignoring the differences between the different elements within the population. The British government, knowing the scepticism that existed in the press and among public opinion at home, put a good deal of effort into persuading everyone that the election was a success and that the great majority of Iraqis were happy with the new system. The British embassy in Baghdad was headed by people who knew perfectly well what the real state of affairs was, and were honest about it. But Downing Street put its own people into the embassy to make sure the 'right' message was put out.

So the Downing Street machine organized a press trip so that the large number of journalists who had come to Baghdad for the occasion could see the people of Iraq voting. Nothing wrong with that, except that the trip was to a particularly strong Shi'ite area in the south.

There was never any doubt that the Shi'ites would turn out in very large numbers and with the greatest enthusiasm to vote. Throughout the Saddam Hussein era and even before, the Shi'ites had been barred from any kind of political power or influence, even though they formed the clear majority of the population. They understood that the American and British invasion had smashed Sunni minority power in Iraq, and that this election was their first chance to take control of the country themselves. So of course they turned out in their millions; and it was a moving and impressive sight to watch them.

But for the British and American governments, the television images of large numbers of Iraqis voting would by themselves validate the invasion. Saddam Hussein had been a tyrant; now the people of Iraq were free to express their real political views. Fine: but of course to call them 'Iraqis', without specifying what kind of

Iraqis they were, was completely misleading. It gave the impression that the nation had come forward as a whole to take advantage of its new freedom.

In the Sunni areas, by contrast, a majority of people was planning to stay at home on election day. There was a distinct threat to any Sunnis who wanted to vote. This wasn't the message that the White House and Downing Street wanted broadcast.

Most of the British television and newspaper journalists who had come to Baghdad to report on the election accepted the offer of free transport to the Shi'ite south without even thinking about it. The pictures they obtained told the story; but it wasn't the full story, and it wasn't even the true story. For my colleagues and me, the important thing was what happened in the Sunni areas. If people there turned out in large numbers, then that really would be a ringing endorsement of the British and American invasion.

But of course they didn't. Some Sunnis voted, but in their areas there was something approaching a boycott.

'I hear you're planning to skulk in your office rather than run the risk of coming down south with us,' a more than usually insinuating and aggressive figure from Downing Street said when she called the BBC bureau. For some time afterwards we had to contend with the suggestion that we had somehow underplayed the huge success of the election. As for me personally, there was an implication, sometimes put into words, that I was a contrarian, a naysayer, an ingrained critic. Memories were stirred in Downing Street of the time in 1999 when I had been based in Belgrade during the NATO bombing and had reported that the bombs were hardening people's will to resist rather than weakening it. Plainly, I was an enemy, and had the basest political motives.

Slowly, though, the reality in Iraq became clearer. People began to understand that this election and the two later votes in 2005 simply made the sectarian divide fiercer and more obvious. Iraqis were forced to decide, sometimes for the first time, whether they were basically Shi'ite or Sunni, and whether they would express their religious identity by voting for their sect. The elections were the main achievement of the invasion. And although it was a wonderful thing to see people voting freely for the first time, the act of voting in fact made the violence and the divisions in Iraq all the worse.

Was this inevitable? No, I don't think so. Certainly a number of senior British diplomats, thoroughly schooled by their service's long tradition in the dubious skills of hedging and fudging the differences between hostile groups of people, felt it would have been possible to devise elections which kept Iraqis together rather than emphasize the differences between them. But Paul Bremer III was impatient with these convoluted, decadent, mandarin ways. Like his patrons in Washington, Dick Cheney and Donald Rumsfeld, he believed it was easy. Just allow people to vote, and that will sort everything out.

But it didn't.

§

I may not have lived in the Green Zone, but I sometimes spent the night there. To report on the trial of Saddam Hussein, for instance, we had to turn up in the Green Zone at seven in the morning. That was the time when the car bombs used to go off, and although I was willing to take my chances with them, the likelihood was that all the approaches to the Green Zone would be closed down as a precautionary measure. I could have found myself stuck outside the Zone for hours.

So I would stay at the Al-Rasheed Hotel, in the heart of the Green Zone. Uncomfortable and decaying though it was, this was always something of a pleasure for me; I had spent six of the most exciting and professionally rewarding months of my life there, between August 1990 and March 1991, reporting on the run-up to the first Gulf War, a small amount of the war itself, and a sizeable part of its aftermath.

In those days it was crowded with people (though almost all of them vanished when the war began) and was run with great professionalism. There were spies and listening devices everywhere. A friend of mine, a British banker who oversaw the deal between Saddam Hussein's government and the Swedish company responsible for the original furnishing of the hotel, warned me that there was an item on the bill to cover the installation of small video cameras in the television sets in some of the rooms.

Evidence for this came later. The security men who watched the guests in their rooms realized they were on to a good thing when wealthy honeymoon couples came to the Al-Rasheed to spend their first night there. The security men developed a profitable sideline as peddlers of pornography, by selling the videos in the souks. The story supposedly came to light when one recent bridegroom, for reasons we can only speculate about, was browsing through the stock of one dealer in porn and found the video of his own wedding night there.

Now, though, as in Iraq itself, things had gone downhill in the Al-Rasheed. Scarcely a penny was spent on maintaining it. The thick carpets, stained with the activities of sixteen years, were frayed and rucked-up. The lifts worked erratically and alarmingly, and on some floors pressing the call button gave you an electric shock. The rooms smelled of sewage. On several occasions I found myself itching badly after spending the night between the rough, darned sheets, and after that I used to bring my own sleeping-bag and pillow.

The Americans took it over, as they took over most of the buildings in the Green Zone, and ran it as a hotel for soldiers and officials. In 2004 Paul Wolfowitz, the deputy defence secretary and co-author of the plan to overthrow Saddam, spent a night on the tenth floor and was lucky to escape when a missile hit the hotel close to his room. That gave rise to a good deal of black humour, particularly among the American soldiers.

For a while, the hotel was a little cleaner and a little better run, though there was little electricity and often no water, whether hot or cold. The man in charge was a reservist colonel from New York, who realized that the Iraqi staff were thieving from every room. His solution was a radical one. He ordered that every cleaner who entered a room there should be accompanied by one of the former Gurkha soldiers who at that stage ran the hotel security.

The Gurkhas were armed, and the cleaners were told they would be executed on the spot if the Gurkhas caught them stealing. The Gurkhas themselves, wonderful, intelligent, polite, neatly turned-out men, seemed entirely incorruptible, and anyway spoke a language unknown to any other race. You could see them as you walked down the corridor, standing menacingly behind the cleaners, watching their every move, rifles cradled in their arms.

The colonel who organized this was a magnificent archetype, a Polish New Yorker who felt that everywhere else in the world was a spittoon. When you checked in at the Al-Rasheed, you had to go to his office first, in order to be briefed. We will call him Kowalski. He loathed everything about the job, and he was obliged to be there for a whole year. Broad-shouldered but short, his hair *en brosse*, wearing a mixture of military and civilian clothes, he was a fountain of articulate hatred. He would tell you, angrily and without any sign of humour, about his most private concerns; and yet if you greeted him in the hotel lobby twenty minutes later he would stare at you as though he had never seen you in his life before.

'I hate this fuckin place. I hate the people. I hate this fuckin hotel most of all. They're just animals here, stealing everything they can lay their hands on. Animals. They can drown in their own shit as far as I'm concerned.'

After a while, I learned to draw him out, and encourage him to let rip; it was one of the few unalloyed pleasures of being in Iraq. He always had the same complaints to make, as though he had never spoken to you in his life before.

'I wouldn't be in this fuckin country at all if it wasn't for my fuckin ex-wife and her fuckin lawyer. I hate the bitch. Took me for everything I had. Here in Iraq, I got a gun. There in New York is where I need it, to go round and blow her fuckin head off. I got two fuckin kids, a son who does nothing and a daughter who does everything. With everyone.'

He handed out the forms as he spoke.

'I don't want to know your names. They mean fuckin nothing to me. You may be a big cheese back in your country, you may be nobody. I don't care. Here you don't have a name, in case they get to hear about it out in the city, and put a rocket through your window. If that happens, the blame belongs to you, not me. Got it? So when you hand in this card to the mother-fuckin Iraqis on the desk, who I don't trust any more than I can remember their fuckin names, and I can't remember any of their fuckin names, you'll see you're just down as "Kowalski". For them, everyone staying in this hotel is a fuckin Kowalski. It's the biggest collection of fuckin Kowalskis in the world.

'And if you lose the fuckin card I give you, or take it with you when you go as a fuckin souvenir of this shit-hole, I'll never forget it. If ever you come back, I'll hold you fuckin responsible. Do I make myself clear?

'Right. Now *she*'s going to tell you something.'

'She' was his assistant, Alice: a heavily overweight former school-teacher in her late forties from somewhere in the Mid-West. At first, she seemed to be a true believer in the invasion and its benefits, though slowly, I felt, she began to understand what was really going on. She lost some weight, and became better company. In the end, I came to like her, and admire her for her staying power and her bullet-proof confidence and her armour-plated niceness.

But she never lost her little-girl voice; and it was that, I think, that made Kowalski hate her more than anything else. He watched her move slowly across the room with a loathing in his face that he never took the trouble to hide.

'Hi there, everybody,' she said, like a junior-school teacher talking to a class of backward six-year-olds.

'Hi,' we answered.

'Now we have some rules in this hotel, because it's very different from other places you stay in. The people in this country have a lot of difficult problems, and we are here to help them. They are very wonderful people, and we want them to be able to look after themselves soon. And because this is a desert country, we have to be very careful with the water.'

Across the room, sitting at his desk, Kowalski snorted. He knew as well as we did that a series of insurgent bombs had damaged the water supply, and that so far no one had been able to repair it. In fact, they never did manage to repair it.

But for Alice, it was as though some naughty older boy had committed an act of vandalism.

'You see, there are people in this country who don't want democracy to succeed, and occasionally they do things which make life difficult for everybody.

'And so sometimes the water will be off, but then it will come on at times when you don't expect it, so you must always make sure the faucet is turned off when you leave your room. And to help you remember which way to turn the faucet when the water is off, we have a little rhyme in the United States which you should try to remember. It goes: "Leftie loosie, Rightie tightie".'

She twirled her hands in the air, as though to emphasize its poetical, aesthetic qualities, and to demonstrate the methodology of turning the taps on and off.

'Have you got that? "Leftie loosie, Rightie tightie".'

I glanced across at Kowalski, and thought I had never seen such naked, undisguised feeling on a man's face in my life. He must have listened to Alice saying these words a dozen times a day, but they never became easier for him to bear.

'Leftie loosie, Rightie tightie', and the little-girl voice, and her forgiving, uncomprehending attitude to the Iraqis whom he hated, not for who they were as individuals or even as a nation, but because they were different from the New Yorkers he wanted to be with, were all compounded like some poisonous recipe with the malignancy of his ex-wife, the crookedness of her lawyer, the laziness of his son and the loose morals of his daughter, to make the whole place completely unbearable for him. Perhaps he really did want the Gurkhas to shoot the thieving cleaners.

After he went, and the hotel was handed back to the Iraqis, everything got worse. And then, on the few occasions afterwards when I saw Alice, who had bravely signed up for yet another tour of duty, I missed him badly. And I felt a surprising rush of affection for her. But she never repeated the rhyme again. It occurred to me that she might only have said it to upset Colonel Kowalski.

§

In 2003 and the start of 2004, it was still possible to find real optimism among some people in Baghdad. It never occurred to them, I think, that the most powerful nation in history could fail when it set its mind to something. Slowly, though, this changed. The awkwardness and widespread lack of elementary social skills among the American soldiers began to enrage ordinary Iraqis. The majority treated all Iraqis as enemies, just as their predecessors had once treated all Vietnamese, then were surprised to find that most Iraqis did indeed come to hate them.

As a Westerner, it took a little time to understand all this. In my case, it happened early in 2004, when a friend of mine drove me to areas I knew from the past.

'You know, Iraqis are very afraid of Americans now,' he said conversationally as we drove along.

'I don't think there's much need to be.'

My friend looked at me sideways, and then looked ahead at the road.

'Would you like me to show you?'

I agreed.

He left the road we had been on, and turned onto one of the motorways which ring the city. Ahead of us I could see a line of American Humvees.

'This is dangerous, John,' said my friend. 'You are OK?'

'Of course,' I said.

I had the window open, and stuck my head out. They could see from my face, my clothes, my waving hand that I was a European.

He pulled out to overtake the column. As we got to within thirty yards of the last American vehicle, the gunner on the roof with whom I had exchanged a smile and a wave lowered the muzzle of his gun until it pointed directly at our windscreen. My friend dropped back again.

'You see?' he said, his faced contorted with anger. 'This is how they treat us in our own country. It happens every day.'

I asked around. It did happen every day and it was the single worst thing the Americans did. This should have been a war for the hearts and minds of Iraqis. But it was fought by soldiers who were trained for aggression, and who were usually exonerated if they maintained they had opened fire because they thought their lives were in danger. You don't win hearts and minds by firing at civilians. On the contrary, you have to be prepared to be fired at forty-eight times out of fifty without firing back. There are no better soldiers to have alongside you than the Americans if you are fighting an all-out war against enemy soldiers. They are tough, brave, and very committed. In the Second World War they were much more aggressive than the British army, and could never understand the British soldiers' habit of surrendering when they ran out of ammunition, rather than fighting to the end with any weapon that came

to hand. But if you are in a war against a shadowy enemy who fire
at you from around corners and behind innocent civilians, whose
language and habits you have to understand, then it is better not to
have the Americans around.

Over the years the situation grew worse and worse, until the
Americans announced that when their convoys or those of the Iraqi
army were patrolling the streets, every vehicle on the road had to
stop, or else stay a hundred yards back. The Iraqi cars creep forward
meekly, nervously, their eyes fixed on the rear gunner. He has the
power of life or death over them, and they hate him for it. And
if he, or sometimes she, decides that there is anything suspicious
about one of the cars that are discreetly following from a distance,
there will be no real problem about opening fire. The rear gunner
possesses the power of life and death. 'If you have them by the
balls,' said a sign on the office wall of a particularly aggressive
general in Vietnam, 'their hearts and minds will follow.' He couldn't
have been more wrong.

§

There was nothing special, or even particularly interesting, about
Ali. If you walk down the street in Baghdad, or any one of a dozen
Iraqi towns and cities, you will see twenty like him: slightly built,
dark, probably unshaven. I didn't meet Ali, but I gather he looked
shifty. He had done several years in Saddam's gaols, and that
marked every Iraqi it happened to.

He had spent five years of his life as a prisoner, but wasn't a
criminal, any more than seven years in the army, fighting the
Iranians, had made him a soldier. He had served entirely without
distinction, though he was slightly wounded twice and had to be
patched up and sent back to the front like a soldier in the First
World War. He hated the army as much as he hated prison, but
between them they had taught him never to step out of line.

The offence which saw him arrested, tortured and thrown into
a dark and crowded cell in the north of Baghdad was to have been
the cousin of a small-time Shi'ite insurrectionist. When Saddam
seemed about to fall in March 1991, after the catastrophic end of
the first Gulf War, Ali's cousin heard the US president's call for all
Iraqis to rise up. With the Americans behind them, Ali's cousin

thought, they couldn't fail. But General Colin Powell, who was then Chairman of the Joint Chiefs of Staff, advised President Bush that too many American lives would be lost if the US got involved in Iraq's internal wars, so the Shi'ites and the Kurds found themselves fighting alone.

Ali's cousin was captured and shot in the back of the neck. The mass grave where he was buried probably hasn't yet been discovered. Then the hunt was on for everyone related to the insurrectionists, whether or not they had been involved in the uprising. Ali lived in a mud-brick house in a village on the edge of the Shi'ite holy city of Najaf. One morning, at five o'clock, the army trucks rolled up; soldiers loyal to Saddam Hussein jumped out of them and started kicking in the doors of the houses round about. A lieutenant, who like so many of the officer corps was a Sunni, had a list in his hand. A pathetic figure on the end of a rope identified the men whom the soldiers pulled out into the open. Ali's name was on the list.

No one ever seriously accused him of being involved in the Shi'ite uprising. Nor was he systematically tortured. But one of the soldiers broke his leg with a pickaxe handle as he lay on the ground, and the journey on the back of an open truck over bad roads to the holding centre was as bad as any torture. His leg was never set by a doctor, but other prisoners helped him when they thought it was safe to do so. Ali still walks with a limp.

Like anything else, you can become habituated to prison life. Ali endured it with the stoicism which comes from the realization that resistance will not have the slightest effect. And then one morning, without any warning, one of the gaolers came to the crowded cell where he spent twenty-four hours a day, six days a week, and told him he was free to go. They pushed him out into the noisy sunlight, and left him to fend for himself.

Back home, he married a local girl named Fatima: quiet, modest, uninspiring, loyal. He was much older than she was, his youth wasted in the army and in prison. Now he was thirty, and she was only nineteen. Over the next six years they had four children: a boy, two girls, and finally another baby boy.

For no reason that anyone could see, the elder boy, Hosayn, captivated his father's heart and his attention. Hosayn was Ali's pride and joy. The other stallholders in the little market in the centre of Najaf, where Ali made a scarcely profitable living out of selling stolen cigarettes, laughed at the way Ali would take Hosayn everywhere with him, even to the men's baths, limping along with Hosayn holding his hand.

And then came the invasion. Ali obeyed the instructions written on the leaflets the Americans dropped, and stayed at home. Iraqi army trucks came round a couple of times, picking up former soldiers and forcing them back into service. They didn't want Ali because of his record.

There was a little fighting on the outskirts of Najaf, but because it was a Shi'ite city most people were glad to see the American troops as they drove towards the city centre. The idea of having Western soldiers near the holy shrine at the heart of Najaf wasn't very attractive, but they were glad to be rid of Saddam.

Life changed slowly at first. Then the bombings started. Sunni extremists would drive trucks into the city centre, especially when big religious processions were taking place. Many of the men Ali knew joined militia groups in order to defend their community, but Ali had had enough of being told what to do.

Besides, he liked to be with Hosayn. They talked about everything together. Hosayn knew there had been nothing wrong or discreditable about his father's time in prison. He was a clever boy, I was told, not just a sharp-minded street urchin, but someone who thought about things carefully. Again, you wouldn't think he was anything special if you saw him running an errand for his father, or pushing the small barrow when Ali's leg hurt him. Ali was almost in awe of him, he was so clever. He wanted to know complicated things, like how far the moon was from the earth, and why the Americans were so much taller than the Iraqis were.

And then, one day, there was an announcement that anyone who wanted to join the police force should present themselves in front of the local police-station at 7 a.m. on a given date. Ali talked to Fatima about it, and to Hosayn as well. They both thought he should try to join. There was regular pay, and it was quite good: six times as much as Ali could get from selling his cigarettes outside the grand mosque. Hosayn thought the uniform would be very fine.

At 4.30 on the morning of the big day, Ali went to the police station, taking Hosayn with him for company. Such was the enthusiasm and the need for a decent salary that some men had been there since midnight. There was pushing and shoving, jovial enough at first but more and more angry and desperate as the hours wore on. For Hosayn's sake, Ali tried to stay out of it, but he dared not lose his place in the queue.

It wasn't until early afternoon that the side door of the police station opened, and a policeman stood on the steps and shouted to the crowd to come forward. There was real fighting then. Hosayn tried to protect his father, but he was too small and weak; in the end, Ali ordered him to leave. Slowly, the foremost group, in which Ali had managed to get himself, got closer to the steps, and a couple of policemen pulled men out of the crowd at random and kicked them one by one into the interview room.

Ali's record, which had always counted against him so strongly, now looked quite good. There was no mention of his injured leg on any of his papers, and since he stood up straight in front of the three senior officers, no one guessed there was anything wrong with him. The captain stood up to hand Ali his certificate.

Ali was reaching out to take it when the entire wall of the police station burst inwards, and after a second of appalling noise and dust and confusion the flat roof collapsed, burying them. A Sunni suicide bomber, no older than eighteen, riding a motorbike with around fifty pounds of high explosive taped under his coat, had forced his way into the crowd and blown himself up. Afterwards, one eye-witness said the young man had smiled as he pressed the plunger.

In the stink of the high explosive and that terrible, unforgettable smell of blood, it took more than two hours to extricate Ali from the ruins of the building. The captain was dead, but Ali had suffered only a broken finger and a nasty gash to his arm. All he had asked them as they were pulling him free was if they knew anything about Hosayn.

'Were any young boys hurt?' he kept asking.

'No, friend, no young boys. But a lot of men died. Maybe a hundred. God grant that no brother of yours was killed, my friend.

Now be patient for a little longer, and you will be free of this heavy beam.'

Ali knew he wasn't expected to take the numbers of dead literally. But the knowledge that no young boys had been hurt kept him going through the pain of being freed.

They took him to the main hospital. The floors of the corridors swam with blood, and groans and screams filled the place. I have seen this kind of sight many times, and, believe me, you never forget it for as long as you live. The most you can hope for is that it will cease to haunt you eventually.

It took several hours for Ali's injuries to be attended to, because his injuries were relatively slight. All together, twenty-seven people had been killed and more than sixty injured: by that stage, a moderate death toll. I was in the BBC bureau in Baghdad that day, and although we had some terrible pictures of the aftermath of the explosion, thanks to the courage of the Iraqi cameramen who worked for the two big news agencies, APTN and Reuters, I couldn't persuade my colleagues in London to take a report from me about it.

'If more people had been killed . . .' someone said to me regretfully down the line from Television Centre.

The days when five or ten deaths in Iraq seemed worth reporting were long past. Now it had to be seventy plus. Murderous bomb attacks in Iraq were only to be expected, like winter snow in Switzerland; it was only if there was more snow than usual, or none at all, that anyone took notice.

As for what happened to Ali, I gathered his entire story from an Iraqi friend of mine who was there for APTN. Fatima had been too frightened to come to the hospital to look for her husband, and Ali assumed she had kept little Hosayn with her. At last he was bandaged up and allowed to leave the hospital. And as he limped down the corridor, he glanced into the room near the entrance which was being used as a temporary morgue.

There was a small body there. The blood was seeping through the white sheet that wrapped it as it lay on the floor.

Ali knew who it was. He ran into the room, knelt down and started pulling at the sheet to see the face beneath. A couple of old men who were laying out the corpses tried to stop him, but not before Hosayn's white face, his eyes closed, had been revealed.

'O God, take my worthless life but give me back my son,' he shouted, beating his chest and his face in his agony.

The old men held on to him, and a crowd of people gathered to watch and sympathize.

'My life isn't worth living if you are dead, Hosayn, my wonderful son,' he shouted, screaming now with the pain of his terrible loss.

§

When the pictures of Ali's grief appeared on some television screens around the world that night, many people no doubt wondered if he was putting it on for the sake of the cameras. Not in Britain, though, and not in the United States: the two countries which, more than any other, had started the chain of events which led to some fanatic destroying himself and others, and taking away the life of Ali's son Hosayn. British and American viewers didn't see Ali that night, not because there was any kind of active censorship but because at that moment Iraq wasn't a particularly important news story. The news bulletins were full of other things: stories about supermarkets and crime and government manoeuvrings and crises elsewhere.

Anyway, the world saw so many people weeping and shouting in the news coverage from Iraq. This stuff about Iraq seemed so foreign, so hard to comprehend. All they did was kill each other; we should leave them to it, if that was what they wanted.

I never met Ali, but I have known plenty of people like him. All my information about him and his life and the death of his son Hosayn comes from my friend, but what happened to Ali and Hosayn is not much different from what has happened to hundreds of thousands of people in Iraq.

My son Rafe wasn't born when Hosayn was killed, but now that I have a child of my own again, I understand just a little of how his father must have felt. Life is so important, so valuable, so sacred, that there is no crime comparable with taking it away.

Especially not for political or religious reasons. I know that filthy stench of high explosive so well, that after decades of reporting on bombs which have been exploded for some high purpose, I have come to loathe everyone who has used it: the IRA, the UVF, ETA, and a dozen other collections of stupid initials; the intelligence services of a dozen countries; al-Qaeda; the air forces of Russia, the United States, Britain and all the others. Back there in the government buildings, up there at thirty thousand feet, down there in the secret hideouts and safe houses, it all seems so clear-cut: make a statement, save lives, express your nobility of purpose. 'The armed struggle,' said a South African song which, God forgive me, I once used to like until I thought about the words, 'is an act of love.'

Bullshit. Stupid, bigoted, irreflective, ignorant, blind, wicked bullshit. Armed struggles, of whatever kind, mean hospitals with blood flowing down the corridors, and ordinary people like you and me and the rest of us, decent or stupid or dishonest or loving or bewildered, lying there on the floor, our arms or legs pumping blood, the stench of that filthy explosive in our nostrils still. The screams of others, injured worse than us, pounding in our ears. The fear and despair of the small number of doctors who have to deal with so many life-or-death cases, and know they are condemning many of them to a slow, painful, untreated death in their own blood and shit. And then, afterwards, the dreadful moment, like a kick in the stomach, when we find out who has died.

'I think it was worth it,' said Madeleine Albright, the American Secretary of State in Bill Clinton's administration, talking about the deaths of Iraqi children as the result of the sanctions which the US and Britain so enthusiastically called upon the United Nations to impose in the 1990s. But I saw some of the results of that particular policy, and I defy anyone to look those dying children in the eye and congratulate them on having the good fortune to be part of a wider benefit for the world.

'It was certainly the right thing to do,' said Tony Blair, talking about the seventy-seven-day bombing campaign against Serbia and Kosovo, inspired by President Clinton in 1999. But I saw the ruins of the Belgrade television station, bombed by the Americans, with the legs of the make-up lady who used to put powder on my forehead before a broadcast sticking out from under the rubble, and heard the children scream when the bombs started falling.

'They have had the honour, by God's grace, to be in Paradise,'

said the deputy leader of al-Qaeda, Ayman al-Zawahiri, speaking
of the latest group of suicide bombers who had just murdered
dozens of innocents. But I have seen the broken bodies, the broken
lives, which the daily bombings in Iraq have brought. And to me,
though I understand that the motives and even the justifiability of
these things are different from one another, all these people use the
same weapon: explosives. And they all use the same argument: it's
unfortunate that ordinary people's lives have to be sacrificed, but
there is a greater good that we must bear in mind.

There are few arguments more despicable.

I'm not in any sense a pacifist. I think that having a good
defence is the best assurance against having to fight a war. And I
think that one or two wars have been absolutely necessary.

But not this business of treating the innocent as a target, in
order to strike at the people who govern them. In the past, I may
have condoned it; I remember, to my shame, cheering the news that
the Clinton administration was going to bomb the Bosnian Serb
towns and villages in the former Yugoslavia to bring their siege of
Sarajevo to an end. The siege was in itself a disgusting crime,
because it held a quarter of a million people hostage, and systematically starved them of food and water. But one day, I am certain,
the world will decide that the act of deliberately setting out to
bomb towns and cities, knowing that civilians will die, constitutes a
crime too.

The idea that some civilians are decent and righteous, while
others deserve everything they get, is something I can't any longer
accept. It could be my own son who is trapped in the rubble, or
whose blood stains the white sheet.

And I don't care any longer what the cause is. I care only about
him, and about the people like him. I'm sorry if that sounds pious
or sentimental; I don't mean it to be. But I have finally understood
something, through the almost unlooked-for blessing of having a
child of my own, so late in life. It is that life itself is immensely
valuable; not just the lives of people who think and look and
worship like us, people who are attractive or well educated or rich,
people who are the right type of Christian or Muslim, but all lives.

It must all sound as obvious, as commonplace as the three or
four lines of homily at the end of a *Reader's Digest* article. Still, just

because it's obvious doesn't always mean it's entirely valueless. And I can't end this without adding something else: that my time in Baghdad, and my time with my little son, Rafe, have finally taught me that the lives of the poor, the stupid, the old, the ugly, the failed, are no less precious to them and to the people around them, than Rafe's life is precious to me.

7

BOERS

There was the crack of a large-calibre revolver just outside the house. I hurried into the kitchen where the housekeeper, Vuyo, a quiet, firm, pleasant-looking Xhosa woman in her late twenties, was standing at the sink, calmly washing the dishes.

'Did someone fire a gun?'

'That was me,' she said. 'But not a gun. One of those baboons came to the door, and I threw a firecracker at him to make him go away.'

She went on scrubbing at a cooking dish.

We'd seen the troupe of baboons the previous day. There were twenty or more of them, patrolling the boundary fence which separated our garden from the thick, almost black forest which rose five hundred feet up the hill behind us. They clambered up on their hind legs, peering over at the house, looking for a way in.

Chacma baboons are handsome creatures, four or five feet tall, with light grey fur and dark, angry, pointed faces. There is absolutely nothing cute about them. If you threaten them, or worse still trap them, they can blind you or even kill you. To sit in a car while they swarm over it, punching it and kicking and wrenching off the windscreen wipers and radio aerial, is an unforgettably alarming experience.

This particular troupe reminded me of a patrol of Red Indians scouting a settler's house. They plainly realized that the Great Dane which usually lived here had gone away, and had decided that the place was no longer properly protected.

And so, when he thought no one was looking, the leader, an elderly male, hoisted his grey bulk over the fence and dropped down into the garden to check out how difficult it would be to get into the house.

But Vuyo had seen him. Quietly, hiding behind the door, she lit the firecracker from a packet which had been left handy on the breakfast counter, then stepped out in the open and flung it onto the patio. It landed just a foot from where the baboon was crouching, inspecting the place, and went off like a hand-grenade.

He gave a wild, angry scream and ran hard for the fence. The rest of the troop, panicking, hurled themselves back into the safety of the thick forest. You could hear them crashing through the branches for several minutes after, squealing angrily. They wouldn't be back for a good long while. Vuyo, armed with a firecracker, is much more formidable than any Great Dane, and baboons have excellent memories.

Nature's Valley, on the southern coast of South Africa, is a wild place. There are *boomslangs* in the trees, green snakes which are normally somnolent and unaggressive, but have a bite so venomous that no serum exists that can save your life from it. Puff adders, handsomely marked, slow-moving and inclined to lie out in the pathways across the garden, are also highly poisonous. There was one which lived in the woodpile from which we had to get our firewood daily. A Cape cobra reportedly haunted the woods near us. Beautifully dark yellow in colour, it can rear up almost its entire five feet six inches, open the hood just below its bleak little eyes, and strike at you.

Bush pigs, less nimble than the baboons but just as fierce in their way, grunt irritably in the forest beyond the fence at night as they root for morsels in the ground. They too are handsome creatures, with large drooping ears and fluffed-out side whiskers like a Victorian rural dean. And there are scorpions everywhere: efficient, machine-like black creatures, looking like armoured robots with their stings probing and turning.

All sorts of insects, benign and malign, treat the house as their own. In the dark gap between the refrigerator and the dishes cupboard a particularly large hornet seems to be making its nest. It flies ominously through the kitchen with its undercarriage hanging down, looking like an attack aircraft coming in to land.

Since hornets are reputedly almost unkillable and their sting is certainly virulent, it seems safer (if a little feeble) to allow it to go about its business. So, like meek householders peering through the net curtains at the drugs dealers doing their deals in the street outside, we just stand aside when the hornet flies in through the open door, and watch it zoom in to its dark retreat.

Our landlord, Dr Smuts, runs a campaign to save the leopards of the area, but it is proving a difficult job. The leopards find it hard to resist the temptation to attack the lambs and calves on the surrounding farms, and the farmers put out traps for them. Dr Smuts is trying to persuade them to use humane traps, which imprison the leopards without injuring them. One farmer who agreed with him caught a leopard recently. Dr Smuts tagged it and took it away to be released into the wild, and as a reward he named it Niels, after the farmer.

The great majority of the animal life in Nature's Valley stays out of sight. You can read in the guidebooks about the caracal and the genet, the Cape porcupine and the Cape clawless otter, the water mongoose, the blue duiker and the bontebok, but you almost never see them.

What you do see, though, are the magnificent birds. If I stand beside our fence, looking up into the dense forest, there is a constant racket: piping trills, whistles, croaks, the relentless chattering of the wood hoopoes with their brilliant green feathers and their red bills, the 'woop, woop' of the Knysna lourie, the 'whee' of the sombre bulbul, the infuriating, repetitious call of the red-chested cuckoo, which the Afrikaners think sounds like the words *piet my vrou*. The sea-birds are entrancing here, from the hamerkop with its hammer-shaped head and large, ungainly beak, to the avocets, sand-pipers, stilts and whimbrels which stalk elegantly along the sands on their spindly legs.

Africa is not for the feeble – among whom I count myself. Although I spend much of my professional life going to the kind of place that sensible people avoid, I usually draw the line at spending my own money in order to risk my life or be needlessly uncomfort-able. But my wife Dee is South African, and feels the pull of her native soil. And so we are spending Christmas on the south coast, a hundred and twenty miles from Port Elizabeth, at a place called Nature's Valley: a suitable enough name, given the baboons, the warthogs and the nesting hornets.

This is not the South Africa of the new tourism, the booming places like Cape Town and the Natal coast, where the prices are on a level with Europe, and you hear as many German, French and British accents in the shopping malls as South African ones. This is something much older and more basic. The only language you hear here is Afrikaans.

§

When I was based in South Africa in the dark days of 1977 and 78, when apartheid was at its height, many Afrikaners regarded the BBC in general, and its local representatives like me in particular, as their natural enemy. Even then, though, I knew enough liberal-minded Afrikaners to realize that the moral opposition to apartheid was not a matter of ethnic origins. Large numbers of English-speaking whites, who as a community were regarded abroad as more liberal, were in fact perfectly happy with apartheid. Many British people had emigrated to South Africa from Britain in the 1960s and 1970s precisely because they wanted to take advantage of it.

So although the basic concept was an Afrikaans one, and sprang from the ideologues of the National Party, the irreducible enemies of the British and their conquest of the Boer Republics in the war of 1899–1902, apartheid was never the exclusive doctrine of the Afrikaners. And plenty of Afrikaners fought it, and suffered as a result.

In its ignorance, though, the outside world assumed that all Afrikaners were like the fierce, embittered old characters who imposed and supported apartheid, and the brutal ones who administered it. This was never the case. Afrikaners were also some of apartheid's greatest enemies, and even many of those who never took a stand against it opposed it in their hearts.

During the period of the great election of 1994, which brought white rule to an end, a telephone engineer came to the BBC office in Johannesburg to wire it up for all the extra broadcasting demands that were going to be made. He was an Afrikaner in his mid-fifties, who had everything to lose and nothing outwardly to gain from a handover to majority rule. He was on his knees in the corner of the office, clipping the main telephone cable. One of my colleagues asked him what he thought about the political changes.

'I feel as though a great weight has rolled off my conscience,' he said in his strongly accented English, without looking up, his hammer tap-tapping at the little tacks fixing the cable to the wall.

Young Afrikaners are some of the new South Africa's most enthusiastic supporters, and are the most prepared to stay in the country and work for it. As a group, Afrikaners are supporters and belongers, and they have taken the new South African flag to themselves, even though it represents the indigenous and British traditions of the country, but scarcely seems to hint at the Boer tradition. Perhaps because they are individualists and loners, they seem to need symbols of their own to unite behind with intense enthusiasm: rugby, cricket, beer, the culture of the barbecue. *Braai*-ing, or barbecuing, is the Afrikaner's great national activity.

Yet it's really unwise to generalize too much about Afrikaners. Again and again, they defy the efforts of outsiders to fit them into easy categories. If apartheid was an Afrikaner invention, it was also Afrikaners who helped defeat it. And you could never be quite certain even about those who were apartheid's front-line defenders. When I was based in South Africa I found various policemen, government officials and soldiers who showed a private hostility to apartheid.

Altogether, Afrikaners have always been hard to categorize. In 1977 I interviewed Nelson Mandela's then wife Winnie in the town of Brandfort, where she had been exiled. The interview was illegal, since she was subject to a 'banning' order. On the way back to Johannesburg we were stopped by the police. I was questioned by a gross-looking Afrikaans police sergeant with a thick neck and fingers like pork sausages, which he drummed irritably on the counter as I answered his questions. He didn't like me, he didn't like the BBC, and he especially didn't like Winnie Mandela. I had him marked down as a brute and a torturer.

Somehow, though, as we talked I felt there was something else which lay unspoken behind his questions. It took a long time to surface; but after perhaps half an hour he suddenly asked me if I had ever been to Canterbury Cathedral. I said I had. Had I ever looked at the stained glass? Again, yes.

'Because my wife and I make stained glass, and it is my lifelong ambition to go to Canterbury and help restore the stained glass there.'

I almost laughed aloud. The secret of this brute of a man was that he was a creator, a conserver, an appreciator of one of the finest but least-known treasures of medieval England, an aesthete.

I'm not suggesting that beneath the unprepossessing exterior he was gentle and loving. No doubt he kicked and punched the truth out of suspects with as much relish as the worst of his colleagues. All I'm saying is that there was something else there as well, a complexity which you had to take into account if you wanted to understand him, and people like him. It is unwise to be too certain that you really know what motivates any human being; but with Afrikaners, in my experience, there tends to be a more complex intellectual hinterland than there is with most other people. It is a great mistake to take them for granted.

Nelson Mandela had a lifelong respect for them. When my wife Dee met him at a dinner at the Mansion House in London, he told her in Afrikaans that she should go home because South Africa needed its Afrikaners.

'We can understand each other,' he told an Afrikaans friend of mine, 'in a way that neither of us can understand the English.'

Mandela's spoken Afrikaans was excellent and courtly, and he chose a ferocious blonde Afrikaans woman called Zelda to be his personal assistant – perhaps because he was always inclined to say yes to every request. Zelda loved saying no, and she once ordered the South African high commissioner in London to grab me and stop me talking to Nelson during a visit he made to Cambridge. Having had to deal with professionals, from Russian and American secret servicemen to Chinese ones, a tug at the tail of my jacket was scarcely very intimidating. Zelda herself would have done it much more effectively.

The old apartheid regime effectively ended when Nelson Mandela was released from Victor Verster prison in 1990, even though it was four more years before majority rule came in triumph to South Africa. South Africans, black as well as white, found that their passports, which had once been so much of a liability abroad that they were known as 'green mambas', were suddenly acceptable; and more than that, were actively popular everywhere they were shown.

Nowadays Afrikaners fill all sorts of strange ecological niches around the world which other people, even the British and the Australians, instinctively avoid. I have come across Afrikaans traders and pilots and doctors and security men in countries as diverse, but difficult, as Colombia, Afghanistan and Iraq. An Afrikaner is the biggest catering contractor for the American forces in Iraq, providing everything from three hundred-man tents to knives and forks and washing-up liquid. Another has a contract to fly UN personnel to the kind of place in Africa and Latin America which other charter companies wouldn't consider.

I've already described how I was flown to Baghdad for the opening of Saddam Hussein's trial by a South African crew in an ancient chartered Fokker. After that experience I took that route to Baghdad almost every time; the crew gave me a certain feeling of confidence, and a great deal of amusement.

Typically, the pilots are Afrikaners and the cabin staff are a mixture of Zulus and Afrikaners. There is often a startlingly beautiful blonde among them. The seats are narrower and less comfortable than anything a modern traveller will have experienced, and as the plane taxis and takes off the meal trays tend to fall into your lap, and the overhead luggage bins often spring open. No one seems to care very much.

The flight takes much longer than it used to, because instead of flying almost due east, the direct route, the plane heads south to the Saudi border and hugs it until it is directly south of Baghdad. That way, it flies over as little Iraqi territory as possible.

As we approach Baghdad, a voice with pinched vowels of Afrikaans English comes over the address system. Sadly, the cabin staff have stopped talking about 'corkscrewing down to Baghdad International Airport', possibly because of the laughter it provoked. Instead, the voice simply announces that we will soon be landing.

Still, a certain amount of corkscrewing is done. The greater the passengers' nervousness, no doubt, the greater the pilots' enjoyment. This is real flying, as opposed to the routine stuff most commercial pilots endure nowadays. In other words, it's just the kind of thing that is likely to appeal to the Afrikaaner mind. Getting out of my seat and queuing to leave the aircraft, I always look to see if the cabin staff look in any way rattled by what they have gone through. They never do.

'*Totsiens*,' I said recently to the archetypally Afrikaans stewardess as I left the plane at Baghdad.

'Oh, how did you know I was from South Africa?' Her voice had the singsong quality that you often hear in Afrikaans women when they speak English.

'Just a lucky guess,' I answered.

§

The house where we are staying in Nature's Valley belongs to the grand-nephew of the greatest Afrikaner of all, Jan Smuts. The old boy's pictures look coolly and quizzically out at us from the rooms and passageways, clever and slightly other-worldly with his little white pointed beard, looking more like a pioneer psychiatrist than a politician. This was the man who, after fighting a fierce and highly effective guerrilla war against the British at the turn of the century, decided to accept the offer of reconciliation and build a new South Africa within the British Commonwealth. Nowadays many Afrikaners have an instinctive dislike of him, for being too close to the British; though the vengeful Afrikaner nationalists who eventually defeated him and imposed the apartheid system were pygmies compared with him.

During the First World War, Smuts was a member of the British government's War Cabinet. The prime minister, David Lloyd George, asked him to gauge the mood of the front-line troops in 1917, when the other Allied armies were starting to mutiny. Smuts spent a lot of his time with the men in the trenches, listening to them. Then he reported back, completely accurately, that although the troops had many grievances which should quickly be addressed, their basic morale was rock solid. The War Cabinet accepted his say-so, and gambled everything on it; he turned out to be triumphantly right.

In 1939 he brought South Africa into the Second World War on

Britain's side and again served in the War Cabinet alongside his close friend Winston Churchill, while Nationalist politicians like John Vorster, who was to become prime minister in the 1960s and 70s, were in prison for their pro-Nazi sympathies. But in 1948, exhausted and extremely unpopular, Smuts was voted out of office. The National Party kept themselves in power for forty-six years, until white rule was set aside and a genuinely multi-racial state was created. Having seen the repression at its worst and most brutal here, my heart still lifts when I visit the new South Africa – in spite of its many failings.

Nature's Valley is where well-to-do Afrikaners take their holidays. Unlike the places where they live and work – Cape Town, Johannesburg and Pretoria, for the most part – it is almost entirely free from the robbery and murder which are integral to the new South Africa. And so in the evenings the lanes of Nature's Valley are thronged with tall, big-boned men and women and children, strolling around at times when, back at home, they would be inside their little domestic fortresses, behind the barbed wire and the electronic alarms. You only occasionally hear English spoken. And although there are plenty of black servants, it is rare to see black people on the beach.

Altogether, being in Nature's Valley is like being kidnapped and bundled back into the 1950s. The little shop at the end of the village cannot have changed in any significant way since the days of D. F. Malan's crazy, unfolding system of apartheid, and Sir de Villiers Graaf's feeble opposition to it, or the endless, inconsequential debates in Natal about whether to break away from the new Republic of South Africa.

Nowadays the newspapers in the shop carry very different stories, about hijackings and murders and accusations of corruption in Cape Town and Johannesburg, and most of the faces on the front pages are black. But the shop still sells much the same things: *takkies* (plimsolls, we would have called them in the fifties), t-shirts, the same postcards with the same views, the same antique-looking chewing-gum in bright yellow wrappers called Chappies. The unmistakable holiday smells of washing-powder, rubber soles and ineradicable dampness fill the place, just as they always have.

The same sort of people go to the same pre-Christmas carol service in the open air by the charming lagoon, and sing the same carols. Verwoerd might perfectly well be running things in Pretoria still, and the Group Areas Act might still be on the statute book.

Afrikaners are a strange and interesting breed. Like Irish Protestants, whom they resemble politically, they are a settler nation, small in numbers, sometimes angry and defensive, yet with an extraordinary diversity of opinions and talents, and a particular self-mocking sense of humour. Like the Irish Protestants, they have a remarkably large gene pool for a small tribe, which gives them a remarkable variety of backgrounds, abilities and looks. I am biased, of course, but it seems to me that there is statistically more real beauty among Afrikaner women than among any other population group I know; with the possible exception of Somalis, Cambodians and Irishwomen, both Protestant and Catholic.

The Hollywood actress Charlize Theron, a quintessential Afrikaner, has chosen to adopt an American accent even off-screen, and used it to great local irritation when she paid a triumphal visit to her homeland after winning an Oscar. But curiously she hasn't changed her name, which shrieks her origins on the wrong side of Afrikanerdom's tracks.

Whenever she is interviewed for American or British magazines she gives the impression that she grew up on a farmstead in a dusty little *veld* town called Benoni, near Johannesburg. In fact, for the past fifty years Benoni has been a dreary, featureless outer suburb, a South African Croydon or Hoboken. It takes a certain courage to admit you come from somewhere quite so unglamorous.

If Afrikaans hadn't been the language of *apartheid*, foisted on blacks and Indians and 'coloureds' and English-speakers alike by the Nationalists, it might have been more widely known and admired outside South Africa; and like the Protestant Irish writers who have dominated the list of Nobel Prize winners for literature, Afrikaners might have claimed a greater share than they have. (J. M. Coetzee is so far the only Afrikaans-speaking laureate, but several others merit the title.) Like the people who invented it, Afrikaans is a forthright and muscular language, and the poets and novelists who have used it deserve to be better known.

The people who wander down towards the beach at Nature's Valley in their shorts and *takkies* are practical and tough. People say that is why there are no armed robberies or murders here: who would want to risk a hue-and-cry among people like this? And of course it takes a certain toughness to spend your holidays in the company of baboons and Cape cobras, or know that great white sharks are likely to be patrolling the inshore waters of the ocean you are swimming in.

But Afrikaners are used to living with danger. Their forebears trekked across southern Africa to found the Boer Republics of the Transvaal and the Orange Free State. (One of Dee's ancestors was Andries Pretorius, who founded the city which is still South Africa's capital; though now it is called Tshwane, and the name 'Pretoria' applies only to the collection of rather pleasant government buildings in the city centre.) The Boers fought the British almost to a standstill in a war that nowadays seems more and more reminiscent of George W. Bush's invasion of Iraq: only with gold and diamonds as the objects of imperial desire, instead of oil.

This evening, though, the Boers are not heading for the beach. Their t-shirts are slightly cleaner than usual, and sometimes their shorts over the tanned legs have been carefully ironed. There is a church fête, with the best of traditional Afrikaner cooking on sale: pancakes, *koeksusters*, almost intolerably sweet twists of dough soaked with honey, *melktert*, delicious tarts with a filling of gentle cinnamon-flavoured milky custard, *boerewors*, tough, splendidly gamey sausage, and *biltong*: strips of chewy air-dried meat.

The crowds are gathering outside the undistinguished little church on the edge of Nature's Valley: cheerful, familiar, full of jokes as broad as themselves. Most of these people know each other well, and have seen each other here year after year, through all the political changes that have come over the country. The tables have been set up outside the church, and are covered with good and interesting things. Still, it's impossible to get too close. The crowds in front of them are six or seven deep.

Exactly at six o'clock the *dominie* or minister comes out and stands on the doorstep of the church. He looks at his watch, and calls for silence. The crowd goes quiet, and everyone closes their eyes. The *dominie* intones a prayer in the slightly nasal tone of Protestant pastors the world over. The words are all about gratitude and the richness of God's gifts.

The familiar Nature's Valley joke is that while the Boers pray, their eyes tightly shut, their hands are already straying over the goods ranged on the table-tops, ready for the moment when the *dominie* stops talking and the buying can begin. It isn't, I can see, entirely true; but only because the most determined buyers have already taken up their station in front of the things they most want, and know perfectly well where they are.

'. . . in the name of Jesus Christ, Amen.'

There is scarcely a beat between the 'n' of 'Amen' and an outburst of shouting, laughing and appealing. Twenty-rand notes are waved in the air, packets of *boerewors* and *koeksusters* are thrust under the buyers' arms, there is turmoil in the crowd as the successful customers push their way out and others compete to take their place. The supply does not anywhere near match the demand; and within six or seven minutes the tables have been swept clear of food.

The entire business is finished within fifteen minutes. The triumphant ones carry off their trophies, laughing at the ferocity of it all; the rest trail home, with the faint sense of having been done down. Afrikaners like winning, and most were brought up to expect it. Losing, whether well or badly, is not part of their culture.

Most Afrikaners, like most Americans or French or British people, are unremarkable enough, with nothing in their habits or opinions or appearance to single them out. Yet as with the American South, there is a distinctly caricaturable quality to rural Afrikanerdom, and the sophisticated Afrikaners of Johannesburg and Cape Town enjoy making fun of them.

In the big town near Nature's Valley there is a vast religious-goods store which is usually cavernously empty, even at Christmas. Entire sections of it are filled with Bibles, others with hymnals and prayer books and religious tracts. There are racks and racks of CDs by people with strange hair-dos and oddly out-of-date clothes, rejoicing and praising and worshipping. An enormous mural covers one entire wall, with a panoramic view of mountain peaks and a large and rather surprised eagle which has clearly just landed on a rock to one side and seems about to leave again now that he has been spotted. A shop-long biblical quotation about rising up on wings of eagles explains why it's there.

But you don't notice any of this when you walk in. You don't even notice the sudden chill of the air conditioning, or the tenor singing 'Climb Every Mountain'. Your attention is seized by one thing only. Right across the gallery on the mezzanine floor, opposite the entrance, is a row of very large stuffed animal heads: a buffalo, a warthog, a kudu, a hippopotamus, and a giraffe. In fact, the giraffe motif is pretty heavily stressed, since in front of the heads stands an entire, rather large male giraffe, now losing much of its hair. Maybe the giraffe head just behind it was related to it; perhaps not. The fully formed one has, I notice, no genitalia. Not only does he have to stand, day in and day out, listening to Kumbaya music, but his wedding-tackle has been snipped off in case it might cause offence.

I bought something cheap, because I was too embarrassed to show I had only gone in there to make fun of the place. The man behind the counter may possibly have been the owner. His head was completely bald, and on it he had planted a large, fuzzy and very obvious wig. Clearly, if I wanted to ask anything about the giraffe, or the giraffe's balls, or the idea of limiting the expression of God's love to people and stopping short at the animal kingdom, this was the man.

But I didn't ask him anything. I paid up and turned away.

'God bless,' said the man with the improbable rug, affably.

The guilt that plenty of older Afrikaners used to harbour about apartheid has changed now. They feel they handed over power to majority rule freely and generously, and that they have been repaid with crime, social violence and the kind of affirmative action which means that white people are being edged out of their jobs. Young Afrikaners are often impatient with this kind of approach, and they have accepted the new South Africa with enthusiasm. For a few years it looked as though Afrikaans might die out altogether as a language, but the success of Afrikaans-speaking radio and television stations has changed that entirely. A new generation of garage bands – so called because they usually begin life in the garage beside the house of a band member – has become immensely popular among young Afrikaners, who find the music and the language very much to their taste.

§

As clever and as stupid as the rest of humanity, but noticeably more complicated and diverse, Afrikaners have shown that they can adapt to the fiercest, least hospitable environments. As they play on the beach at Nature's Valley, or splash in a sea that is like chilled champagne, dodging the jellyfish and always distantly aware that a great white might be lurking somewhere in the long green rollers, the people here are living out an older relationship with Africa for a week or so in their Christmas summer holidays.

This place is how things once were, before air conditioning and microwaves and the eradication of the mosquito. In fact, far from being eradicated, mosquitoes have as easy a time of it in Nature's Valley as humans do. The kindly *dominie* of the local Dutch Reformed Church, the one who blessed the *koeksusters* and *melk-tert* at the church fair a nanosecond before the tables were cleared of everything, has set aside his pond in the middle of the village for the use of mosquitoes, refusing to drain it or spray it. As a result, the least attractive of God's creatures roams as free here as the bush-pig and the chacma baboon.

Nature's Valley is a little enclosure, a Lost World where old habits rather than dinosaurs have been shut in and protected. Ancient yellowwood trees tower up out of the tropical undergrowth, as straight as the ship's masts they were once used for. Ironwood and stinkwood are here too, as good as yellowwood for making fine furniture.

But as you leave the valley with its moss-grown trees and climb to the plateau above the sea shore, you find yourself in an altogether different eco-system: the fynbos. There are six floral kingdoms in the world, most of which cover entire continents. The Cape floral kingdom is the smallest of them all, and by comparison with the others, tiny; it consists simply of the fynbos in the Cape Peninsula and a few hundred miles to the east. Yet it is the richest and most diverse of all, with several hundred more plant species here than in the whole of Europe or North America.

Some of the world's most familiar flowers and plants originated

here. They spread out on either side of the road in a great swathe
of heathland: king proteas, geelbos, sugarbush, spider orchids,
candelabra flowers, watsonia, carpet geraniums, rose-scented
pelargonium. *Anoplolepis custodiens*, the pugnacious ant, works
aggressively away in the fynbos, burying the seeds of the different
plants so that they will survive and germinate in the aftermath of
the bush fires which regularly ravage the area.

However fanciful it may be, it's impossible not to see some kind
of mirroring process going on here. The Afrikaners, as pugnacious
as any fynbos ant, have made themselves indigenous in this part of
Africa over the past three hundred and fifty years – just as indigenous as any Xhosa or Zulu, who have also travelled hundreds of
miles overland to settle here, but mostly more recently than the
Afrikaners.

Are they wanted? Probably not. After Mandela ceased to be
president, his successor, Thabo Mbeki, lacked his warmth, forgiveness and inclusiveness: precisely the qualities which Jan Smuts
had shown towards the British, a hundred years earlier. Again
and again, mostly in small ways but sometimes in large ones, the
Afrikaners have been shown that the new South Africa isn't interested in them. But their hard work and entrepreneurialism and
imagination are precisely the qualities South Africa has a desperate
need for.

For now, the white tribe of Africa seems to have decided to stay
put, always hoping that the next president, like Nelson Mandela,
will realize how much better off the country will be if they remain.
Afrikaners are difficult, complex, tough, and often unforgiving; but
it would be an act of great, self-defeating foolishness on a par with
Robert Mugabe's onslaught on the white farmers of Zimbabwe if
South Africa failed to keep the Afrikaners where they belong.

8

AMERICANS

It was starting to rain, and the fans were flowing out of the Nashville baseball stadium when I arrived. I was a little late, as ever, and had just driven in rather fast from the airport. But the BBC producer, when I finally met up with him, had arranged everything.

'I thought you'd get some good answers if you vox-popped the crowd,' he said.

'Vox-pop' started out as an old BBC term, in the 1930s or perhaps even earlier. You can tell it was the BBC that invented it: it's slightly self-conscious, it's ponderously jokey, and it's in Latin. And maybe, just maybe, there's a hint of divine purpose about it, since it comes from the expression *Vox populi, vox dei*: the voice of the people is the voice of God. Not even Vatican Radio or one of those embarrassing evangelical stations in America is quite so certain of having divine authority behind it. The BBC is the most self-assured broadcaster on earth.

And by 2000 the BBC had made its mark on America. Once, if you stopped people in the street there and said you were from the BBC, they would react as though the very initials were disturbing and incomprehensible. Now, though, it was piped into the State Department and the White House itself, and people were watching its programmes on many different outlets across the country.

With Dee beside me, and the cameraman ready, I stopped the first likely looking fan who passed.

'What do you think of George W. Bush as a presidential candidate?'

It had been some time since I last worked in the streets of America. I had done plenty of political reporting from Washington, but I hadn't ranged around the country with a camera for a long time. As a result, I had forgotten what a joy it is to vox-pop Americans. Maybe television has taught them to speak in neat, well-expressed sound-bites; maybe they half-expect to be asked questions for television, wherever they are; maybe it's just a natural gift. Anyway, the man I spoke to had a perfectly formed answer, well phrased, witty, and clearly understandable.

'Would you want a man who thinks "Grecian" is the adjective from "Greece" to be leading *your* country?'

Not all the others were quite as good as this one, but after speaking to four people we had everything we needed. That constitutes some kind of record, in my experience. Usually, you have to interview at least twelve people in the street, because half of them cannot speak good enough English and another three cannot speak anything like sense.

There were still ten days to go before the 2000 presidential election. People had a very clear understanding of George W. Bush's limitations in foreign policy, because they had heard him trying to speak about the subject on television and his inadequacies had been much trumpeted in the liberal press. But beyond that, they knew remarkably little about him; so little, that his image makers, led by the pollster and spin doctor Karl Rove, had been able to present him to the country as a caring, middle-of-the-road conservative. In order to be elected, he was prepared to sail under colours which were very different from his true ones.

His background in oil, even though everyone knew about it, was allowed to fade. His links with the religious right were scarcely mentioned. He had few clear policies that anyone knew about. But he had one great advantage: he wasn't Al Gore.

Al Gore was the Democratic candidate, and had been the vice-president in the previous administration of Bill Clinton. Clinton's questionable dealings, his well-publicized sexual misconduct and his willingness to pardon some of his dodgiest associates in the last days of his presidency had disgusted many people: including, it seemed, Al Gore himself. Gore had seemed embarrassed and awkward during the last couple of years of the Clinton administration. Amid the sex and the scandal, he looked on uncomfortably from a distance, like a Christian schoolboy at a raunchy prom night. Yet, after Clinton, people found him boring. As it happened, he was far from boring, and anyway the charismatic, good-looking president who was soon to step down had shown that abundant charisma and charm didn't necessarily signal good government. Gore certainly seemed stiff and ill at ease, but perhaps it was the newspapers rather than the public who decided he was boring. In any event, everyone soon came to believe it. America, despite its self-image, is at heart a conformist society, in which people like to do and say the same as their neighbours, and – as George W. Bush's advisers knew – they are easily led. The opinion polls soon picked up the change.

Not quickly enough for me. I usually report on the campaign of the candidate who is likely to win, because the contacts you make are valuable when the new administration comes in. When, at the start of October, I had to decide whom to follow, Gore was well ahead in the polls. Perhaps, in the end, he was the rightful winner; the voting figures were so uncertain and so contested that we will never know.

A few years later I had to chair a conference in Cairo at which Al Gore was the main speaker. He was much more charming and much funnier in person than I had ever imagined; perhaps a slight woodenness in his manner gave the impression that he was boring and dull, but he certainly wasn't. At the conference an Egyptian delegate, perhaps trying to needle him, asked what the best form of democracy was.

For a moment there was a silence. Then slowly and a little ponderously Gore, sitting beside me on the left, shuffled his papers and spoke with more than his usual hint of a Tennessee accent.

'I think the best form of democracy is when the fellow who has received the most votes wins.'

It brought the house down.

§

Nashville shocked me. It was pleasant enough, if rather featureless, but it seemed remarkably old-fashioned and run down. The gleaming, wealthy face of America portrayed in Hollywood movies can blind you to the fact that this is not necessarily the widespread reality, any more than most people are as beautiful, slim and well dressed as they are on the screen.

The camera, as every television reporter, director and cameraman knows, cleans up the image, burnishes it, makes it gleam. If you ask a cameraman to get you some shots of a slum, with heaps of rubbish in front of the houses and burned-out cars in the streets, the result will be an estate agent's image. Especially if the sun is shining.

'I'd better put the gloomy filter on,' a cameraman friend of mine used to joke.

But the gloomy filter rarely seems to work with a digital camera, so when we went filming in the old centre of Nashville, the result was a cheerful distortion. Even the closed shutters, covered with spray-painted graffiti, and the untended heaps on the waste ground, seemed quirky and charming when we looked at the pictures later.

Before election day, though, I had a hint that things might not go altogether smoothly. In a middle-income suburb of Nashville we went to a polling station which was being set up at a school. The regional overseer was there, and I talked to him at some length in private. He was worried. The electronic voting machines, when they were tested, turned out to have all sorts of problems. And the method of punching holes against the names of candidates and referendum issues was causing him anxiety too. For the first time I heard the expression 'hanging chads', meaning the little circles of paper which ought to be punched out and allowed to fall to the ground, but which tended to stay connected to the ballot paper.

And indeed when the election took place it was a hopeless, shameful mess. If the gap between the candidates had been greater, the deficiencies and technical failures in the voting system wouldn't have mattered so much. But since there were only a matter of a few hundred thousand votes separating them, right across the nation, almost every close result turned out to have been affected either by technical failings or by the questionable activities of local officials who had manipulated the voters' register or interfered with the completed ballot papers. In many areas the Democrats were just as guilty as the Republicans. They had had more than a century's experience in vote-rigging. The election of 1960 between John F. Kennedy and Richard Nixon was decided by the votes in Cook County, Illinois, where the results were flagrantly distorted by the local Democratic Party boss, Mayor Richard Daley of Chicago. Yet in 2000 the Republicans were no less bad, overall, and no serious action was taken by those at the top of the party to discourage such gerrymandering.

And so for night after night, while wind howled round me on the shaking scaffold which the world's press was using as a studio set in front of Nashville City Hall, I had to tell a British and international audience that nothing much was happening here, and that the real action was going on among the lawyers in Washington. Finally, the Democratic camp issued a two-line statement which I was able to read out on camera. It said that after much consultation Al Gore had decided not to continue challenging the result. Florida had been his Illinois, and although everyone suspected that crooked things had gone on there, Gore had decided that any further delay in deciding the presidency would be disastrous for the country. At the time, he seemed to be right.

But by the time I met him, the feeling was already growing that George W. Bush's administration was one of the worst in American history.

'Do you regret giving up the challenge like that?' I asked him as we sat side by side on the podium in Cairo.

'Sometimes I do,' he answered. 'My legal team told me we had a real good case, and I knew that things weren't right in states like Florida. But I have to tell you, it was a kind of liberation too. I failed to reach the peak of my ambition, but there were so many compensations. And you know what? I think I'll live longer and be happier as a result.'

But when Gore conceded, there was the deepest gloom among his election team. We walked around the building the Democrats were using – one of the pleasures of working in America is that a television camera is a passport to go almost anywhere – filming the election-workers as the realization sank in that everything they had worked for had come to nothing.

'What would you have done differently if you'd known what was going to happen?' I asked the man who had organized the entire national campaign for Gore.

'What wouldn't I have done differently? It would all have been different,' he answered, with an appealing honesty. Compared with the smooth, carefully prepared approach of the Republicans, for whom appearance was everything, Gore's Democrats were almost touchingly frank.

But they felt angry and robbed of a victory which they felt should have been theirs. Later, when the Democrats stayed so quiet, and voted meekly for legislation which was the reverse of much of what they stood for, or the invasion of Iraq which many of them privately opposed, I remembered this mood of utter despair, back in November 2000. It seemed to play an important part in the decision of most Democrats to cease their opposition to a president who, they believed, had stolen the election from them. In other words, it was a collapse of will; and the Democrats became so rudderless, so lacking in any ideas of their own, that they could only follow where the Bush administration led, with political consequences which were to prove both disastrous and long lasting.

§

The first election I ever reported on, anywhere in the world, was the US presidential election of 1964; but although I called myself a reporter, I was really just a student trying to give myself a bit of status. At that time, though, scarcely any European students could afford to travel to America, and it was only because of the extraordinary generosity of my chronically hard-up father, and the fact that I had fallen in love with a girl from southern California, that I was there.

In later years the 1964 election took on an added interest, because it was the first time a candidate avowedly from the far right had been put forward by the Republican Party. In today's America, Senator Barry Goldwater would scarcely be regarded as from the far right at all; he would simply be a conservative, perhaps, or just possibly a neo-con (though that was always a rather silly expression, almost entirely meaningless). He had views which seemed at times to border on the racist (though others denied this on his behalf), and his attitude towards the Soviet Union seemed to most people in Europe to be reckless and dangerous.

Yet it didn't matter, because all the opinion polls showed that he would only attract a very small proportion of the vote. The story went the rounds that he had been put forward by more moderate

Republicans in order to show how suicidal it was to let Goldwater's wing of the party have its head. His fanatical and, I felt, completely uninformed hatred of communism and the Soviet Union seemed ludicrous rather than worrying. I talked to quite a lot of ordinary Americans, as well as some academics and a few journalists, from New York right across to southern California, and I found that they all dismissed him as crazy.

'Don't imagine this is how real Americans feel,' someone said to me.

And indeed, America in 1964 seemed a remarkably liberal-minded, go-ahead country, with a far more progressive attitude than Britain, which was still locked into its old class warfare and was finding it hard to come to terms with its loss of status and the end of empire. In the South there were still diners and restaurants and buses and public lavatories and park benches which black people couldn't use, but this was clearly part of an old, discredited system which was on its way out. The full force of the US government had been directed against segregation, and although there were dreadful figures from a different past who controlled the police and the courts in some southern states, discrimination had received its death sentence. America was a young, vibrant, and – a European would have said, using a word which soon became tainted for Americans – liberal society.

Goldwater was duly swept away by the predicted landslide, his brand of extreme conservatism dismissed out of hand by the voters. Lyndon Baines Johnson, still recognizably a New Deal Democrat, won a four-year term which, most people hoped, would help the country get over the mood of shock and bitter introspection which the assassination of President Kennedy had created.

'This is the end of extremism in our country,' said a charming old journalist I met in San Diego.

I wrote it up for my student newspaper, and felt very pleased with myself.

Later, my fiancée's father, a gentle, frail and slightly discouraged professor from the local university, would inveigh every night at dinner about the governor of California, Ronald Reagan, who seemed to want to cut back on everything to do with higher education.

'That son-of-a-so-and-so,' he called him. It was about as abusive as he ever got.

But Reagan seemed absurd as well, a former actor whose most famous line, when he played the part of a double amputee, was 'Where's the rest of me?' and who had once made a film with a chimpanzee.

'Sometimes they had a problem knowing which of them was stupider,' said my father-in-law-to-be.

There was no reason to think that either Goldwater or Reagan represented anything significant in American life. Far from creating a common front, they didn't even like each other. 'Irrelevances', I called them grandly in my student newspaper. That showed how much I understood about American politics.

In 1980 Reagan, who was about to become the oldest president in American history, beat the incumbent Jimmy Carter, partly because Carter's presidency had been marked by ill luck and apparent lack of determination and direction, and partly because Reagan was much less clever than him. As with the old, pre-Thatcher Tory Party, being too obviously intelligent was a disadvantage in America.

Reagan struck the killer blow against Carter during one of their television debates. With much of the nation watching, Carter began a well thought-out, rational answer to a question about policy, backed up by the necessary facts and figures.

'There you go again!' Reagan interrupted gleefully, as though there was something self-evidently useless and absurd about having accurate information at your fingertips.

That interjection seemed to finish Jimmy Carter off; he too was swept into oblivion by a landslide. Under Reagan, America's shift to the right, the growing power of the religious fundamentalists, the willingness of government to ignore the legal niceties, all began to show. A mood of cynicism took over in Washington, a mood which George W. Bush's administration was to share a quarter of a century later. It seemed perfectly natural for the president to sanction an arrangement whereby America, having announced that it would never negotiate with terrorists, secretly agreed to sell missiles to the Islamic Republic of Iran in order to secure the release of American hostages in the hands of pro-Iranian groups. Iran's money would then be spent on equipping Contra guerrillas to undermine the elected government in Nicaragua. Reagan's administration claimed that it gave only moral support to this particularly vicious group who murdered and raped at will. Reagan himself compared them to the Minutemen who carried through the American revolution.

George Bush senior, as president, seemed to represent a return to older Republican values: calmer, much more middle-of-the-road, and more sensitive to the views of the outside world. During the run-up to the first Gulf War, after Saddam Hussein's invasion of Kuwait, Bush's diplomats managed to persuade both the Egyptians and, even more remarkably, the Syrians to join the coalition against Iraq. But Bush understood how important this delicate relationship was, and he was anxious to keep the goodwill which he had created for the United States around the world.

So when the Iraqi army fell apart and fled headlong from Kuwait, President Bush didn't send his forces into Iraq to finish off Saddam. He knew that the US didn't have the support of the UN Security Council to do that. He also knew that his carefully built coalition would collapse if he acted without the backing of the UN. And if the American forces on their own overthrew Saddam Hussein and had to run the country, he understood that that would be a disaster. Everything his son did in Iraq after 2003 showed that Bush senior was entirely right.

President Clinton, who beat him in 1992, had a problem. He had avoided serving in Vietnam by going to Oxford as a Rhodes scholar, and as a result he was vulnerable to right-wing attack if he put US forces in harm's way. (George W. Bush, who also dodged the draft, seemed to have no such problems.) Clinton, therefore, had to find other means of intervening in foreign countries. He used the US air force and navy to bomb Serbia, while against Saddam Hussein he used a combination of bombing and sanctions. No one knows how many Iraqis died as a result of this campaign, but it must have been many hundreds of thousands. Children and the elderly died in vast numbers, but since Saddam Hussein rarely allowed foreign journalists to visit Iraq after the end of the Gulf War, the outside world had very little idea of the full horror of Clinton's hands-off approach.

America is a country with an extraordinary ability to reinvent itself. Every four or eight years, when there is a new president, it's as though the past has been completely wiped away. Everything is new: the president, his advisers, his officials, his policies. In France, Jacques Chirac stayed at the top of politics for thirty years, as prime minister and president. In Germany, the same faces tend to stay around for decades. In Britain, the faces might change but the policies and the civil servants show a lasting continuity.

Not so in America. Once the previous president has gone, it's as though he never existed. Presidential officials usually come fresh to Washington, and have to learn from scratch how it works. Senators and congressmen often keep their jobs for decades, but under the presidential system they have little control over the president and his policies. It is the White House that runs things.

A system like this needs a chief executive with wisdom and judgement: one who listens to his advisers and makes his decisions accordingly. Bill Clinton was a man with the intelligence and grasp to oversee the whole of his administration, but because he couldn't keep his hands off women, in an essentially puritanical country where everyone's life is open to scrutiny, and because he had large numbers of unforgiving enemies, his attention was increasingly directed to keeping himself in office.

George W. Bush, who followed his father and Clinton into the White House in January 2001, lacked most of the qualities that seemed essential for an American president. He had a short attention span, no experience of national government, a very moderate intellect, and an odd lack of judgement. An American journalist who trailed him during his election campaign in 2000 was shocked to see that, when Bush was invited to the funeral of a senior political figure, he winked and gave a thumbs-up to the journalists sitting in the congregation. The little smile which accompanied even his most serious speeches seemed strangely out of place.

Once president, Bush appointed Dick Cheney as, in effect, his prime minister. Cheney was a man who, many American political observers believed, didn't seem overburdened with scruples. A Saudi government minister told me, a month before the invasion of Iraq in 2003, that he had pleaded with Cheney not to go ahead. Cheney had told him there was no alternative.

'All right, then, tell me why you have to invade Iraq,' the Saudi minister said.

'Because it's do-able,' Cheney replied.

In other words, attacking Iraq was an easy way of demonstrating America's strength. After the weakness which the attacks of 11 September 2001 had revealed, it was necessary to hit back at someone and show America's strength. People in the West ignorantly thought of Iraq as strong, with its supposed weapons of mass destruction, but in fact it was an extremely feeble opponent. The US could hit it hard and impressively, and yet not risk anything by doing so.

With Cheney and Donald Rumsfeld, the Secretary of Defense, fiercely in favour of a demonstration of overwhelming American power, it was the job of the president to listen to their proposal and make his judgement. Part of that judgement should have been to ask, 'And what happens on the day after we overthrow Saddam?' In other words, who would run the country, and how long would American troops stay as an occupying force? These were the questions which had persuaded the president's father to leave Saddam Hussein alone.

They shouldn't have been hard to answer. Colin Powell, Bush senior's military chief of staff, had warned that America would have to control Iraq like an imperial possession for an indefinite time, and that a resistance movement would arise to challenge American power. Bush's father had listened to him; but when the same questions came up a little over a decade later, Bush himself didn't. As the chief upholder of the US Constitution, he was nevertheless perfectly prepared to overlook the restrictions of the law, if the wider interests of the government and the country seemed to demand it.

And so Cheney and Rumsfeld, with the help of like-minded officials, created a prison system which was outside the control of the US government, and developed a method of detaining suspects around the world and transferring them to secret holding places where they could be questioned. They introduced a system which, if necessary, would permit these and other prisoners to be tortured, even though the word was never used. Methods like half-drowning and near-asphyxiation had been favourites of the Gestapo and the KGB. Abu Ghraib was a torture centre under the US as under Saddam.

All of this was made possible by a new legal structure, the PATRIOT Act, which, together with other legislation, had the effect of neutralizing the traditional controls the American system had previously maintained. Newspapers and television stations investigating these methods would often find that companies which supported the Republicans would threaten to withdraw their advertising.

Through all of this, the president, the upholder of the Constitution, watched what was going on, signed the necessary legislation into law, defended it in simplistic but strong language and smiled his way through the speeches in which he told the people of the United States what was being done in their name. Most of the leading figures in the Democratic Party were afraid that Karl Rove, the president's chief electoral strategist, would accuse them of weakness where the country's safety was concerned, so they went along with it all. The problem with the presidential system, in the US and in many other countries, is that opposition to the government is usually pretty badly organized, and can easily be attacked as disloyalty or even treason.

America, as I have said, is a country where people prefer to do what their neighbours do, and politicians share the same instinct. In the early 1950s the fear of communism produced McCarthyism – a witch-hunt that only the most extreme American politicians would nowadays regard as justifiable. At the start of the twenty-first century the instinct produced a security panic during which many things happened that Americans would later be ashamed of. As a result of a highly questionable election in 2000 it had become a very different country from the one I visited in 1964: no longer relaxed and liberal, and no longer the kind of society which young foreigners like my former self would admire and envy.

§

I have never met George W. Bush, though I expect that, as with most former US presidents, I shall come across him at some stage in the future. Nor have I been able to meet Donald Rumsfeld or Dick Cheney. The American political system (which the British political system unfortunately tries to copy) keeps foreign journalists away from the topmost figures in any administration, while allowing quite junior reporters from America's regional press and television regular access to them. It is much harder to meet the American president than it is to meet the Pope.

It's quite easy, though, to meet people a little further down the scale; and I've been fortunate enough to meet most of those who were responsible, in one way or another, for the decision to invade Iraq in 2003. The Secretary of State at the time, Colin Powell, seems to have been at least partly against it, though his speech to the UN Security Council not long before the invasion, in which he went into considerable detail about the weaponry which Saddam Hussein didn't actually have, played a part in swinging a good deal of opinion in favour of the invasion – in Western countries, at any rate.

Not long ago, I chaired a meeting in Stockholm at which Colin Powell was the key speaker. There was a reception, and then we all boarded a boat and sailed down the river to the main conference hall. On the journey Powell was pleasant and amusing, and gracious in his praise for those of us who work for the BBC. I felt almost awkward at having to put some tough points to him about the way the policy he had apparently supported had turned out. As it happened, I was leaving Stockholm the next morning to fly to Baghdad, and had my flak jacket and helmet in my hotel room, ready for the trip.

There is nothing like a little personal experience of a big international problem such as Iraq, and I was able to tell him and the other speakers and guests what things in Baghdad were like at first hand. At the same time I was able to say that if some of Powell's proposals to President Bush – inasmuch as we knew them at that stage – had been put into operation, the situation in Iraq would probably have been a great deal better. But there was no getting over the problem that Powell's UN speech had opened the door to the invasion.

Afterwards, when Powell replied, I was a little anxious. Leading politicians are understandably sensitive to what is said about them, and although I prefer to stab people in the front rather than the back, it's hard to blame them for complaining. Powell didn't complain at all. In fact he agreed with the things I'd said, and afterwards he was even more forthcoming.

We are too ready to assume that every senior member of a government is a supporter of what is done in that government's name. Powell was given the job of Secretary of State in 2001 in order to provide the impression that the Bush administration was relatively malleable and open to ideas. It took the outside world some time to realize that Powell had scarcely any power at all, and certainly no influence with the White House. The only weapon he had was the threat of resignation, and Powell was too much of a gentleman, and perhaps too much the loyal military man, to use it. Instead, he stayed with a policy he detested, alongside people he had nothing in common with, and went quietly and with some relief when George W. Bush was re-elected.

His successor was Condoleezza Rice, a woman portrayed by cartoonists around the world as an iron lady, tough and brooding, with a hair-do that could have been constructed by a steel worker. I first met her when she was in charge of Stanford University, a few months before she became a part of George W. Bush's first administration. She had a certain toughness of character; you can't rise to these heights unless you can deal firmly with your own staff and with your own and other governments. And she was naturally a strong defender of her future boss.

'Doesn't it matter to you,' I asked her, 'that he didn't actually know who the new leader of Pakistan was?'

'It mattered not one whit whether he knew the name of General Musharraf or not,' she replied. 'That's a misunderstanding of the function of a president. In dealing with foreign policy, even President Bush [senior], who was one of the best-equipped presidents in that way, had to rely on his advisers to supply him with options. Then he would exercise his judgement and set an agenda, and he would have smart aides to take that agenda forward.

'That's what a president does; he relies on his aides. Governor

Bush of Texas is very capable of setting an agenda, bringing people together round it, and carrying it out.

'I think the world will be pleasantly surprised by George W. Bush, his views of it, and his familiarity with it.'

Not, perhaps, the most accurate of forecasts.

Condoleezza Rice scarcely seemed to me like a politician-in-waiting. She was interested in ideas, and pursued them to the point where, I felt, she could get into trouble. Personally, I prefer academics to politicians, and I like people who concern themselves with ideas and don't worry about saying things which aren't necessarily very circumspect.

Politicians, on the other hand, are usually concerned with justifying themselves ('As I told the House on 5 October . . .'), and those who admit to being wrong or to having changed their minds rarely make good politicians, or stay around for long. Jimmy Carter was unusual in that he had a regard for honesty and readily admitted when he had been wrong. Yet at the time he was unpopular (his popularity rose again after he left office), and it was partly his honesty which people disliked.

American politics are very different from European ones. The professional politicians who sit in the Senate or the House of Representatives can have a career spanning decades; Senator Strom Thurmond lasted until he was 100, and shifted from being an almost avowed racist to being a self-styled supporter of the human rights of African-Americans and many other groups. Whether he was sincere in any of his changes of heart scarcely mattered; it was the fact that he spoke the language of integration and human rights with apparent sincerity that got him re-elected.

But the government of the United States is run at the upper levels by people who in Europe would be regarded as amateurs. Many of them come from the big liberal or conservative think-tanks in Washington, some moving in and out of government several times over the years. For Europeans, it is hard to see the advantage of this. It encourages a hardening of the ideological arteries, so that the senior people in any administration are chosen for their political line rather than their experience and their ability, if necessary, to change their approach. It also means that there is a certain other-worldliness about them. Most academics live in the realm of ideas, and while that is very charming and very necessary for academia, it can be a problem in the real world.

Condoleezza Rice seemed to me to be the exact opposite of her reputation. Far from being a tough operator, she wanted to agree and to be agreeable, and she used her remarkable intellect to do it. When I interviewed her she didn't, of course, concur that George W. Bush was a man with no serious understanding of the world outside America; I wouldn't have expected her to do that. She defended him as someone who was fascinated by foreign affairs, and was informing himself about it constantly. But beyond that? There wasn't, I think, another question which she didn't agree with me on: events in the Middle East, in the Far East, in Europe, even in Iraq.

Agreement in conversation is a very pleasant thing; people who disagree with you habitually are, by definition, rather disagreeable. But not in politics. A good interview with a politician is one where there is some friction, where ideas are tested and examined, where a little light is shed as a result. But Condoleezza Rice wasn't a politician, she was an academic.

She had come to the attention of George W. Bush's father when, as president, he had had to decide how to behave towards the politicians in the Soviet Union in the days after the Berlin Wall came down and a new and potentially unstable world was starting to emerge. Her advice was clear and effective, and he marked her down for advancement. The fact that she was a concert pianist helped to make her a charming guest at the White House, and soon after that a close family friend.

So far so good. But the American presidential system creates an atmosphere rather similar to a royal court. The king can select his courtiers from anywhere, usually because they agree with him; and they only keep their jobs, and their proximity to the throne, if they continue to think as he does. Under the parliamentary system, prime ministers can select their ministers only from among members of the governing party, who may or may not be his political allies. George W. Bush chose his courtiers from among his own friends and those of his father, though at first much of the choosing seems to have been done by his vice-president, Dick Cheney; who in turn seems to have been imposed on Bush by his father.

So Condoleezza Rice, a clever woman and family friend with many graces and attributes, was made National Security Adviser in the first Bush administration. At first, before the attacks of 11 September 2001, it was her job to give the president clear advice about the threat of terrorism; except that, before the attacks, this was self-evidently not what he was interested in. As a member of his court, therefore, with her position resting on the degree of influence she had over him, she doesn't seem to have given him the firm warnings he should have had. Nor did she demand from him the kind of action a president should have taken to defend the country.

She might have seemed tough to the outside world but, inside the court of George W. Bush, Condoleezza Rice mostly seems to have told him what he wanted to hear. In 2002 the big decisions were being taken about whether or not to invade Iraq. Dick Cheney and Donald Rumsfeld were loudly urging the president to do it. Condoleezza Rice knew it was a highly questionable course of action, and she saw much of the intelligence which made the CIA, for instance, very dubious about the whole enterprise. She may well have been tempted to agree with Secretary of State Colin Powell that the invasion of Iraq should either be done very differently or not at all. But she could also see that the president was determined to go ahead, and her position depended on doing what the president wanted. So that is what she did.

This was the woman I saw and interviewed: highly intelligent, articulate, supremely well informed, charming – but not independent minded. The desire to agree was all too evident, and the job she was given was altogether the wrong one. In the governmental structure of the United States the best National Security Advisers are tough and self-confident, awkward coves who insist on saying their piece without fear or favour: Henry Kissinger, Zbigniew Brzinszki, Sandy Berger. A National Security Adviser who prefers to go along with the general opinion instead of giving unwelcome advice will inevitably be weak. Condoleezza Rice wasn't an awkward cove.

§

Neither Dick Cheney nor Donald Rumsfeld was the author of the original plan to invade Iraq. That was Paul Wolfowitz, another academic who moved easily into the Bush administration. Cheney and Rumsfeld were aggressive, powerful, self-assured men; in Rumsfeld's case, too self-assured. No one liked him, not even George W. Bush, to whom he was inclined to be patronizing. (Dick Cheney, though tough and overbearing by nature, was always careful not to make that mistake. Bush might be weak and lacking in self-confidence when he dealt with his closest courtiers, but he still had the power to hire and fire.)

But Wolfowitz was no Rumsfeld; he would never have been selected as his deputy if he had been. I met Wolfowitz only once, but I was as surprised by his softness and lack of real fibre as I had been by Condoleezza Rice's malleability. The British television tradition is to ask tough questions, and in the case of a man like Wolfowitz, whose approach was profoundly unpopular in large parts of the world, it was essential to be firm with him.

He seemed to have no real answers beyond his brief. Worse, he found it hard to answer probing questions, and smiled awkwardly almost as if he were asking me to have mercy on him and stop. At the end, I felt I had elicited neither answers nor even clever evasions. I had just got the answers his advisers had provided him with. But our interview made that absolutely clear; he didn't come out of it well.

The intellectual drive behind the plan to invade Iraq came from another academic, Douglas Feith. Feith was a strong supporter of the Likud Party in Israel, and approved wholeheartedly of its policy of war to the knife towards its enemies. He was Wolfowitz's deputy, the man who did the hard thinking and planning, and whose input persuaded Wolfowitz, and then Rumsfeld, and then Cheney, that invading Iraq would be an easy business. The Iraqis, he said, without specifying which ones, would shower the invading troops with roses.

As we have seen, the news that the Iraqi population was so deeply divided, both ethnically and in terms of religion, seemed to come as a surprise to the Bush administration, quite late on. Rumsfeld, Wolfowitz and Feith all had a certain contempt for Europe, but their experience was largely drawn from there and from the

Israel–Palestinian conflict. Ethnic and religious divisions were not things they had much interest in, or awareness of. Rumsfeld, in particular, had been much influenced by the collapse of Marxism–Leninism in Eastern Europe, and he made it clear he expected Saddam's rule to collapse as tidily and satisfactorily as Moscow's had. The rest of the Arab Middle East could be expected to follow. The CIA and the State Department, who knew better, weren't consulted.

After the invasion was over I began making a documentary for the old *Panorama* programme about the war in Iraq. In the BBC system, these long-form documentaries can sometimes be something of a trial. The idea is that the film is the reporter's view of the subject, and I was indeed asked for my personal account of what was happening in Iraq. Since I was travelling there to report regularly, I had plenty of ideas about it all. But in the BBC current-affairs tradition, the producer is really in charge of the whole thing (unlike the news tradition, where the correspondent is in charge). No doubt these distinctions seem pretty small beer, but the result was that my personal view of the situation in Iraq very quickly became the producer's view. He and I got on well, and the result was probably a better film than I would have made if left to my own devices. I was certainly keen afterwards to take as much of the considerable credit as I could. But it was different in some ways from what I would have done, unaided.

As part of the film, we wanted to interview Paul Bremer, the American viceroy in Iraq. But these big set-piece interviews can have awkward consequences; another *Panorama* correspondent had interviewed Bremer some months before, and given him a hard time. Bremer had a very high opinion of his function, and of himself ('He was unbelievably pompous, silly and arrogant,' said a British official who had dealings with him), and he was deeply affronted that anyone would press him for an answer in a television interview. As a result, Bremer refused to speak to the BBC again, and although I tried half a dozen times during his year in office, he would never see me.

In this case I wanted to speak to him for our documentary, and went to see his British deputy, Sir Jeremy Greenstock, to ask for help. Sir Jeremy was the precise opposite of Bremer, and said he would go and ask Bremer to change his mind.

We were sitting in Greenstock's office in Saddam Hussein's old palace, which had once been the office of Saddam's deputy. It was separated from Saddam's office, where Bremer had installed himself, by a large typing pool full of administrative people. I watched Greenstock walk across the open area to Bremer's office. A US Marine sergeant who was regularly on duty there, and must have seen Sir Jeremy twenty times a day, watched him walking over. Then he checked the identity card he was wearing, glancing from it to Sir Jeremy's face and back to the picture on the card.

A couple of minutes later Bremer's door opened and Sir Jeremy came back through the typing pool. He shook his head: Bremer still refused to speak to the BBC, even though his deputy, a highly distinguished diplomat, had asked him to see me as a personal favour.

So instead of Bremer, we had to settle for Douglas Feith in Washington. At the Pentagon, the BBC's reputation was high, and as we were led through the confusing, oppressively low-ceilinged corridors, the major who escorted us said some kind things about our programmes. The last time I had been there, a year earlier, it had been to see the admiral in charge of the operation which ended in our being bombed by the American navy in northern Iraq. At that time work was still going on to repair the damage done by the plane which crashed into the Pentagon on 11 September 2001, but now that was finished. We were shown into a small room where our interview with Douglas Feith would take place, and the cameraman set up his equipment.

I had never met Feith before. Typical of so many of the ideologues who worked in the Bush administration, he stayed out of the limelight; although I knew roughly what he looked like from photographs, I had never seen him interviewed. His intellect was celebrated, though General Tommy Franks, who led the invasion of Iraq, had famously deemed him 'the stupidest fucking idiot in the world'. It seemed unlikely to me that he was anything of the sort. Franks was a larger-than-life, swaggering character who liked men's men; Feith was an intellectual, slightly built and with a rather high-pitched voice, who had the power to tell Franks what to do.

The cameraman needed time to get ready. When he had finished setting up the lights and the seating, we told the major, and he went to get Feith. The man who had been the intellectual driving force behind the invasion of Iraq walked in.

'Good afternoon.'

His handshake was disconcertingly limp, but he had a pleasant smile and it was clear to me right from the start that he was clever. I had prepared my questions carefully. We needed some information, but mostly we wanted an able, articulate defence of the invasion and occupation of Iraq. Even at this early stage in the war, things weren't going well and we had the material to prove it. Apart from anything else, we had narrowly escaped being ambushed while the American military convoy we were embedded with was driving through north Baghdad.

Yet as soon as the interview began, I could see that Douglas Feith wouldn't be able to provide us with the robust defence of American policy we needed. He might have played a major part in creating the policy, but his words carried little force because he seemed so feeble. Clearly, he expected me to take what he said at face value. Everything was going to plan in Iraq, he told me, and naturally the people of the country were grateful for what had been done for them by the United States.

All this started to irritate me. The invasion of Iraq had cost unknown thousands of lives. From reporting there on a regular basis, I knew it was starting to look like a disaster in the making. And yet the man who had persuaded the Bush administration that the invasion would pass off smoothly was giving me answers that were much too easy. Worse, he clearly didn't understand what the invasion had done to Iraq. I could feel the anger welling up in me.

'If it was so good for the people of Iraq that this invasion should have taken place, why are there more Iraqi children living below starvation level now than there were under Saddam Hussein?'

Feith panicked.

'Stop the recording, please,' he said, waving at the camera.

The public relations major who had arranged the interview looked stricken. He knew as well as I did that putting a hand up into the camera lens and asking us to stop filming was the worst thing Feith could possibly do. It was an acceptance of weakness, a damaging surrender. Viewers who didn't remember anything of what he said would certainly remember this.

'I didn't know you were going to ask me that kind of question. I don't deal nowadays with what's happening on the ground in Iraq. I'm not briefed about this. I don't know if it's true what you say or not. I'll have to get more information.'

No politician in America would have said, on camera, that he didn't know anything about an issue as important, as devastating to his own position, as the death of large numbers of children from malnutrition. But, like Condoleezza Rice, Douglas Feith wasn't a politician. He was another academic who had been brought into government for his ideas. Even if he was personally saddened by the issue, in this context it was essentially a matter for documentation, for study, for filing away somewhere.

No doubt I could be accused of ambushing Feith unfairly. It was true that he had had nothing to do with the administration of Iraq after the invasion. Yet he had been so sure that the invasion of Iraq was in Iraq's own interest, as well as America's, that he had convinced everyone above him in the governmental structure, from Wolfowitz to Rumsfeld to Bush himself. So what happened as a result of the invasion was something that went much wider than Feith's own administrative brief. And it didn't seem altogether outrageous to ask someone so involved in public affairs to defend a view that had cost hundreds of thousands of lives.

To interrupt a television recording like this is, for any figure in the public eye, from a leading politician to an actor or a rock star, very unwise. The organization which is recording the interview has full rights over the video, and for Feith to show he had no idea about the Iraqi children who had died as a direct result of his own advice was quite shocking.

Worst of all, it was naive. It revealed an innocence which might, in another context, be rather charming. Feith was an academic, so cut off by his own studies that he had no idea of what was going on the real world. But given that he was the ideas man who helped to make the invasion of Iraq a possibility, it wasn't charming at all.

The interview wore on. I asked him why, if things were going as well as he claimed they were with the administration of Iraq, oil should be rationed in Iraqi cities. Again, the hand in the camera, the anguished face, the plea that he hadn't realized I was going to put questions like these. More naivety, more self-revelation.

Finally, it was over. No one accused me of acting in bad faith or sharp dealing. On the contrary, Douglas Feith apologized profusely for not having performed better. If he had railed at me afterwards, I might have found it easier to deal with. Feith was, in his way, very otherworldly, like a cloistered monk in the seventeenth century, largely unaware of the horrors that were happening on the other side of the monastery wall. In other circumstances, I might even have liked him. But he was the kind of person who shouldn't be allowed out without a minder.

Iraq wasn't just a place to be read and theorized about. It was full of people who needed food and electricity and petrol to stay alive and healthy. Anything that interfered with their supplies could well threaten their very existence.

And when things broke down, and they started dying in large numbers, it didn't really seem quite adequate for the person who thought it all up to say he didn't know what was going on there and hadn't been fully briefed. As though it had all been just an experiment. As though he could rub it off the blackboard now, and start an entirely new experiment from scratch.

§

The lives of most people of my age were touched by the Vietnam War. In America, young men had to get their fathers to pay for them to go somewhere safe to avoid being sent to Vietnam; young men, that is, like George W. Bush. Those who didn't have the money or the influence had to take their chances. More than fifty thousand died, and nearly a million had injuries of a physical or mental kind which affected them for most of their lives.

Outside America, the Vietnam War radicalized an entire generation. A few remained radicals for the rest of their lives. With many more, the effect didn't last. For the majority, I suppose, it meant they never wanted to be on the side of the big battalions, no matter what the issue might be. And it left many people in the US and in other Western countries convinced that the American military leadership would always fight any war unintelligently and disastrously. It's one of the big regrets of my professional life that I didn't report

on the Vietnam War. It was one of the most formative events of my
career, and I have been trying ever since to work out what really
happened, as opposed to what books and newspapers and documentaries tell me happened.

The Vietnam War was always a presence in Iraq. It hung in
the air like a low-level sound wave, insistent and disturbing.
On the RAF Hercules from Kuwait to Baghdad there would usually
be, aside from the soldiers and the occasional official, a contingent
of Americans in their late fifties and early sixties, strapped into their
seats along the sides and down the centre of the cathedral-like
plane, sweating heavily in the fifty-degree heat, chewing gum. They
were American security contractors, onetime soldiers who had
signed up for the difficult and dangerous job of guarding people
and protecting buildings. Their heads were often shaven, or else
they wore their hair long and in a pigtail. Their faces were often
shaven too, except for a little integral moustache and beard. Like
many of us at this age, nearly all had a big gut. They tended to be
tattooed with strange patterns or depressing slogans.

They laughed a lot among themselves, and drank a good deal of
beer out of cans. One or two of them left messages written in
ballpoint pen on the walls of the flimsy green plastic latrine cabins,
which stank in the heat. I jotted one down which I read at the
holding area where we all had to wait for our flight to Baghdad:

> Got me three gooks in Nam in 72,
> Got me three more in Iraq too.

'Gooks' are locals: the distinction between insurgents and the civil
population they were supposedly there to protect was as tenuous in
Iraq as it had been in Vietnam; with the same results on public
opinion, and on the eventual outcome of the war.

Iraq wasn't a new Vietnam, in the sense that a huge American
military force would be defeated in the field and at home, and that
people would cling pathetically to the last American helicopter out.
I once wrote a long report for the BBC on why Iraq didn't have to
become another Vietnam; yet even while I was writing it, large
numbers of tattooed and shaven-headed men, in uniform and out of
it, who thought everyone was a gook and a fair target, were making
sure that Iraq would be just as much of a disaster, and would leave

similar amounts of hatred and destruction behind them when they pulled out.

American soldiers are much too inclined to behave like the German army in France in 1870, 1914 and 1940: they believe there are *francs-tireurs* all round them, and they open fire accordingly. Slowly, the American and British press began to turn up evidence of various massacres which individual American soldiers had carried out in Iraq; I myself discovered one, and broadcast the details. And although revelations like this obliged the officers to stop their men carrying out full-scale massacres, there were always individual killings which caused even greater anger and bitterness. Iraq, after all, is a country where the concept of blood-vengeance is very strong.

Until I began to meet them, I assumed that the generals who ran the Iraq War were like those who ran the Vietnam War; and I based much of my assumption on what my American first wife's brother, a US Marine Corps captain in Vietnam, had told me about his own general, a shaven-headed little man who was anxious to impress the flow of American politicians who came through. To do so, he used to send small detachments of Marines into enemy-occupied territory, so that they would be surrounded and have to fight for their lives. My ex-brother-in-law, who was a helicopter pilot, then had to go in and rescue the wounded. It was an immensely dangerous business, and his best friend, also a helicopter pilot, was killed in action. My brother-in-law heard his screams over the radio as he burned to death.

Gradually, though, I began to rethink my 1960s assumptions about senior American officers. It started at the vast Saddam-era conference centre in the Green Zone. I had seen Saddam Hussein give a speech here, not long before the war of 1991. After the American invasion in 2003 the conference centre had become a meeting place for Iraqi politicians, journalists and occasionally American civilians and military people. In those days the government, or the Americans, used to prepare lunch for anyone who happened to be around.

The conference centre was a depressing place, which seemed to follow the fortunes of the country itself. At first it was reasonably well lit, and the lunches gave it a festive atmosphere. There was a vast banner hanging on the balcony of the top level, over the open atrium, which carried the love and good wishes of the children of American to the children of Iraq. When the Iraqi parliament took over the building the banner came down, because Iraqis found it offensive.

The carpets became more stained and torn. The toilets began to jam up and stink. The electricity failed more and more often, so that when you walked around the building, even in daylight, you needed a torch. It was hit many times by mortar shells, and the repairs always took a long time. Then the Americans pulled out altogether, and the place was left to Iraqi politicians and Iraqi journalists. It seemed to me to be haunted by the failure of everyone's attempts to take control of Iraq, and the ghosts wander, mocking the living.

Shortly before Christmas 2003 I went there to get my accreditation, and to see if I could meet up with any interesting people. While I was there, lunch was served, and I decided to have a bite to eat. The only empty seat was next to an American Marine colonel. I was reluctant to get into conversation. I didn't want to start an argument with a gung-ho soldier who knew nothing more about Iraq than he saw on Fox News.

But he was polite and pleasant, and turned out to be a dedicated listener to the BBC World Service. And soon he was telling me what was happening to his men, and what he saw from touring his sector of the country; for, contrary to what I had assumed, he wasn't a Green Zone pen-pusher but an active commander in the field.

'This isn't going well, you know,' he said, keeping his voice down for much the same reason that I had been reluctant to get into conversation in the first place: he didn't want to start an argument with some of the officers who were sitting round us. 'This certainly isn't a war for hearts and minds, and if it is, we've lost it already. I was in Vietnam, and I saw what went down there. And we're making exactly the same mistakes now that we made then. You mark my words,' he said, leaning closer to me, 'it's all going to be another disaster. In fact, it already is.'

In the years that followed, I met a number of senior military men, from the generals who ran things in Baghdad to General David Petraeus, who was eventually promoted to command the entire American operation in Iraq. The more of these people I met

and interviewed, the more impressive I found them to be. They were
not mindless, gung-ho characters careless of civilian losses or the
actions of their own men. They knew perfectly well that the entire
enterprise was likely to fail, and they did their best to tell the
politicians in Washington what was happening. Many of them,
I later found, had a deep hatred of Donald Rumsfeld, who as
Secretary for Defense had got them into this war without sufficient
resources, and who treated them with great vindictiveness if they
made their own views in any way public.

The professional soldiers, headed originally by General Eric
Shinseki, had warned that the occupation of Iraq would take at
least twice and perhaps three times the number of troops Rumsfeld
had allocated to the job. Others, such as General George Casey,
made it increasingly clear to Congress that the war was going
badly and might actually be unwinnable. Casey's successor, David
Petraeus, had had a highly successful war, and was the leading
advocate in the US forces of the policy of winning hearts and minds.
But right from the moment he took over in February 2007, he made
it abundantly clear in his public statements that he didn't expect his
mission to be successful.

The generals weren't the villains of this war. They were the men
who understood how bad things were likely to be. And many of
them paid a price for saying so.

The centrepiece of the case for the war, put forward by Rumsfeld, Wolfowitz and Feith, was that the mere act of toppling Saddam
Hussein would bring the overwhelming majority of Iraqis over to
the American side, and that a big occupation force would simply
not be necessary. The head of British intelligence, Sir Richard
Dearlove, visited Washington and realized early on that this was
the administration's plan. He duly warned Tony Blair about it.

But Blair failed to use what ever influence he had with George
W. Bush to persuade him that it would be a disaster, and Bush
lacked the foresight to anticipate the problem himself. The top
American military men understood it very well, though. They went
ahead with the invasion and the occupation because those were
their orders, but they knew they were being asked to do something
that would turn into a disaster. Later, Casey and others had their
revenge by making it clear to various congressional committees that

in their view the fault lay with Donald Rumsfeld; when the mid-term elections of November 2006 went seriously wrong for President Bush, Rumsfeld had to go.

After that, the course the war was taking was scarcely a matter of controversy any longer. American public opinion decided by a sizeable majority that it was a serious failure, and the issue was then how quickly the US forces should pull out: immediately, or over a period of time. General Petraeus was given a big new force – 'the surge', as it was known – even though many senior generals warned that this wouldn't succeed in taming the insurgency in Iraq. And of course it didn't. After forty years I had learned that it was possible, after all, to believe what American generals said.

§

Much of the problem sprang from the US army itself. The quality of its recruits was low. It included a sizeable proportion of Latin American and other immigrants who joined up in order to gain American citizenship, and there were many who had volunteered because they had a criminal record and wanted it expunged. The equipment and basic training of the US forces was for the most part excellent, and as an aggressive force they were second to none – the best in the world. But when it came to patrolling the streets of Iraqi towns and cities, they were decidedly second rate.

'I can't believe this, I just can't believe it.'

The former regimental sergeant-major of the Coldstream Guards, who was now working as a security adviser for the BBC in Baghdad, was escorting my cameraman, my producer and me to Baghdad airport by road. These trips were always slightly nerve-racking, since we had to travel along Route Irish, with its daily suicide bombings and ambushes.

The RSM was sitting in the back of the vehicle with the three of us, his gun on his lap. In the front sat one of our Iraqi drivers, and an ex-SAS man. All four of us peered out through the windscreen. Our vehicle was indistinguishable from most of the other Iraqi cars on the road; and although this meant it was dangerous to get too close to any American convoys, which would open fire on us instantly if they thought we were travelling too close, we were much safer from ambush or bombing than the big white armoured 4x4s which some of the American defence contractors still used. And we did have some protection: big sheets of Kevlar, discreetly stretched along the inside of the vehicle where we sat.

What the RSM couldn't believe was that the Americans had simply left Route Irish to the insurgents.

'In Northern Ireland we would have four or five packets of men on either side of this road, moving in and out all the time, without any kind of pattern to it, so the IRA would never know where we were.

'All this lot do is drive up and down the road in their armoured vehicles. So of course they make themselves a target. They could clear it in a couple of days. But they don't have the training.'

I spent some time, before and afterwards, with American special forces units. They, I found, were very different, and highly critical of the tactics and behaviour of the ordinary infantry. The US special forces could have achieved a great deal more in Vietnam, because they understood the importance of winning the trust and support of local people. In Iraq, too, they did their best. But they were never allowed to run the operation. Instead, they were kept for special occasions, and looked on while the regular army alienated the great majority of the Iraqis they came into contact with.

9

JAPANESE

Suitably enough, it all started in the most sumptuous place in the world.

Even the least royalist among us would experience a twinge of nervousness at driving through the gates of Buckingham Palace. The policeman on the gate looks at your invitation, then stands back and salutes. You drive past the front section of the palace, which faces onto the Mall and contains mostly offices, and into the large, open, gravelled courtyard behind it. Now you can see the other half of the Palace: the more important part, hidden from public view. A *porte-cochère* covers the entrance, and your car drops you off under its shelter. On one occasion I drove my disreputable old banger through the Palace gates myself, but no one seemed to mind or even to notice when I parked it alongside the Bentleys and Rollers. There are, thank God, one or two countries left where you aren't automatically judged by your possessions; though once you have listed Britain, Ireland, France, occasionally Spain, and the east coast of the United States, you have pretty much exhausted the list. In Britain, if you drive into the grounds of Buckingham Palace in a tatty old Rover, you are more likely to be an earl than a BBC journalist.

This evening, though, Dee and I were being taken to Buckingham Palace by a BBC driver for a state dinner in honour of the president of Brazil. It was hard to say who of us was the more nervous. The driver probably thought he would crash into something, or run over the Duke of Edinburgh. Dee was dressed up to the nines, but was scared that some false move might rip her dress. I was haunted by the same fear that had gripped me when I went to an investiture after the first Gulf War, and had to take a couple of steps backwards from the Queen; I had read not long before about the courtier who had broken wind loudly as he descended the steps from Elizabeth I's throne. When he returned after seven years wandering the globe to expiate his embarrassment, she said to him, 'Greetings, Sir William – we have forgot the fart.'

Nothing about my rig felt right. White tie and tails is a rarity nowadays, and it is far too expensive to be worth buying a set. I went to Moss Bros in Covent Garden, and had the impression that every other male who was going to the state banquet had got there before me. My suit fitted – I think the gentlemen in the hiring department at Moss Bros would make a citizen's arrest on you rather than allow you to walk out with something that didn't – but it was distinctly uncomfortable, with buckles and bits of elastic in strange and illogical places. I had tied my white bow tie myself, since I loathe made-up ones, but I had a constant fear that it was turning on its axis and coming undone. The elastic on my white waistcoat seemed to pull my head forward, and the braces which held my trousers up pulled me back. I felt like the Millennium Dome in a gale.

Only after we had passed through the *porte-cochère*, climbed the grand staircase and joined the crowds of people standing around in the vast gilded saloon did I realize that virtually every other male was in the same state. Men were standing awkwardly wherever I looked, pulled in different directions simultaneously by the inner workings of their Moss Bros suits. Furtive hands went up to adjust wayward white ties, or down into pockets to pull unnaturally tight trousers into a slightly less uncomfortable position. Even for ambassadors and genuine courtiers, I guessed, white tie and tails was an unfamiliar rig. As for the rest of us, we might as well have been sporting the doublet and hose and gigantic ruff as worn by Sir William the wind-breaker. The strange thing about having a monarchy is that most people support it in general terms (it's colourful, it's cheap, it's good for tourism, and it means not having to have President Thatcher or President Blair) until they come into contact with some of the stranger practices associated with its daily workings; and then they sometimes feel less enthusiastic.

Dee and I made our way through the crowd. I don't enjoy big receptions very much, after losing my hearing in one ear. Having to make intelligent conversation with someone whose accented voice

I can scarcely take in, while a crowd is baying all round me, has become a particular type of hell; in addition, the shrapnel wound near my hip usually starts to ache, in order to remind me that I'm not enjoying myself.

At Buckingham Palace, though, it isn't like that. The salon is so high and so spacious that you don't feel under any great pressure. The drinks are generous, the snacks delicious. There were plenty of people to talk to, and we found ourselves caught up in several conversations. Politicians like to talk, and diplomats quite like to listen, but all of them were more interested in Dee, because she looked so good, than in me. But in order to get to her, they had to start with me, and I'm certainly not averse to the sound of my own voice. Altogether, then, it was a pleasant and comfortable progress through the room.

We ended up with a senior figure whom I have met several times, and whose company I particularly enjoy. There are people in high positions who are adept at talking to you openly about important subjects, and giving the impression that they are giving you valuable new insights. Often, of course, when you reflect on the conversation afterwards you realize that all you have been given is what you already knew; but there is a pleasant sense of having been close to the horse's mouth, and any journalist enjoys that.

We talked to him for a good while. I was faintly aware that the crowd behind me was thinning, but he was so important that I felt nothing could begin without him.

Then he said, 'I'd better be heading off. I'm not going to the banquet, so I'll leave you to it. Enjoy yourselves.'

That was awkward. The saloon was now entirely empty. All of the other guests had been through the reception line, and the reception line was now waiting for us alone.

As we walked quickly in the anteroom, they were standing in a little half-circle, as at a wedding. From the right, closest to us, was the Brazilian president's wife. Then came the president. Then the Queen. Then Prince Philip. Then the Queen Mother. At that stage she was ninety-nine, and leaning on a walking-stick; and we had kept her waiting. In fact, we had kept them all waiting.

Dee went first. She was nervous, and probably annoyed with me for delaying us by talking too much. She took the hand of the

Brazilian first lady, who was, if anything, more nervous still. As a result, perhaps because each recognized the other to be an outsider and wanted support, they stayed together for a fraction too long. And they managed to get too close to each other. Somehow a brilliant and rather large diamond brooch which the president's wife was wearing hooked itself to some lacy material on Dee's dress, and stuck like Velcro. When Dee moved away to shake the president's hand she found she had gained a Siamese twin. The President's wife moved with her, her eyes wide with the horror of it all, and the two of them froze, afraid of destroying something absolutely vital.

My reactions dropped to paralysis level. Everything seemed to be working in slow motion, as though I'd pressed the wrong button on a video editing machine. The president, too, seemed completely overcome. He opened his mouth, but couldn't speak. The Queen had turned away and was talking to Prince Philip, so she wasn't aware that anything was wrong. The Queen Mother, who must have seen far worse things over the decades, smiled serenely.

Only the Duke of Edinburgh, characteristically, took action. He strode the two or three steps across, took Dee with one hand and the president's wife with the other, and pulled. They came apart and stood there, speechless. Then we shook hands with everyone, and went in to the banquet.

Fortunately, perhaps, since an unsympathetic judge might have said it was all my fault, Dee and I were sitting on different tables. There were no recriminations. I found myself next to the Japanese ambassador. He was quite remarkably polite, but every now and then he would surreptitiously take out his watch and make a note. I looked at him and waited for an explanation, but none came. For a while I talked to the person on my right, but he turned out to be so boring, and so hostile to the BBC, about which he seemed to know nothing of any significance, that I turned back to the Japanese ambassador and his watch.

'The first course took twelve minutes and four seconds from start to end,' he suddenly announced in excellent, almost unaccented English.

'Surely you must have been educated in Britain,' I said.

He smiled politely.

'And the serving of the wine took only forty-five seconds.'

'Very good wine,' I said. The Buckingham Palace cellars are better, in my experience, than those of the Elysée Palace; though it is distinctly possible that on the occasion I dined with the French president they weren't putting out the really good stuff. It was a dinner for a British delegation.

'Mother's milk,' I added for effect.

The Japanese ambassador almost did the nose-trick, something I had assumed Japanese diplomats were genetically incapable of. Managing not to choke, he turned back to his watch and started making some more calculations, which he then jotted down.

In the end I had to ask him what it was all about.

'Ah. The Emperor of Japan is to make a state visit here later this year. I must make sure to explain to his officials how everything works.' There was a pause. 'The main course comes in at precisely eight fifty-seven.'

'But it probably won't be like this at the next banquet,' I said. 'When I was here last it was all different. It was dark, and a man played the bagpipes as the pudding came in.'

The Japanese ambassador looked at me as though I was describing a Ku Klux Klan ceremony.

'Bagpipes?'

It was true I had drunk rather deeply of the superb Buckingham Palace wines, both then and now, but that's what I thought had happened.

'And all the lights were out, except for the candles.'

He wrote something down on his little piece of paper, but it didn't look to me as though he believed it.

'What time did this happen?'

'Unfortunately I didn't have my watch on it,' I said, with a hint of sharpness.

There was a silence. In order to break it, I touched on a difficult subject.

'I suppose there'll be demonstrations when the Emperor comes here.'

'There will?' He looked panic-stricken.

'Well, maybe not. But not everyone will be happy.'

I thought of my dear Uncle Alan, who had been a leading light in the association that kept the Old Chindits together. The Chindits were an elite group of British and Indian soldiers who were trained by a brilliant, if wayward, brigadier called Orde Wingate to fight behind Japanese lines in the jungle, living off what they could find and carrying out raids which terrified the enemy. To call Uncle Alan anti-Japanese scarcely began to touch his emotional response to the country. I remembered coming home and telling him, after my first visit to Tokyo in 1979, what a wonderfully civilized place it was. I thought he was going to have a major infarction.

'Bloody animals,' he spluttered. It was some moments before he felt strong enough to pick up his gin and tonic again, and he scarcely spoke to me for the rest of the evening.

Fortunately for the ambassador, and even more fortunately for the Emperor, my Uncle Alan had died quite soon afterwards. I'm not sure the imperial life would have been entirely safe if he had been alive when the state visit finally took place.

'Not happy,' the ambassador repeated uncertainly.

'You know, old servicemen and so on.' I put on a sanctimonious look. 'They haven't always changed with the times.'

The ambassador shook his head. 'We are worried about it,' he said. 'Everything must go perfectly.'

'Hence . . .' I nodded towards his wristwatch, a beautiful Breuguet, as it lay beside him on the perfectly starched table-cloth.

'Exactly.'

Something came to me; it often does at these times.

'You know, the reason why there is still opposition to the Emperor here is because the people of Britain know so little about him. Why not, in the month before he comes here for his visit—'

'With the Empress,' said the ambassador.

'With the Empress, let me spend some time with them with a BBC camera. A documentary about the Emperor at home – and the Empress, yes – would have a big effect on British public opinion. You might well find that everything was completely different afterwards.'

I wasn't trained as a lawyer, but the careful use of words is just as valuable to me in my profession.

'You think it would make a difference?'

'I think it might make a very considerable difference.'

He jotted that down, too.

Then, suddenly, the lights were dimmed, and only the candles lit the room. Down the long corridor from somewhere in the interior of the Palace came a cough and a whine, and then the magical sound of a set of bagpipes playing. The piper, a huge man in a splendid kilt, strode into the room with a great pudding on a silver dish behind him.

'Ahhh,' said the Japanese ambassador beside me. Now he understood.

He made another note; a long one this time.

'Nine forty-one,' he said, to no one in particular, as though that just summed everything up.

There were speeches, which he timed with the utmost precision, and some outstanding dessert wine, and cheese of a kind I didn't think the British or even the French were capable of making. There may have been other things too; by this time I scarcely noticed.

Afterwards, Dee and I met up in the nearby drawing room for coffee. To forestall any remarks about her experience with the Brazilian president's wife, I told her what the Japanese ambassador had said.

'Tomorrow he's going to contact the Minister of the Imperial Court and ask him to let us do a fly-on-the-wall doccie with the Emperor. There might be a bit of work in it for you.'

That did the trick. There was no inquest into the great brooch disaster after all. Not till later, at any rate.

§

My trip to Japan in 1979 had been a bewildering one for me. By that time – I was thirty-five – I had travelled widely throughout Europe and Africa, and was starting to know about Russia and the Middle East. But the Far East was still completely closed to me.

I went to Tokyo to see the Japanese prime minister, a man who made little mark even on Japanese history. Nevertheless he was about to host the G7 summit, as it was in those days, and he agreed to be interviewed.

The hotel where the summit guests would be staying was the most extraordinary and advanced place of its kind I had ever been in. The New Otani had only just been opened, and it contained every new feature it was possible to conceive of. Nowadays it seems quite staid and run of the mill, and I have seen plenty of hotels which are far more innovative. But in 1979, to be awakened by recorded birdsong, to have your own personal butler, to take in the sensational gardens with their cobblestones and delicate bridges and huge extraordinarily coloured fish which put their heads above the surface if you clapped your hands, to eat at one of the four little restaurants dotted about the gardens, each offering a different Japanese cuisine, to find weird gadgets in the bathroom which needed an instruction manual to tell you what they were for, let alone how you might work them, and to have a mini-bar which counted the things you took out of it and charged them automatically to your bill, all seemed close to magical.

I was in Tokyo with a delightful man named George Walker, who was well into his fifties but was immensely lively and hard working, and very good company. He sold BBC2 the idea of an interview and reporting programme called, not very adventurously, *Correspondent*. He chose me to present it, and together we did a lot of interesting things (apart from anything else, we did one of the very first television interviews with Colonel Gaddafi in Libya, and another with Ayatollah Khomeini before he went back to Iran). Nowadays BBC television doesn't have any kind of programme like that. The last one, also called *Correspondent*, was axed by a woman called Jane Root, who was the controller of BBC2 at the time. She said the name reminded her of some Old Etonian in a white linen suit. She left the BBC soon afterwards, and now works for an American channel. I don't expect anyone wears suits of any material on her programmes.

George and I had travelled with an old-fashioned television news crew consisting of two men, a cameraman and a sound recordist. There are times, even in today's stripped-down, cut-price days, when I miss having a sound recordist: it means the cameraman can concentrate on the look of the interview, and doesn't need to worry about microphones and leads and sound levels. This particular sound recordist, though, managed to foul up the entire job.

After we had done our interview with the Japanese prime minister and flown back to London to get it developed (these were still the days of film, which nowadays seem indistinguishable from the New Stone Age), George and I discovered that the sound was hopelessly wrong: scarcely even present. I could see what had happened. The sound recordist had put a little lapel microphone on the beautifully tailored suit of the Japanese prime minister, and another on mine. (Not so well cut, but I was very fond of it; it was light grey, with a very faint stripe, and I bought it in Piccadilly from a tropical-wear specialist called Airey and Wheeler. The BBC, in those privileged days, paid for it. The very name had a kind of lightweight sound, as though it might have provided me with precisely the kind of white linen effort that Jane Root disliked so much.)

Then, as the interview began, the sound man recorded my questions on the Japanese prime minister's lapel mike, and his answers on my lapel mike. Since we were sitting a good five or six feet from one another, the sound was not strong. My guess is he realized what was happening quite early on, but was too embarrassed to interrupt us and ask us to start again. Back in London, when George and I confronted him with the fact that we had taken him right round the world to do this one job, which he had signally failed to do properly, all he could say was, 'I thought that was how you wanted it.' Soon after that, sound recordists began to be phased out; this one had scarcely done much to prolong the survival of his profession.

George Walker was wonderfully civilized, ever optimistic, Pickwick-waisted, indefatigably jovial and inclined to wear his green Harris Tweed sports jacket and baggy grey trousers even in the steaming heat of a Tokyo summer. I loved him very dearly, and missed him a good deal when he retired. One of his best points was that he realized how important it was to understand a country if you were going to interview its political leaders. As a result, he spent a good deal of money on getting me to Tokyo a week or so before we saw the prime minister, and insisted that I should acclimatize myself while he got on with the mundane business of fixing a place for the interview and organizing translators.

So I just went out and walked the streets. I knew very little about Japan, its people or its culture, and nothing about Tokyo as a city. It shocked, challenged, delighted and surprised me. For a start, I had never been anywhere so expensive. The taxi journey

from Narita Airport to the New Otani Hotel cost me, I calculated, the equivalent of three days' wages and took two hours, less
because of the traffic than because it was just such a very long way
away.

Nowadays, as I write this, it's London that shocks the visitor
with its prices: 'A hundred dollars to get from the airport to the
centre of town?' said an American businessman sitting next to me
at a dinner recently, adding patronizingly, 'Where do you people
get that kind of money from?' But in those days it was Tokyo which
was unthinkably, insanely expensive.

The taxi driver wore white gloves, and he had a gadget in his
cab which warned him gently but insistently that he was on the
point of exceeding the speed limit. When we arrived at the hotel
I paid him, and added around 10 per cent as a tip. He carefully
counted out the money, and handed the tip back to me.

'Thank you,' he said in surprisingly good English, 'but I am
sufficiently paid already.'

Then he pressed a lever and my door opened to let me out. I
was dismissed.

Late that afternoon, after I had listened to the birdsong in the
hotel and had drunk a cup of green tea, I ventured out for a walk.
It made me feel very ignorant and untravelled. I couldn't understand
a single street sign or shop sign or notice. There were huge crowds,
but no one bumped into each other. A kind of mass politeness
ruled; people would stop and bow to their acquaintances, but no
one complained, or shout at them.

There was virtually nothing I could understand. I went into a
huge store that sold electronic goods, but I couldn't even work out
the purpose of most of the gadgets. Passers-by drooped in armchairs, receiving an automated massage. You could listen to music
on small taperecorders: I had stumbled across the Walkman. It felt
as though I had just arrived from some primitive backwater. The
gap between Japan and Europe would narrow over the following
decades, but when Dee and I went to Tokyo, shortly before the
Emperor's visit to London in 1998, we still kept our mobile phones
out of sight: they seemed like bricks compared with the minuscule
ones the Japanese carried.

As evening drew on, and I was still wandering the streets, I began to get hungry. But what were the rules of engagement? I knew nothing about Japanese food, except that they ate a lot of raw fish, and that didn't sound very appetizing. Several times I saw a place that seemed as though it might suit me: the cooks looked friendly, or there was a table free, and the other customers were well dressed. But I was too ignorant and embarrassed to go in. I just walked on.

In the end, hunger forced me into a quiet-looking little place. A couple of businessmen in dark suits sat side by side at the bar. I pointed to a table and raised my eyebrows; the waiter nodded and fussed round me. It was only when I sat down that I realized how small everything around me was, and how big I was. I felt like Alice after she'd eaten her mushroom.

Fortunately, I had brought a book to read. The menu was only in Japanese, but there were photographs of the available dishes, and I pointed to some of them. I must have committed all sorts of solecisms, but the waiter was too polite to tell me. From the reaction of the cooks, though, it was clear that this wasn't how you ordered Japanese food.

I looked round at the other customers. The two men at the bar were just drinking solidly: no food for them. At some of the other tables, people were getting their heads into the trough in a pretty intense way; I could hear them right across the restaurant. In later years, when Japanese people started coming to Britain to study and work and live, and Japanese restaurants became familiar sights in the streets of London, I used to eat a lot of Japanese food. By that stage it had been explained to me what you do and how you do it, and I no longer felt like a country bumpkin.

Once, in one of my favourite Japanese restaurants in Covent Garden, I sat on my own, near an attractive Japanese girl whose almost perfect English when she ordered showed that she lived in London. Her parents were with her, obviously visiting from Japan, and although her mother was attractive and well dressed, her father was a pretty rough diamond. To her obvious embarrassment, he slurped his noodles with loud relish, gripping his chopsticks in a big hand. Her mother, who might well have done the same back home, appreciated that she had to eat more quietly and carefully in a Western restaurant; the girl herself looked at me as though she were mortified that I had seen the reality of the life she had left behind her.

In that first Japanese restaurant I ever went to, in Tokyo back in 1979, slurping was *de rigueur*. At that stage, I didn't know what to do with the little white or green cones of condiment, or when to drink *sake* or green tea. But having nowhere else to go, I sat there for a long time, looking round and trying to work everything out. So long that the two businessmen drinking Scotch got completely, utterly legless. They raised their voices to a level I had come to think that no Japanese person would reach. In the end, one of them slumped down on the counter, and the barman and the other businessman helped him through the door. A taxi took them off into the night.

Several days later, when our translator began to explain things to me, I realized I had been witnessing one of the most important, and perhaps necessary, rituals of company life. One of the two businessmen was the boss, the other was an employee. During the day you would treat your superior with the greatest respect. But after work, by mutual agreement, you could go to a bar with him, drink a lot and tell him everything you thought about him. *And it didn't count.* The next morning you would greet each other with the usual politeness, and there would be not the slightest indication that only a few hours earlier you had been telling him in the greatest detail what a swine he was. It's a remarkable tradition, which is now starting to fade a little; but it makes office life bearable in a country where there are few other ways of letting off steam.

§

It had never happened to me before, and it has never happened since, but when I went to Japan in 1998 with the notion of making a film about the Emperor and Empress, I was the only male in an otherwise all-woman team. I don't know what the Japanese thought about it, but I found it delightful. Dee was with me, because we were hoping to do at least two editions of our programme, *Simpson's World*. The news producer was Sarah Whitehead. The researcher was Farne Sinclair, who was in charge of my office at Television Centre in London. And the camera work was to be done by Louise Kerslake, who was slightly built and very attractive, and the exact opposite of the traditional idea of a television camera operator, big and tough and very male. Yet Louise had worked in some dangerous and difficult places, and lugged all the gear around as well.

We had been given two minders by the Japanese government: a senior official in his fifties, and a young woman in her twenties who was probably his equivalent of Farne Sinclair. They met us off the long flight from London, and seemed not to have realized that four of our team would be women. But if they were surprised, they certainly didn't show it. In fact they didn't show anything very much, then or later.

They were charming and quite conversational as we set out on the two-hour drive to the New Otani, but it was clear to us right from the start that they weren't there to ensure that we got what we wanted. Instead, their job was to stop us making a nuisance of ourselves. They listened with the utmost politeness to all our ideas about what we wanted to do, and nodded judiciously, and talked about making a note of it and ensuring a satisfactory result.

But by the following day we would understand that nothing we wanted was going to happen. My initial idea, of spending a day with the imperial couple, had never been a starter; that I soon realized. But the polite enthusiasm everyone had shown gave me the clear impression that we would at least be able to follow the Emperor and Empress around for a few days, and film them at public occasions when they met people and went about their duties.

Still our minders had their own very clear ideas about what we should do.

'Today we have arranged an opportunity for you to film Japanese *ikebana* ceremony. This will be very good for your programme.'

'What's *ikebana*?'

I cursed my ignorance and stupidity, but I had an idea I shouldn't agree to his big proposal until I knew exactly what it was all about.

'Flower arranging,' Dee hissed.

'I see. So the Emperor is going to be there?'

There was a momentary silence.

'His Imperial Majesty will not attend.'

'So why are we going to film it?'

'It will be very interesting for you.'

'Not if the Emperor isn't there, it won't be.'

He smiled politely, as if I were a tiresome six-year-old.

'We should leave in one hour's time.'

I looked at the others. We didn't have any alternative to propose; we were in the minders' hands.

'Then I suppose we could come back at around lunch-time and make some arrangements to film the Emperor tomorrow.'

Another of these brief, alarming silences.

'What time will we get back?' Louise asked.

'The *ikebana* ceremony will last six hours. A hundred women will be taking part.'

I'm not at my best in circumstances like this. I lack the gene for patience. Also for politeness under stress. But the more I fumed, the more polite our minder became, and the more mask-like his face looked. By now he had lost the faint Westernness that he had originally shown. He had taken to bowing when he met us, and when he left. He would take a sudden step back, and just as I was starting to take a step towards him to close the gap, his head would go down very politely and very low. Sometimes our crania missed each other by a fraction of an inch.

I remembered what an American translator I had hired in Beijing at the time of the Tiananmen Square demonstrations had told me. He was a delightful man of around thirty, whose major (perhaps sole) interest in life was getting Asian girls to go to bed with him. This had led him to learn both Mandarin and Japanese, and it had worked so well that several Chinese people – girls, as it happens – told me that his Chinese was almost flawless. A Japanese newspaper correspondent said the same about his Japanese. When I asked him, in a rather facile moment, to compare the two countries, he told me that speaking Chinese drew Chinese people to him more closely; in this case he didn't just mean girls. By contrast, he said, when Japanese people found his Japanese was so good, they would retreat behind a second line of defence to keep him at a distance. The language was a great barrier, but there were so many others that they were always successful.

As for the barriers between us and the imperial couple, they seemed to be greater with each day that passed. Two more British journalists, witty and pleasant, arrived from London to join us. The chief minder referred to us collectively as 'the Pens'. We started to work as a group, *The Times*, the *Daily Telegraph* and the BBC together, in case that gave us greater leverage. It gave us, of course, nothing of the sort.

But it did give us a sumptuous, memorable lunch. The three of us went to see the head of the imperial household, a man of immense grandeur and courtesy, whose English was as good as mine, if not better. He had studied at Oxford, like a number of the top civil servants we came across, and he had a very clear understanding of what we wanted. And yet, as the lunch went on and on, and more dishes came to test our ingenuity and appetite, it became obvious that there was nothing doing in this quarter either.

The two journalists, Alan Hamilton and Robert Hardman, must have grown very bored with my sales pitch, yet we all believed in it to a greater or lesser extent. If we had access to the Emperor and Empress, we could all report about their charm and kindness and erudition and general peace-loving qualities, and this would present a very different and far more positive view of them to the British public. I outlined the ghoulish possibility of the Emperor riding down the Mall during his state visit and being yelled at and hissed by large numbers of ex-prisoners of war and their families.

'This is something we all want to avoid,' I said piously, though I was really only using the whole issue as a ticket to meet and film the Emperor. Still, I rather liked what I had heard about him, and genuinely hoped his visit would be a success. It would be nice if it also led to some attractive television.

The august figure on the other side of the table let slip that the Emperor himself was quite nervous about the possibility of some kind of physical or verbal violence.

'Well, there's an easy way of ensuring it doesn't turn out like that,' I said, and the other two Pens nodded.

'You see, there are wheels within wheels,' replied the head of palace protocol, or whatever he was, in his perfect English.

Here, it seemed to me, was a case of a reverse linguistic barrier. The imperial official spoke such wonderful English that he knew how to be evasive in my native tongue as well as his.

By this time I was getting really desperate. This was an expensive trip, and we hadn't turned over a foot of film. (Expressions like this merely show my age. Not only have we not used film in British television news since 1980, but video isn't and couldn't be measured in feet and inches.) The Emperor must be doing something which we could film in the next couple of days.

'I'll look into it. I'm sure he will be. And I'm equally sure you will have a ringside seat.'

That sounded good, and it wasn't just the *sake* talking, or listening either. I went back to my all-female team and boasted of my success. They cheered up too.

Even the minder seemed to unbend a little. His bows, I felt, were a little less solemn; perhaps, I told myself, they were even getting a bit perfunctory. We were working on him successfully.

The next day he came to the New Otani immediately after breakfast, and was positively enthusiastic.

'It has been arranged. Their Imperial Majesties will attend the opening of a chrysanthemum nursery – you say nursery? – tomorrow. It is near Tokyo. We will drive there, and you will have everything you have been asking for.'

'What, everything? We'll be able to film the Emperor and Empress, and meet them?'

'Such is my understanding,' he said, in his gorgeous but slightly antiquated English.

Somehow, listening to him always reminded me of staring at a hugely expensive vintage Jaguar or Bentley through the window of a car showroom in somewhere like Berkeley Square. He spoke showroom English of a particularly grand type. It certainly wasn't for everyday use. I don't suppose he had ever intentionally used a slang expression, except in verbal inverted commas.

But for the first time since I met him, I felt happy. I even tried a little bow of my own, though I stood back far enough to avoid a clash of heads along goalmouth lines.

§

Before this glorious and, I was made to realize, entirely unprecedented opportunity arose, we were to film an edition of *Simpson's World*. We had already recorded one, walking with the BBC Tokyo correspondent along one of the main shopping streets in central

Tokyo, and ending up in a sushi bar, talking to anyone who would speak to us. It had turned out particularly well, and was as interesting visually as it was in terms of thoughts and ideas. I was proud of the way we went about filming *Simpson's World*, and to my surprise it had proved to be both popular and, within the television news industry, influential.

I have always hated the artificiality of television programmes: that dreadful, stupid business of having male and female newsreaders sitting side by side and reading alternate paragraphs off the autocue, for instance. They look like two parrots; what is worse, each gazes at the camera or at the other reader with an entirely ersatz affection and interest when not reading the autocue. They talk in a kind of mad journalese: 'Going to ground – how three coal miners found themselves trapped in Scotland,' or 'The forty-one-year-old father of three later explained to us what he was doing.'

Or there is that ludicrous business when the newsreader introduces some other poor freak who is standing in the studio, and the poor freak begins as though he's talking to the newsreader – 'Well, Arthur, it happened this way' – but then turns creakily to the camera and starts addressing the rest of us, as though we've just been eavesdropping up to that point, and don't really count. Who behaves like this in real life? Or doesn't television have anything to do with real life?

Then ... but I shouldn't get started, it's probably bad for my blood pressure, and it's certainly bad for my career. In any television organization, not just the BBC, they expect you to enthuse about the fashion of the day, as though you actually like it. Well, I don't like it. I think television ought to be as relaxed, as free and easy, as natural and calm and pleasant and understandable, as speaking to someone in your own office or sitting room. I don't like television news to be artificial. It feels like one of those people who smile at you as you are walking down the street, but only to get you into conversation so they can extract money from you for a charity you've never previously been interested in.

When we started *Simpson's World* I wanted to create a programme which would be natural. Where I could just tell people where I was, and why, and start to show them what it really looked like. It would be a half-hour in the life of the place where I happened to find myself. It wouldn't be edited or polished up, it would just be what it really was. Real life: I suppose I should describe it as anti-television.

And it proved moderately successful. Television organizations around the world imitated the formula; there is even an exact copy on Iran's 24-hour English-language news channel (I bet you've never thought Iran would have a 24-hour news television channel in English – confess it), and an old boy with white hair introduces it. If that's not a rip-off, I don't know what it is; except that the Iranians were charmingly open about it and, I liked to think, proud of it. And once, when I was in Iran, they actually had me as a guest on it. What was more, the old boy (who was probably a few years younger than me) asked me some really good questions.

> *Interviewer:* Now, Mr Simpson, you have said several times that the BBC is completely independent of the British government. But I would like to ask you, how can it be independent if it is paid for by the British government?
>
> *JS (taken by surprise, since we had just been talking about something entirely different):* Well, most of the BBC is paid for by the people of the United Kingdom, who have to pay a licence fee. Only one part of the BBC is paid for by the government, and that's the World Service on radio.
>
> *Interviewer (smiling, because he thinks he's got me on the ropes):* But the British government must tell it what to say.
>
> *JS (now a bit more settled):* No, because it is made up of the same people and uses many of the same reports as the rest of BBC News does. And the same rules about impartiality apply to BBC World Service as they do to the rest of the BBC.
>
> *Interviewer (cunningly):* I don't think many people here would understand this. If your government pays out a lot of money for the BBC, then surely it expects to get its money's worth? It must want the BBC only to say the things it wants?
>
> *JS (slightly desperately, because this is a good argument which, although not actually true will appeal to most Iranians, and turning a fraction nasty as a result):* That might be true here in Iran. But in Britain the government and the people value the

BBC's independence, and think that is part of the benefit the government gets for its money.

If only, I thought, successive British governments had always been mature enough to value the extraordinary benefit of having an independent broadcasting service. But of course the Thatcher government and the Blair government, in particular, put immense pressure on the BBC; and so did other political parties from time to time. The only way to deal with that is to show toughness in reply. The following dialogue is reconstructed from various accounts, and while I can't vouch for the precise wording, the level of menace and aggression is certainly right, and so is the response. It happened during the years of the Blair government, immediately after one rather fraught programme had just ended.

> *Phone rings. The programme editor looks round the room; no one else is available to pick it up.*
> *Editor (in a tired voice, as though he shouldn't be troubled like this):* Yes?
> *Political Spokesman:* That was a fucking shameful piece of shit you just broadcast, and you should be fucking ashamed of yourself for putting it out. Your standards are getting lower and lower, and you can't tell the difference between the truth and a piece of shit lying on the pavement. That stuff about . . . [and so on and on, with the scatological and faecal element heavily stressed].
> *Editor:* Can I just make a point here?
> *Spokesman:* Go on.
> *Editor:* Fuck off. *(Puts phone down.)*

That, believe me, is the way that people who behave like this should be dealt with. I don't necessarily advocate the bad language, but when it is liberally poured over your own head, that is sometimes the only fitting response. What doesn't work, if you have people like Alistair Campbell or his imitators around, is meekness, or worse, something that can be mistaken for contrition. That is a betrayal of the principle of independence. The only response to a bullying and aggressive government is to be robust.

I would have liked to tell this story to the *Simpson's World* rip-off on Iranian television, but I felt it might not be entirely understood.

We recorded the programme, incidentally, walking round and round the lobby of the Laleh (once the InterContinental) Hotel in Tehran. It was two o'clock on a July afternoon, and the heat outside was ferocious. Even so, if my team and I had wanted to film something at that time, we would certainly have done it outside, and sweated the necessary buckets. Perhaps there is a touch of 'Mad Dogs and Englishmen' about it, but the looks of the programme do come before our own comfort, and a half-hour discussion filmed walking round and round a hotel lobby is, to say the least, boring for the viewers. It also goes against the grain of the original idea. *Simpson's World* was designed to ensure that people would have something interesting to look at. Not matter how much I like the Laleh Hotel, and I certainly do, the reception desk, the transport desk and Mr Mozafarian's antiques shop exert only a limited fascination.

This business of wanting to get an interesting background can go too far, though. A year or so ago I recorded a *Simpson's World* in Baghdad with the Iraqi foreign minister. As we had expected, his officials wanted us to record the interview in his office, with him sitting behind his desk. Impossible, I said; we will have to walk round somewhere. But it's dangerous round here, the officials replied; we think there are snipers in the building opposite. Oh, I said patronizingly, I very much doubt that. But if there are, we'll make sure to keep out of their line of sight.

The officials were still resisting when the minister himself came into the room.

'Well,' he said to the officials, 'if the BBC wants to film it outside, walking round the little garden, that's fine by me.'

'But minister, it could be dangerous.'

'I said I'd do it.'

'But—'

We did it outside. I was a little surprised by the numbers of heavily armed bodyguards the minister brought with him, but they added to the interest of the shot.

Particularly when a bomb went off nearby, and there was a wild outbreak of shooting. The bodyguards ducked and jinked around behind the minister, but he kept on talking and answering my questions as calmly as if we were in St James's Park in London. By mistake, I took a wrong turn in front of the building, and of course everyone – minister, our team, his team – had to come with me. We continued to stroll along, with the cameraman moving elegantly round us. This time, I noticed in passing, we didn't have so many bodyguards with us. Eventually I led us round the corner of the building and in through the main entrance. There was quite a lot of shooting by now, and even I realized it was pretty close.

'Well,' said the minister calmly, 'that was all very exciting.'

He didn't mean my questions. We had spent the last four or five minutes in clear view of the flats where snipers were indeed operating, and quite a few shots had been fired in our direction. No wonder some of the bodyguards had decided it wasn't worth the risk of coming with us. I was impressed by the foreign minister, though. He'd known just how close the bullets were coming, but he kept on answering the questions calmly. And me? Well, there are definite advantages to being a little deaf.

There would be no gunfire on the soundtrack of our second *Simpson's World* in Tokyo. We would film it in a beautiful little park, and then go into the magnificent Shinto shrine which stood on one side of it. Our guests were a Japanese woman who spoke excellent English, plus three elderly men who had fought with the Japanese army in the Second World War. They had all been in Burma, where my Uncle Alan had done his fighting. How annoyed he would have been with me! Yet he would certainly have wanted to watch the programme. One of the reasons he suffered his fatal heart attack, thirty years earlier, was that he had been dashing back to see me appear on *University Challenge*.

The old men were remarkably well preserved, and looked good in their identical dark blue blazers and light-coloured trousers. I had turned down one of the guests our Japanese fixer had suggested: a leading light in the former Kamikaze pilots' association. I felt that too many of our 300 million viewers would share my feeling that he represented a classic case of failure.

The subject of our programme was the Emperor's forthcoming

visit to Britain, and the after-effects of the war on the way Japanese and British people thought about each other. The Japanese had often behaved with outrageous cruelty, most of it directed at prisoners and at Chinese and other people in Asia. Recently, for instance, an elderly Japanese doctor confessed that during the war he had cut out the livers, kidneys and other organs from living people in the Philippines, including young girls, using no form of anaesthetic. An army officer ordered him to do it, and watched as he did so. The doctor says he realizes now that it was wrong, but at the time he was just obeying orders.

My courage failed me as I spoke to the three gentle, dignified old boys in their blazers, as they sat there in the dappled sunlight in front of the shrine. Could they have committed any atrocities themselves? Perfectly possibly. But I hadn't invited them onto *Simpson's World* to be interviewed about that, and it seemed unreasonable to spring such a question on them. Alan would have been proud of me, I know, but a large number of viewers would certainly have thought it was in bad taste.

'Do you think the Emperor and Empress should visit Britain?'

They did. The war had ended a very long time ago, they said, and Britain and Japan had had the friendliest relations ever since. Even at the time, they said, they had had no bitterness against the British; they had merely been soldiers, under orders, and they believed it was exactly the same for the British.

I asked them a few more difficult questions, about reparations for the countries the Japanese had invaded, and about the so-called 'comfort women' who had been forced to prostitute themselves to the Japanese soldiers. But their answers were calm and unexceptionable and dignified: yes, if the Japanese army had done things that were wrong, they should pay for it. That was only right.

One of them had even been to Britain and had met a group of British ex-soldiers from the Burma campaign. Face to face, the elderly Japanese man said, the British had been very polite and correct. It seemed that they hadn't asked any awkward questions either. Perhaps, like me, they found his air of calmness and dignity impossible to penetrate.

'Would you be prepared to sacrifice your life for the Emperor now?'

'Ah, things have changed so much in Japan and in the world. I
cannot think I would be called on to make such a sacrifice.'

'No, but if you had to?'

But I wasn't getting anywhere. And of course he was right. You
had at least to be in your late seventies to have much idea of what
Emperor-worship meant. Not many of the old attitudes, and scarcely
anything of the old Tokyo, had survived the war and the devastating
bombing Japan had suffered. For the most part, it was a new country,
with new attitudes. And the attitudes which had gone before were on
their way to being forgotten.

§

It was starting to look good for our hopes of filming the Emperor
and Empress in some fairly close up and intimate way. It wouldn't be
the fly-on-the-wall access I had originally asked the Japanese ambassador for at the Buckingham Palace banquet, but you never get
everything you ask for. Being able to accompany them on their visit
to the chrysanthemum nursery would be fascinating. Of course we
would have to be discreet, and make sure we didn't block their way
or irritate them, but Louise had had plenty of experience of filming
the British royal family, and she would, I knew, be tactful.

As for me, I would probably have to fade into the background
most of the time. A large Westerner getting between the imperial
couple and the crowds would probably be most unpopular. But in
television journalism the important thing is that the camera should
be able to see the event. Often, it's only when you look carefully at
the pictures a few times that you begin to understand what you have
witnessed with your own eyes.

Only Louise and I were to be allowed to go to the chrysanthemum
nursery, together with Alan and Robert. The rest of our team were
barred. I took that as a good sign: they would never tell the others
that they couldn't come unless we were going to get really close to
the imperial couple.

It took us a long time to reach the nursery, which was on the
distant outskirts of Tokyo. The nearby town was mostly modern, yet
it had been rebuilt after the bombing along the old lines. Late that
afternoon, as we arrived, people were shuffling down the street to the
public bath in their slippers and dressing gowns; quiet and earnest as

they went, relaxed and pink from the hot water and laughing noisily as they came back.

The morning of our encounter with the Emperor and Empress was cloudy, and we could scarcely see Mount Fuji from where we were. It reared up quite close to the little town, almost absurd in its beauty, its indented top white with the snow that scarcely ever melts. We were lectured again about not getting in the way of the imperial couple, not speaking to them, not filming them if we were asked not to, not coming between them and anybody who wanted to speak to them. It was all completely self-evident, but in order to keep the swarm of officials happy – they gathered round us like midges, each with his or her little piece of advice and warning – we nodded and smiled and said of course that was how we would behave.

'The important thing,' one of them confided to me, as though he knew this was a very difficult thing for me to grasp, 'is not to trouble the Emperor in any way.'

'Or the Empress,' I added gently.

Having been rebuked so often myself for leaving her out of the conversation, that felt good.

'Ah, yes, or the Empress, of course.'

At long last we boarded the bus which was to take us to the nursery.

'Why are there so many snappers and cameras here?' Louise said to me. 'I thought this was just intended for us.'

I'd thought the same thing.

'We will have good access to the Emperor, won't we?' I asked the most senior official there – a mildly obsessive character who did a lot of head-counting and had told me at least three times that we mustn't obstruct the people's view of the Emperor.

'And the Empress,' he said. 'Yes, you will have very clear access. No one will be in your way.'

'Thank you,' I said, but I still felt a little unsettled. After all, we would need enough material to fill a twenty-five-minute programme; that meant we would have to film for at least fifty minutes or an hour. In the normal way you discard at least three times as much as you use. Nowadays, with video so cheap, no one cares about the old business of usage ratio, but in the days of film you had to husband your footage very carefully because it was so expensive. Anything more than a three-to-one ratio was looked on with disapproval.

In a way it was good, since it encouraged precise and thoughtful filming. Yet somehow the camera was almost never switched on when something vital happened.

A film magazine lasted little more than fifteen minutes, and changing it was a complex and time-consuming business. Some of the world's most important events happened when a cameraman had his hands inside a black changing bag, winding the film on. Even in these days of instantaneous everything, there are some cameramen who always seem to be switched off when something important happens, just as there were cameramen in the days of film who never seemed to miss anything, just as there are now. It's not a technical question, fundamentally; it's a matter of what Jeeves would call the psychology of the individual.

I have never seen so many chrysanthemums in my life. They filled the enormous glasshouses with their magnificent, noble blooms in every imaginable colour. Sometimes, in a florist's, I smell that distinctive, almost musky perfume and am instantly transported back to the vast nursery where we first saw the Emperor and Empress. It was like being in the hot-house at Kew Gardens. The temperature was distinctly warm, and the smell of the flowers made it heavy. It was the kind of place where, if you had to wait a long time, you would want to look for somewhere quiet and comfortable to lie down. The Japanese especially, since they are adept at taking cat-naps in the most unusual places. I was once invited to a lunch in order to brief the Japanese foreign minister before a major international conference about what was happening, and should happen, in Iraq, and just as I was getting to the good part I saw him nodding off over his prawn tempura. I quite often have that effect on people, but I do expect them to show a bit of embarrassment afterwards. Not the Japanese foreign minister. He seemed to feel the briefing had gone particularly well, so perhaps it was better that way.

There must have been a couple of dozen cameramen and photographers at the nursery, all of them Japanese. Everyone kept looking at us, or, more precisely, at Louise. No one I asked seemed to recall seeing a camerawoman before.

'I suppose they'll pull us out of the crowd and take us to where the Emperor comes in,' I said doubtfully to her.

I could see she didn't feel any too confident either.

'Just as long as they let me move around and get some decent shots. And we'll have to get in quite close for the sound.'

Directional microphones of the kind Louise had brought are quite good, but if you are making a twenty-five-minute programme you need high-quality sound. And that means getting reasonably close – within fifteen feet, say.

Louise is slight, not particularly tall, and looks delicate; but I had seen her operate before, and knew how good she was at getting in close through a crowd of policemen and minders and other journalists. It's not a matter of bulk or size or strength, it's a matter of intelligence and attitude. The justly famous, long-serving photographer of the *Observer*, Neil Libbert, was one of the quietest and most polite of men; yet I was once at an important meeting in London which John Major, then prime minister, was to attend. For some reason, the entire world's press was barred from seeing what was going to happen. All the other photographers were carrying electronic cameras with monstrous lenses; Neil just had his small, battered Leica hanging unprofessionally round his neck. If he had any accreditation, he had hidden it away. He walked over to the line of policemen who were pushing the cameramen back.

'Excuse me,' he said to the sergeant in his usual gentle manner, 'but I wonder if I might . . . ?'

'Yeah, go on, dad,' said the sergeant. 'Now then, not you lot.'

Neil ambled through, pursued by the angry shouts of Fleet Street's finest, and got the essential picture of the occasion.

Louise was more assertive than that; as a woman, she had to be. But she too got her pictures by wit, not by muscle power.

We took up what we hoped would be an easy position for the officials to call us out and take us over to the Emperor. We were on the right-hand side of the longish line of press.

One of the worst of the minders now appeared: fussy, querulous, obsequious to her own authorities but inclined to be imperious with us. My spirits drooped like an unwatered chrysanthemum.

'I have to be with you,' she said. It didn't sound as though she'd volunteered. 'I will tell you what you must do.'

Louise and I exchanged a pessimistic glance.

'You must stand here. You must not talk or call out. You must not put your feet across the line here' – for the first time I noticed there was one – 'and when I tell you to stop your camera, you must stop it at once.'

For an instant neither of us could speak.

'But we can't just stand in one place,' Louise said at last. 'We've got to move about in order to get interesting, varied pictures. Anyway, how far away will the Emperor be?'

'He'll be over there. With the Empress, of course.' She pointed to a spot about twenty yards away, through the chrysanthemums and the thick atmosphere.

'But we'll never get a decent shot of him at that distance. And we won't be able to hear anything he says.'

The minder didn't seem to feel that was her problem.

'One more thing. I will tell you to stop after two minutes. No more filming after that.'

I finally found my voice.

'Two minutes? That's absurd! We've got to make a twenty-five-minute documentary out of this.'

The minder didn't seem to feel that was her problem either.

There was no real point in arguing much more. She was the most senior minder in sight, and it would be absolutely impossible for us to break away from the line of cameramen on our own.

At that moment, it became clear the imperial couple were on their way. Louise focused up on the place where they would appear.

There was nothing for me to do except curse under my breath. They knew perfectly well what we wanted; they seemed to have agreed to give us at least some of it, but now we would have less material than we would need for a brief and boring news report of the Emperor and Empress examining a few flowers. It was probably the farthest I had ever travelled, and the most money I had ever spent, to record such a minor, untelevisual occasion. I was in a frenzy of anger and recrimination; but the minder put her finger to her lips.

'There can be no talking when His Imperial Majesty is present.'

That was clearly untrue, since the other journalists were all grunt-

ing and sweating in the heat and muttering to each other as the
Emperor and his wife came nearer.

Because Louise is a clever camerawoman, she managed to get
some beautiful and crafty shots from the one immovable position in
which she had to stand. But it was pretty hopeless.

She wasn't going to surrender easily, though.

'Stop filming now!' hissed the minder.

Louise took no notice. The imperial couple wandered on, with
various obsequious characters showing them more and more different types of flower.

'I said you must stop filming!'

Still no notice.

'There can be no talking while His Imperial Majesty is here,' I
said. That made me feel better.

Even so, we got only about four minutes of pictures. I eventually
found the head of the minders and began to rail at him. He smiled
politely, he apologized, he rebuked me in the gentlest, nicest way for
being hostile to our minder, and he was sorry if I had misunderstood
what had been arranged.

'You will, however, have the honour of being presented to Their
Imperial Majesties this coming Thursday.'

That calmed me down immediately.

'Will we be able to film?'

'Alas, no. But there will be an imperial cameraman on hand who
will record everything.'

'And I can use the pictures?'

'Most certainly.'

'Ah.'

I stopped complaining.

Yet strangely our complaints bore immediate fruit, of a small but
exquisite kind. No one told us what was happening, but the minders
somehow managed to get rid of everyone else, and set us down on
the platform of the nearby railway station.

'You should put your camera here,' one of them told Louise.

She set up her tripod, obedient but mystified.

Fifteen minutes later, just as we were suspecting a further waste
of our time, the train in which the imperial couple were travelling
back to Tokyo drew in and their carriage stopped immediately

opposite us. More than that: they were sitting at the window just where we had set up. The Empress was facing the engine, the Emperor had his back to it, and they were looking at each other and talking quietly as Louise filmed them.

And then something delightful and rather magical happened. The Emperor happened to glance round and see us. He turned back to the Empress, and told her (I later discovered) that the BBC was there; both of them were enthusiastic viewers of BBC World. Then they turned to us and our camera, and bowed their heads in greeting. It was one of the most charming things I have ever seen, to watch these two delicate, beautiful, highly bred people greet us with such exquisite politeness. Their heads were still inclined as the train began to pull out of the station.

§

Despite the appalling destruction wrought in Japan by the Allies at the end of the Second World War, despite the conscious efforts of the Americans to rebuild the country in America's own image afterwards, despite Japan's immense success in becoming the second richest nation in the world, it has somehow managed to keep a stronger grip on its own character and its past than any other of the world's economic powerhouses.

Dee and I once took the train from Tokyo to the old capital, Kyoto. No one in Japan seems to know what foreigners mean if they call it 'the bullet train'; in Japanese it is called the Shinkansen, meaning simply 'the new trunk line'. At the terminus, immensely crowded and yet surprisingly quiet and orderly, we fortified ourselves for the trip by buying some sushi and a couple of *bento* boxes at one of the long line of food stalls. We pointed at things, and the girl behind the counter packed them all neatly into a couple of paper bags, together with chopsticks, pickles and napkins. She was efficient and businesslike, though hardly friendly.

No one took any notice of us, and to find the platform for Kyoto I had in the end to stop a hurrying passer-by with an apologetic '*sumimasen*'. He stopped, pointed quickly, and hurried on his way. But that doesn't constitute rudeness in Japan; what does, is bumping into people or staring at them aggressively in the eye. In other words, Westerners behave remarkably rudely in Japan without meaning to.

Fortunately the Japanese know enough about the outside world nowadays to understand that we are not being deliberately impolite.

The train was clean in a way that only those of us in Britain who can remember the 1950s could imagine, and for once it wasn't too full. Now that Europe has trains of its own which travel at more than 250 miles per hour, the Shinkansen no longer seems unthinkably advanced, except in its service. A hostess, flawlessly made up, pushed a little trolley down the aisle. It seemed to contain everything, from American fizzy drinks to quite rare single malts. Two salary men opposite us ordered whisky, and were given crystal goblets to drink it from.

Kyoto survived the war virtually intact. There is a modern section, which is indistinguishable from any other city in Japan, but old Kyoto is one of the most charming and interesting places on earth, largely unchanged from the fifteenth century. Our taxi driver, who managed to turn his few words of English into an expression or two of quite remarkable charm and politeness, took us in his quite preternaturally clean and shining cab into Gion in the old part of Kyoto, with its narrow cobbled streets and its houses which lean towards one another and almost touch. He left us, still smiling and bowing over the steering wheel, and we crossed a little bridge, only a few feet wide, over a narrow waterway, the Shirakawa canal. The bridge led directly to the front door of the *ryokan*, or inn, where we would be staying – the Shiraume. Its little *noren* curtains, hanging over the entrance, showed it was open for business.

We pushed our way through them. In the small hallway, a young maid in a kimono greeted us on her knees, bowing her head to the polished floor. Bowing is an arcane art, and a Japanese friend of ours had warned us not even to try it.

'People don't expect you to, so they won't be put out if you don't. But if you do bow, and you get it wrong, they might well be offended.'

The way you make your bow, the deepness of it, the time you spend with your head lowered, are all carefully calibrated according to the relative age and importance of bower and bowee. And because no one would indeed have expected me to know these things, I just stood and smiled, and Dee did the same.

The *ryokan* was owned and run by a woman and her daughter, who had once worked for JAL as a stewardess and so spoke a certain amount of English and was familiar with the alarming and curious ways in which foreigners, particularly Westerners, behaved. The young woman led us, down a narrow wood-panelled corridor to our room, and slid open the *fusuma*, the rice-paper and bamboo door. It made not the slightest sound as it moved. The room was entirely empty except for a small low table, a flower arrangement and a couple of *zabutons*, or floor cushions. This was where we would eat and sleep.

Everything combined to make me feel vast and clumsy: my clothes, our big cases (though we thought we were packing remarkably lightly), my great clumping shoes which I had handed over at the entrance, my entire being, which seemed to take up at least half of our six-*tatami* room. (A *tatami* is a mat of woven straw, made to a standard shape and size so that it is usual to measure a room by how many *tatamis* it requires to cover the floor.) At this stage there were no futons for us to sleep on. They would be brought to the room and laid out later.

When did we want our *on-sen*, our bath, and when did we want *kaiseki*, our dinner? At six and seven respectively, we said, and the onetime stewardess backed out through the silent *fusuma*, bowing as she went. Dee and I looked at each other: this was stranger than anything we had imagined. At that moment the *fusuma* opened again, and a maid appeared with a teapot and two cups and two rolled-up hot towels. She was in the room and on her knees before we had realized it.

The *on-sen* was less of an ordeal than I had expected, though I still had the feeling of being in a completely wrong dimension as we shuffled down the corridor in our *yukatas*, thin cotton dressing gowns. The sleeves on mine only just came below my elbows, and I felt as though I might burst out of the entire thing at any moment. As we passed we glanced out at the tiny, delightful courtyard with its carefully raked sand, its minute tree, and its solitary, minuscule rock. The bath, fortunately, turned out to be just the right size: quite a lot bigger than a Western bath, but the same general shape, and made of some impervious wood.

It was full of near-boiling water, clear and green, and seemed to be the source of a strong and very pleasant smell of camphor. But Dee, who had been shown around earlier by the ex-JAL stewardess, warned me not to get into it yet. The bath was for relaxing, not washing; that was done on a tiny stool, under a shower.

It was dusk by the time we emerged, wearing our dressing gowns and shuffling along in our slippers, though I could scarcely be said to be wearing my slippers at all since they were far too small and merely balanced on my toes.

We took a brief stroll before dinner. The narrow streets seemed magical in the thickening light, and three or four geishas emerged from their houses, their faces white and their valuable kimonos wrapped around them, picking their way carefully on their delicate sandals. They scarcely looked at us as they passed. It was a heart-stoppingly beautiful sight, and one that seemed too good to spoil with flashlight and photographs, as though the geishas were beautiful animals in a zoo. The impression they made was on the mind and the spirit and the emotions, not on an electronic disc.

Once there would have been dozens of them, going off to amuse tired and bored males with their conversation, their music and their beauty. Now, the art of the geisha is well in decline; yet perhaps we should be more surprised that it has lasted as long as it has, and kept the past alive so faithfully and beautifully. And we should be glad that, in the degraded age of McDonald's and Starbucks, such traditions are maintained at all.

Kaiseki was everything Dee, who had been to the Shiraume before, had promised me it would be. The daughter, with her gentle looks and her pleasant English, would come in silently with course after course – twelve of them altogether. They were designed to appeal to each of the senses, and the little plates they were served on imitated the nature of the dish itself. They took us through a range of culinary experiences, from the bland to the spicy to the sweet, from the broiled to the roasted to the steamed. I stopped trying to remember them individually, and surrendered to the overall effect, which is what one is supposed to do. And every course would be preceded by hot towels, so that you would feel entirely cleansed and prepared for what was to come next.

Afterwards, the futons were brought in: not thick and lumpy, like those found in British stores, but thin and delicate. I could feel the floor through mine, but I could also hear the water flowing gently below the floor; and that sent me to sleep quickly and easily.

The following morning, we went out to buy prints. I had always been interested in what I called, in my ignorance, kabuki prints. Kabuki is a type of stage performance, highly formalized and unyieldingly traditional, and in the eighteenth and nineteenth centuries in particular its stars were celebrated in woodblock prints. That these were not necessarily regarded as great works of art at the time is evident from the fact that they were used in their hundreds to pack Japanese chinaware which was being exported to the West. Yet as the prints were unpacked in Europe, and saved instead of being thrown away, they helped greatly to feed the growing interest in things Japanese. Their correct name is *ukiyo-e*, which translates as 'images of the transient world'; or, as we would say, 'ephemera'. (The word is Greek, and in the Middle Ages we adopted it to mean a fever which lasts only a single day.)

There was, we knew, one particularly famous dealer in old prints in Kyoto. His shop is the oldest of its kind in the city, though it is in the newer section and is now depressingly surrounded by souvenir shops. Toru Sekigawa-san's shop, Nishiharu, is tiny: a one-*tatami* room, which opens onto the street. Getting into it – after, of course, you have taken your shoes off – feels like climbing into a Punch-and-Judy booth.

Sekigawa-san has a few cabinets, that is all. But if you tell him you are interested in, say, *bijin-ja*, portraits of beautiful courtesans, or the work of Kuniyoshi or Hiroshige, you can expect a cup of tea and a spread of a dozen or more prints to show you. In our case, though his English was halting and our Japanese virtually non-existent, he introduced us to the work of the members of the various members of the Toyokuni family, who produced woodblock prints from the 1790s to the 1860s.

There was, of course, no haggling, but the prices were anyway lower than you would pay outside Japan. He sold us three charming Toyokunis: a Kabuki actor playing the part of a courtesan (in Kabuki, the women's roles are all taken by men), a group of actors looking at the blossoms on a plum tree, and the geisha Naga-taifu. There is a delicacy about the Toyokuni touch which I think I can now recognize. And toothy, smiling, greying Mr Sekigawa himself, kneeling on his mat with the delicate, gently coloured prints laid out in front of him, was a sight as unforgettable as the geishas hobbling elegantly to their evening's work in the gathering dusk.

§

At long last, together with the two other Pens, Alan Hamilton and Robert Hardman, we were to be taken to meet the Emperor and Empress. I would be greatly humiliated if people thought I was a social snob, although I notice from my writing that I am a considerable name-dropper. (Not, I hope, in private conversation, but the habit is quite dangerously catching, and as you get older you like the sound of your own voice even more. Age has many afflictions, and this is one of them.) Snob or not, I found the prospect of meeting a genuine emperor distinctly engaging. I had met and interviewed Emperor Bokassa of the Central African Empire (which reverted to the Central African Republic directly he was overthrown by the French, who, having sold him his entire regalia, found him a bit embarrassing). But that didn't count. There have been dozens, perhaps hundreds of emperors in human history, and for a brief while until 1947 the British monarch was also an emperor/empress – of India. The Queen Mother, whom Dee and I saw at the dinner at which my efforts to make a film about the Japanese imperial family began, was the last of them.

But Japan is the only true empire left. Akihito, born in 1933, succeeded his father, Hirohito, to the Chrysanthemum Throne in 1989 as the 125th emperor of Japan. The Japanese imperial tradition supposedly goes back to 660 BC when the first emperor, Jimmu Tenno, is said to have established his reign. In 1959 Akihito, Hirohito's eldest son, caused great controversy in Japan by marrying a commoner, Michiko, the daughter of a flour magnate. Even to this day there are Japanese people who feel that the monarchy has been somehow damaged by the union.

We were coached beforehand by the court chamberlain about what to wear – just suits and ties – and how to address the imperial couple. In fact, it all seemed very relaxed; none of the business of not speaking until you're spoken to which hangs around the British royal family like a rather tedious cloud from the past.

'It will be very relaxed. His Majesty the Emperor prefers it that way.'

'But will we have to bow?'

'No, no, not at all.'

I understood why this was, of course. In the presence of the Emperor, you are supposed to bow very profoundly. The court officials, knowing that we Pens would certainly get it wrong, felt it would be better if we didn't do it at all.

'And will there be a video camera there?'

'That is certainly the intention.'

'So it will be?'

'We have requested one.'

I let it go, for fear of being a bore. But I think I knew what was going to happen, even then.

The imperial palace is an attractive building, but scarcely impressive or grand. Like so much of Tokyo, it was built in the 1950s, when ornamentation was out and red brick was in. It reminded me rather of one of those colleges at Oxford or Cambridge which were founded or rebuilt after the war; suitably enough, since the imperial couple were rather academic people. Emperor Akihito was an expert on certain types of Japanese fish, and Empress Michiko studied silkworms.

We walked through a line of rooms, pleasantly furnished with items that were probably priceless, and finished up in one so very like a Master's drawing room in Oxford that I expected everybody to be dressed in academic subfusc. Instead, the courtiers wore morning clothes, the daytime equivalent of the white tie and tails I had hired for Buckingham Palace. My slightly baggy grey suit, pressed and cleaned by the hotel laundry, scarcely seemed to match up.

There was no fanfare of trumpets, no squeal of pipes. One moment I was standing with one hand in my trouser pocket, talking to a Japanese grandee with an impeccable English accent, and the next moment we were all in a line watching the slightly built, gentle couple greeting people and bowing back to them. The Emperor passed along the line, and it seemed pretty clear that we Pens were the guests of honour. Should I bow or not? I inclined my head, and if I committed some terrible gaffe everyone was far too polite to tell me. Losing face is such an appalling thing in Japan that you are likely to be the last person to realize it has been lost. And anyway, as a television journalist, I have become accustomed to doing some pretty dreadful things in public. Losing face is no big deal if you've never had much face in the first place.

I looked round: the idea, I had been told, was that the cameraman would video the great moment when the Emperor shook hands with the three British journalists. No cameraman. 'That is certainly the intention,' the grandee had said. He was obviously just being polite and non-confrontational.

All there was, was an old-fashioned photographer with a rather elderly camera, who was wearing a morning suit which didn't fit him terribly well. He seemed constantly in danger of treading on the cuffs of his trousers. But at least he had taken some pictures of the three of us. Given that I had been hoping to get a twenty-five-minute documentary out of this, three still photographs plus a usable thirty seconds of the imperial couple at the chrysanthemum nursery and twenty of them bowing to us from the train window seemed distinctly on the short side: twenty-four minutes short, I would say.

'Come, please.'

A cup of tea was placed in my hand, and I found myself standing with the Emperor and Empress.

'Ah,' said the Emperor.

They both seemed tiny and very fragile, and their skin was almost transparent. But they were wonderfully dressed. You had to be close up to see how wonderfully. While I was registering these things, the Emperor was speaking again. It took me a moment to register.

'My wife and I always watch BBC World, so we saw you.'

'We appreciate BBC World very much,' the Empress murmured.

I didn't quite know what to say.

'But we like most of all the programmes the BBC does about nature. You do them better than anyone else in the world, you know.'

I bowed, like someone in a Jane Austen novel.

'The programmes about fish?' I ventured.

'Ah, yes.'

That was it for a while.

But the Empress seemed to realize I had things I wanted to ask them. She made a beautiful turn in the conversation, like a bird altering direction in mid-air.

'I suppose you are here because of our visit to London.'

I looked at her gratefully.

'Well, I had been hoping to make a documentary . . .'

'Ah,' said the Emperor, with sudden energy, 'but the Court, you know . . .'

'So you knew about our request?'

'People don't always feel these things are, well, suitable.'

His answer was as beautifully tailored as his suit.

'How do you feel about your visit to London?'

'Well, to be honest, I am a little – shall I say nervous?'

'Not for himself, of course,' the Empress said quickly. 'He just hopes there will be no unfortunate incidents which might have a bad effect.'

'That was why . . .'

'I know,' said the Emperor.

And then someone else with a teacup was escorted forward, and it was my time to leave them.

Afterwards I asked the court officials for the photographs of our meeting. They were sent round to our hotel a few hours later. The photographer had managed to station himself in line with the rest of us as the Emperor shook our hands, so in each case what you saw was the Emperor, inclining his head gently and smiling, and an arm and a hand sticking out and shaking his hand. We knew that the hands belonged to the Pens, but it would be hard to persuade a television audience of that.

It was the end of the road. We used the other pictures to quite good advantage, and the imperial couple bowing from the train was much remarked on in our news report. But there was no fly-on-the-wall documentary. Our viewers never heard a word the Emperor or the Empress spoke.

People, as the Emperor said, don't always feel these things are suitable. The court officials had won, hands down. My guess is that they always do.

§

It was a fine, slightly blustery morning in April 1998. I was standing in the Mall in London with a cameraman who was a particularly good friend of mine. He was filming the crowd which had gathered to watch the state procession as the Emperor of Japan drove to Buckingham Palace with the Queen sitting in the coach beside him.

The part of the crowd we were concentrating on was composed of elderly men and women, all of them well turned out, the men mostly in blazers and slacks. Some of them wore their medals. They looked remarkably like the old soldiers I had interviewed in Tokyo.

'We are here,' said the man who seemed to be in charge, 'to register a dignified protest against the visit of the Japanese Emperor to Her Majesty the Queen. As prisoners of war we were often very badly treated, with friends and comrades who never came back, and we have never been properly compensated. We feel it is an insult to us that this man should come here.'

'Well,' I said, 'I've met him, and he's very charming.'

'I'm sure he is, but it's what he represents. His people treated us like savages, and we should never forget that. But as I say, our protest will be very dignified. We don't want to insult Her Majesty in any way.'

'No,' agreed one or two of the others.

'So what are you going to do?'

'Well, in the PoW camps the guards would beat you or even shoot you if you turned your back on them. So as the coach comes past with him in it, we're going to about-turn smartly, and show him our backs. That's the way we're going to get our own back for what was done to us.'

I was about to ask another question, but one of the women called out, 'They're coming now, Charlie!'

We all looked down the Mall. The Queen's coach, and the others with it, was coming towards us. Around them were the Life Guards, their cuirasses shining brilliantly in the morning sunshine, their horses magnificent to see. An officer rode between the coach and the crowd, and when he saw our group he fell back just a fraction. It was skilfully done, and you scarcely noticed it; but it meant that he was blocking the Emperor's eyeline at the critical moment as he came up to our group.

The former PoWs came to attention, and the man I'd interviewed barked an order.

'Company, a-bout turn!'

The old men in their blazers, their medals swinging and clashing on their chests, turned their backs as one. It was their revenge: quiet, peaceful and dignified.

But there were a couple of men with them who, at the last moment, couldn't bring themselves to do it.

'Yah, you old bastard!' they shouted, and flashed the Emperor a V-sign.

It might have been a real insult if the Emperor had noticed. But their V-signs were given to the flanks of a particularly handsome horse of the Life Guards, and the only response was the amused glance of the officer in the saddle.

'Did you get the V-sign?' I asked the cameraman.

'Did you really want it?'

'I'm not sure. I suppose so.'

'Well, I'm afraid I didn't.'

Like so many events in this story, it somehow didn't quite happen. But let's not think the Japanese are the only ones who turn a blind eye to what they don't want to see.

10

CONGO

'We never belonged here. It was foolish of us to think we could make our lives in a country like this. It's too threatening. It's too wild.'

The speaker was a woman in her forties: Belgian, blonde, long-featured, angular but rather stylish in a linen shirt and slacks. They were only slightly stained and torn by the ordeal she had been through. She was sitting on the floor of the airport at Kinshasa, the capital of what was then called Zaire, beside a couple of bags and some things wrapped up in a garish Zairian table-cloth. The Red Cross had plucked her out of Kisangani the day before, and flown her here.

Around her were a hundred other refugees, all white, all desperate to get out of the country. There was a full-scale rebellion going on in the interior, and anyone who found themselves in the way of it was liable to be murdered, especially if they were white. Her husband was dead, and she was lucky to have escaped. She had watched him being butchered.

'Frankly,' she went on, not caring what she said now that she was on her way to safety, 'you can never trust these people. They will always slit your throat if you can't defend yourself properly. I never slept a single night in safety while I lived here. And I was just as scared of our own servants as I was of the rest of them.'

Her tenses showed that, even before she had left the country, she was finished with it. I didn't need to ask her if she'd be coming back when the present emergency was over.

'How long have you lived here?'

'I came to join my husband here when he was just starting. Nineteen years ago. My poor Raoul.'

Tears came to her eyes, and I waited a little while before speaking again.

'And you never felt safe?'

'Never for a single moment. Every day of every week I was afraid.'

I thanked her, and went in search of someone else to speak to. But afterwards, in the quiet of my hotel room, I listened to the tape of my interview with her particularly carefully. Her voice, her tone, her look had had something more to it than just fear and hatred and sorrow at her husband's death. But what was it?

It took me some time to identify the quality I had heard, and it wasn't what I had expected. There was guilt in what she had said. She felt, I was sure, that it had been wrong to be there, and that she had somehow suffered as a result of it. A kind of dread lay behind her words – a dread of the forest, of the dark forces that dwelt there, of the dark emotions that had been stirred up and had boiled over. It was no place for us, she had added when she spoke about her time in the little outpost on the edge of Kisangani with her husband. She didn't just mean that the climate was difficult, or that the two of them hadn't fitted in. She meant that it was wrong for them, and for white people like them, to intrude into such an alien, hostile, dark world.

After that, in other parts of the continent, I heard the same tone. Sometimes it was in the voices of people who had once lived in Africa but had been forced to leave: a *pied noir* from Oran in Algeria whom I came to know in the South of France, for instance, or a former settler from Rhodesia who left when it became Zimbabwe and went to live in the Northern Transvaal; or people from Johannesburg and Pretoria, who felt that there was no future for them in the new South Africa.

None of them seemed to feel that there had been anything wrong about the way they or their fellow settlers had behaved towards the local population, or with the white governments that had represented them. That all seemed to be secondary. The primary offence was trying to make a life in a continent which was so alien. Even though they felt that they themselves and the structures their people had brought with them were entirely justified, there was something of the intruder's sense of nervousness about them; as if they were admitting: 'We are suffering for our intrusion.'

Joseph Conrad, in his novella *The Heart of Darkness*, which is

a study of this sense of trespass and what it reveals about the
trespasser, describes one of his characters travelling up the Congo
in a small steamboat, and making a

> gesture that took in the forest, the creek, the mud, the river –
> seemed to beckon with a dishonouring flourish before the sunlit
> face of the land a treacherous appeal to the lurking death, to
> the hidden evil, to the profound darkness of its heart. It was
> so startling that I leaped to my feet and looked back at the
> edge of the forest, as though I had expected an answer of
> some sort to that black display of confidence. You know the
> foolish notions that come to one sometimes. The high stillness
> confronted these two figures with its ominous patience, waiting
> for the passing away of a fantastic invasion.

A fantastic invasion: it had been that exactly, and especially
here along the banks of the Congo. Europeans went to other parts
of Africa for a variety of reasons: to stop other Europeans taking
them over, to find wide open spaces for farmers and entrepreneurs,
to find souls to care for and convert, to bring them the blessings of
European civilization, to hack out the riches of the land, to dominate people too cowed to resist. But they mostly came to the Congo
to make themselves rich.

A good friend of mine, a former Belgian ambassador in London,
has promised me that if I go with him to the museum in Brussels
which deals with Belgium's colonial past, he will be able to prove
to me that King Leopold II's motives in colonizing the Congo were
not at all mercenary, and that the allegations of insanely cruel
mistreatment of the natives by the Belgian authorities and the
adventurers they encouraged to go there were largely false.

Well, because he is a friend of mine and because I admire him,
I have listened to him, of course, and one day I hope to go to the
museum with him. But the evidence is pretty strongly against that
line of thinking; and the photographs of severed heads and hands
stacked high after some minor transgression by the locals, and of
the wretched survivors crawling around after indiscriminate punishment had been handed out by the colonial government, seem
moderately conclusive to me.

It's odd how often you come across the word 'dark' in references to the Congo. As it happens, much of the country isn't dark in the slightest. It has large swathes of beautiful open savannah, under a clear sky, as fine as anything in Kenya or South Africa. The forest itself is wonderfully varied, with gorgeous flowering plants and excitingly different species of animals and insects. If you float up the Congo river by boat, the forest does indeed look dark on either side of you, but no darker than the Amazon or the Mekong, where the forests constantly tempt you to stop and amble down their secret paths.

Many emotions and perceptions go to make up the European's feeling about the Congo. Part of it is a perfectly justified sense of fear. The crowds in its cities are indeed something to be really afraid of, and their mood can turn from one of calm to ferocious rage within seconds: faster, I think, than any other crowds I have seen. And in the forests you unquestionably have a sense of foreboding, of violence preparing to spring, which follows you round and seems to hide in every thick bank of bushes, behind every tree.

It's partly the ancient panic fear, which the Greeks believed was inspired by the god Pan, which seizes hold of us when we're alone in the depths of the forest and makes us run madly through the undergrowth, tearing ourselves on the branches and falling over tree roots, until we are too exhausted to run any further. And only then do we slowly come to our senses, and realize that it was something in ourselves we were running from. In the Congo, we always seem to be aware of the fear that lurks in the forest, the diseases that can leap the boundary from animal to human.

Maybe the people of the forest themselves felt this, and showed it in their art-forms. Ever since I first went there, back in the 1970s, I have made a collection of Congolese masks, buying them whenever I have come across them. There is a graphic ferocity about these masks which sets them apart from the art of most other parts of Africa. The anger and fear seem palpable. The gods of the forest are violent and irrational, and we have come to believe that the people who worshipped them must be violent and irrational too.

These may be our feelings: yet my experience of the people who actually live in the forest is very different. The people we dismissively label pygmies have a gentleness in them which reminds me very much of the Bushmen – also a derogatory name – further south in Namibia and Botswana. Other forest people too seemed peaceable and generous. But when they leave the forest, and come to live in the towns and cities which the colonialists have established, they become unpredictable and angry, and easily moved to dissolution and violence.

So it's for this reason, as well as others, that I believe one of the basic emotions felt by Europeans in the Congo is guilt. White people often ran to excess there, lashing out and murdering and torturing in order to ward off their fears. Mr Kurtz in Conrad's short story dies with the words 'The horror' on his lips, and the horror has come from his realization of the savagery that lies within him. The vast majority of Europeans who have lived in the Congo during the hundred and twenty years since it was first claimed by the Belgians probably never committed any act of violence themselves, but they knew that their very presence there was an unnatural assault on the territory and its people.

Colonialism nowadays seems bewildering, almost inexplicable to us. How could we have treated Indians as second-class citizens, or put up notices in Shanghai parks to say that dogs and Chinese were not permitted? Whenever I go to Iraq I am reminded that the British and Americans there behaved in the way of most colonists, obtained their prizes through violence, in which crowds were fired on and basic liberties were stamped on hard. No doubt we are inclined nowadays to forget how much more there was to empire than aggression and greed and brutality; if that's all there was, why should Jawaharlal Nehru have issued an order, in the earliest days of India's independence, that 'God Save the King' should be played first at all government occasions, and the new Indian national anthem only afterwards?

But colonialism was always based originally on might rather than right, and usually on a desire for raw materials. It was the Congo's raw materials – wood, ivory, minerals – that drew the Belgians there, and made them rich. No one in the seventy years of its existence as a colony troubled themselves much about raising the standards of the Congolese themselves, let alone educating them. So when the Congo became independent in 1960, there were only a dozen university graduates in the entire country.

To this day it is a place which makes you feel guilty and scared in equal proportion. People gather round you in the streets of the cities when you venture out on foot, thrusting the cheapest things at you and demanding pathetically small amounts of money which you know will ease the poverty of their lives just a fraction that day. And yet, worried that the sight of money will work them into a frenzy, you push them and their maps of the country and their day-old newspapers and their pictures of the president aside, and hope that a policeman will come over and kick them away so you can get through the crowd unscathed.

Everywhere you go, the fear goes with you. I was once delayed at the customs desk at the airport, negotiating the size of the bribe I should pay the officials to recover my suitcase, and then found it was getting dark outside. At night, the Congo seems twenty times more frightening than by day. The road to the centre of the city was lined with fires, which lit up the passers-by in the darkness resulting from the almost continuous power cuts. I could see my taxi driver was scared, but he needed the fare and chose not to warn me that the journey was dangerous. Every mile or so there was a road-block manned by soldiers, and at times of trouble the soldiers are more dangerous than anyone else.

Some could be bought off with dollar bills or small-denomination notes. On the outskirts of the city, though, we were stopped by a group of soldiers who were more drunk than the others had been. One of the soldiers jabbed his rifle through the open window – the temperature was in the high thirties – and pushed the muzzle against the side of my face.

'*Fume, fume,*' he shouted, in a kind of French.

This was not a good time to explain that I didn't smoke. A small note satisfied him just as well, but it had seemed like a close-run thing.

Soldiers demanded cigarettes from me at two more road-blocks. Once, the driver produced a couple of cigarettes of his own. At the other one, the fact that the street-lights were working here and the closeness of the city centre encouraged him to put his foot down, and we flew through the checkpoint. I braced myself for the shots, but none came. When I finally reached it, my hotel, built during the boom of the 1950s when the Belgians seemed likely to stay in the

Congo for ever, felt like an island of civilization and safety in this wild sea of darkness and instability.

§

I had made various attempts to interview the leader of this extraordinary country. President Joseph Mobutu was the same generation and had the same background as Emperor Bokassa of the Central African Republic: a sergeant in the French army who had risen with his country's independence and eventually seized control. This progression is characteristic of many societies in a state of political meltdown; it happened in ancient Rome during the political upheavals of the third century, when a huge centurion named Maximinus Thrax, formerly a shepherd, was elevated to the rank of general for his strength and wrestling abilities and then seized power from an inexperienced emperor who was still in his teens.

Mobutu had a wonderful public relations system. He introduced a system which he called 'Africanization', in order to be in tune with the times, though he clearly preferred Europe, especially as a place to put his money. And he took the name Mobutu Sese Seko Kuku Ngbendu Wa Za Banga, which has been translated (with what accuracy I have no idea) as 'The All-Powerful Warrior who, because of His endurance and unyielding will to win, will go from conquest to conquest, leaving fire in His wake'; from which we can only assume that Kikongo must be a remarkably succinct language.

But what he mostly left in his wake, apart from fire, was an empty treasury. He robbed his country blind, selling off its mineral wealth as though it were his own property, siphoning the money into his various personal bank accounts, and generally living the life of a billionaire, much of it in France. A report issued in 1984 showed that Zaire's national debt amounted to $4 billion. And $4 billion was the estimate for Mobutu's personal wealth at that time.

In this enormous country of his, the size of much of Europe, the spot where he chose to build his favourite palace was seven hundred miles north of Kinshasa at Gbadolite, on the southern bank of the river which separates Zaire from the Central African Republic: Bokassa's old fiefdom. In other words, Mobutu was always poised for flight, and he stayed as close as possible to the emergency exit. At his palace he maintained a fleet of fast boats which could whisk him to safety within minutes of hearing that his rebellious people were coming for him. But although he was hounded from the country and ended his days in Morocco, it was his own body that killed him, not the people he had dominated and fleeced for thirty-two years.

In 1993 his private office invited me to Kinshasa to interview him. We arrived under conditions of great secrecy, and landed in the neighbouring country of Congo Brazzaville, so no one would know we had arrived. Mobutu's chief private secretary met us at Brazzaville airport, and escorted us to the port on the River Congo which divides Brazzaville from Kinshasa by a couple of miles. There we boarded a speedboat and were taken to Mobutu's personal port, on the edge of Kinshasa.

We were told to prepare ourselves for an interview with the president the next day, but it didn't happen. Days passed, and two things became disturbingly obvious: first, that the president wasn't even in the country (he had gone, we were told, to consult his dentist in Cairo, but would be back very soon) and second, that our hotel bills were going to be disturbingly high. At that stage, to stay in the Kinshasa InterContinental cost more than a night at the Ritz in Paris, and my budget and that of *Newsnight*, the programme I was working for, simply couldn't take the strain. We left the following morning.

Eventually it became clear that the problem hadn't been Mobutu's teeth at all. He had prostate cancer, and had been flown under conditions of the greatest secrecy to Switzerland for treatment. In 1997, four years after I had tried and failed to interview him, the President for Life died, and the small measure of stability he had brought to Zaire died with him. The country descended into a form of anarchy, and has never been entirely free from it since.

I was very sorry about missing him. My personal stock went down badly with the BBC, of course. It always does if you promise something, spend the money, and then come back with your hands empty. In this case it was even worse, since, at the time when it still seemed certain we would get the interview, I wrote an article about Kinshasa for the *Spectator*.

'So all I got for my three thousand quid,' raged the editor of *Newsnight*, who had commissioned me to interview Mobutu, 'was a sodding, ill-phrased thousand-word article in a crap, pretentious, overwritten right-wing rag.'

'Eight hundred words, actually,' I said. Well, you have to be correct about details.

Much, much worse, though, I had lost the opportunity of going to see Mobutu's palace at Gbadolite. It was a personal gift to the All-Powerful Warrior from that scourge of wealth and bourgeois power, Chairman Mao Zedong of China, and its design was based on that of the Forbidden City in Beijing; not, therefore, entirely in tune with the local ambience. (Mobutu also borrowed Mao's own title for himself – the Great Helmsman. Since they both steered their countries to devastation and death on a grand scale, his instincts were clearly right.)

A town grew up around the palace at Gbadolite, because the little army of government ministers, suitors, con-men, journalists and arms salesmen had to live somewhere while they were waiting to attract the Great Helmsman's attention. You could change your traveller's cheques at any of three banks, and there were two hotels to stay in: one expensive, one for the people who had been waiting a long time. There was also an airport, with a runway capable of taking Concorde. It landed there quite often at one stage.

When Mobutu was finally chased out in 1997, a brief battle took place at Gbadolite before the loyalists joined the rebels in trashing the palace and the town. There was a lot to trash. Jean-Pierre Bemba, a serial rebel who fought against both the presidents who came after Mobutu, led the attack on Gbadolite and liked it so much he decided to stay there. His army was probably the most dangerous force in the whole of the Congo, but I met someone who went there and lived to tell the story.

He maintained that the doors of the various Chinese-style palaces had been ripped off, and that excrement filled the corners of most of them. The contents of the palaces had long since been stolen, broken or shot to pieces, but if they were like the ornaments and furniture at Mobutu's palace outside the town of Goma, then most of them will have been cheap fakes, often plastic. As happened with Saddam Hussein's palaces, the contractors ripped him off royally. Which was only fair, considering what both Mobutu and Saddam did to their own countries.

§

In 2004 the magazine *GQ* gave me an award for one of the books I'd written. It came completely out of the blue. At the age of sixty, I scarcely seemed like the kind of person whom *GQ* or its readers would be interested in. It's stylish, young, and interested in clothes and gadgets and cars; I am not. At the awards ceremony, I was the oldest person by some decades. Yet I had a splendid time, meeting all sorts of people whom I would probably never have come across otherwise: the author Alan Hollingsworth, for instance, and the singer Badly Drawn Boy, and a startlingly beautiful model called Heidi Klum. I felt like a time-traveller, but it was highly enjoyable, all the same.

As a result, *GQ* magazine commissioned me to write an article about the most frightening place I knew. There was no question about where that was: it had to be the Democratic Republic of Congo, as Zaire had now been renamed. My brother-in-law Mark, who had come with me to Madrid to see the lottery fraudster, would take the pictures.

But since our time would be limited, we needed someone in Kinshasa to make the arrangements for us; these weren't things you could easily do over the phone, and anyway the phone system in Kinshasa is very much what you might expect it to be in a city which is subject to constant power cuts, regular deluges of rain and occasional attacks by rebel armies. Mobile phones are the answer, of course, but there is no telephone directory to help you find the numbers you need. You need to have them first, before you can start negotiating; no phone numbers, no negotiations.

Fortunately, though, the BBC had a correspondent in Kinshasa; not just an ordinary journalist, the kind of adventurer who settles in a place and starts writing or broadcasting from there, but one of the best of his kind that I have come across.

I first met Arnaud Zaitman at Bayeux, in Normandy. He had just received an award for his remarkable reporting on a pitched battle in the Congo between rebel forces and the government. Listening to it, I tried to imagine what reserves of courage would be required to stay there, so close to the places where the bullets were hitting. Especially if you were white, and very slightly built.

The BBC is an extraordinary outfit. It employs people who are honoured and admired all round the world, but sometimes the organization scarcely registers their existence itself. In Arnaud's case it's partly because, as a native of Belgium, his English, though excellent, is quite strongly accented, so he rarely reports for the main English-language services. Arnaud reports from Kinshasa for the BBC French service, and his work is remarkable.

I don't want to go on about his height, but he is certainly small, Hollywood-actor sized, and very slender. Of course, slightly built people are no less likely to be courageous than bulky ones, yet somehow there is a much greater poignancy about them, as though they can't look after themselves as well as someone bigger. Arnaud Zaitman can look after himself very well. But in his little beaten-up car, with his notebook thrown on the back seat and a pile of papers on the front one, he looks too young and fragile to be doing a job as dangerous as this one.

'So are there times when you are the only foreigner covering a story?'

'Yes, quite often. You have to be careful, of course.'

'Oh, you do, do you?'

Arnaud didn't get the irony.

He made all our arrangements for us, and met us at the airport.

Kinshasa airport, at nine in the evening, is a vision of hell. It is swelteringly hot, and there are people everywhere shouting and pushing and trying to sell you things, or steal from you. It takes a very long time for your bags to come off the plane, and a sweating customs man tries to tell you you can't take them through until you have paid him a *douceur*.

The airport building itself is rather attractive – another product of the boom of the early 1950s. But it is suffering from heat and dampness, and blisters have formed under the surface of the paintwork. The once attractive lino has long ago worn away at the edges. The luggage carousel squeals and protests as it starts up. As you are being pushed around by the other passengers, and by the soldiers who are there to keep order but don't, you are aware of being

stared at by the dozens of people who are climbing over each other
to get a glimpse of you from behind the bars which separate the
baggage hall from the arrivals hall. The sight of so many seething,
sweating people watching you as though you, or else they, are in a
gaol or a zoo, is unnerving. And the noise of so much shouting
makes it all far worse.

There was a single white face peering at Mark and me from
between the bars as we walked out, with dozens of hands trying to
tear our suitcases from our grasp. It was Arnaud's. Perhaps he had
lived in Kinshasa too long, but he seemed charmingly aware of the
Hieronymus Bosch impression it all created on us.

'It is good to see you again,' he said, gripping my hand.

I remembered his accent: English as spoken by a Bruxellois.

I suppose I had expected him to have a driver. But he grabbed
our bags himself, telling the porters to go away in a tone so fierce
that they left us alone immediately, and marched ahead of us in the
dark to the place where he had left his car. I was to become quite
fond of his car over the next few days, but at that moment I was
just surprised. I had forgotten how little the BBC pays its news
stringers, even in places like Kinshasa.

He drove us with a little of the local wildness through the
darkness. We hit potholes and avoided unidentifiable mounds of
stuff that littered the roadway. Cars passed down the other side of
the bad road, swerving to avoid obstacles, swerving back to avoid
us, their headlights dark yellow. Some had no lights at all, and were
just shapes faintly outlined by the feeble lights of the cars behind.

'Is this how you live?' I asked in the end, as a girl who had been
walking in the road threw herself out of our path.

Arnaud looked round at me. An oncoming car lit up the
puzzlement in his face. Of course this was how he lived; what other
way was there? I felt ashamed of myself for asking, as though I was
some Californian or other who had suddenly landed here.

And then I understood. This was how I had been myself when I
was a foreign correspondent. You discover in yourself a burning
love of the place, a defensiveness about its failings which makes you
at times entirely blind to them. This is the way we do things here,
you want to say; you're not in the Champs Elysées or Regent Street
now. At other times, of course, all you want to do is describe the

failings of the country where you are based, but in this first hour, when the impressions hurt, you are instinctively protective.

'I like it here, you know,' said Arnaud.

And since he must have understood what both of us were thinking, he went on, 'It's an exciting place. Very interesting. And the lifestyle is good,'

Well, I've found myself staying in apparently unpleasant places before, and realizing their good qualities after a while. Moscow in the bad old Soviet days, for instance: after I had spent a few weeks there, I could begin to see why so many of the foreign diplomats and journalists had such a powerful affection for it. For one thing, the difficulties of life – food shortages, the climate, having to queue for everything, the rudeness, being followed around by spies and *provocateurs*, and treated by the government and its agents as an enemy – brought you together, as a family and as a group.

'You know, looking back,' said a journalist friend of mine whom I had first met when he was his newspaper's Moscow correspondent, 'I don't think I've ever been happier than when I was there.'

Arnaud, it seemed to me, felt rather the same. Kinshasa was a difficult, sometimes frightening place, but it was his patch. He knew just about everything about it, and he knew everyone there who mattered. As far as the BBC's French service was concerned, he was the king of the Congo. And that counted for a great deal.

§

Sunday: breakfast at the Memling Hotel. The food is surprisingly good, the service pleasant enough but otherwise indifferent. The dining room is full of large white people: a few businessmen, and a dozen or so men in some unidentifiable uniform, presumably from the United Nations. The only Congolese in the room, apart from the waiters, sit at the table next to ours. When I try to listen to what they're saying, they sound like politicians. They certainly want to persuade the senior figure sitting with them about something to do with their region, which seems to be in the east of the country.

Mark and I sit with Arnaud and plan our programme. He has organized every single thing we asked for: a boat to take us upriver, a visit to the resting place of the old colonial statues, an outing to meet the child wizards of Kinshasa, and a UN flight to Kisangani; but he also has some other things in mind.

'You know that the big new thing in Kinshasa, and all over the country, is religion. They are Protestant, but not from the big churches . . . What do you call them?'

'Evangelists,' I say, and he shakes his head.

I have to think a while.

'Pentecostalists?'

'*Ah, oui, c'est ça*: *pentecostalistes*. You know, they are taking over in the Congo, not just here but everywhere. Would you like to see one of these?'

We would.

'I'll take you to see Fernand Kutino. He's one of the biggest – maybe the biggest of all. He denies, it but everyone says he was a big gun-runner in the Angolan war. Then in the late nineties he started his movement, which is called L'Armée de la Victoire, the Army of Victory. Very big, and very, very rich, but they say he's making more money as Bishop of L'Armée de la Victoire than he did when he was selling guns to Angola. They also think he wants to be President someday.'

It's the rainy season in Kinshasa. Every season seems to be the rainy season here, of course, but this is worse than the rest. The water sweeps across the roadway like a dam that's burst. The orange mud at the side of the road boils up and covers everything. The wheels of Arnaud's little car whip it up into circles that almost overlap.

Even before he turns onto the coarse grass beside the crumbling road and stops the engine, we can hear the bishop's voice roaring over the loudspeakers. Security men, snappily dressed, usher us into a big expanse under a huge corrugated-iron roof, held up by steel poles. In this heat, an open-air church is a necessity, especially if you can attract the kind of numbers Bishop Kutino does.

The speakers through which his voice reverberates dizzyingly are as big as some of the huts we've seen along our way here: the homes, no doubt, of some among the crowd of several hundred who have assembled to hear him; simple people, mostly women, dressed in their best clothes, fanning themselves against the heat, a look of concentration, and sometimes of rapture, on the shining faces they turn to him as he stands at the microphone.

His electronically amplified bellowing has taken on a new tone: a high-pitched note which is almost unbearable. He is shrieking something about guilt. Something about everlasting suffering, love, forgiveness, miracles, heaven. Something about the possibility of redemption. Something about how you obtain it. And then, finally and most emphatically, something about money.

Bishop Kutino is a shaven-headed bull of a man, awash with sweat. It has darkened the armpits and sides of his expensive dark blue shirt, and you can see those stains linking up with the ones spreading from below his throat and the back of his neck. Soon the shirt will be black, not dark blue, and the grey waistcoat which stretches across his chest and stomach as tautly as a sail in a high wind will be as dark as the rainclouds above the corrugated-iron roof. It's a very nice suit he's wearing, but it must be a one-off use. The God business certainly keeps him in good clothes.

It is hotter here than you can possibly imagine, and far, far louder. Bishop Kutino's voice reverberates through your head like the sound through a cheap wooden speaker cabinet, so distorted that you can catch only the odd noun or occasional instruction in the great tsunami of sound that flows from him. But that doesn't matter. It all boils down to one thing: God wants his plastic buckets filled.

They are expecting that, and so money is thrust at him by his sweating, excited, suffering congregation in great waves of guilty relief. Now the air above their heads is darkened by the dirty Congolese ten-franc notes they are waving in the air. They know the price of redemption, all right, and now they are throwing it into the buckets which his acolytes are handing round by the dozen. Many notes fall to the ground, but no one touches them. The acolytes will collect them later.

The bishop screams into the mike which he holds parallel to the ground, pointing directly at his mouth, like a karaoke singer, and looks eagerly round at the congregation, his eyebrows raised, waiting for them to scream back at him. And they do. By God they do. The women scream back far louder than the men, who mostly seem to be tame little creatures. The women, by contrast, are big and confident and assertive, and they are getting seriously worked up.

They half-stand in their places, the spittle showering the row in front
of them, yelling the amens and the praise-the-Lords and the *ah-ouis*.

Occasionally a woman in a brilliant red or yellow or green dress
clambers heavily out of her seat and wriggles towards the bishop
on her knees, yelping orgasmically. He reaches out an equally heavy
hand, the back of it shining with sweat, and lays it on her forehead.
She yelps and squirms under its weight, then wriggles back again
across the hard concrete.

When the screaming dies down, the rain starts again, beating
down on the corrugated iron like hammers. Or perhaps the noise
was there all along, and we couldn't hear it before. Now the
congregation sits quietly on the neat little chairs, still breathing
heavily. And for the moment the bishop isn't bellowing; he's talking
into his microphone, just loudly enough to be audible over the rain.

He's telling them about the victory they're winning. Strange
how the former gun-runner can't stop talking about fighting; but
then, the whole country is dominated by warfare. Here, the signs
all over the walls bray about it: '*Nul ne tiendra contre nous*',
'*L'Armée de Victoire*', '*Je donnerai la Paix, dit l'Eternel des
Armées*'. Nothing can stand against us. The Army of Victory. The
Lord of Hosts. Surrender your will, your soul, your money.

Pentecostal churches are taking over the Democratic Republic
of Congo, and Fernand Kutino is one of the leading generals in
God's high command.

'Jesus Christ is king in Kinshasa!' he screams.

So far he's only got one radio station and one television station,
but he's looking for more. He's also interested in the mobile-phone
boom. Fundamentalist religion and wireless communication: the
only two growth industries in a country which is otherwise prostrate, devastated, raped, abandoned.

§

A day or so later, the driver Arnaud has found us, a crafty but
devoted old boy called Pierre, with a courtly turn of phrase, takes
us by a back way so we can see the kind of things ordinary people
like and want: not the tinned and frozen goods from the centre of
town, where the high buildings are. Here, the alleyways are lined
with people selling things from sacks. Things that move and crawl

over each other: dark brown caterpillars that you can fry and eat, or that are pre-fried. I've eaten mopani worms in Zimbabwe, and found them quite bearable, so I'm not against larvae on principle. But these weren't to my taste. I thanked the lady in the brilliant print dress for the offer of a free handful, and shook my head.

The road ran alongside a railway line, down which came a train moved with exhausted slowness, crammed inside and out with passengers. Most of the people you could see hanging from the doors and open windows and roof were young; the Congo has a remarkably high proportion of young people, though no one knows quite how many of them there are. Mark started to take photographs, and a howl of rage went up, people screaming and pointing and beating their own heads and faces in rage. Some dropped down onto the track and started angrily towards us. Mark continued taking pictures for an instant, then we ran for the safety of Pierre's car. We backed at speed down the road between the women selling their caterpillars, then swung round and headed off for the centre of town, with a few fast runners in pursuit.

'They are thinking you are capturing their souls when you are taking photos,' Pierre said when the last one had dropped away behind us.

As I say, anything here can ignite an explosion. Living in the Congo is like working in a nitroglycerine plant: the slightest piece of carelessness or bad luck can blow the entire place up. At best, there is an atmosphere of strained and watchful silence, your white face gleaming in the huge dark crowd where you don't belong. At worst, the rage bursts out like boiling, undirected magma, sweeping away and destroying everything with it.

There is always something new and frightening about this country. Until recently it was child soldiers, ten-year-olds with the firepower of an AK-47, who could blow you away without understanding the first thing about what they were doing or why they were doing it. Armies from Rwanda, Zimbabwe and Uganda invaded the vast, sprawling, paralysed body like viruses, entering its abrasions and wounds and working their way through its veins and nervous system, infecting it, weakening it, almost killing it. They gave the child soldiers their chance, and poisoned their minds and their futures too. Two million people died as a result of the war, and untold thousands or maybe millions more were hacked and shot and chopped into useless beggary. What happened here made even Iraq look peaceful.

And when a deal was finally done, and the child soldiers were disarmed and sent back to primary school with so much death and horror on their consciences, most of the guerrilla groups which had massacred each other's followers were roped together into a coalition government. It proved reasonably stable for a surprisingly long time.

But some elements were so wild, so unprepared to give up the intoxicating business of destroying villages and burning their inhabitants alive, that they remained unreconciled, outside the agreement, either by their own choice or by the choice of others. One such group operated near Lubumbashi, in the southern province of Katanga. This group was particularly proud of its handiwork, and liked everyone to know it had passed by. When its men captured people, they carved their faces off with painstaking care and left them like that, to live or die.

Welcome to the Democratic Republic of Congo.

§

In the beginning was the river: dark, resentful, fast-running, thick and brown and warm. At Kinshasa, the Congo is a mile across. Great clumps of green water-hyacinth float on its dull, unreflecting surface as fast as a man can walk. They seem like phlegm spewed up from the impossibly distant, unimaginable interior.

The river *is* the country. It is its only reliable route, its main source of livelihood, the one thing that holds a vast, crazy, violent, rich and vandalized country together. The government can't do that. Nowadays there are no roads left between one city and another; they all peter out into grass and rank weed a few miles from the outskirts. The Congo is the only way to travel long distances, and those parts of the country which are not touched by it can't be reached in any other way than by air.

Yet until recently there has been very little trade along the river, and almost no travel, because the warlords would fire on any boat that moved by daylight; and any boat that moved at night was in danger of foundering on the shifting shoals and sandbanks. From the safety of the air you can see the wrecks that litter them, as white as stripped skeletons. Joseph Conrad's travellers only had to face poisoned arrows from angry tribes along the banks. Now the unseen enemy has Kalashnikovs. There may not be much trade in the Congo, but there is always the arms trade.

Like many twentieth-century names in Africa, 'the Congo' is a European misunderstanding, the name for something altogether different. The people who live along its banks call it 'Nzere', the Swallower, because it drains all the other rivers and streams which flow into it over an area larger than India. The river is a gigantic tapeworm, reaching 4,700 miles into the deepest guts of Africa, curling in a gigantic bend across the continent. It contains five hundred different species of fish, some of them twelve feet long, stingrays, water snakes, crocodiles and hippos.

The Portuguese, who were the first Europeans to reach the mouth of the river, turned 'Nzere' into 'Zaire', and for nearly thirty years President Mobutu Sese Seko called the country that because he was annoyed at the confusion with the small, former French colony on the opposite bank of the river, Congo Brazzaville. Strange, in a world where so many states chose to get rid of their colonial names, that one country should be called after a Portuguese mishearing of a perfectly good local word, while the other's capital should still be named after its (admittedly attractive) European founder, Brazza. When Mobutu was replaced by another plunderer, Laurent Kabila, his country got its old colonial name back again, and the confusion between the Congos returned.

Down the River Congo has come everything good or bad that the country produces: diamonds, gold, uranium, ivory, rubber, wood, and perhaps a dozen awful diseases. There is a theory, though now pretty much discredited, that AIDS jumped the species barrier just before the Belgians left, as the result of an experiment carried out by Belgian and American doctors in Stanleyville, now Kisangani, on the northern bank of the Congo; a quite good book and a rather dire Hollywood film have been devoted to this proposition.

Other diseases, equally vile, have certainly made their way down the length of the river to Kinshasa, like a parasite travelling through the national gut. Ebola, for instance. This is another disease which, like AIDS, can spread from animals to humans if there is contact through the mouth or through a wound. In the Congo, monkey meat is particularly favoured, and Ebola spreads that way. If you contract it, you begin to gush blood through the mouth, ears, anus and genitals. It is the most appalling and terrifying disease imaginable, and death is the almost inevitable outcome. If someone catches it in the Ivory Coast, where I once made a film about Ebola, the custom is to shut up the victim and his or her entire family in their house, nailing up the windows and doors. Then everyone waits until the disease has run its course and all inside are dead. I asked Pierre, our driver, if that was what they did in the Congo too.

'*Oui, bien sûr, c'est normal,*' he said, using the French expression which just means something like 'it's a matter of course'. It can sound chillingly impersonal and brutal to British ears.

Yellow fever, monkey-pox, breakbone fever (in which your limbs become so painful it feels as though you've broken them): all these and others have made their way out of the depths of the dark forest and downriver, where they have infiltrated the human biosystem on a grand scale. And from the mouth of the Congo they have spread everywhere. Are there other diseases lurking in the forest, just waiting to jump from animals to humans and infect the world? Almost certainly. It all adds to our sense of fear and guilt at our intrusion into the heart and soul of Africa.

The Congo was the last great territory in Africa to be subdued and penetrated by Europeans. It seems natural to use the vocabulary of sex and domination here: this entire naked, vulnerable region, splayed out across the continent, was raped and mutilated on the personal orders of King Leopold II of Belgium. At the very time when he was convincing international opinion that he was bringing enlightenment to the darkest part of the dark continent, and fighting the slave trade there, he was himself enslaving huge numbers of Congolese and using them to rip out its rubber and ivory. Hundreds of thousands of elephants were slaughtered in order to make the piano keys which entertained and enhanced the snobbery of late-Victorian England. If you have a piano which was built between 1885 and 1920, the chances are that its keys are made of ivory torn from the skull of a massacred elephant in the Congo and dragged through the forest for hundreds of miles by unpaid labourers urged on by the whips of their overseers.

The slavery which King Leopold brought to the Congo was not the kind that populated the United States, the Caribbean and Latin America, dreadful though that was. He pioneered new, industrial methods of slavery on a mass scale, which predated the labour camps of Stalin and the concentration camps of Hitler. The full extent of the horror was revealed by an Anglo-French journalist, Edmund Morel, and a British consul in the Congo, the Irishman Roger Casement. Casement was much honoured in Britain for his dedicated work in uncovering the truth about the methods of slavery there, though the government which knighted him hanged him for treason fifteen years later, after he had tried to help the Germans invade his native Ireland during the First World War.

In 1899, heavily influenced by the work of Morel and Casement, Joseph Conrad published *Heart of Darkness*. Its hero, Charlie Marlow, travels up the river from Leopoldville, now Kinshasa, and begins to understand the appalling cruelty which the European colonists have visited on the Congo. Marlow is in search of Mr Kurtz, the great white hope of the large trading company he works for. He discovers in the depths of the Congolese forest that Kurtz has been driven mad by the power he exerts over the local people, and by the revelation of the depths of his own brutality and violence.

It was fiction, of course, and it prefigured the dreadful excesses of violence which supposedly civilized Europe was just about to turn upon itself in the twentieth century. But it was scarcely exaggerated. Kurtz, who had ordered that the pathway to his house should be marked out with human skulls, was representative of plenty of white settlers and traders up-country in the depths of the Congolese forest. Faced with the terrifying immensity of the country, with the degree to which they were outnumbered by the Congolese population, and with the sense of their total power, and driven on by the expectations of company bosses back in Europe, some white colonialists turned into monsters of cruelty. For Kurtz you could read Rudolf Hoess, the commandant of Auschwitz, or Franz Stangl of Treblinka, or any of the nameless commissars in charge of hundreds of Soviet labour camps.

Yet Belgium ruled the Congo for only the blinking of an eye: little more than seventy years. Tens of thousands of Belgians, and a few hundred Congolese, lived through the whole drama, from the start of Leopold II's venture to the bloody dissolution of colonial rule in 1960. During that period, the forest terrors of the 1890s and 1900s were transformed into urban terrors. In the 1950s, when Kinshasa was still named after its original oppressor, the Belgian colonialists felt perfectly safe as they walked the clean, neat, well-policed streets of Leopoldville. Today the pavements are broken and decaying, and sudden overpowering rainstorms flood the deep potholes in the surface of the roads. Rank grass and bushes thrust their way up through the cracks in the paving and the corners of buildings, and a dark green mould spreads over the cement.

There is no real law here. The police are usually unpaid, so they make their living by arresting passers-by, especially Europeans, and extracting money from them. The Kinshasa wits call it 'direct taxation', and every foreigner in the city seems to have an anecdote about it.

In the usual way, there is not too much open violence in Kinshasa, unless you summon it up by, say, taking people's photographs unasked, or refusing to buy something that is offered to you. The violent crime of Johannesburg, Durban or Cape Town, where gangs target the wealthy and if necessary murder them, is quite rare here. But that is because South Africa has adopted a Western pattern of crime, and exaggerated it beyond anything known in the West, including even the United States (which would be a moderately peaceful country if there weren't any guns). In the Congo, crime is mostly unplanned. It simply erupts without premeditation, as though the violence is always silently swimming along just below the surface, simply waiting for a sudden, unexpected eruption.

In 1960, when the Belgians, under pressure, decided to give the Congo its independence, this was one of these moments. In that instant of weakness and indecision, the hidden rage exploded, turning into a wild cruelty of a kind which mirrored the tactics of Leopold II's colonization. Women were raped and men and children were butchered, just as the Congo itself had been raped and butchered. This might not be an excuse, but it is a kind of explanation.

World opinion was horrified by it all, and the British and French both decided that their empires in Africa, which they had previously expected to control until the end of the twentieth century, should be given independence as quickly as possible. Thus began an unseemly race to get rid of the African colonies, long before there were proper structures in place to take over from colonialism, and when there were very few university graduates up and down the length of black Africa. Much of the poverty and failure which has marked the continent ever since dates from this panicky withdrawal in the 1960s and early 70s, as though the violence of the Congo had somehow created the pattern for the rest of Africa.

And at the same time, Europeans learned to associate the Congo once again with darkness and the most extreme violence. This perception has remained unchanged for nearly fifty years. So when, at the start of the new millennium, a civil war was raging there, at the cost of two or even three million lives, people in the West scarcely even noticed. Civil war, Europeans felt, was the natural condition of the Congo. And the more they heard about what was going on there, the more they shrugged: what else could you expect from the Heart of Darkness?

§

Leopold II, clever and mendacious, remade the Congo as a business venture and was the chairman of the board; but its first managing director, the man who turned it into a reality, was born John Rowlands, the illegitimate son of a local solicitor at St Asaph's in north Wales. (He took the name Henry Morton Stanley only after emigrating to New Orleans.) His escape at the age of fifteen from the workhouse where he grew up, his boundless determination to succeed, his unbearable bumptiousness, were all part of the Victorian legend of the successful man of action; the nineteenth-century equivalent of the American dream. Yet Stanley lied relentlessly about his past, claiming for instance that he had punched the overseer of the workhouse before leaving; in fact he was the much admired head boy. He went to America because Victorian England was inclined to look down its nose at him, and in order to win the affection of the first in a succession of unlikely American heiresses, he travelled to Africa to be an explorer.

Quite how much he understood of King Leopold's intentions is unclear; but whether he was the king's first dupe, or the king's cunning fixer, he was the man who opened up the Congo. Stanley believed as an article of faith that the river was navigable for the entire 2,900 miles from the point at which he built a town – Stanleyville, of course, now Kisangani – right down to the settlement called Leopoldville, now Kinshasa. He proved himself right, though it was sometimes a near-run thing, in an epic journey in 1877.

Henry Morton Stanley was a self-publicist, a twister, and an incorrigible boaster. Yet he certainly succeeded in navigating the Congo, and he certainly found Dr David Livingstone at Ujiji, beside Lake Tanganyika, in 1871, though whether Livingstone quite understood that he was supposed to be lost is unclear. Stanley may well have lied about some of the details of their famous meeting, and since Livingstone died soon afterwards we only have Stanley's word for what happened.

Stanley was capable of being a good and loyal companion. He could also be as cruel as almost every other white man in the Congo at the time. If his African porters annoyed him, he is said to have enjoyed whipping them and chaining them up, though this has been disputed by his latest and best biographer. Once, when his favourite dog, goaded by the heat, did something Stanley didn't like, he cut off its tail himself, ordered his servants to cook it, and made the dog eat it. That would scarcely have worried the Congolese, though. They eat dog meat with almost as much enthusiasm as they eat monkey meat, and the butchers' shops in Kinshasa have plenty for sale. Yet who are we, who eat hamburgers made from the meat of cows for whom the forests of Latin America have been cut down, and chickens and turkeys which are bred and slaughtered under conditions reminiscent of a concentration camp, to criticize their taste?

Stanley died, worn out and prematurely aged at sixty-three, in 1904. Throughout the seven decades of the colonial period, his statue and the iron boat which carried him on his epic voyage, the *Aia*, were placed side by side on a promontory overlooking the river. Then, after 1960, the boat was moved and the statue knocked down, and they disappeared, together with the other memorials of Belgian rule.

Arnaud Zaitman, of course, knew where they were stored. He arranged for his driver, Pierre, to take us there. Pierre grumbled and joked about the Congo the whole way, but in a sly, oracular fashion that was distinctly amusing. I could see immediately why, although he wasn't much of a driver, Arnaud employed him.

'This is a bitch of a country. When it isn't raining, they rob you. They would rob you when it's raining, too, except that they are too lazy to carry an umbrella.'

'Don't tell me you think the place was better under the Belgians?'

'Well, at least things worked then. They were bastards, but their police didn't stop you for doing nothing. And of course you and I were both young in those days, so things were really good.'

He had a sly way of laughing, so you were still trying to work out what he meant when you saw he was nodding his head up and down soundlessly.

'Would you want them back?'

'Would they want to come back? The answer in both cases is no, my friend. We are on our own here.'

We had reached a compound beside the river. Behind the rusting wire and the cancer-ridden concrete posts which held it up stood a building that had once been a bus depot. On the forecourt, and under a large lean-to with a weather-damaged corrugated-iron roof, stood thirty or more buses. Their windscreens had long since been smashed, and their tyres had been stolen or taken to burn on some cold night in the distant past. The paintwork, once the cheerful blue of the kind you see in the streets of happier, more peaceful cities, had faded in the sun of many years until it was almost white.

The buses had been the gift of the European Union, at a time when Europe cared about the Congo. But Kinshasa isn't Stockholm. No one paid their fares, there was rarely any fuel, and maintenance didn't cross anyone's mind. In a society like this, public initiatives scarcely exist. The people of Kinshasa get around by cramming themselves into private taxis and minibuses. The cost is minuscule, as it has to be, and the system works very well – give or take the occasional robbery and rape.

And so the buses had been turned into housing. They had neat little curtains, and there were cooking pots around the doors where northern European passengers once clambered in and out of the sleet. Washing lines had been attached to the steering wheels at one end, and to anything handy at the other. Little stoves stood on the ground in front of the radiator grilles. Nothing had been left unused; inside, curtains were strung from the straps that commuters once gripped and swayed with.

Pierre approached a man who, long years before, had been the watchman at the depot. Now, it seemed, he rented out the buses to suitable families; they had become his property, because no one else wanted them. But we had come to see him not as the entrepreneur of the buses, but as the keeper of the old colonial statues which had been dumped just behind the depot in 1960, and then forgotten.

Some folding money went into his receptive hand, and he led us through the decaying buildings that were once intended to be repair shops and offices, canteens and rest rooms. In an open area stood a dozen or more statues and reliefs: kings, queens, princes, princesses, Belgian heroes hacking their way through the jungle, and grateful and obedient Congolese on their knees to them all. If only the sculptors could carve a political future for us, how noble and contented and good looking we would all be! But instead we carve the future for the sculptors, and they try to make it seem attractive to us.

Above them all, the smiling queens and the straining blacks, stood a vast statue of a man on a horse. His aggressive spade beard, jutting out at an angle, identified him as Leopold II. Gawkily mounted, fifteen feet high, he looked out over the ruins of his act of public theft and cruelty, his right hand crooked and grasping, as though he could sense that there was money and men's lives to steal, even here, even now.

But there was no sign of what Mark and I had come to see and photograph. These were the statues and reliefs from the centre of Kinshasa; I was looking for the grand statue of Henry Morgan Stanley, and the *Aia*, in which he had successfully navigated the Congo. A moment's puzzlement, then the guardian of the place spoke to Pierre in the local language and another wedge of folding money went into a hand as grasping as the bronze Leopold's.

'*Là-bas,*' he said to me, pointing down towards the riverbank, way past the other statues and buildings.

Pierre was more precise, and much more courtly.

'*Voilà ton compatriote.*'

Anxious to reach my compatriot before someone decided to ask us for more money, I strode ahead of the others through the rank grass, which rasped as I brushed against it. Then the grass itself faded out, and there was nothing but the ochre ground.

Stanley was in a bad way. Someone had sawn through his legs at ankle height and (I imagine) an enthusiastic crowd had pushed his statue down. The steel supports inside his legs were bent and strained. I could imagine the sudden fury that had had that effect on solid metal. Then, their passion slaked, they had taken him a little further down the river which he himself had opened up, and hauled him up here. And on the riverbank they had given up the effort. They had simply tipped the statue, amputated at the feet as though he were one of the slaves who had refused to haul the requisite amount of ivory (foot-chopping was a frequent punishment for those who wouldn't walk), into his iron boat.

It was one of the weirdest sights I have ever seen. Stanley lies with his head, still protected by a regulation solar topee, pointing towards the *Aia*'s bows. His left arm is raised. When he was upright it would have shielded his fierce, mustachioed, triumph-of-the-will face from the equatorial sun. Prostrate, it looks as though he is in the middle of a swimming stroke, and is turning his head to take a mouthful of air. His right arm hangs down over the side of the boat. The overall effect is of a man swimming desperately, trying to get away from this place but never managing it.

Serves him right. Stanley, the most famous explorer of his time, the discoverer of Livingstone, used his famous name to make money out of the Congo and lend Leopold II's venture a little spurious respectability, rather than expose the horror or try to stop it.

And so, a century later, the Congo has had its revenge on him, far more effectively than if the mob had just smashed his statue to pieces. It has turned him into an absurdity, a silly joke. It's what he deserves.

§

Life in Kinshasa, like one of Bishop Fernand Kutino's addresses to his flock, is all about fighting. Unlike the bishop, who rakes in the money, it's mostly about extreme, grinding poverty: scraping the barest of livings in the most hostile of urban environments. Noise, dirt, disease, violence, cruelty, betrayal are the basic givens. It is Thomas Hobbes' *Leviathan* exported to equatorial Africa – a war of all against all. In these circumstances, you join with others only at times when individual violence becomes mob violence. The rest of the time you are on your own.

Even in the family there is no stability. Marriages break up continually. The average relationship, someone has estimated, lasts six years. When a man takes another wife, and takes his children with him, the chances are that she won't want them around if they are boys. Girls are different: they can be useful around the house, and later they can earn money working for others, or as prostitutes. So Congolese society has developed a mechanism for getting rid of unwanted boys. They are thrown out of the house on the grounds that they have turned into *sorciers*: wizards.

'What,' asked a recent opinion poll (for such things exist, even in Kinshasa), 'are the signs by which you can tell that a child is a *sorcier*?'

Wetting the bed, 23 per cent.

Disobedience, 24 per cent.

Throwing up in church, 38 per cent.

Being denounced by a man of God, honourable and reliable people like our friend the Bishop, 50 per cent.

But the best sign of all, according to no fewer than 80 per cent of the respondents, was if the child admitted it himself.

Absurd, you might think. Why would a young boy put himself in danger of getting thrown into the street, to live or die as fate chose, by admitting he was a wizard? Yet, as I discovered, this is exactly what can happen.

Arnaud knew who to go to. He gave us the address of a small European aid agency which specialized in helping street children, and the name of one of its workers. Jean-Marc turned out to be smart, nicely but not particularly expensively dressed, and he spoke good English. He had started out as a street child himself, and had been helped by the agency. At first he had worked for nothing, in return for food and shelter. Then he was given a full-time staff job.

According to Jean-Marc, there were thirty thousand street children in Kinshasa. Almost all of them were boys, and the great majority had been accused of being *sorciers*. Could he find one or two for me to speak to? No problem. He took us to a police station, where we waited, and was back in fifteen minutes, trailing behind him a small group of six ragged boys aged between ten and twelve.

'*Voilà*,' he said with a flourish, '*tes dit-sorciers.*' Here are your alleged wizards.

I interrogated them one by one, as though they were witnesses to a crime. And that, of course, is exactly what they were. It was a crime against themselves.

As a group they were competitive and jolly, nudging each other and giggling and making private jokes as they sat in a row on a wooden bench in front of me. But when I explained to them what I was going to do, and sent the others off into another room, each of the boys turned out to be quiet, reflective and melancholy, brought face to face with the small tragedy of his life. The cases were all depressingly similar.

Yannick Leblanc, for instance, was a slight, dreamy boy, small for his age, wearing a dirty white t-shirt several sizes too big for him. Most of the time he played quietly and thoughtfully with a piece of string tied round his wrist. But every now and then he would look me intently in the eyes, as though I were the one who was being interrogated. I felt uncomfortable. Like some psychiatric tourist, I was putting the boy through a difficult cross-questioning for my own selfish purposes and profit, asking him intrusive questions which it hurt him to answer. And he seemed to understand all this.

Yannick came from Congo Brazzaville, the former French colony just across the river. His mother died when he was eight, and he was sent to Kinshasa to be looked after by his uncle. The uncle was fine; it was the aunt who was the problem. Yannick played more intently than ever with his piece of string as he told me about the day when his aunt had announced there was no more money to look after him. He couldn't go and live with his father, who was last heard of in Gabon. All Yannick's clothes, except the rags he wore, had already been sold. His aunt hit him and called him a *sorcier*.

By now Yannick seemed to be paying the closest attention to the string. He was nearly crying, but didn't want me to see. He couldn't stop talking; the story came tumbling out of him. At first, to avoid his aunt's verbal and physical attacks, he would stay out all day, going to the market to beg for food, and coming back to their hut only late at night to sleep.

'Ah,' said the aunt, 'you're not at peace with yourself. That's a clear sign you're a *sorcier*.'

She hit him, and bit him, and broke his arm. He stretched it out to show me: the bone was bent out of true. After that, with his broken arm untended, he ran away to his grandparents. They were sympathetic, but they didn't have enough to feed themselves and him, and they all went hungry. In the end he knew he couldn't stay with them. He went and joined the street children.

By now the tears were very close, and if I'd been able to stop him I would have. But there was something else that troubled him badly – something he wanted to tell me even though it hurt.

'You know, I used to go to school. I was in the fifth grade.'

He cried unchecked then. He was deeply ashamed of his fall from education and grace, a Congolese David Copperfield.

The children's case histories were all depressingly similar. Two others wept as they told me their stories: the loss of a parent, or their home; the violence and cruelty; being driven out, or electing to leave. Perhaps they exaggerated, or blamed the wrong people. But they believed their own accounts of separation and suffering, and this ripped apart their tough, self-sufficient show and gave a glimpse of the wounded children they really were. I found the hour we spent interrogating them painful and disturbing, and I have never been able to forget it. Now that I have a son of my own, it cuts even deeper.

Yannick denied that he was a wizard, and so did the other children. Yet they didn't doubt that such things really existed. In fact, they said that another of their group, whom they called Pamuké, really was a *sorcier*. They told a confusing story about how he had flown through the air, and burned them with something while they slept. They had thrown him into a pool of water, but he had come out dry. That proves it, they said eagerly, looking for me to believe.

We went out to find Pamuké. Directly the boys got into the street, their adopted home, they became completely different from the vulnerable, melancholy children I had talked to earlier. Out here, among the mud and the stink of rubbish and the spray from the tyres of passing cars, they were pushy and tough, streetwise, near-adults.

Pamuké, when we found him, turned out to be an engagingly funny boy of twelve, with irregular features and teeth which were still too big for his child's face. Last week, he announced, some kids had accused him of killing and eating his own father.

'Is it true? Did you?'

Pamuké shrugged.

'Are you really a *sorcier*?'

A pause, then a tentative nod of the head, then a series of much more vigorous nods.

'What can I do?' Pamuké asked. 'I get into other people's dreams. I can't control my powers. I don't want to hurt people, but it just happens.'

'How does it happen?'

Silence. He looked at me, shifting his eyes to look into each of mine in turn searchingly. I found it quite disconcerting. Then another shrug.

I tried to think of something else to ask him, when he broke in.

'One day, maybe, the other kids will kill me.'

He wasn't laughing now. Pamuké, at the age of twelve, had discovered what we comfortable Westerners cannot bring ourselves to consider: that peace, protection, companionship, love, security, happiness, satisfaction are just artificial constructs which we make for ourselves, and we either possess them, or pretend we do.

There was no pretending for Pamuké. He knew he was entirely alone in the world, and he had foreseen his own future: an ugly, nasty, lonely death in a ditch at the hands of the children he consorted with. Perhaps, as I write this or as you read it, he will already be dead. His body will have been cast aside somewhere and carted off to be thrown into the ground, like any other piece of garbage. His life will have been nasty, brutish and very short.

Yet for now he was full of life, jumping around and laughing and playing tricks on the other kids, as though he had no thought that they might soon be his executioners.

The gang proudly showed us the little sleeping quarters they had created inside the walls of a ruined building by the roadside. They slept in pairs or trios in little hutches like dog kennels, built using things they had salvaged from the heaps of rubbish on every street corner, as jolly and happy as kids out of some nice childhood story: *Peter Pan and Wendy*, perhaps. That, at any rate, is how someone with a comfortable middle-class home and a happy family might imagine the experience. But suppose all the support systems and all the comforts and all the love were suddenly to evaporate, as they had for Yannick and Pamuké and the rest of these lost boys? Their reality wasn't nice and comfortable at all. It was dirt and sores and a private grief which could never be healed.

And then, as we were saying our goodbyes, an odd thing happened. Mark was taking his last pictures of the group of boys as they bunched up together in front of us, laughing and joking. But then they started to play up to the camera, acting the part of the zombies they had mostly denied they were. They staggered towards us like extras out of Michael Jackson's old video 'Thriller', their faces distorted, their arms reaching out to grab us and turn us into *sorciers* ourselves.

§

The Nautic Club was an absurd little outpost of tidy colonialism. The grass leading down to the River Congo was carefully mown. Everything was newly painted. A postcard on the notice board beside the door of the clubhouse said 'Madame Laure: Piano Lessons By Arrangement', as though King Baudouin was still the master of the country and Leopold was still on his horse in the centre of town. At the bar, the clink of the ice-cubes in my gin and tonic was louder than the noise coming from a few dozen yards away.

Because the ludicrous thing was that the real Kinshasa lay just on the other side of the Nautic Club walls. Swarming, noisy, easily provoked masses of people were trading, buying, stealing, banging, shouting, hooting, playing loud music, unbearably distorted, in the sweltering damp heat, while the dark green leaves dripped water on them like a rain shower. The club wasn't a haven so much as a fantasy for the rich and, mostly, the white.

We had gone there to hire a boat for a trip on the river so Mark could take some photographs. The Congo moved slowly beneath our rented vessel like a single living creature, vast, lead coloured, oily, its movement marked only by the clumps of water-hyacinth which were moving effortlessly downstream at a speed of three knots. They were all that marked the difference between the grey water and the grey sky.

Suspended on the mirrored surface of the river, we overtook a little steamer, like something out of *The African Queen*, packed with people who surely wouldn't all have room to lie down on the decks at night. They were making the dangerous journey to Kisangani, not having the money to fly there. It was longer, much more risky, and far more testing physically and mentally than a trip to the moon. They too believed that Mark was stealing their souls by taking their photographs. They roared at us across the water, shaking their fists with a rage that, at that distance, seemed rather comical.

Closer up, I would have been scared; so much sudden, unregulated anger emanating from fifty or sixty people is a shocking thing. But distance detracts from that, just as pilots say it detracts from any sense of common humanity when they drop bombs on their targets. The people on the boat would never be able to catch us, so we could stare at them with impunity, and take their pictures too, as though they were bacilli, edging their way through the African bloodstream to the very heart of the creature, and we were studying them through our microscopes.

Not having the time or the courage to go by boat, we flew with the UN to Kisangani. Soon afterwards, it was attacked by rebel soldiers, who burned down the compound where we stayed. But at this time it was still relatively peaceful: apart, that is, from the usual sense of impending violence and eruption.

Kisangani must once have been pleasant enough, when it was Stanleyville; if, that is, you were a white colonist. Since the pre-independence boom, though, no building of any significance had been erected there. The houses of the European traders and planters were slowly decaying and collapsing where they stood, the damp from fifty years of unresisted rains staining the once-white fronts, the rich, untended greenery thrusting its way through roofs and doors and windows, showing who was master here.

And just as the forest strained and spread and reasserted itself, so the local population displayed an almost silent rage against intruders which it would have been foolish to ignore. Terrible things had happened in Kisangani over the years: massacres, mutilations, cruelty on a scale that showed it was meant to be exemplary. I have always felt liberated in Africa, as though I am free to act and speak in a far more natural way than I can in Europe or North America. It was in Zimbabwe that I first learned how easy it was to drape my arm over a man's shoulder; something I would never have done in England. But Africans are free and relaxed and easy, and it was a revelation to me to be among them.

Kisangani, though, wasn't like that. It was openly angry and hostile, and (unlike Kinshasa) its barely controlled ferocity wasn't covered by any appearance of ordinary day-to-day activity. This was a town which was waiting for the next eruption, and knew it wouldn't be long in coming. Even walking down the street past the diamond dealers and the money changers – because Kisangani is an important trading centre for gems and minerals in its own right – sweating in the ferocious, moist heat of the afternoon, felt danger-ous. In Kisangani, the slavery and cruelty of Stanley's day have left a long shadow.

And so, when I was there, had the peaceable and well-intentioned efforts of a group of Belgian and American doctors at the medical faculty of Stanleyville University in the 1950s. Opinion among scien-tists researching the origins of AIDS eventually turned against the theory that the disease might have crossed the species barrier from primates to human beings here in the medical faculty, but it was an engrossing one for a time.

The plan had been to develop a polio vaccine by testing it out first on chimpanzees. But during the process of inoculating thousands of people in the town and its surroundings, the story went, the AIDS virus which had existed in the chimpanzees was passed to human beings, and thence, eventually, to the world. It was said that the blood samples from the original experiments were still faithfully kept at the medical faculty building in Kisangani, and that they contained the proof that people here had first contracted AIDS. We knew that French and American researchers had been trying recently to obtain the samples, but it had been too dangerous for them to get to Kisangani and collect them.

For a short while, though, conditions in the town were peaceful enough for Mark and me to go there. The medical faculty was set a little outside the town. I had seen a photograph of it in a book which detailed the theory of the AIDS species leap: *The River*, by the medical historian Edward Hooper, and knew it was a clean, efficient-looking, white-painted building set in well-tended grounds: the kind of place you could find at the time in any of fifty African cities governed by white colonists.

When our taxi delivered us there we were shocked to see what time, neglect and Africa had done to it. The building had been quite badly damaged during the recent fighting, and the surrounding forest, which the Belgian colonists had ordered to be hacked down, had begun to reclaim it. Full-grown trees had established themselves on the roof, in the hospitable dampness where the gutters had once been. It had been necessary to cut a new path through the under-growth in the old garden so people could reach the main entrance.

Because, in spite of its wrecked appearance, it was still the medical faculty of Kisangani University. There were even feeble attempts made to teach students there, though most of them had fled or been killed during the recent fighting. We made our way down the path through the waist-high bushes, and pushed open the protesting door. Inside, the ancient plaster, untouched since the Belgians left, was erupting in a series of gigantic white sores. The ceilings in the corridors had billowed out and sometimes collapsed, and no one had swept away the debris. The doors had been shot open by the first soldiers to capture the place, and then shot open again when it was recaptured.

An elderly man with a bad shave and a mobile Adam's apple sat there, his face shining in the afternoon heat. He seemed completely unaffected by our sudden arrival, after all the months, even years, in which no European had come here; in fact it didn't seem to interest him. All he cared about was the camera Mark was carrying.

'Photographs are forbidden because of the war,' he said impassively, his Adam's apple the only really animated thing about him.

'But the war is over. The soldiers have gone.'

He smiled. It wasn't ill will which prevented him from letting us in, it was a rigid, faithful adherence to the last set of orders anyone gave him.

'You must have permission.'

Fifty years of national independence had done nothing to make him less dependent on higher authority.

It took a little time to track down the head of the university and get permission to photograph anything we wanted. He, at least, was a jovial man who understood that the security situation had improved. And he saw the possibility, perhaps, of a discreet profit for his bankrupt, poverty-stricken campus.

He introduced us to the dean, a big man in a bright red shirt who was carrying a French magazine about astronomy under his arm. He guided us up the damaged concrete staircase, with its missing steps and its bullet holes, to the laboratories on the first floor. One was almost entirely empty and smelt of the jungle. At the far end was a solitary shelf at chest height, on which stood several open boxes thick with dust and cobwebs. You wouldn't want to put your hand in them without looking very carefully first.

'*Voilà les lâmes que vous cherchez*,' said the dean, with a theatrical air. Here are the slides you are looking for.

He took one out gingerly. It was a strip of discoloured glass a little larger than a Tube ticket. I peered at it. It enclosed a small, rosy splodge. Attached to it was a small strip of browning paper on which was written in spidery French when the blood sample had been taken and whom it had once belonged to.

'We have looked after these things very well,' said the dean in a sanctimonious voice which made me realize he was hoping for some money from us. 'The world should reward us for keeping them,' he added, as though I mightn't have got the point.

For him, we were representatives of the international community, and could be expected to express the gratitude of the entire world. I nodded politely, but said nothing. We stood there for a while, examining more of the slides, while he went off and looked out of the window at the decay and vibrant new growth all round the building.

Downstairs, in the remains of another laboratory, we found a middle-aged man in a dirty white coat. I was touched by that: it seemed to represent an affirmation of duty and the continuity of scholarship. He was going through the motions, for our benefit, of examining something through a microscope. This must have been how educated local people in Europe behaved after the Romans left, I thought – hanging on to the forms of civilization while everything broke down around them. Yet it pained me to find myself regarding the colonization of Africa as civilization, since it had so clearly not been intended that Africans should be entirely civilized until very late in the colonial day; and now Europeans like me would come along and look down on the people they encountered for being deficient in civilized qualities.

Near the man with the microscope sat a very old man who seemed to have no function whatever. He was, someone explained, the janitor, and he had worked here in the 1950s, during the Belgian occupation. I asked him a question or two, but his replies were so listless and brief that I could scarcely understand them.

Then I asked what it had been like to work in this building during the old colonial days. His face lit up at once, and a sense of sudden animation came over him in this hot, dusty, humid room, filled with the smell of decay: the decay of dead creatures, of dead vegetation, of dead bricks and plaster, of a dead culture.

'It was wonderful – so clean, so tidy. Not at all like the dirt you have here today. And the Belgians and Americans – they were so civilized, so well dressed, so educated.' He sighed, and looked away. 'And now . . .'

§

There was one last place I wanted to see in Kisangani. In 1950 Katharine Hepburn, Humphrey Bogart and John Huston made *The African Queen* on this stretch of the river, and I had heard that the house they lived in during the shoot was still standing.

We drove along the riverbank for a mile or so to the west of the town, where a line of grand, decaying mansions stood. I spotted the Villa Regina at once: a charming place, set apart in its own grounds, but as stained and crumbling as all the others, vegetation thrusting out in the angles of the building like armpit hair.

Dozens of families lived here now, their washing hanging from the architraves, their children and chickens and listless dogs padding around outside. Everything seemed to be moving at half-speed in the damp heat. Idle, resentful men gestured at us and shouted, only it was too hot for them to bother to come across and attack us.

Somehow, it seemed emblematic of everything that had happened to this rich, magnificent country in its half-century of independence. After the decades of neat colonial brutality, the Congo had been reclaimed with a vengeance. Here, more than anywhere, I found I couldn't get that phrase of Joseph Conrad's, 'fantastic invasion', out of my head, imagining Hepburn in her starched white dresses with blue or red sashes, and the after-shoot drinks with Bogart and Huston on the verandah, while the sun went down over the river and the white-coated servants politely murmured that dinner would be ready in twenty minutes.

As late as 1950, they could never have imagined a world as wild, dangerous and unkempt as this. Now, though, the fantastic invasion is comprehensively over – at least in its colonial form – and little is left except despair, anger and the rank growth of the forest, coming back to reclaim its own.

As we left the Villa Regina, our car got stuck in a large pool of standing water by the entrance. Spinning the wheels simply drove us deeper into the mud. As Mark and I jumped out to push, a group of twenty people suddenly manifested itself around us to help us. At the third effort, we succeeded, and the wheels sprayed us all liberally with muddy water. Everyone laughed. The driver, whom we had hired in Kisangani, disdainfully threw a handful of notes out of the window, and adults and boys fought each other for a moment or two to get them.

A tall, spare figure in his early thirties stood watching them. I'd noticed him earlier, with his sardonic expression and his head shaved like an American Marine. He hadn't helped us push the car out. He looked at me as though he understood perfectly what I was thinking; and he was right.

'The Belgians built this place,' he said, nodding towards the Villa Regina and the people camping in its once attractive rooms and corridors and balconies. 'We Congolese have improved it. In our own special way, of course.'

This is a beautiful, rich, terribly damaged country, betrayed and tortured by everyone who has tried to control it. Nowadays it encompasses gangs which slice off people's faces to demonstrate their power, clergymen whose religion consists solely of milking their congregations of cash, children who are driven out to live or die in the streets because they are a nuisance to feed, diseases which burst out of the forest and haunt the entire globe.

The Congo must have a future, because everywhere has a future. Every week dozens of earnest bureaucrats from the outside world come here in the hope of constructing one. But it most certainly has a past. And that past gives the Congo its dreadful, violent, unchanging present.

11

BUSHMEN

In 1950, when I was six years old, there were 2.7 billion people in the world. By 2050, if we continue the way we are now, there will be nine billion of us; and by the end of the century the figure could be thirteen billion – an unthinkably large, highly destructive population of people who care nothing for each other, or for our small and fragile planet, or even for our own long-term interests.

It may well not happen, either because we learn how to control ourselves, or else because some major plague arrives to wipe most of us out and restore a certain harmony to the planet. But it is certainly one of the strong possibilities we face. We are so successful as a species that we are breeding and consuming our way to the earth's utter destruction.

Yet this isn't the first time in our history as a species that human beings have faced the possibility of being wiped out. There were, of course, the moments within living memory when we seemed to be in danger of all-out thermonuclear war, though nothing of the sort happened. But the period I mean was something like 80–100,000 years ago. Perhaps because of some major disaster such as a volcanic eruption or a strike by a meteorite, or maybe because of suddenly changing weather conditions, the human population dwindled to a very low level indeed: perhaps 2,000 individuals all told.

In the past few years, researchers from Stanford University in the United States and the Russian Academy of Sciences took DNA samples from more than fifty areas around the world. These confirmed that we are all descended from a very small number of ancestors, and that as a result our genetic pool is, relatively speaking, tiny. A group of twenty or thirty chimpanzees is likely to have a greater genetic variety than all six billion human beings in the world today.

The evidence now shows incontrovertibly that we are all related to each other, and fairly closely at that. 'Am I not a man, and a brother?' was the slogan of the anti-slavery movement, almost certainly formulated by Dr Peter Peckard, the Master of Magdalene College Cambridge in the 1780s. He meant it idealistically, but it has turned out to be more true than he or anyone else could have suspected. Just as DNA findings have shown that every dog on earth, from a Chihuahua to a Great Dane, is descended from wolves which became domesticated, so we, Inuits and Aborigines and Caucasians and Africans and Chinese, all have a common ancestress, Mitochondrial Eve, who lived a short but remarkably productive life somewhere in sub-Saharan Africa.

The Stanford/Academy of Sciences study found that hunter-gatherer groups began separating off from farmers in Africa as long ago as 140,000 years. An earlier genetic study suggested that humans first started to leave Africa, perhaps following the shoreline north to the Gulf and thence to India and beyond, around 66,000 years ago.

These were the headline findings of the study. But there were others; for instance, that the Mbuti pygmies of the Congo basin and the Khoisan Bushmen of Botswana have a close genetic kinship. They were, said the researchers, the oldest branch of modern humans which they had studied.

So pygmies and Bushmen – both of them derogatory terms, though both groups seem actually to prefer using them – are our brothers too. A few decades ago, scarcely anyone would have wanted to believe this. There are certain quite strong physiological differences between Bushmen and Africans or Europeans. Bushmen in general have particularly baggy skin, and the men tend to have permanently semi-erect penises: something of a problem, apparently, when they hunt. They also have less cartilage in their noses than the rest of us.

Yet you only have to spend a short time with any so-called primitive people to realize that the differences between us are minimal. It happened to me when I first visited Amazonia, and spent some time with a tribe of Indians called the Ashaninca, close to the Brazil–Peru border, in some of the most remote territory on earth. These Indians had never seen people who were not themselves

Indians before, and they were almost entirely unaffected by the outside world. Living, as they did, seven days' journey by river from the nearest town, the dense forest cut them off from outside influences.

To my shame, I suppose I expected them to be some kind of hominoids, primitive and wholly undeveloped. Instead, I found the Ashaninca village where I stayed to be full of exactly the same kind of individuals I knew from my life in Britain. There was the eternal optimist, who used to stride through the forest whistling a cheery tune and slashing at the long grass with his stick; there was the miserable older man, very much under his wife's thumb; there was the attractive younger woman, who was teased by the others for the amount of time she used to spend every morning painting her face with the juice of the bright red urucum berry.

She and the others would spend hours looking at and playing with the beads and mirrors we had brought with us to trade for the beautiful headdresses they made from parrot feathers. Yet even when we went away for two days and a night, not a single one of the beads disappeared. I asked the village headman why not.

'The other people in the village wouldn't like it. I wouldn't like it.'

As in an English village at any time down to the nineteenth century, everyone knew everyone else's business. If a single imitation pearl bead had disappeared, the others would have been aware of it immediately, and would have insisted that whoever had taken it should hand it back in order to preserve the village's good name. Our vastly increased numbers, and our greater sense of privacy and individuality, have changed all that, and because we are reluctant to face up to other people ourselves, we employ a police force and a legal system to do it for us.

So pygmies and Bushmen and Amazonian Indians are closely related to us, but are simply at a different level of development. Technically, of course, they are a thousand years behind us, yet when you see these three groups, and others like them, you wonder if they really are behind us at all. The Ashaninca cured me of the paralysing effects of a very painful insect bite simply by picking a leaf and squeezing the juice onto the wound. And when my brother-in-law Mark and his wife, Dee's sister Gina, broke down in the

Kalahari Desert and were in serious danger of dying from thirst or exposure, they were saved by a small group of Bushmen, no larger than children, who appeared from nowhere, lifted their Land Rover bodily out of the sand where it was stuck, and set it on the track again. They may scarcely have seen a car before, but they knew exactly what to do to rescue one.

Yet the Bushmen, like the pygmies and the Amazonian Indians, are regarded by their neighbours as effectively sub-human. President Festus Mogae of Botswana once asked in a public speech, 'How can you have a Stone Age creature continuing to exist in the age of computers?' The Botswanan government forced them off their land and rehoused them in dreadful camps where they quickly succumbed to alcohol and AIDS. Many people suspected it was because diamonds had been discovered in the part of the Kalahari which the Bushmen had been given in perpetuity by the British.

Like many of us, I had been attracted to the Bushmen by the books of Laurens van der Post and, more recently, Sandy Gall. Then I became a patron of a small but highly effective medical charity called Health Unlimited, which ran a clinic for the Bushmen in north-eastern Namibia, and took advantage of that to go and see them.

The Kalahari covers an area of more than half a million square kilometres: about the size of France. It overlaps several countries: Angola, Botswana, Namibia, South Africa, Zambia and Zimbabwe. Altogether there are thought to be about 90,000 Bush people, divided into several groups. They speak a wide variety of languages, almost all of which use various types of tongue-click. They don't feel that they form a separate group, different from other people, and they don't call themselves by any collective name. In recent decades, realizing that 'Bushmen' was derogatory, Westerners began referring to them by the names which were used for them in the countries where they lived: 'San' in Namibia, 'Basarwa' in Botswana; I suppose it sounded more authentic. Yet both these terms are contemptuous or insulting too, and all the Bushmen I have asked about it prefer to be called just that: 'Bushmen'.

'This is what we are,' one of them said. 'We are men who live in the bush.'

Everywhere they live, they find themselves at the bottom of the social order, despised and segregated and pushed around. It has always been like this. The Bushmen once occupied almost all of southern Africa, and may have lived in part of East Africa too. Yet each new wave of immigrants pushed them further and further aside. They are physically small, but they are also essentially peaceful, and abhor the killing of other human beings. When the South African army used them as trackers in the guerrilla war before Namibia's independence, they were occasionally compelled to kill. Those who did usually suffered from serious psychological problems which often led to their own deaths.

So all they could do when the Bantu spread downwards into southern Africa, at roughly the time the first Europeans were settling there, was to fall back into less and less hospitable territory, until in the end there was nowhere left to go except the Kalahari itself. Only the Bushmen had the necessary skills to survive in one of the fiercest deserts on earth.

Yet even there they aren't entirely safe. In Namibia, tough and assertive cattle farmers from the Herero people are moving illegally into the area of the Kalahari called Tsumkwe West. The government wants to turn part of the area into a refugee camp. And an Australian prospecting company says that diamonds are likely to exist in Tsumkwe East, one of the Bushmen's last havens.

It's just the latest of many threats to their existence. In nineteenth-century Namibia, then called South-West Africa, the German colonizers organized regular hunts to kill them. After the First World War, South-West Africa was given to South Africa to administer. In 1948 South Africa imposed apartheid on the country, and moved the Bushmen off their land in order to create game reserves and white farms. After Namibia received its independence, the black farmers were just as hostile to them. The Bushmen are now threatened on all sides.

§

I spotted them instantly in the crowd. The school bell rang, the children came pouring out into the playground, laughing and joking and pushing each other. But the last children to leave stayed together by the door, about a dozen in number. They didn't join in the games and they didn't laugh. They were smaller than the others, and much lighter in colour. Their skins were apricot, and their features seemed almost Asiatic, with high cheekbones and slanted eyes. The Bushmen children were quiet and earnest and used to being bullied. They were at the back of the line for everything: education, food, health-care.

'Sometimes I think they live in a dream world,' said the teacher. 'They don't answer my questions, they don't play with the other children. But when I speak to them on their own, and they don't have to compete for my attention, they are quick and bright.'

She shook her head sadly. Unlike most teachers here, she cared about them and wanted to help them.

I walked closer, trying not to be too obtrusive. I could hear the clicks they made, light ones from the front of the mouth, deep ones formed by making the mouth into a deep cavern. But when I went and stood beside them, they stopped talking, as though the sounds gave them away. Like hunters, they wanted to merge into the background. The language they were speaking was Zu/'hoasi; the punctuation marks are an attempt to represent particular clicks and glottal stops.

The names of the surrounding Bushmen villages stretch conventional orthography to its limits; !Xo, for instance. Later, my Bushman translator taught me how to pronounce it, but I could only do it by trying to achieve the sound you would make to a child if you tried to express sympathy and annoyance at the same time. In fact, it is almost entirely irreproducible.

The Kalahari is not a sand desert, like the Sahara. It is sparsely covered with trees and bushes, though there are occasional outbreaks of sand dunes. At first it can look almost hospitable – until you start to walk in it. Then you realize that everything here is utterly harsh and resistant, from the thorn-covered scrub to the low bushes and the small, bent trees. There is nothing on them that is spare or apparently edible, yet the Bushmen know how to use every part of these plants.

They are hunters as well as gatherers, though the government now restricts what game they can take, and how often. Duiker, a deer the size of a large dog, are their favourite prey; yet when you look around you at the few thin bushes in the empty landscape, you wonder how they could possibly get close enough to kill them.

In !Xo and some of the other villages I found the people were pleasant and welcoming, clever at seeking out herbs and fruits, and adept at hunting duiker with their small, poison-tipped arrows. But others were much more depressing. In the camps they had been moved to, most people had surrendered to alcohol and drug dependency. The deciding factor seemed to be the strength of their culture. The stronger their traditions, the less likely they were to sink into despair and give themselves up to drink.

In the strange little colonial town of Gobabis, where Health Unlimited had its local headquarters, I talked to a girl called Joanna Nawadoes. She was only the size of a ten-year-old, but in fact she was eighteen, and sufficiently educated and self-confident to be an instructor for Health Unlimited. In particular, she was very good at persuading other Bushman teenagers to go to local clinics to get advice about avoiding HIV/AIDS. At a lecture she gave there was a lot of embarrassed laughter as Joanna showed them, using a suitable model, how to get a condom onto a boy.

She was completely unflustered. When I spoke to her on camera for a promotional video Health Unlimited was making, I found she was sharp-minded and outspoken. Yet qualities like these had failed to protect her against the exploitation and ill treatment which are all that most Bushmen can expect from the rest of the population.

Joanna told me that she had paid the headmaster of a Catholic school an advance of 220 Namibian dollars (£14 – quite a large amount for a young woman like her) in advance for a term's teaching. But her mother fell ill and she had to nurse her, so she couldn't attend the course. She went to ask the headmaster if he would agree to put her money towards the next term's tuition fees. But although he had been happy to see her before, he refused to meet her now.

Instead, his secretary told Joanna that the rules wouldn't allow what she wanted. They wouldn't allow the school to refund the money either. I told her she should complain, but she just shrugged. That was the kind of thing that happened to Bushmen. And when I told her I would go round and have it out with the headmaster, she begged me not to; there are so many ways a man like that can get back at you in a small town like Gobabis, she said.

Health Unlimited, working with the Namibian government, had

achieved one important success there. (Forgive me if I boast about it; the BBC has nowadays forbidden the people who work for it to be associated with charitable organizations or campaigns of any kind – suppose, the argument went, you had to report on something bad your outfit had done? I can see the sense in that, even though it saddened me greatly to cut my links with Health Unlimited, Amnesty International and Prisoners of Conscience. But I would just like to blow the HU trumpet one last time.)

The Bushmen are particularly susceptible to tuberculosis, but in Tsumkwe there has been a remarkable degree of success in curing it. To treat TB properly, you usually have to move the patient to hospital. They need to take a variety of pills at particular times, and most people are too careless and forgetful to do that without supervision. But Bushmen are wanderers by nature, and unwilling to let themselves be bundled up and put into an institution. Most of them would rather die; and they did die, in large numbers.

Health Unlimited trained people like Joanna to raise teams of volunteers, most of them Bushmen themselves, to monitor large areas, tracking individuals who were suffering from TB and treating them on a regular basis. HU's achievement was that 84 per cent of sufferers had been cured like this: a world first.

We drove out from Gobabis into the depths of the Kalahari. After a lifetime of travelling, I am fairly phlegmatic about it, but the roads of Namibia frightened me. It is a vast country, almost the size of western Europe, yet not much more than a million people live there. I have never seen roads so empty of both traffic and habitation. Someone in Gobabis told me that a couple had broken down in their car on a drive between one town and another; their skeletons were found, picked clean, beside the car some weeks later.

Maybe that's simply the kind of thing people in Namibia say to freak out susceptible Europeans; if so, it worked on me. I was simply terrified on these long roads, with the sun burning down on us and only a couple of bottles of water in a cooler on the back seat. Gangs of armed and masked brigands I can take: I have great faith in my ability to talk my way out of trouble. But there is no arguing with the sun, or with a pack of hyenas.

Our engine held up, and Dee and I and our cameraman and a couple of Health Unlimited people finally reached an utterly

featureless place in the road which our Bushman translator recognized at once. We trudged across the harsh ground for some way
until we saw a hut with a grass roof, and then another and another.
There was a fence, though what purpose it served wasn't clear, and
as we followed it round we found a group of twenty or more people
sitting outside the main hut, quietly working at various types of
handicraft and talking softly among themselves.

From a distance, because there was no threat of any kind to
them here, the Zu/'hoasi they were speaking sounded like the
twittering of birds and the clicking of a dozen gates. The village
was named Sonneblom, the Afrikaans word for 'sunflower', presumably by some upbeat administrator in Gobabis or far-distant
Windhoek. Bushmen have to speak several languages if they are to
fit in with the people who run their lives, but the main one, apart
from their own, is the lingua franca of Afrikaans.

The people here formed a nomadic band, made up of six families
in all. There were plenty of children running around or lying in
their mothers' arms; no danger, for the foreseeable future, that the
Sonneblom group might die out. They lived here in the area the
government had set aside for them, around a water-hole. They were
waiting to greet us, dressed in their best clothes. Their faces were a
cameraman's dream, with sharp eyes in the light skin and wrinkles
that seemed deeper than ours: almost, but not quite, like tribal cuts
on their cheeks. I asked the headman of the village what it was he
was carving from a piece of yellowish wood. He held it up to show
me: it was a small guinea fowl, delicately done. He explained in
Afrikaans that it was a gift for his baby son, so he would know
what was good to hunt when he was older.

'I'd really prefer it if he spoke Zu/'hoasi when we're filming,'
I told the translator; I wanted the audience to be able to hear the
language for themselves. The translator explained, and the headman
at once slipped into the complex sounds of the Bushmen.

We moved over to where the oldest inhabitant of the village sat,
munching toothlessly. She was, the translator said, ninety-nine years
old.

'How different were things when you were a girl?' I asked.

Her little eyes, scarcely perceptible among the wrinkles, checked
me out and then slowly moved off to the horizon. She carried on

chewing for a moment. Then she spoke, very quietly, with the clicks almost imperceptible.

'The game was plentiful then,' the translator said, with his usual schoolmasterly precision. 'We would kill eight animals, and that would be enough for everyone for a whole month.'

'And now?'

'Now they only let the men take a few duiker.'

Everyone nodded; it was a heartfelt complaint at Sonneblom that the government wouldn't let them hunt in the way they used to.

But there was no doubt that hunting was still the most important thing in their lives. As we were talking, a young man aged about twenty arrived, whistling. He carried a bow and arrows in a quiver made from an animal skin on his back. Through the translator, I asked the man if he would show us the contents of the bag, and he tipped them out: a bow, only about two feet long, a little tortoise shell full of some kind of powder, and twenty or so small arrows, unflighted, but with well-made iron heads. The Bushmen buy the arrowheads at a store on the edge of their area. Before they were available, they used a particular type of wood for their arrows, which was difficult to find. It could be cut to a point that was almost as sharp and durable as iron.

But the real weapon was the poison they smear on the tips of their arrows. Made from crushing the larvae of Chrysomelidae beetles, it acts as a paralysing agent, entering the quarry's bloodstream, slowing down and eventually stopping the action of the muscles. Then the Bushmen have a chance to catch up with their prey. But the poison is weak and slow acting, and after they shoot a kudu or an eland they often have to chase the animal for four or five days before it drops from exhaustion.

'We don't keep the poison here in the village, in case the children get hold of it and it gets into an open wound,' said the headman.

I could see he didn't want to talk about it.

'Where do you keep it?'

But that was as much as the headman was willing to say on the subject. He turned back to whittling his guinea fowl.

The young man was putting his arrows back into his animal-skin quiver.

'Would he mind showing us how he hunts?'

I knew it was a little crass, but these hunting skills may not survive too much longer, and I wanted to be able to show them on camera.

A couple of boys went running off and hung some kind of cloth in the bushes, forty yards away, to signify an animal. The hunter entered entirely into the spirit of the thing, like someone playing charades. Everything he did was delicately exaggerated, from miming the pulling out of the bow, choosing his two favourite arrows, pretending to smear the mysterious poison on them, and then throwing himself on the ground and wriggling his way to the shelter of an upturned tin bath. But the rest of the Bushmen were too noisy and excited by his display, and he had to turn round to hush them. Then he raised himself very slowly, with his elbow on top of the bath, and, holding his bow at an angle, he loosed an arrow at the target.

There was an instant's pause; then the cloth fell, and was carried away in triumph by the two boys. Everyone clapped their hands together and shouted the marksman's praises. He grinned, and retrieved his arrows from one of the boys.

Here, at least, the Bushmen could be themselves, and could feel they were of value. On the farms, when they went for work during the bad times of the year, they were treated little better than animals. Often their pay would consist of nothing more than a bag of sugar or mealie-meal, and perhaps a bottle of the roughest alcohol.

Among their own, though, they have proper status. The others respect them for their skills. Their name for themselves is 'the real people'. I smiled when I heard that, because the name 'Ashaninca' means precisely the same thing. To ourselves, we are always the real people, and everyone else is a little weird or unfathomable, and perhaps a little less than real.

§

It shocks the human spirit to find that a well in the desert has been deliberately destroyed. I was standing near the largest, and sometimes the only, well in the Central Kalahari Game Reserve. From a distance, the square concrete basin where the water lay looked like a small swimming-pool. Up close, I could see it was full of sand. The pipe that once filled it had been hacked open, and sand dripped out of its mouth in a dry yellow parody of water. The job of destroying the well had been done with a thoroughness that seemed to border on anger. You have to be pretty angry to want to make sure that anyone left in the area will die of thirst.

Especially if they are a small group of harmless men, women and children who simply want to remain on their ancestral lands, given to them legally and in perpetuity. These lands were vast, and there were only sixty Bushmen left on them. But the government of Botswana had deemed that they should be relocated, and it had given them the effective choice of moving or dying. It all seemed so unlikely. Botswana wasn't Zimbabwe, run by a vicious and corrupt thug; it was a quiet, effective, prosperous democracy – one of the showcase nations of Africa. In every other respect, it was an exemplar. Yet somehow, for reasons one could only speculate about, it had chosen to employ tactics against the Bushmen which were as bad as the ethnic cleansing which used to go on in the former Yugoslavia.

The government started moving against the Bushmen in 1996, claiming that they would be better cared for in resettlement camps. It wanted to turn the Central Kalahari, where they had lived and hunted for 10,000 years, and which was ceded to them formally by the British in 1961, into a game reserve. There were thought to be diamonds under the land – a possibility that soon turned into a certainty.

In February 2002 the government sent in lorries and troops to clear out the thousand or so Bushmen who had resisted the earlier deportations. The great majority of them went without a struggle. Many revealed afterwards that the soldiers had threatened to burn them alive in their huts if they stayed. They were taken away in army lorries. Then the soldiers turned their attention to destroying the wells.

I visited the Central Kalahari Game Reserve, where these people came from, a few months later, not with a television news camera-man but with a large and very pleasant film crew. It was a curious business. The news desk had been uninterested in my suggestion that I should report about what was happening to the Bushmen in

Botswana, but at that very moment the people in charge of filming on-air promotions for the BBC asked me if I would be prepared to make a short film for them, showing how the BBC's two television news channels, News 24 and BBC World, operated in the field. Since promotional films are the BBC's equivalent of advertisements, they are very short indeed – rarely more than forty-five seconds long – but they are made to the highest standards of the advertising industry, and as with most commercial advertisements there is a huge budget for them.

Where in the world, the producer asked me, would I like to go in order to be filmed filing a report to London? The question came at exactly the right moment.

'I'd like to go to the Kalahari Desert,' I said.

We did a deal. I was going to be in Johannesburg reporting on an international conference, and the team would join me there. They would hire the vehicles, tents and everything else we would need, and then we would head off together to the Kalahari for a few days. In between filming me, they would also film the Bushmen for a news report I would make. It suited everyone: they would get a genuine, rugged set of images for their advertisement and I would be able to report a story I thought would be of great interest around the world; a story which wouldn't otherwise be told.

These advertising teams are never small. They don't need to be, because the money involved is always plentiful. (In news, by contrast, we are always trying to squeeze the final drops out of an already thoroughly squeezed orange.) This team was actually quite compact. There was a director, a producer, a script person, a cameraman, an assistant cameraman, and a sound recordist. They turned out to be delightful people, experienced, funny and highly efficient.

Collaborations like these are usually intriguing for both sides. News people always feel crude and dull and workaday next to film people, and film people always seem to feel that they are just butterflies, concerning themselves with trivia, while we are deeply serious and doing work of international importance. It was a little like my friendships with actors and comics – they spend the whole time trying to show how serious and well-informed they are, I spend my whole time trying to make them laugh. In this case, the crew had wonderful stories to tell of Hollywood and the British film industry, while I could only talk about the news. But we all got on extremely well.

We drove to Gaborone, the Botswanan capital, then set off the next morning for the CKGR, as we came to call it. The Botswanan government had tried to prevent journalists from going to see the remaining Bushmen, but because Botswana is otherwise a free and relaxed country there was no police system in place to monitor us or get in our way. The entrance to the reserve was manned by a team of wardens, who were all very polite and correct. I couldn't forget, though, how some of these wardens here at the gate had treated the Bushmen in their charge. They had beaten up several of them, including the women, and there had apparently been some nasty injuries: broken bones, ruptured spleens.

After the water supply was blocked off at Gugamu, one of the two villages whose inhabitants had decided to stay, the Bushmen had to buy their water. They had, of course, very little money – they have no need of it in the usual way – but managed to scrape enough together by doing small jobs of work and selling some of their animals. The nearest trading-post was forty miles away, well outside the boundaries of the game reserve. The men of Gugamu made the long trek there on foot, and each of them carried several gallons of water on his back on the return journey. At the gates, the same polite, pleasant game rangers we saw stopped them and poured out all the precious water onto the ground in front of them.

If you or I looked at these Bushmen, small and sinewy and gentle, our hearts would go out to them. They are strong, immensely resourceful and incomparably knowledgeable about the desert, but in most other ways they are like children, defenceless against our world and its ways. Perhaps this sounds patronizing; and there is no need to patronize men who are capable of lifting a Land Rover bodily out of the sand. But even if they were breaking the law by staying in Gugamu, and it was never clear that they were, you would think that common humanity would ensure that the Botswanan authorities would allow them to have water in a desert.

But common humanity seemed to be oddly lacking, from the country's leader down. As we have seen, President Festus Mogae called the Bushmen 'Stone Age creatures'. In a single sentence, he gave two damaging impressions: firstly, that he didn't seem to regard the Bushmen as being entirely human ('creatures' is scarcely the word most of us would use to refer to our fellow men), and secondly, that it wouldn't entirely worry him overmuch if they died out altogether. His next sentence was as follows: 'If the Bushmen want to survive, they must change, otherwise, like the dodo, they will perish.'

Many people would think that the Bushmen were one of the great glories of Botswana, a group to be cherished and supported and helped to continue their lives as they chose. Instead, Mogae – who was their president as much as he was the president of every other citizen of Botswana – seemed untroubled by the possibility of their extinction.

There is an undoubted racism directed towards Bushmen, in whatever country they inhabit. Their neighbours mock them, attack them, prey on them, laugh at them. The governments that are supposed to protect them are often happy to evict them from their lands, if those lands are found to contain something worth having. They rarely do anything to protect the Bushmen from strangers who want to move in on their hunting grounds, and they are not good at protecting themselves against abuse by the farmers who employ them. They are, all too often, treated as sub-humans; and because their tradition has always been to slip away into the bush rather than to make a stand, they have devised no other form of resistance.

But the Botswanan president and his people were apparently not the only ones irritated by these people who seemed not to want to be a part of his new computer-driven world. For instance a member of the House of Lords, Lady Tonge of Kew, who in a former life had been a Liberal Democrat MP, Jenny Tonge, spoke about them in a debate on Botswana in 2006. She echoed the line about the Stone Age – the Bushmen, she said, wanted to cling to it – and she accused them of holding the Botswanan government to ransom by resisting their eviction from the Kalahari.

Lady Tonge knew all this, it transpired, because four years earlier she had visited one of the camps into which the Botswanan government had resettled the Bushmen. According to another speaker in the debate, Lord Pearson, who was also on the trip (which had included first-class air travel), the visit had been funded by an organization called Debswana, a joint venture between the Botswanan government and the diamond company De Beers. Debswana owns the rights to mine diamonds in the area. Her guides at the resettlement camp were officials from the Botswanan government. Lord Pearson had hired his own independent translator, so he was able to speak directly to the Bushmen about their experiences; Lady Tonge had not.

My team and I camped in the CKGR, and I was filmed driving around and talking to the BBC in London on a satellite phone. The Land Rover I was using wasn't sufficiently muddied for the shots, so we had to throw some more on it. That's the great thing about advertisements: they aren't real life, they're what real life would be if it conformed to our aspirations. I enjoyed myself hugely, and we had a thoroughly good time.

And, fulfilling their side of our bargain, the crew threw themselves into the business of shooting a news report with great enthusiasm. In News, we haven't used sound recordists for a long time because we can no longer afford them, and the benefit of having one, and someone to assist the cameraman and someone else to check on every detail of the story, was quite remarkable. So was having a director with an international reputation. This promised to be a very good report indeed.

Using only the vaguest of maps, we set off for Gugamu to film the few Bushmen who were holding out to the bitter end. On our way we passed another village, surrounded by a fence of thorns. It was deserted, and the grass-roofed huts were already starting to disintegrate. A few months earlier the Botswanan army had arrived here in trucks at dawn and rounded up everyone they could find. This was, I was told, one of the villages where they threatened to burn the inhabitants alive. The ground was still littered with things that people who were used to making do with almost nothing would have wanted to keep: a kettle, a small shoe, even a knife.

Surely, I thought, the Bushmen would have wanted to take these things with them, if only they had been allowed to. I found a little hand-carved doll, its hair made of some light fibre from one of the bushes around us. Nearby lay an arrow, just like the one the young hunter in Namibia had shot to display his skill. I picked it up in memory of all these people who had been forcibly removed from their homes, and put it in my bag. I have it still. My sentimental hope was to take it back to the village one day, if ever the Bushmen were allowed to return. It seemed very unlikely.

In the heart of this lovely country of Botswana, where the government is, for the most part, benign and impartial and relatively incorrupt, and the people are easy-going and pleasant, something had happened which reminded me very much of the worst of Bosnia. There, too, soldiers would arrive and take people away under threat of death if they resisted. There, too, you would find the ground littered with small, unconsidered things afterwards, and the houses would be empty and decaying. There, too, there were camps where the people were taken, and did not always survive.

It's as well, I feel, to steer clear of excitable expressions like 'genocide', and even 'ethnic cleansing' is better avoided; yet when you come across a place where people have been forcibly removed because of who they are, rather than because they have committed some crime, then it becomes harder to find alternatives.

We drove on without talking. The team I was with hadn't seen sights like this before, and they were more shocked and depressed even than I was. I had a feeling that until we stood in the middle of the empty village, with the little abandoned objects at our feet, the others thought I had been exaggerating.

Not long after that we came across the smashed cistern and the broken well. I had been angry before; now I was enraged. What kind of person gives orders to destroy a well in the desert? What kind of person obeys those orders? Most of us would never sleep again if we did that. What is more, we wouldn't deserve to.

I learned later from the Bushmen themselves how they survived. At the village of Metsiamonong, another place where some of the Bushmen had stayed behind, they got their water from natural depressions where the occasional rains sank into the ground and could be drawn up for about four months each year. They stored the remaining water in ostrich eggs, which they buried in the sand. But in the years when the rains were light, they had to leave the game reserve and buy their water from the store, forty miles away. There was always the risk that they, too, would run into park rangers who would take the water away from them and pour it onto the ground.

The bush stretched away into the distance all round us: harsh, thorny bushes, occasional small trees, tall anthills and the reddish-brown earth which is almost sand. You have to be strong and brave to live here, and very determined. Yet even with my soft, city background I could understand why the Bushmen would be so determined to stay. It had nothing to do with some kind of primitive longing for the Stone Age. For 10,000 years the Kalahari had made them what they were. It defined their culture, their understanding, even their physicality. To leave it was to leave themselves.

Nowadays, most of the surviving Bushmen in southern Africa are not the Stone Age hunter-gatherers of President Mogae's and Lady Tonge's imaginings. They live as herdsmen, farm-workers and servants. Many have integrated with other Africans as fully as President Mogae would like. Yet their characteristics, their past, their beliefs about themselves, their knowledge of the bush, remain with them, helping them to keep their sense of identity. And the bullying they almost always receive from people who are not like them reminds them constantly who they are. They know they can only really be at ease with other Bushmen.

The Central Kalahari Game Reserve was the last big area where the Bushmen of southern Africa were free to roam and hunt as they had always done. Even here they were not entirely cut off from the outside world, and they chose to live in villages rather than in their smaller, more traditional groups. Still, they could be themselves, rather than the servants and employees of others. That was the important thing about being in the CKGR. For them, the land is the key element in their lives, just as it is with farmers and cultivators on every continent in the world. The land made them who they were, and in taking the land away from them, the Botswanan government has helped to destroy the existential quality of the Bushmen as a people.

I could see a large tree in the distance, towering over the rest of the bush, and, as we got closer, a group of the Bushmen's grass-covered huts, still clearly occupied. This was Gugamu.

There were no men around; they had gone out to hunt and see if they could find water. Only women, girls and babies lay under

the tree's shadow. The temperature was in the upper thirties, and
they needed shade. The apricot-coloured faces turned to us, and the
furrows beside their eyes deepened with pleasure. They had seen
people like us before – visitors from aid agencies mostly. They
identified us at once with sympathy and help. We were, I think, the
first television team they had seen.

They mostly wore cast-off Western clothes: blouses and colourful wraparound skirts. The babies were naked. An old woman
had been talking to the group, and they had carried on listening
intently to her even when we drew up and got out. Now, though,
they gave us their attention. Our translator explained that we
wanted to film them, and they gathered round, fascinated by what
we were doing. One woman stood out from the rest. She had been
talking animatedly, and now she sat on her heels, her baby at
her breast, looking at us. She looked determined and strong, but in
front of the camera she was understandably shy. Her name, she
said, was Gaboshediswe.

'We have no more money to get water, and the hot weather will
soon be here. I am afraid. I think we will have to die here.'

'So will you leave?'

She shook her head. I couldn't get her to say anything more.

We gave them money, of course, and almost all our water; we,
at least, could go and replenish our supplies quickly and easily.
There was a lot of it, and with luck and careful rationing they
would have been able to get by for quite a long time.

They allowed us to explore the thorn-fenced village, filming
them and their huts, watching the way they cared for their babies.
The children followed us round, much more quietly and soberly
than most village children in Africa would. Bushmen are born with
the talent for quiet observation.

It was well into the afternoon by the time the cameraman was
satisfied. I knew these pictures were going to be excellent, and the
sound of animals and the drowsing noise of insects was faithfully
recorded. The cameraman looked at me, to check that there wasn't
anything else I wanted him to film. And at that moment the girl
arrived.

We had got almost everything, but I knew we hadn't got what
a news producer would call 'the killer synch': we hadn't interviewed

anyone whose words would sum everything up for us, and perhaps add the stirring quality which something like this demanded. These people weren't just defying the government and the army by staying here, they were defying a very real threat to their lives. Even if they had been dying of thirst, it was plain that the park rangers wouldn't help them. They were here illegally, the government would say; they must take the consequences. We needed someone to tell us that they understood all this, but that staying here on the land was more important even than an agonizing death.

Dingongorego gave us our killer synch. She was twenty, though outside the Kalahari she might have passed for twelve. Nevertheless there was something indomitable about her, a strength of character which, I could see, would require a careful approach. She had, I felt, the stuff that martyrs were made of. Yet there was nothing fierce or challenging or overbearing about her; just a sense that you could never make her do something that she thought was wrong.

I once came across a mayor in a small coca-producing village in Peru who refused to take any part in the cocaine trade, and told the local military and the big drugs dealers that he was going to report them to the government. He too was small and frail looking, but when I interviewed him I had the very definite feeling that I wouldn't want to cross him on any important moral issue.

I felt the same with Dingongorego. She was studying at a school outside the reserve, and I doubted very much if anyone bullied her. She was slight and tiny, but her curiously gold eyes looked straight at mine. She seemed instinctively to understand everything about the business of being interviewed for television, though she told me it was her first time. Even at the school, she said, she hadn't seen a television, though the other pupils, none of them Bushmen, had described one: pictures that you could see in your house. Then she waited quietly for me to start asking my questions.

'Why do you insist on staying here, when it could cost you and everyone else in the village your lives?'

There was fire and beauty in her answer.

'The government wants to take our land, the land we were promised, the land our forefathers were promised, the land of our ancient ancestors, and make it into a park for animals. Why? It belonged to our grandfathers and our grandmothers, and now it belongs to us. I will never leave it. I will be proud to die here. More than proud.'

Her eyes flashed as she spoke. Even at the time, I thought that if she was indeed among the last of the true Bushmen in the Central Kalahari, this was the finest epitaph her people could have.

'But the government is providing you with a place to go. Why don't you want to go there?'

'If we leave here, we have to go to another culture. They drink alcohol and get AIDS there. Our culture is strict for us. We are not allowed to have two men. We live in the traditional way, and stay with one man. I wish to live my life decently and honestly, like my ancestors did. To go there would be death to me. Better to die here, on our own land. I am ready for that.'

There was nothing remotely primitive or Stone Age about Dingongorego. She was magnificent, and she put the denigrators to shame.

A couple of mornings later, we slipped out of the Central Kalahari Game Reserve by a different gate. I wanted to see for myself the place that Dingongorego felt was so destructive to her people. Perhaps, I thought, it was all a bit exaggerated; perhaps her response, and the response of the other people of Gugamu and Metsiamonong was indeed just a reactionary one. What sort of life, after all, could be more difficult and hostile than trying to eke out an existence in a desert? Maybe the Botswanan government was right to move the Bushmen out of the empty, inhospitable desert; maybe it really was for their own good.

Of the two resettlement camps which we could get to, Kaudwane and New Xade, we chose the first. Conditions at New Xade had often been described, and were known to be dreadful. Perhaps things in Kaudwane would be better. It loomed ahead of us, its brick-built huts in a neat row, people walking aimlessly across the road. It didn't look very attractive, but maybe, I thought, I was looking at it with over-critical eyes. Quaintness and picturesqueness are wonderful qualities, until you have to endure them.

Then we got closer. The people in the road were weaving from side to side in a state of drunkenness. We stopped, and I got out. Between a couple of single-storey huts I came across one of the most horrible sights I have ever seen. Four Bushmen who looked like old men but were probably in their forties were drunkenly jostling to get to a window in the side of one of the huts. From the window a man was selling brown paper cups full of beer. In his haste and aggression, one of the men spilled his beer on the ground. He slumped down onto the wetted earth and started weeping. The others laughed at him, then pushed each other aside to get to the window themselves.

I went back to get the cameraman. This was going to be difficult; we had been told there were plenty of guards around, and the Botswanan authorities really didn't like this kind of filming. Our large, professional camera was a real giveaway; we could scarcely say we were just tourists, here to film the wildlife. If we were arrested, we could lose everything we'd filmed, including the promotional video. The crew knew that, and I knew it, but they had become as committed to our news report as I was, and they knew that this was the clincher.

Who could watch the drunks fighting each other for a paper cup of sorghum beer at twenty pence a throw, and think that putting the Bushmen into places like this was somehow in their interest? It made me angry even to think about it. What kind of officials would force gentle, unworldly people like these off their land and sell them alcohol so cheaply and so easily? What kind of foreign observer would come to a place like this and not realize the nature of what they were being shown?

A place of death, one of the Bushmen had called New Xade, the other resettlement camp. Kaudwane was a place of death too.

The cameraman spotted a young girl coming drunkenly over to join the men. They messed around with her, fondling her breasts and putting their hands up her skirt. She looked emptily into the camera lens. She wasn't there, I realized. Her body might be, and it would no doubt contract AIDS and other sexually transmitted diseases, and spread them round the camp, but she herself, the real person, had long since gone. She laughed stupidly and started kissing one of the men.

Everything Dingongorego had told us was true. This wasn't just a barren, soulless place, it was a death camp. A slow-death camp. A camp where an ancient and magnificent culture, 10,000 years old, was being killed. And you had to be very generous indeed not to feel that the killing was deliberate.

We got the pictures we needed, pictures which would later be shown around the world. When our report was broadcast, the Botswanan government accused me of all sorts of offences, and various loyal Botswanans either felt compelled or were encouraged to write me letters saying (as such letters always do) that they had greatly respected my work until this point but would never be able to believe anything I said in future.

Yet no one, not even the government, accused me of lying or distortion. No one claimed these things hadn't happened. What they did allege, again and again, was that I was deliberately trying to harm the reputation of a good and upright nation. I replied that I liked and admired Botswana and wished it well – but that it wasn't I who was doing such damage to its reputation. Eventually the Botswanan government included me in a list of fifteen people who would require special permission to visit the country in future. I hate being banned from countries – it's bad for business if your job is travelling around the world to report on the news – but in this case I treated it like a badge of honour. And I was in auspicious company: the list also included a senior human-rights official from the United Nations.

But all this lay in the future. Now we drove back to Gaborone in silence. Usually, when you pull off a difficult coup, getting pictures of something that is meant to be hidden, discovering an important story at a certain amount of risk and getting away with it, you talk it over endlessly afterwards, laughing and remembering little details about who did what, and praising the achievements of the team. Not now. The sight of the Bushmen fighting each other to get a little more drunk, or pawing at the expressionless girl whose life was already finished but still required some unpleasant and painful disease to finish her off, was too strong. I'm not even sure the rest of the crew was glad to have done all this. We had put images into our minds that we would have preferred not to see.

§

With the help of dedicated organizations like the excellent London-based Survival International, a team of equally dedicated lawyers from southern Africa helped a small group of Bushmen to challenge the legality of their eviction from the Central Kalahari Game Reserve. The case dragged on for years, and some of us began to believe that the Botswanan justice system, which had always had an excellent reputation, had succumbed to the influence of the government. There was a real danger that if the case were allowed to drag on indefinitely, it would bankrupt the groups fighting it.

And then, on a magnificent day in December 2006, the appeal court decided by a majority of two to one that the removal of the Bushmen from their appointed lands had indeed been wrong, and that they could return. I was in Baghdad at the time, and I remember jumping up and clapping my hands when I read about the judgment on the internet, and then having to explain to my colleagues what I was making all the fuss about. I felt that everything people had said in defence of Botswana and its legal system had been right.

But that proved not to be the end of the matter. The government interpreted the judgment as meaning that only the small group of Bushmen who had brought the appeal could return to the reserve, not all the people who had been forcibly removed from it nearly five years earlier. And, using the powers it undoubtedly possessed, the government also issued an order that the Bushmen would not be allowed to hunt animals there. They could, the government explained thoughtfully, hunt anywhere else in Botswana where hunting was legal – but not in their ancestral grounds.

As I write this, in 2007, further appeals have started, and may or may not succeed. While President Mogae is in power, the government is unlikely to relent; one of the great disadvantages of campaigning for the Bushmen, or of doing the kind of filming I did, is that it is liable to confirm a strong-minded old man in the view that he must push ahead with his policies regardless of the bad press he gets.

So are 10,000 years of an ancient culture, one of the great jewels of Africa, now doomed? Strangely enough, I feel a small amount of confidence and hope. Not because I trust the Botswanan justice system, though it stood up to its test of impartiality brilliantly well, but because of the Bushmen themselves. Of course their culture and way of life are under enormous and probably irresistible pressure. Yet we shouldn't make the mistake of thinking that although the

Bushmen themselves seem so small and weak, and so vulnerable to
the modern world's plagues and diseases, that their grasp of their
own culture is equally weak. In one of the villages I visited in
Namibia, I asked the headman about the young Bushmen who were
leaving for work in the nearby town (actually it was fifty miles
away).

'But they always come back,' he said.

'Why?'

'Because of the hunting. They can't forget it when they are in
the town, and they always come back for it.'

Later, I met a group of three young Bushmen, dressed in shirts
and jeans, on the road to the village. One of them, I noticed with a
sinking feeling, was carrying a case with an electric guitar in it.

'We've formed a band in the town,' one of them said.

My heart sank even more.

'What sort of music do you play?'

'Oh, we write songs about hunting eland and kudu.'

The Bushmen are not a pure, untouched race of hunter-
gatherers, romantically free of links with the outside world,
behaving exactly as they have always behaved for thousands of
years. On the contrary, they have had to accept a degree of
integration with their surrounding enemies for aeons. Dingongorego, the magnificent-looking girl who proclaimed her determination to die in the Kalahari if necessary, wore her school uniform
when we interviewed her. But the villagers who had remained, and
the elders who had fought their legal battle, and those who had
miraculously managed to avoid the alcoholism, the drugs and the
diseases of the Botswanan camps, had not given up their nationhood
or forgotten the old ways, even under the greatest possible pressure.
Far from dying off, I believe the Bushmen can survive, and perhaps
one day even thrive.

'Look at this land,' Dingongorego said, gesturing to the open
desert all around us. 'This is ours. It always has been. It is in our
hearts, and it can never be taken away from us.'

12

EXECUTION

It was 5 November 2006. In the courtroom in Baghdad the press box was already full, and starting to heat up. The curtains which the Americans had insisted on installing to prevent our seeing anything that happened outside the actual court proceedings were pulled back, and the familiar stage set was revealed.

The prosecution, the defence and the junior court officials were already in place. The clerk of the court, a squat, heavily muscled man in his fifties who plainly relished his job, called out that we should all rise. At first there had been some resistance among the journalists, who like to feel they are independent even of the people in charge of the proceedings; but early on we had been told that we too must stand, and must not talk when the judges filed in.

The chief judge, Raouf Abdel Rahman, came in first, and glanced proprietorially around before sitting down. The other judges, four of them, followed. Rahman whispered to the judge on his right, and then to the one of his left.

'Call Saddam Hussein al-Majid,' he said matter-of-factly.

The clerk of the court, enjoying the drama of the moment, shouted, 'Call Saddam Hussein al-Majid.' The pride that he might have the small degree of power involved in repeating the judge's command, and oblige the dictator he would formerly have worshipped to come into court for sentencing, was palpable.

Everyone stared at the door. At first when Saddam was on trial there had been a real sense of tension in the seconds before he appeared. That had faded over the months, but now that he was about to be sentenced, the tension was back. Even the judges went quiet, and looked across at the door. This was the most important moment in their lives too, and the consequences of what they were doing today would stay with them for ever. And no one knew how Saddam Hussein would react to being sentenced to death.

Saddam halted in the doorway for the length of a heartbeat, and then came into the courtroom. He was, if anything, dressed more smartly than usual. His black suit, which had been sent to him by the tailor in the Gulf he had used since his days of supreme power, was beautifully pressed. His white shirt was buttoned up to the collar, but he wasn't wearing a tie. His shoes, small for a man of five feet ten, were highly polished. He carried his Koran in his right hand, and some papers in his left. His black hair seemed to have been newly dyed, but he had allowed the grey to show in his beard. I hoped for a glance from him, but he was concentrating on making a grand entrance. He greeted one or two of his favoured co-defendants, waited for one of the special guards to open the gate of the empty dock for him, and sat down in his usual place.

Even at this historic moment, the unseen American agent inside the box to our left was interfering with the television coverage of the proceedings. Saddam denounced the invasion of his country and the overthrow of his government, but the video feed was cut several times in the next few minutes in order to prevent anyone outside the court hearing or seeing Saddam.

Then he sat down, and stayed sitting when the time came for the verdict to be read.

'Make him stand up,' the judge ordered the guards. At this point the video recording was stopped again, but there was a struggle. There was a certain ritual about this. At each of the key moments in his trial, knowing that everyone's eyes were on him, Saddam Hussein would stage a little contretemps with his guards. Most of the time he did not resist when they held him by the arms; but when it mattered, he did. Now it mattered more than at any other time in the trial.

'Leave me alone,' he shouted. 'Don't grab my arms.'

'Let him be – he's standing up now,' said the judge.

'It's useless talking to you,' Saddam snapped at the guards.

Perhaps Rahman was distracted by this sudden show of anger. For whatever reason, he neglected at this critical moment to declare that Saddam had been found guilty by the court. All he said was,

'The court has decided to sentence Saddam Hussein al-Majid to death by hanging.'

In the press gallery, from the small number of foreign journalists and the much larger contingent of Iraqis, there was a sharp intake of breath. One or two of the Iraqis talked to each other in low, urgent voices. We had expected nothing else, of course, and yet the final certainty of his death was a definite jolt to all of us.

The judge, head down, not looking at Saddam or any of the others in the dock, started reading out the long judgment in a harsh monotone, as though he expected to be interrupted.

He was.

'Long live the people! Long live the nation! Down with the collaborators!'

Saddam Hussein waved his Koran in the air, half-turning to see the effect on the defence lawyers, then turning back to roar at the judge again. It was, I think, the loudest I had heard him shout during his entire trial.

Things quickly degenerated. The judge, head down, read out a judgment which no one could hear properly yet everyone knew the import of, and Saddam Hussein yelled his accusations.

'Down with the invaders! Down with the collaborators!' He brandished his Koran again. 'Get out, you and your court!'

I have noticed over the years that moments of high drama in human affairs are often punctured by the absurd. It is as though we find it impossible to sustain the same degree of intensity for long, and have to bring everything down to a more manageable level. Now, one of the defence lawyers chose this moment to interrupt the judge and complain that a security guard standing alongside Saddam Hussein was chewing gum and grinning.

'It is an outrage,' said the lawyer, perhaps more pompously than he intended, 'and deeply offensive to human dignity.'

At that, everyone smiled: the judges on their bench, even Saddam, who was still half turning. For an instant, the tension was broken. The judge waved at the guard, ordering him out of court with a single gesture. Then he took up where he had left off in his judgment. After letting him speak for a phrase or two, Saddam shouted out a defiant phrase he had used in his speeches before Iraq was invaded in 2003: 'We're ready for you!'

It was his equivalent of President George W. Bush's challenge to the insurgents of Iraq, after the formal invasion was over: 'Bring it on!' In both cases the result was much the same: violence and humiliation.

By now the judge had finished reading out the reasoning behind the verdict, and had moved on to the sentence. Even though everyone knew perfectly well what was going to happen, there was complete silence. Even Saddam himself was quiet.

'For the crimes against humanity listed in this judgment, you are sentenced to two terms of seven years each.'

Saddam found his voice again.

'We're the ones in favour of humanity. They [meaning the Americans] are the enemies of humanity, and so are the people who collaborate with them. God is great!'

There was a pause. The judge plainly wanted silence when he read out the main sentence, so he allowed Saddam to have his say now on the lesser sentences.

Saddam, too, had a strategy. It seemed entirely out of character.

'I should like to say this to the Iraqi people: you should forgive those who have taken the wrong course. You should forgive your enemies.'

Perhaps it was a desire at this critical moment in his life to present himself as statesmanlike, above the strife, even saintly. If so, it would not be long before he returned to the old anger and pride. But not just for the moment.

'The sentence of this court, therefore, is that you should suffer death by hanging.'

'I say to the Iraqi people,' Saddam called out, almost as though he had not been listening, 'that you shouldn't hate the people of the countries which are occupying Iraq.'

But the moment of forgiveness was quickly over.

'You're not taking the decisions here,' Saddam told the judge. 'You're just the servants of the invaders. Life is for the Iraqi people, death is for our enemies.'

'Take him away,' ordered the judge.

'Long live Iraq! Long live the Arabs!'

Saddam was still shouting and struggling with the guards as they took his arms and steered him out of the courtroom, a condemned man. That was the point at which he passed me, a matter of inches away, and I saw him smile.

It had taken only five melodramatic minutes to condemn to execution the first Middle Eastern leader ever to be tried for human rights offences in his own country. Within two months, Saddam Hussein would be dead.

§

From 1979 onwards, during the years of his power, Saddam and his doings were some of my main professional concerns, and I reported on them regularly. Yet before his trial I only saw him twice in the flesh: once at a party, and once when he made a speech. On both occasions he struck me as formidable and dangerous, yet distinctly human; too human, in fact, since his whims and his sudden storms of temper could launch an invasion or the slaughter of a hundred thousand people.

The speech I saw him make was highly effective. He was witty, natural, folksy, and he knew how to be tough when he chose. It helped that he was speaking to a thousand people from across the Muslim world who all regarded him as their great hero. Every joke he make was greeted with great howls of merriment, every threat was accompanied by a low, intense rumble of thoroughgoing agreement.

His voice was undisguisedly ugly and rasping, and his Arabic was, I was told again and again, no better than that of any peasant. But his opponents always treated him with a certain disdain, which did him no harm but often made it harder for them to understand him.

He was tall and well built, and made for command. His habit of parading in front of crowds with his right arm out before him, palm half-turned to the sky, gave him a grandly imperial air, welcoming and domineering at the same time.

His doings were invariably the lead story on the nightly television news, and on the front page of the following morning's newspapers; this held true even when he had done nothing of interest, and there was some news item which would have been of overriding importance anywhere else in the world.

No one treated him familiarly, not even his dreadful sons or his equally dreadful half-brothers. His deputy, Izzat Ibrahim al-Douri, a strange-looking, skeletal, red-headed man, who assumed the presidency after Saddam had been executed at the end of 2006, was treated familiarly by Saddam, but responded with a certain deference even when Saddam was holding his arm or laid his hand on his shoulder. There were one or two ministers who had the right to kiss him on the cheek, but most kissed his shoulders or his hand.

Below them came more junior ministers who would never raise their eyes to his. Why not, I asked one after Saddam's fall? Because he might have interpreted it as a challenge, even a threat, he answered. You stared at his shoes, that was all.

I went to a reception which Saddam gave, and stood on the edges of a group around him, though no one offered to introduce me. I didn't thrust myself forward; you could get into serious trouble like that. Everyone around him seemed extraordinarily meek, with a kind of reverential smile on their faces. He had a fierce sense of humour, and would sometimes say something outrageous and unheard-of, allow everyone to agree, and then say, 'What a stupid idea – who suggested that?' There would be a brief silence, and then he would break into loud laughter. Everyone then joined in with relief, of course.

Foreign journalists who interviewed him (I was due to be one of them, but the BBC refused a demand to broadcast the whole interview unedited, and so I lost the chance) found him cold and hard and completely unresponsive. His notion of giving an interview was to talk until he had said everything he wanted to say, and then to allow you to ask him about something else. As far as I know, no one ever interrupted him, and even challenging something he had said made him angry. There was no question of interacting with him, or forming any kind of personal relationship.

An interview with Saddam was as grand and hieratic and ceremonial as an audience with King Ashurbanipal, his Assyrian predecessor. The entire camera crew, plus reporter and producer, sometimes had to spend the preceding twenty-four hours at a secure location, while their equipment was carefully examined. They were obliged to wash their hands and faces in special antiseptic, to guard against any attempt to poison him.

When they met him, and the correspondent shook hands with

him, Saddam deliberately held his hand out low down, which meant that the correspondent had to bend slightly to take it. Saddam's personal photographer was primed to take a picture at this precise moment, so that in the following day's newspaper it would look as though the visitor was bowing to Saddam. He demanded a degree of subservience which no other head of state in the world required.

His image was as sacrosanct as his person. Anyone who defaced a portrait of Saddam was regarded as having committed treason. A drunk who stopped off as he made his way home and urinated against a concrete buttress which held up one of the omnipresent street portraits of Saddam was arrested, tortured and died from repeated electrical shocks to the offending genitals. A man who wrote someone's phone number on a ten-dinar note and managed to let his ballpoint stray onto Saddam's portrait was sentenced to die in an acid bath. Even the executioners thought this a little unfair, when he told them what he had been charged with. They decided to dip him in the bath for just a few seconds, then take him out again. His back was terribly burned, but at least he lived.

Sometimes it sounded like the rule of a maniac. Yet Saddam was entirely sane. Horror stories like these were the result of policy, not of insanity. He was a dedicated disciple of Stalin, and he knew that unless he were ferocious in the way he controlled the country, his regime would eventually go down the slow path from popularity and strength to weakness and military coup. It was the path which every other Iraqi government had taken since the brutal overthrow of the monarchy in 1958.

At first he even had a sense of humour about himself and the source of his power. Early in his presidency, a friend of mine went to interview him at his palace in Baghdad for an American newspaper. Gradually, nervously, my friend raised the subject of human rights. Saddam grabbed him by the arm and pulled him out of the room. But instead of having him executed, Saddam hurried him downstairs and into the front seat of the presidential Range Rover.

Bewildered bodyguards threw themselves into the vehicles behind as Saddam drove at terrifying speed to the centre of town, near Saddoun Street. In the square at the end of the street, an ugly 1960s creation, Saddam pulled up near an old man who was

walking along. He jumped out, pushing the American correspondent out as well, and stuck his swagger-stick under the old man's
chin.

'This American thinks I'm unpopular; what do you think?' he
asked.

The old man could scarcely find enough words to describe his
affection for Saddam.

'You see?' said Saddam, and roared with laughter. Then they
went back to his palace to finish the interview.

So if Saddam wasn't mad, was he evil? That is the kind of word
that only a few unthinking politicians and the writers of tabloid
newspaper headlines use nowadays. I don't vote for politicians like
that, and I don't buy that kind of newspaper. Saddam certainly did
many things which were wicked, and he presided over a system
that made wicked things commonplace. His son Uday was a vicious
gangster who enjoyed killing people.

But Saddam was different. Three unconnected people who saw
him with his family at home described to me how he loved playing
with his grandchildren, going down on all fours to give them rides
on his back. Shortly before his death, he told the American army
nurse whom the US had assigned to him that he used to give his
daughter Raghad medicine to help her sleep when she had a cold or
a stomach-ache.

Raghad remained one of his most devoted followers, even after
Saddam had allowed Uday to arrange a shoot-out in which
Raghad's husband and his brother (married to another of Saddam's
daughters) were killed. Raghad hired lawyers to defend Saddam in
court, she wrote articles praising him and she turned up at the
demonstration in Amman which followed his execution.

'He wasn't what you people in the West thought he was,' a
former member of his household said after he was hanged. 'He was
a strong man with a good heart, that's all.'

A susceptible heart, too. He had at least three wives, and two
well-known mistresses. Uday threatened to kill him because he set
up his new mistress, whom he later married, a little too blatantly.

He himself believed that the women of Iraq were the mainstay
of his support, and for many years he may have been right. He went
out off his way to make himself presentable in public, dyeing his

The Emperor and Empress of Japan.

A passenger boat on the River Congo.

Bishop Kutino of the
Army of Victory prays for cash
in Kinshasa.

The dean of
Kisangani University
with the slides which,
according to one theory,
were part of an
American–Belgian
experiment that
may have caused the
AIDS virus to leap the
species barrier
to humans.

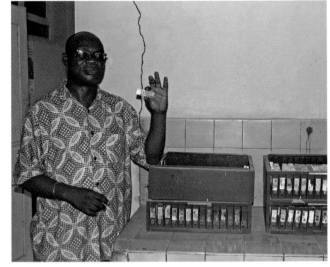

H. M. Stanley's statue, now horizontal in a field beside the Congo.

Child wizards of Kinshasa, trying to spook us out. The one in front is Pamuké.

The house in Kisangani where Humphrey Bogart, Katharine Hepburn and John Huston lived during the making of *The African Queen* in 1949.

Camping in the Central Kalahari
Game Reserve.

Giving water to the Bushman
families of Gugamu who
have resisted the Botswana
government's efforts to drive
them out by hunger and thirst.

Dingongorego, who was determined to stay on her ancestral lands until death, if necessary.

An abandoned shoe at one of the Bushmen villages: evidence that they had been forcibly evicted by the Botswanan army. No Bushman would voluntarily abandon something as useful as this.

People in the crime-ridden Johannesburg neighbourhood of Hillbrow crowd round us – to complain about crime.

Mrs Joy Judes, one of the few remaining white inhabitants of Hillbrow.

'Shi-i-i-ine!!!' A teacher at Hoernle Primary School in Soweto shows what good teaching can do.

Interviewing General David Petraeus, the commander of coalition forces in Iraq.

Lord Butler, former head of the civil service, attacks the Blair government's use of intelligence to justify the invasion of Iraq. His speech was scarcely reported.

Um Zuhail is comforted by Zahra, her granddaughter, as she tells us about her kidnapped son. He was kidnapped and murdered, even though the family paid a ruinous ransom for him.

Christmas Day, 2006: Dee and Rafe on the beach at Nature's Valley in South Africa.

hair and insisting that each of his ministers had to spend time every day in the gym until their figures matched his. When one or two of them, over-eager to please, became slimmer and better toned than he was, he told the cabinet to stop wasting time and get down to some proper work.

§

Throughout the long years of his power, there were no census returns in Iraq. No one, accordingly, had any clear idea how big each of the main population groups was. Officials, if you pressed them, would say that Sunni Arabs, Shi'ites and Kurds were all roughly equal in numbers. It was only after the Americans over-turned the Iraqi applecart in 2003 and held free elections, thus making it possible for opinion pollsters to travel the length and breadth of the country, that a realistic picture emerged: Shi'ites 60 per cent, Sunni Arabs and Kurds around twenty per cent each.

For three decades Saddam, a Sunni himself, used the Sunnis to rule the country. They were the backbone of the officer corps in the army, and they provided the heart of the civil service. It was certainly possible for Shi'ites to become generals and senior civil servants, but there was always a sense that they were not fundamentally reliable. The numbers of Kurds in the topmost levels was much smaller, and the suspicion of unreliability far greater.

Saddam never trusted anyone, and – as his two sons-in-law showed when they drove off in the night in 1995 to Jordan, and informed the world about Iraq's weapons of mass destruction – he was wise not to. But he trusted Shi'ites and Kurds even less he than trusted anyone else.

The years of obsequiousness from everyone around him affected his judgement badly. He genuinely did not believe that the Americans and British would be able to invade Iraq successfully, and when, during the 2003 invasion, he was told that their forces had been repelled near Nasiriyeh, he fully believed it. It was a genuine shock to him to discover that the Americans had captured Baghdad airport a few days later.

And yet his overthrow liberated him as well. On the day Baghdad fell, Saddam appeared in the streets of an overwhelmingly Sunni part of west Baghdad, with just a few security men guarding

him. For the first time in years Saddam appeared in public looking
entirely at ease. This wasn't Hitler peering out of his bunker,
twitching every time a Russian shell landed. This was a man who
had once been used to life on the run, and was now throwing up
everything in order to go on the run again. He knew he could do it,
he knew the plans for his escape had been laid with the greatest
care, and he relished the prospect of pitting his skills against those
of his enemies.

And for eight months, he was at liberty. We now know that
careful, relentless police work tracked down every weak link around
him, and that his old bodyguard Mohammed al-Musslit was
arrested, interrogated, and agreed, not as the result of torture but
of relentless questioning, to betray his former chief. He seems to
have made no money out of the deal, but he has started a new life
in the United States, together with his family.

And so Saddam was discovered in his hole in the ground near
Tikrit, and was pulled out of it saying 'I am Saddam Hussein,
President of the Republic of Iraq, and I would like to negotiate';
not, you might think, one of the stronger bargaining positions to
find oneself in. But Saddam was used to fighting from a position
of weakness, and he usually managed to turn things round to his
advantage by sheer guts and determination.

In this case, though, he was delusional. One of his fixed ideas
was that the Americans would eventually realize that Iraq was too
complicated for them to control, and that they would be obliged to
bring him back to sort out the mess for them. This seems to be
what he had in mind when, grubby and wild-haired, he emerged
from the foxhole talking about negotiating.

In the months and years that followed, people who visited him
in prison reported that he still clung to the notion that, as the
security situation in Iraq worsened, the Americans would have to
reinstate him; and it may be that he expected something of the kind
to happen right up to the end.

In this, he was only human. We all manage to convince ourselves
of the most unlikely propositions, for no other reason than that it
would suit us if it turned out so. Even if we are the least suitable
candidate for a job, we think someone will see our special quality
and hire us. We feel certain that our marriage will finally take a

turn for the better, even though it has long been clear to everyone else that it has broken down irrevocably. And we have a clear feeling that although our particular form of cancer offers only a 5 per cent survival rate, we will be in that 5 per cent.

'Our own death is, indeed, unimaginable,' wrote Sigmund Freud in 1915, 'and whenever we make the attempt to imagine it we can perceive that we really survive as spectators.' Just so. And Saddam Hussein, humiliated, dirty, hungry and short of sleep, was certain on 20 December 2003 that he would survive and prosper even in defeat. It was this, I believe, that prevented him from shooting himself or making a last-ditch stand when he was discovered.

But for more than a year his former supporters believed it had been a failure of will on his part.

'His two sons [Uday and Qsay] fought the Americans and died a man's death with their guns in their hands,' an Iraqi army officer, a Sunni, said bitterly to me. 'Yet their father, who had told us all so many times that we had to shed our life's blood for him, wasn't prepared to make any sacrifice himself. He climbed out of that hole like a cowardly animal, instead of dying like a man.'

A great many Iraqis felt the same way, whether or not they had previously been supporters of Saddam Hussein. Yet he clearly felt that the game wasn't over – that there was still a way out, still a way to regain the initiative. And indeed, as his trial and execution showed, he was right; though not in the way he had expected.

There was an ugly triumphalism about Saddam's capture. Vice-President Dick Cheney had helped to foster the belief among Americans that Saddam bore ultimate responsibility for the attacks of 11 September 2001 in New York and Washington. Yet Cheney didn't create that belief. As we have seen, an opinion poll carried out immediately before the invasion of Iraq in 2003 indicated that 21 per cent of Americans thought Saddam Hussein and Osama bin Laden were one and the same person.

No matter that bin Laden had called for the overthrow of Saddam and regarded him as a traitor to Islam for stamping down hard on Islamists in Iraq, for claiming that there was no difference between Sunni Islam and Shi'ism, and for fostering Western habits like the open sale of alcohol. No matter that, under different circumstances, Saddam might have been a valuable ally for the

United States against Islamic extremism, and had quietly been regarded in Washington as a bulwark against Ayatollah Khomeini's fundamentalism in Iran. Americans like a clear-cut enemy, and Saddam Hussein filled the bill.

So when the Americans pulled Saddam out of his hole in the ground, many of them will have thought that they had finally captured the man who had planned the unprecedented attack on their country, and show how vulnerable it was. There was a savage joy in watching the pictures of their ultimate enemy being treated like an animal, the inside of his mouth examined for poison capsules and his scalp checked for tracking devices.

Yet according to the American public affairs officer who was present at Saddam's capture and filmed his examination, he was courtly and rather grateful to his captors for not killing him or beating him up. Perhaps he was still surprised to find himself alive. He did complain, though, that his head hurt. When he was hoisted out of the foxhole he had hit it a couple of times on the wooden planking, and thought his skull might have been fractured. The examination of his head, crude and intrusive though it was, was intended to find out whether he had indeed suffered any cranial damage.

I arrived at the scene of his capture three days later. A few journalists had already been shown Saddam's hiding place, climbing down into the foxhole to do their pieces to camera and examining the well-camouflaged cover which, in spite of the skill with which it had been made and fixed over the entrance to the hole, had eventually caught the attention of one of the American soldiers in the near darkness.

My team and I reached Saddam's hideout just as the sun was going down. At that stage it was still possible to drive around in Iraq in relative safety, though there was growing tension. The orange and white taxi which Saddam had used to take him from one hiding place to the next was still there, abandoned, and the hut where Saddam had spent some of his last hours of freedom was still full of the things his minders had bought for him.

An American Marine sergeant was on duty. At first he told us he had orders not to let anyone in. Our producer, Kate Peters,

charmed him by explaining that we had come a long way and
would only trouble them very briefly. At last, still half unwilling,
he swung open the gate and let us drive in. We parked close to the
empty taxi.

If the Americans had not had specific information from Saddam
Hussein's bodyguard, I doubt if they or anyone else would have
found him here. Perhaps the presence of the taxi was a little
suspicious; I had already been told by the Iraqi officials who were
working alongside the Americans in Baghdad that they suspected he
was travelling from hideout to hideout in a taxi. Yet you see taxis
in every town and village in Iraq. It might have been an indication,
but it was certainly not conclusive in any way.

A large Marine followed us around when we got out to investigate the small hut that stood close by the river, set among the date
palms. He told me conversationally that he had been ordered to
shoot us if we looted anything. It wasn't clear to me whether this
was true, or whether he was simply making a heavy, tongue-in-cheek
joke; but ever since it had been recast as a volunteer force, the
humour had vanished from the American military, together with the
concept of using individual initiative. It seemed safer to believe him.

The Marine stood outside while we went into the hut. There
were three rooms: one for sleeping, one for cooking and one for
ablutions. All three showed signs of occupation, and of sudden
flight. The bedroom had two bedsteads, which were covered with
clothes. Some had been worn, others were still in their cellophane
wrappers. Saddam Hussein's minders used to buy new clothes for
him wherever he went. Under the bed was a pair of slippers, almost
brand new yet clearly used very briefly.

It was the ordinariness of it all that struck me most srongly as I
went from one room to the next: the egg shells, the scattered olive
stones, the half-empty tin of sweetcorn, the coffee grounds, the dirty
lavatory of the squatting type. The fugitive who had worn these
clothes, eaten this food, used that lavatory, was no longer some
rarefied being whom I had read about for thirty years, reported on
constantly, and seen a couple of times; he was a real human being,
with habits and preferences like any other. We ourselves place the
aura of strangeness and remoteness around the famous ones of the

world, and we are invariably surprised when we discover how like ours their lives sometimes are.

I looked down into the space where Saddam had been discovered. It was very narrow for a man of his size, even though he had lost a good deal of weight during his eight months on the run. The trapdoor lay beside it: styrofoam, and coated cleverly with mud and paint. If it had not been so regular in shape, the searchers might not have discovered it.

We did our filming, and then I went back into the sleeping room. The slippers were beginning to obsess me.

'What's going to happen to all this stuff?' I asked the Marine.

'Goin' to be junked, I hear.'

That decided me. I waited until he looked away, then bent down, grabbed one of the slippers, and put it in my pocket.

He looked back. Maybe something guilty in my expression made him keep his eyes on me the whole time after that. I was uncomfortably aware of the other slipper as it lay on the floor, but it was simply impossible to get that as well.

I took the lone slipper back to London with me, and had it framed together with a rather vulgar but expensive Italian silk tie which was 'liberated' from Uday Hussein's palace by a friend of mine after Baghdad fell. He sent it to me as a thank-you present after I took him to lunch. The two objects hang on the wall of my guest cloakroom in London. I'm not proud of being a looter, but some objects have an inherent interest. I tell myself, of course, that I stole Saddam's slipper in order to protect it from being destroyed.

And it reminds me, also, that he was not merely a world-famous dictator, an image of defiance to many and of cruelty to others, but a human being who had taken a particular set of decisions which had led him to be a wanderer and an outlaw, hunted down, captured, and finally executed.

§

I had a plan: I always do. And, as happens to about three-quarters of all my plans, it didn't work. I manage to survive professionally on the other 25 per cent.

Iraq, I reasoned, is the natural home of the conspiracy theory.

Execution

Nobody seems to accept anything at face value, and perhaps in some ways they are right. Many people had for instance refused to believe that Saddam Hussein had been discovered and arrested in his foxhole in December 2003. The story went round that the condition of a bunch of dates growing on a palm beside the hole was evidence that the arrest must have taken place months earlier, and kept secret.

You and I might think that nothing can remain hidden for very long nowadays, but the conspiracy theorists rarely take reality into account. And of course to this day no one really knows who was behind the murder of President John F. Kennedy, so I suppose the conspiracy theorists have a point.

The feeling still existed, particularly among Iraq's Sunni Muslims, that the Americans wanted to keep Saddam alive. An Iraqi government minister had suggested to me that when Saddam was hanged, they might ask a couple of foreign journalists who specialized in reporting Iraq to be present, in order to persuade Iraqi and international opinion that Saddam was really dead.

I have a rooted disapproval of the death penalty, and although I have seen several executions I hate the whole thought of it. Yet to be present at Saddam's execution would be an extraordinary experience, and something of importance for the BBC. So after thinking about it I told the Iraqi minister that if his government asked me, I would reluctantly agree. As a Shi'ite and a former exile, he found it hard to understand why anyone would fail to get enjoyment out of seeing Saddam Hussein hanged.

Then the government changed, but the official who was my point of contact where the execution was concerned kept his job. After Saddam had been sentenced to death, I went down the road from our house in Baghdad to see my old friend John Burns, the *New York Times* bureau chief in there. John and I have been friends ever since the days of the Rhodesian war during the 1970s. We have a lot in common: we are both tall, odd, grey-haired, talkative Englishmen of roughly the same age, who have kept on working in weird and unpleasant places long after our contemporaries gave it up and settled for a quiet life. I have great admiration for John's courage and insight, and it seemed to me that the two of us would be a hard combination to beat as truthful witnesses to Saddam's death. He had some very interesting plans of his own, and we agreed to work together.

The next evening, accompanied by some colleagues, I went to see the government official I had been dealing with. To be honest, I had always thought him a bit strange. He had a loud, American-accented voice, and some fairly odd opinions. But he unquestionably had the ear of the Iraqi prime minister, and he seemed precisely the right person to approach.

He gave us a fascinating account of the way convicted criminals were executed in Iraq. It was obviously a subject he took a lot of interest in, and when he told me he would be prepared to execute Saddam personally, it didn't seem too surprising. I had the impression he had already volunteered for the job. I suggested to him that John Burns and I should witness the execution, and he jumped at the idea. He rang the prime minister straight away, and the following day I had an email from him to say that it had been agreed.

But it didn't happen. It was partly because Saddam Hussein's execution was such a rushed business. The prime minister, Nouri al-Maliki, had already told me, in a BBC interview which we recorded a couple of days after Saddam had been sentenced, that the execution would take place before the end of the year. That had been greeted with disbelief in Iraq and elsewhere. 'Just a vague expression of intent,' said one leading observer dismissively.

But it was more than that. Saddam's appeal was turned down on Boxing Day, 26 December. I was in South Africa on holiday at the time, but I got on a plane as quickly as I could and reached Baghdad on 29 December. My colleagues, Oggy Boytchev the producer and Nick Woolley the cameraman, arrived the same day. We had no idea when the execution would take place, but it was obviously going to be very soon.

The government official was nowhere to be found. My big idea, like so many of its predecessors, had come to nothing. But at least I was in Baghdad at the right moment, thanks to the hard work and good contacts of the BBC people who had made the arrangements for me to be whisked through Dubai airport and on to a very questionable Russian airliner which plied daily from Dubai to Baghdad. At times like these, working for a big organization is extraordinarily helpful. Scarcely any other foreign journalists were in town for the biggest news event since the fall of Baghdad.

I woke at six o'clock in the morning, lying on my uncomfortable, creaking bed. Outside, from every Sunni mosque in the area, I could hear the muezzins calling out the prayers for the festival of Eid al-Adha, when the faithful make a sacrificial offering by killing a sheep to celebrate the end of the pilgrimage season. But the muezzins I could hear were Sunni ones; the Shi'ite Eid would not start for another day.

At the precise moment when the muezzins began their call, Saddam Hussein died.

Oggy Boytchev called me seconds later.

'The government television station is saying they've executed him.'

I leaped out of bed, washed and shaved as best I could in cold water and hurried out of the house where we sleep and across the alley that separates us from the house where we work. The sun was rising fast, and it promised to be a bright but chilly day. My colleagues – Susannah Nicol, Peter Emerson, Peter Greste, Oggy and Nick – were already in the office when I got there.

There was no doubt it was true. All the Iraqi television and radio stations were now reporting it as fact, having confirmed it with government officials. The government wanted everyone in Iraq to know that the execution had happened. We got our own confirmation, and started broadcasting.

It was mid-morning before someone from the government rang us to say that video of the execution would soon be made available. It would stop short of showing the moment of Saddam Hussein's death, he said, and there would be no sound. We sat and watched the government television channel for any sign of it.

Even then I felt there was something faintly questionable about it all. I could understand why the government might not want to show pictures of the actual death: that could be on grounds of taste. But why would there be no sound on the pictures? Was it because Saddam had made some last fiery speech which the Iraqi government did not want broadcast?

The video, when it came, was electrifying. The official cameraman was standing on the scaffold as Saddam was brought shuffling up the steps, his feet shackled. There were three or possibly four trapdoors, side by side, so that several people could be executed at the same time; but in this case only the one nearest the steps would be used. Saddam glanced at it briefly and neutrally; the rope with its fat hangman's knot was resting on the railings around the hatch.

He was wearing a black coat, with a white shirt underneath. It was a freezing morning, and perhaps the prison authorities did not want Saddam Hussein to shiver in the moments before he died. Charles I put on two shirts on the morning of his execution, on 30 January 1649, for the same reason.

Four executioners, all wearing black balaclavas, gathered around him. The one who was in charge explained something to Saddam, pointing to his neck; he was explaining that they would put a cloth round it, to protect it from the violence of the drop. Saddam listened for a moment, but you could see his attention wandering. Maybe the government had hoped that he would break down at this point and beg for mercy. Someone who was present at the execution told me later that he had expected it to happen. He had interrogated Saddam in the days immediately after his capture in the foxhole, and Saddam had been very querulous at the time.

But the period of imprisonment and trial had given Saddam back his old self-confidence. Perhaps it had given him back a kind of humanity, too: the American medical orderly who had looked after him every day while he was in prison reported after the execution that he had been very calm, and had talked a lot about his family. He saved small pieces from his bread ration and fed the birds with them when he was allowed out for exercise. He had sometimes watered a patch of wild flowers.

'I was a farmer once, you know,' he told the orderly.

When the orderly's brother died of cancer in the United States, Saddam put his arm round the orderly's neck and held him to him.

'I'll be your brother now,' he said.

The official video of Saddam's execution seemed to emphasize the idea of a quiet, dignified, elegiac finish to his life. It showed the executioner putting the black cloth around Saddam's neck, as he had explained, and holding it as he led him forward onto the trapdoor. Then he placed the noose over Saddam's head. At this point, a few seconds before the trapdoor opened and Saddam fell to his death, the video fades to black.

The official version, then, gave a sense of almost ceremonial dignity. But there were important details which showed the whole affair in a more vindictive light. Executing him on the morning of the Sunni Eid, and thus making sure he was dead by the Shi'ite Eid the next day, seemed like a deliberate act of sectarian vengeance.

And then there was the choice of the execution site. Perhaps it was impossible to hang Saddam Hussein anywhere else in Baghdad, but the place which the Americans blandly called 'Camp Justice', well outside the Green Zone, had previously been the headquarters of Saddam's military intelligence organization. Anyone found guilty of working secretly for the Iranians during Iraq's eight-year war with Iran was executed here. Those who died were almost exclusively Shi'ite. It looked as though Saddam Hussein's hanging was the final revenge for all those thousands of deaths.

§

It was well into the afternoon before we began to realize that the version of Saddam's death we had seen did not tell the full story. One of our local producers, the indefatigable Laith, had been ringing round to see if he could find a witness to the execution for us we could interview. At last, at around three, he managed to find someone who would agree to talk to us: the judge who had presided over the execution. We drove to the Green Zone, where he lived.

Oggy looked at me as we opened the door of the block of flats.

'Just like the old Soviet days,' he said.

It was true. This building, like so many blocks of flats in Baghdad, had been built on the Russian model, and now that they were thirty years old and more they had decayed in exactly the same way. The entrance hall stank of urine and cats. The lifts only worked erratically, so we had to walk up the stairs; the windows were broken, and there were smears of blood on the walls. Inside the judge's flat, the furnishings also seemed a little Soviet: odd lighting fixtures in coloured glass, a small brass Aladdin's lamp, a glass-fronted cabinet containing items that scarcely seemed to warrant display.

Down the hallway I caught a glimpse of the judge himself,

wearing just his underwear: he had obviously thought we would take longer to arrive, and wasn't yet dressed. We sat down and waited. A little girl opened the sitting-room door and walked in, too shy to greet us. She sat down at a desk with a laptop, and started to play a computer game. Nick set up his lights and arranged the chairs to his satisfaction.

The judge came in and introduced himself politely. 'I am Munir Haddad.'

He looked like a judge now, dressed in a dark suit with a wide blue tie, rather than an old man taking an over-long siesta in his vest. His eyes were sharp and wary. He spoke quite good English, but asked us if we would mind if he answered my questions in Arabic. When he was settled, I asked him what his part in the affair had been. He had presided over the execution, he said, and his first duty was to read out the sentence to Saddam Hussein.

'He was normal and in full control. He was aware of his fate, and knew he was about to face death. One of the guards asked him whether he was afraid of dying. He answered, "I have spent my whole life fighting the infidels and the intruders. This is my end, this is the end of my life. But I started my life as a fighter and as a political militant, so death does not frighten me."

'Another guard asked him, "Why did you destroy Iraq and destroy us? You starved us and you allowed the Americans to occupy us."

'His reply was, "I destroyed the invaders and the Persians, and I destroyed the enemies of Iraq. And I turned Iraq from poverty to wealth."'

'So what happened when you were actually in the execution chamber?' I asked.

'He was reciting, as his custom was, "God is great", and also some political slogans such as "Down with the Americans!" and "Down with the invaders!" He said, "We're going to heaven and our enemies will rot in hell." He also called for forgiveness and love amongst Iraqis, though he stressed that they should fight the Americans and the Iranians.'

'What happened then?'

'When he was taken to the gallows, the guards tried to put a hood over his head, but he refused. Then he recited some verses from the Koran. Some of the guards started to taunt him by shouting Islamic words. A cleric who was present asked Saddam to repeat some spiritual verses. Saddam did so, but with sarcasm. These were his last words. And then the cord tightened around his neck, and he dropped to his death . . . He was killed instantly.'

'Are you happy that Saddam Hussein is dead?'

'Do I look happy to you? I was entrusted to oversee the execution, and that's what I did. Yes, I do have my feelings as an Iraqi citizen, but I carried out my duty the best I could, and I gave Saddam Hussein his rights. I wasn't there to seek revenge.'

I tried to find out from the judge what, precisely, he meant about the guards taunting him and Saddam repeating the spiritual words with sarcasm, but since I don't speak Arabic it proved impossible to get any closer to what he meant.

Back at the office afterwards, we went through the words again and again, but without understanding them any better. The judge wouldn't explain, and the various officials who talked about the execution on Iraqi television said nothing to make it any clearer. With nothing else to go on except the video itself, silent, short and apparently calm, it seemed as though Saddam Hussein's execution had been a dignified business.

It was around eleven o'clock the next morning that someone in Baghdad called to tip us off: another video of Saddam's death had been posted on the internet. Nick Woolley found it and downloaded it.

'I think you should come and see this,' Oggy Boytchev said.

Everything about the new video was entirely different. For a start, it had been filmed on a mobile phone, so the quality was mediocre and the picture wobbled constantly. It was shot from a completely different viewpoint, not up on the scaffold like the official version, but from down among the group of fourteen witnesses, six feet or so below. Most important of all, there was a soundtrack.

Altogether they showed that, far from being a quiet, dignified business, the execution of Saddam Hussein had been raucous, uncontrolled and brutal. Saddam was taunted and insulted to the very moment when the trapdoor opened. Watching the pictures felt like watching a public hanging at Tyburn in the eighteenth century.

'I'll show you the whole thing from start to finish,' said Nick. 'It's not very pretty.'

It wasn't. Saddam was still praying when the hatch opened and he fell through. I shouted out with the shock of it, though I have seen men hanged before. The next shot showed Saddam, his neck broken, hanging motionless. He must have died instantly.

We went back over the pictures again and again, working out the details, trying to distinguish the words that were being spoken. Now that we had the sound, two things were very clear from the start: Saddam's own harsh voice, cutting in from time to time, and the shouting of the name Moqtada al-Sadr.

It had not been the government's intention that the execution should be so chaotic and abusive, but things in Iraq are rarely well disciplined, and there was little proper control over what happened. No one was supposed to take a mobile phone into the execution chamber, for security reasons; mobiles were often used to detonate bombs in Iraq. But two people smuggled theirs in, both of them senior figures. One, a top government official, is said to have browbeaten the security man who searched him, and insisted that he had to have his phone with him for official business.

And then the security men themselves, contrary to their orders, pushed their way into the execution chamber to see the hanging for themselves.

Two of them, perhaps more, were followers of the radical young Shi'ite cleric Moqtada al-Sadr, and it was they who started chanting his name during Saddam's last moments. On the video you could hear Saddam's growling voice repeating the name with contempt and irony:

'Moqtada!'

Then, as they continue to chant, Saddam asks, 'Is this the way real men behave?'

'You're going to hell!' one of the guards shouts.

Saddam ignores him.

One of the witnesses, probably the prosecutor Munqith al-Faroun, called out, 'Keep quiet! He's just about to die.'

Saddam Hussein had just handed his copy of the Koran, which he had carried throughout his trial, to al-Faroun, asking him to make sure it was passed to a member of his family.

The Muslim cleric who was present on the scaffold told Saddam he should pray. Saddam began the statement of faith which is essential to every Muslim: 'There is no God but God, and Mohammed is His Prophet.' He finished it, and started again. As he reached the name 'Mohammed' the second time, the executioner pulled the lever and Saddam fell to his death, the prayer unfinished.

Ten days later, a shorter video, also captured on a mobile phone, showed Saddam Hussein's body lying on a hospital gurney, wrapped in a shroud. It was clearly only a few minutes after the execution. Someone pulls the sheet back and reveals Saddam's head. There is a wound on his neck, and bruising and blood on his face. Saddam's supporters immediately said this showed that Saddam had been beaten up before his execution, but that is plainly untrue. The injuries were all consistent with the violence of Saddam's final fall.

His enemies, even some of those who had been present at the execution, tried to insist that Saddam Hussein had faced his death in a cowardly fashion. 'He was a broken man,' said one eye-witness. But this was plainly untrue. Munir Haddad, the judge who was present at the execution, told me during the interview we recorded with him that he had seen Saddam soon after his capture in the foxhole.

'He was very nervous then, and seemed unable to concentrate or take a firm line on anything. I expected him to be like this at his execution. But he wasn't. You know, I have many reasons to hate Saddam Hussein. But I cannot deny that he died a brave man.'

Saddam's execution shocked even the Americans, and brought out some unusual responses. This, for instance, was how the chief of the American military in Baghdad, Major-General William Caldwell, described what had happened when the Americans handed him over to the Iraqis to be hanged. His tone was almost reverential.

'He was dignified, as always. He was courteous, as he always had been to his US military police guards, though his characterization changed at the prison facility as the Iraqi guards were assuming control over him. But he was still dignified towards us.

'And we had absolutely nothing to do with any of the procedures or any of the control mechanisms from that point forward.'

In other words, the American military were distancing themselves as far as possible from the way Saddam Hussein's execution was carried out.

When it was too late, the Iraqi government itself realized that the whole thing had been a disaster. I spoke to the prime minister's senior adviser, Sami al-Askaria, who had also witnessed the execution.

'It was horrible, terrible, because it was a mistake,' he said.

He meant the business of allowing in the guards to taunt Saddam, and perhaps not preventing people from using their mobile phones to film what had really happened. But it applied more generally to the execution itself.

§

There is, if you have the stomach to do the mathematics, a complex hangman's equation to ensure that the thickness of the rope and the length of the drop are proportional to the weight of the person to be hanged. Too short a drop can mean they will be strangled slowly rather than have their neck broken instantly. Too long can mean that they are mangled.

Albert Pierrepoint, the last British hangman, who executed many Nazi criminals after Nuremberg as well as others including James Hanratty and Ruth Ellis, worked out both the equation and the choreography of a hanging so well that the condemned person was dead within ten seconds of his coming into the execution chamber.

I witnessed a triple hanging in Kabul once. It was carried out in front of the eager eyes of thousands of Afghans, and – less excusably – several dozen international aid workers, who all seemed to have really good and important professional reasons for being there. Well, I was there too, so I suppose I shouldn't judge them, but if I hadn't had to cover the whole unpleasant affair for television, I would certainly have stayed away. Dickens and Thackeray both wrote about the unhealthy interest which the London crowd took in a public hanging, and nothing seemed to have changed in a hundred and fifty years.

The three men were all supposedly vicious robbers, rapists and murderers, though one kept proclaiming his innocence in a way that indicated to me that he might just have been included to make up the numbers. One was short, one was of medium build and the third was noticeably tall for an Afghan. The executioners, none of whom knew his trade, had prepared themselves with three ropes of different lengths: short, medium and long. They duly put the short rope round the neck of the short man, the medium one round the neck of the medium-height man, and the long one round the neck of the tall man.

There wasn't even an attempt at a drop, so these three were all going to be strangled. The short one let himself go and died pretty quickly. The medium one put up a little fight, and died slower. As for the tall one, the rope was simply too long even for him to hang. The incompetent fools tried everything, from digging a hole under his feet to turning an iron bar around in the rope to make it shorter. It was one of the most dreadful and cruel things I have seen. Even one or two of the international aid workers found it hard to watch.

The executions of Saddam Hussein and his co-defendants were nothing like that. But when the other two were hanged a fortnight after Saddam, the rope for Barzan al-Tikriti was too long and the force with which it arrested his fall was therefore too great for the weight of his body. As a result his head snapped off and landed a few feet away. He certainly did not suffer any more than Saddam, but it was a disgusting business.

Even Pierrepoint had his failures, and sometimes he used to tell of necks that had snapped or even stretched to an appalling length. Execution is a barbarous business. What civilized person could possibly approve of this or any of the other savage ways of getting rid of the people we have failed to deal with?

§

Saddam Hussein began his extraordinary, melodramatic career as a small-time enforcer from the ugly little village of Awja, beside the River Tigris, close to the town of Tikrit. Born in 1937, he was marked forever by the poverty of his upbringing and the savagery of his drunken stepfather's beatings. Yet his mother adored him, and instilled in him his sense of destiny; it was she who had named him Saddam – 'he who confronts'.

He had risen to extraordinary heights by confrontation, and

made his name familiar to people in every part of the globe. Anyone who approached him, from his own ministers to foreigners like the British politicians George Galloway and Tony Benn, knew that you had to behave towards him with almost grovelling respect. He lived in the grandest style, building palaces he scarcely visited and touring the country he dominated in fleets of expensive limousines. Everywhere he went there were huge statues and portraits of him, smiling at the people he controlled with almost unprecedented terror. Outside the law faculty at the University of Baghdad there was a portrait, twelve feet high, showing him as the still smiling embodiment of justice, with the scales in one hand and the sword of vengeance in the other.

And then, because the business of confrontation made so many enemies for him, he lost everything. He had to go into hiding, travelling round in a beaten-up old taxi and taking refuge in shacks and holes in the ground. Finally, he concerned himself with feeding the birds and tending an unkempt patch of weeds at his prison.

When he died, it was the main news throughout the world. His body lay under a sheet in a prison corridor, and was loaded unceremoniously in a plain deal coffin onto the back of a pick-up truck which took him back to Awja, where his journey had started, sixty-nine years before.

He was buried in a temporary tomb under the floor of a mortuary chapel. If he had been buried in the ground, it was felt, someone might come and desecrate his grave. Not far away, in a desolate corner of the local cemetery, the bodies of his two sons and one of his grandsons lay. I visited them not long after they had been buried in 2003; it very soon became too dangerous for a Westerner to visit the cemetery. The graves of Uday and Qsay, and Qsay's son, lay unmarked except for a single wreath of red plastic roses in the yellow mud, away from the other graves, as though they were unworthy to be in close proximity. One day, perhaps, Saddam Hussein's body will lie alongside them.

In his will, he asked his daughter Raghad to decide where he should be buried: Awja or Ramadi, the heart of the insurgency against the Americans. Raghad chose Awja, for family reasons. Yet Saddam himself had always hated the place. He showered it and its inhabitants with money, so that even when I was there in 2003 it boasted more expensive cars than any comparable village in Iraq. But it was well known that when he drove past Awja on his way to or from the town of Tikrit, which was full of his supporters and his statues, he would turn his face away so he didn't even have to look at it. Perhaps he sensed that one day he would be back here among the peasants he had sprung from, buried in its dusty earth.

If ever it becomes safe enough to go to Awja again, I will make the journey. Almost the whole of my long career has been spent watching and reporting on Saddam Hussein. I could never admire him or sympathize with him. Far too many good people had died or had their lives destroyed as a result of his terrible deeds for that. But he was, in his way, fascinating.

And there was that instant in the courtroom in Baghdad when I met his glance, and saw something more than just a fallen dictator.

13

AN ANATOMY OF REPORTING

I suppose, if viewed dispassionately, my efforts on 25 February 2007 were pretty much a failure; yet I look back on what happened that day with great pleasure.

It all started rather early. Oggy Boytchev, Nick Woolley and I had been invited to the Hyde Park Hotel in Knightsbridge to interview the president of Afghanistan, Hamid Karzai, who was on a visit to London. The other two came to my house and we drove to the hotel from there. The time was 6.40 a.m.

We walked up the front steps of the Hyde Park, and then up the even steeper, even longer flight of stairs indoors. We were laden with equipment, though as ever Nick insisted on carrying the main part of it: something about needing to be balanced because of his back. And there we stood and waited. And waited.

I had first met Karzai in a hotel car park in Islamabad in September 2001. Al-Qaeda's attack on New York and Washington, planned by Osama bin Laden in Afghanistan under the protection of the Taliban, had taken place a week or so earlier. Now the Americans, with British support, were getting ready to overthrow the Taliban.

I was walking with a friend of mine out of our hotel, one of those large, pompous, modern places full of fake marble and fake wood, so featureless that I can't remember if it was a Marriott or a Sheraton. Official-looking limousines were pulling up and leaving: some sort of government do was taking place.

'Good Lord, there's Karzai,' said my friend.

A distraught figure was weaving his way between the black cars. He clearly wasn't heading for the government do; he wasn't dressed for it. He looked pretty rough. My friend introduced us, and Karzai burst out with his story. The Pakistan government, which still had strong links with the Taliban, was threatening to send him back to Afghanistan. That would mean a speedy execution.

'They say they'll make a decision any day now.'

I said something about helping to raise a fuss.

'Would you?' he asked, with hope starting to surface in his anxious face.

It would certainly have been utterly disgraceful if the Pakistani government had decided to send him back to Afghanistan. Karzai had been a minister in one of the unpopular *mujaheddin* governments, and had escaped to Pakistan when the Taliban took over in 1996. He was a pleasant, unassuming man, and a particularly human one: thin-skinned, quick to show his emotions, and equally quick to make up for it. Three years later, when he was president of Afghanistan, he got quite angry at a question I asked him during an interview. Then, a moment later, he apologized on camera for what he had said. For some people, I suppose, that might have made him seem weak or vulnerable. To me it was the sign of a real person, not just a politician with a front. I had liked him before; after that I admired him.

As it turned out, I didn't have to do anything to help him after our meeting in the car park. The Americans and British were looking for someone to install as president, and the British suggested Karzai. A word to the Pakistani government was enough: no one mentioned extradition again.

Britain and America had earlier supported another *mujaheddin* leader for the job, Abdul Haq. He was a splendid man, tough and courageous, who moved around with great dexterity in spite of the fact that he had lost a leg in a landmine explosion. A friend of mine, the well-known cameraman Peter Jouvenal, had paid out of his own pocket for Abdul Haq to come to London to be fitted with a prosthetic, and had thereby launched him on a spectacular but brief political career. Mrs Thatcher, who was prime minister at the time, heard about him and invited him to Downing Street. All this attention, and the possession of a state-of-the-art plastic leg, gave Abdul Haq enormous kudos among the *mujaheddin*, and when he went back he found himself in the ranks of their topmost leaders.

After 11 September the British and Americans together decided that Abdul Haq would make an excellent president for a post-

Taliban Afghanistan. It would be necessary, they decided, to get him into the country while the Taliban were still in power, so that he could establish himself as chief among the internal opposition. Abdul Haq, game and tough as ever, agreed. Then came a terrible mistake. The Americans insisted, against the advice of the British, that their own special forces should escort him back into the country, where he would be able to make contact with the resistance.

Having worked alongside men from the American special forces in various parts of the world, I have learned to have considerable respect for them. But here in Afghanistan the British had much more experience, and suggested different ways of doing things. But the Americans insisted on following their own course. Disregarding Abdul Haq's protests, they took him to the wrong place, contacted the wrong people, and managed to leave him on his own with them. He was captured, and the Taliban executed him soon afterwards.

After that, a new leader was required. The Americans had had their doubts about Karzai, who had never been particularly close to them, but now it was hard for them to find an alternative. With better support and better plans, Hamid Karzai rode across the Pakistani border into Afghanistan on a motorbike. He had a difficult time of it, too, because the Taliban had apparently been tipped off by Pakistan's Inter-Services Intelligence, the ISI, and knew he was coming. But he survived, and eventually became president. Ever since, he had done as well as anyone could, given the difficult politics of Afghanistan.

His position is precarious, of course. He is like the Amir in the poem by the late-nineteenth-century administrator of British India Sir Alfred Lyall:

> And far from the Suleiman heights come the sounds of the stirring
> of tribes,
> Afreedi, Hazara, and Ghilzi, they clamour for plunder or bribes;
> And Herat is but held by a thread; and the Usbeg has raised
> Badukshan;
> And the chief may sleep sound, in his grave, who would rule the
> unruly Afghan.

Yet it always amuses me to read the columnists who complain that Karzai controls little more of Afghanistan than Kabul, the other main cities, and the routes between them. When, since the days of Dost Mahommed or earlier, has any ruler of Afghanistan controlled more than that? The last king didn't, nor did his unruly Afghan kinsmen who overthrew him. The Russians certainly didn't, nor the *mujaheddin*, nor the Taliban. You don't rule Afghanistan, you simply sit in Kabul and soliloquize, like the Amir:

> For there's hardly a room in my palace but a kinsman there was
> killed;
> And never a street in the city but with false fierce curs is filled;
> With a mob of priests, and fanatics, and all my mutinous host;
> They follow my steps, as the wolves do, for a prince who slips
> is lost.

So now the three of us – Oggy, Nick and I – were hanging around at the Hyde Park Hotel waiting for Hamid Karzai, having arrived obediently on the dot of seven o'clock. Seven-fifteen came, and an Afghan official turned up and explained that unfortunately the president was holding a meeting and might be a little time. A tremendous air of apology seemed to hover around us; even the hotel staff seemed embarrassed.

My main concern at that time in the morning was to get a cup of tea, though when the hotel staff summoned up a tray of coffee I drank some gratefully and began to wake up. I didn't really mind hanging around. I liked and sympathized with Hamid Karzai, and knew how polite he instinctively was, like most Afghans. Plenty of well-known names have kept me waiting over the years, and I have paced around angrily, full of nasty warnings that I'd have to leave soon. I don't particularly care about myself – like most journalists I have long become inured to that sort of thing – but I don't like to see any sign that the BBC is being treated disrespectfully.

But I knew Hamid Karzai wouldn't deliberately disrespect the BBC. On the contrary, he had put himself out for it several times. And he was unfailingly pleasant.

Someone from the Foreign Office joined us, and the atmosphere of apology deepened. Then an Afghan official came down, and there was some whispering. It was left to the discomfited Foreign Office person to break the news to us.

'Actually, the President's still asleep.'

No one, it seemed, wanted to wake him up. I just thought it was funny. Oggy and Nick and I had other work to do that day, and it simplified things a good deal if we didn't have to broadcast an interview with Karzai.

'Tell him I'm not at all upset, and that he needs his sleep.'

Maybe 'The Amir's Soliloquy' was still running in my head.

'But tell him I'll come to Kabul soon and interview him there.'

There was relief all round, and much sincere nodding and exchanging of business cards.

Now I felt like taking the other two to breakfast somewhere nice, to make up for getting them out of bed so early. It occurred to me that the Chelsea Arts Club was only a short way away. The Club, for me, is the centre of the known universe. I've been a member for nearly a quarter of a century, and some of my happiest times have taken place there. It is everything a club ought to be; and if some of the big clubs in the centre of town were sensible enough to follow it in allowing women to become members, and relaxing the dress code so you don't have to wear a jacket and tie the whole time, they would be jollier places than they are.

We went in and sat down at the members' table, looking out at the garden. One or two people were there already, looking as though they had slept in the club bedrooms: a rumpled look, combining a Spartan night with too much to drink the evening before. The Chelsea Arts Club provides both. But the breakfast we got was as good if not better than anything the Hyde Park Hotel could have served up, and it cost us only five pounds a head.

The rest of our day now lay before us. The interview with Karzai had been a sideshow, something I had requested months before, when it had been important to get a word with him. Now, Afghanistan had slipped down the news agenda and was scarcely visible. But something else of real importance had taken its place; something particularly relevant to the BBC. I had explained everything to both Oggy and Nick, and we were tense and intrigued about it.

It related to the central issue in recent British foreign policy: the decision to join the Americans in invading Iraq in 2003. The basic reason was strategic. Tony Blair and his closest advisers felt that, when the chips were down, Britain had to stand alongside the United States. This attitude had reaped great advantages for Margaret Thatcher in the 1980s, and for Tony Blair himself during Bill Clinton's presidency. In spite of the serious doubts of the Foreign Office, Downing Street bought George W. Bush's idea that the invasion would be quick and easy, and that although no serious plans had been made for the period after the invasion, there would be such rejoicing at Saddam Hussein's downfall that everything would be all right.

This was a distinctly un-British approach. Historically, British officials may not have got every decision right, but they have always been meticulous planners. Now, though, the Foreign Office was completely ignored. So was the State Department in Washington, which produced a 900-page blueprint for the period immediately after the invasion. The plan was apparently dropped into the waste-bin, unread by the president or anyone close to him.

There was great disquiet in Britain about the whole idea of the invasion, and this went right up to the Cabinet. But Tony Blair, Alastair Campbell and the others in the inner circle decided to use the intelligence provided by MI6, the Secret Intelligence Service, and by other agencies, to demonstrate that Saddam Hussein had to be stopped urgently. Intelligence professionals are trained not to shape or mould their information to fit a particular policy, but to present it in a balanced way.

Tony Blair was breaking with tradition by publicizing the intelligence in order to persuade the British public that it was right to invade Iraq. What was more, he presented it as being much more reliable than it really was. People were given the impression that British intelligence had firm information that Saddam Hussein could launch attacks with his weapons of mass destruction within forty-five minutes – and that these weapons could reach British targets. That actually meant British bases on Cyprus, but you couldn't blame people if they got the impression that Britain itself was suddenly a target for chemical, biological and even, at a stretch, nuclear weapons. Tony Blair told the House of Commons that the intelligence on this from SIS was 'extensive, detailed and authoritative'. It all played an important part in persuading Parliament to vote in favour of the invasion of Iraq.

More than a year later, in May 2004, a reporter for the *Today* programme on Radio 4, Andrew Gilligan, broadcast the findings of an investigation he had been conducting into the government's use of intelligence in the run-up to the invasion. In a live, off-the-cuff remark at 6.17 in the morning – like the Afghans, *Today* keeps early hours – Gilligan had said, in effect, that the Blair government had knowingly exaggerated ('sexed up') the reports from the intelligence community about Iraq's weapons of mass destruction in order to persuade the British people to support the American project to overthrow Saddam Hussein.

Even at the time, I wondered how Gilligan could have been so sure that Blair and his officials and ministers had *known* that they were lying. Only a minister or a very senior official, perhaps from MI6, could have been so certain.

Alastair Campbell, the prime minister's head of communications – a sort of public relations officer on a grand scale – heard Gilligan's words and exploded with rage against the BBC. He was abusive and threatening, and the crisis had begun. It ended with the publication of a report by Lord Hutton and the resignations of the BBC's chairman and director-general. Having played a part in every major row between a British government and the BBC for twenty years, I felt rather left out of this one, though a year or so later scarcely anyone who had been closely involved was still in his or her job. Even so, I wish I had waded in; I've always enjoyed a good fight with the politicians.

Personally, I thought Gilligan's source must be the head of MI6, Sir Richard Dearlove, or perhaps the head of the Civil Service, or the permanent secretary to the Treasury or the Ministry of Defence; I found it hard to think of anyone else who would have been authoritative enough for Gilligan to have taken his or her word for it, and put the BBC's reputation on the line in this way. In the end, as the world was to discover, his source was someone much lower in the chain, an arms-control official from the Ministry of Defence, Dr David Kelly. The Ministry of Defence outed him in a way you or I wouldn't want on our conscience. Isolated, frightened, cast out by those he ought to have been able to trust, he committed suicide.

In my forty years as an observer of successive British governments, I have never known anything quite so disgraceful.

Then, at the end of 2006, as the fourth anniversary of the invasion of Iraq came closer, I had a conversation with a friend of mine from way back, a very senior figure in the government. Our paths had long separated, but I had always liked him. He was cleverer than I, and probably more worldly wise, and nowadays he was a lot grander. Actually, I have always thought that it was one of the saving graces about journalism that it prevents you from getting too grand: it's hard to be pompous if you find yourself standing in the gutter with the rain pouring down, shouting questions at the great ones of the world alongside a bunch of other journalists.

As we spoke, it occurred to me that he was in a position to tell me whether Tony Blair had knowingly exaggerated the intelligence he had been given about Saddam's weapons of mass destruction. I arranged to go and see him, and talk about it some more.

So now Oggy and Nick and I were in Nick's car, still full from our Chelsea Arts Club breakfast, heading for my friend's house outside London. I had originally thought to go alone, but the new editor of the *Ten O'Clock News*, a shrewd, intelligent and highly motivated man half my age called Craig Oliver, suggested that even if there were one chance in a hundred that my friend would agree to say something about it all on the record, I should have a camera nearby. He was right: on something as sensitive as this, people have a great habit of changing their minds after committing themselves. Then they announce that they don't want to comment after all.

On the way we stopped for coffee in a favourite place of mine. There happened to be another BBC camera team in the area, and we met up with them in case there was something they could do to help: some location shots from a greater distance, perhaps. It was all very pleasant and companionable. Then I left them there, and took the lonely walk to meet my friend.

Right from the moment I shook his hand, I could see none of it would turn out the way we had all half-hoped. There wouldn't be any public announcement, and he would clearly never allow me to hint at his identity. We had a delightful lunch, talking about everything except the matter that had brought me there. Afterwards we sat in his kitchen, and he made me coffee in a mug as though we were forty years younger, and discussed the events that had led Britain to invade Iraq.

My instinct had been right. He wouldn't dream of speaking out against the government, or how it had behaved. In fact he seemed still to feel that the invasion of Iraq had been unavoidable. If Britain had sided with Germany, France, Russia and China against the United States, he believed, it would have created a rift in Anglo-American relations which might never have been healed. He supported Tony Blair, and was clearly unwilling to say anything against him.

Yet there was something else that lay behind what he said, and I couldn't work out what it was. I just felt it was there. By this stage I was taking notes. That always alarms people if they are talking to you off the record, because they are worried you might use your notes later and forget their 'deep background' nature, but I had to take the risk because I knew this was an important conversation, and I would later need to recall the full details of it. He was duly alarmed, but I hope he knew he could trust me. I am long past the age where the story matters more than the people involved. For me, the people are all that really matter nowadays. I would much rather have gone back with my tail between my legs than betray my friend's confidence. That must sound terribly sanctimonious, I'm sure, but you wait until you are sixty-two and see if it isn't how you feel too.

And then, just as I was finishing my coffee, there came a moment of pure gold.

'It's one of the great regrets of my career that I didn't challenge the way the intelligence was used,' he said.

He means Alastair Campbell, I thought. He still wants to stay loyal to the prime minister, but he's blaming his closest adviser for distorting the intelligence. For knowingly exaggerating it. For sexing it up. I wrote his words down, and put a little star beside them in the margin.

I promised him at the end that I wouldn't use anything that I hadn't checked with him first. I bet he'll tell me I can't use it, I thought. But it wouldn't affect my friendship with him if he did; people have got to do what they've got to do.

I rejoined the others. They were disappointed at having come all this way and having nothing to show for it, but I went through my notes carefully with Oggy and he saw the value of them at once. They left for London after that, but I stayed behind for a while and went to an antiquarian bookshop to make myself feel better. We all have our different therapies for moments like this. Some people get drunk, some go out and buy clothes. I bought a signed first edition of some poems I particularly like, and my retail guilt about the cost washed away the disappointment.

During the next few days Oggy and I went over the whole story, sometimes with Craig, sometimes on our own. There wasn't enough to make a news report in what my friend had said to me – not even when I put it together with other material I had obtained about the number and quality of British agents working inside Saddam Hussein's government immediately before the invasion. There were, I had been told by someone who knew authoritatively what he was talking about, two or three (which probably meant three) agents on the fringes of Saddam's inner circle who were working for British intelligence, and a larger number outside the circle. I knew, too, that they had been given small but powerful radio sets to send their reports back to London.

Yet no matter how good the British agents were, and they were apparently better and more senior than the agents for the CIA or any other intelligence organization, they didn't know the ultimate secret of Saddam's rule: that at some stage during the 1990s he had smuggled his weapons of mass destruction out of the country.

But where had they gone? Perhaps I had had a clue about that, without realizing it. In 2002 I wrote an article for a British newspaper into which I dropped a little piece of information I had just gleaned from a very senior Arab source. In the article I said I had absolutely no way of checking this or proving it, but was simply putting it in for the reader's consideration: my source, who might have been expected to know what he was talking about, had told me that in the late 1990s President Mubarak of Egypt had written to Saddam Hussein, telling him he should get rid of his 'naughty' weapons (the word 'naughty' was in English, apparently). Mubarak then helped Saddam move the weapons out, possibly to Syria.

I didn't report this for the BBC, because I couldn't back it up; but I felt that by burying it deep in my newspaper article, with all the necessary disclaimers, I had done my duty. A day or so later, everything exploded. The information minister in Cairo gave a press conference denouncing what I had written in the most furious terms. Newspaper editorials spoke of dishonourable, crooked, deliberately damaging reporting. Up to that point, I hadn't really believed the story about the 'naughty' weapons, but the way the Egyptian government reacted to fifty words buried in an undistinguished column in a minority British Sunday newspaper made me begin to wonder.

For the Blair government, though, the key problem was that the intelligence which was so reliable, according to the prime minister when he spoke in the Commons, hadn't been reliable at all. I had been told, by a much more senior source than Andrew Gilligan's, that the head of British intelligence had informed Tony Blair all along that the quality of information from Baghdad wasn't that good. Indeed, the head of MI6 told the Butler inquiry into the government's use of intelligence in the run-up to the invasion that there had been no reliable information about many of Saddam's weapons of mass destruction since 1988.

If I had been able to give the name of my friend who told me it was his great regret that he hadn't challenged the government's use of intelligence, I would have had a big story. But I couldn't. Craig Oliver came up with the solution. We were planning to have an Iraq week in March 2007, marking the fourth anniversary of the launching of the invasion. I was going to be in Baghdad for it; why not broadcast our intelligence story from there, with the anniversary as a peg?

That sorted out the problem. My quotation might not make a news story on its own, but it would be a very respectable and interesting addition to a report about how Britain came to invade Iraq.

And then Daniel Pearl, Craig's deputy, gave us something else to go on. He had heard suggestions that members of Lord Butler's inquiry into the use of intelligence had thought the government might fall as a result of the publication of their report in July 2004 – but that the journalists who covered it had failed to spot how damaging the accusations were. The government had been let off the hook. Sir Michael Mates, a member of the Butler inquiry, felt that the journalists had been expecting that the inquiry would find a scapegoat, and when there wasn't one, they lost interest. They certainly didn't seem to read the damning passages in the report with any understanding.

Lord Butler, himself a former head of the Civil Service, put the knife in even deeper when he made a speech in the House of Lords in January 2007. He accused Tony Blair of being 'disingenuous' in the way he used intelligence to justify the invasion of Iraq. 'Disingenuous' is a strong term for a former senior civil servant to use about a prime minister's words; it means 'deliberately misleading'. You or I might call it lying.

I knew Lord Butler and liked him, and I tried to get him to agree to an interview with me. He didn't return my calls. But he had made his views abundantly clear, and because business in the House of Lords was televised we had him doing so on camera.

All of this was very much what Andrew Gilligan had reported on the *Today* programme that fateful morning in 2004. The trouble was, although the basic facts of what Gilligan had said were true, his source wasn't really strong enough or senior enough for Gilligan's report to be waterproof. It was true that Tony Blair had been warned that the information about Saddam's weapons of mass destruction wasn't as strong as he maintained, but Dr David Kelly couldn't have known it for a fact, and neither could Andrew Gilligan. If you are accusing the prime minister of lying – sorry, of being disingenuous – you have to have pretty strong backing for it.

One last thing remained to be done. I emailed my highly placed friend and told him I wanted to use his quotation. A day passed, and I grew increasingly worried. Then the message flashed up: he had replied. He wanted a slight change in the quotation, that was all. If anything, I felt his change made it stronger.

So I had the kind of backing that Andrew Gilligan had lacked – though of course it was much easier to report all this now, so much later. The pressure had long been off the BBC. Blair was soon to leave office, Alastair Campbell was a busted flush looking for another career. In one of those curious turns that make even the most faithful of BBC employees wonder about the organization occasionally, the Corporation had even bought the rights to make a series from Campbell's memoirs. It felt like searching out someone who had mugged you, and paying him handsomely to describe for you exactly how the crime had been committed.

When we got to Baghdad, Oggy and Nick and I went out into the streets and recorded a piece to camera: that strange, artificial moment when the disembodied voice of the reporter pauses, and he or she suddenly appears, haranguing the audience in person. I usually do my best to make mine as natural as possible, as though it's a conversation rather than a parade-ground rant, but in this case, because I had given my word to my friend to speak his words and no others, I had the quotation taped up on the camera beside the lens, so I could read it out word for word.

The *Today* programme, fittingly enough, ran the first version of my report, but not as prominently as I had hoped, because the programme led on something quite important which had come up. Another version failed to make it onto a radio news bulletin altogether. Well, when so many people had lost their jobs over all this, you can't blame people for being cautious. But the *Ten O'Clock News* came up trumps. The report ran in full, and was given pride of place; I felt proud of it. A lot of people had worked on it, and helped to make it better. And although I don't suppose one viewer out of a thousand thought anything about it, it seemed to me that we had finally put the record straight. Here, just to drive the point home, is the full script:

Transcript of report from 10.00 News, Tuesday 20 March 2007: Baghdad

This was Baghdad today: six bomb explosions, up to twenty dead, dozens of injuries. Four years after the invasion, Iraq is in a state of chaos.

The war was sold to the British people on the basis that intelligence showed Saddam Hussein was a serious threat, and had to be dealt with.

Synch: Tony Blair
The intelligence on which this is based is extensive, detailed and authoritative.

Piece to camera:
Yet now a very senior figure in Whitehall, heavily involved during the run-up to the war, has told me privately it was one of the great regrets of his career, with the benefit of hindsight, that he didn't challenge how the intelligence was used.

I gather from official sources that British intelligence had a couple or more agents, on the edge of Saddam Hussein's inner circle. They would have sent their reports to London by radio.

But they weren't close enough to Saddam to know the best-kept secret of his rule: that at some time in the 1990s, he got rid of most of his weapons of mass destruction. Why should he want to keep that secret? British officials believe it's because he was afraid his neighbour, Iran, would take advantage of his weakness, and invade.

British intelligence was up-front about its lack of good information from Iraq. It told Tony Blair it hadn't known much about Iraq's work on chemical and biological weapons since 1988. That wasn't the impression the prime minister gave to Parliament. He said the intelligence was 'extensive, detailed and authoritative'.

Lord Butler, a former head of the civil service who headed an investigation into all this, was scathing about this in the House of Lords recently – though his speech went largely unreported. He accused Tony Blair of being 'disingenuous' in the way he used intelligence; that's Whitehall-speak for 'deliberately misleading'.

Synch: Lord Butler
He told Parliament only just over a month later that the picture painted by our intelligence services was 'extensive, detailed and authoritative'. Those words could simply not have been justified by the material that the intelligence community provided to him.

But when Lord Butler's committee reported, in July 2004, its criticisms weren't nearly as strong as this. They might have brought down the government – but it didn't happen.

Synch: Sir Michael Mates
Frankly I was rather surprised, I was very surprised that at the press conference which Lord Butler gave and at which we were all

there, nobody asked the killing questions . . . The ones about the intelligence, the ones about the unreliability . . . The media didn't hone in on that. Once we hadn't provided them with a scalp, they more or less lost interest.

What really saved the government was the fact that the British intelligence community had signed up to what Tony Blair told the Commons. Senior officials may have their regrets now about the fact the intelligence was wrongly used. But it was Whitehall's support and discretion which allowed the government to massage the intelligence in order to bolster its case.

John Simpson, BBC News, Baghdad.

(Synch, by the way, is an old film term, long outdated, and simply means a voice is heard.)

There wasn't a peep of complaint from Downing Street, or anywhere else, which merely showed that the story was dead as a political issue. The dreadful damage to the BBC was over and done with. Yet the question of whether the people of Britain had been seriously misled in the run-up to the invasion of Iraq remained. And Lord Butler and my friend had strongly implied that they had.

Someone had suggested, though, that I should contact Alastair Campbell while we were preparing our report, and ask him to respond. I knew Alastair before he became the voice of Tony Blair, and rather liked him in those days. So I emailed him and asked him if he would agree to be interviewed.

He answered, with a curtness I found rude, that the answer was no. I thanked him, and was prepared to leave it at that; but Campbell wasn't. If Andrew Gilligan had asked to interview him, he wrote back, the BBC wouldn't have been in such a mess.

I was furious. To me, the BBC had been placed in a mess at least partly by Campbell's lack of self-control, and the much-condemned report by Lord Hutton into the whole business of Gilligan's report and the hounding of Dr Kelly. The BBC had rebounded quite quickly, but it was no thanks whatsoever to Downing Street. Then I reflected that the best answer to this kind of thing is usually mockery rather than rage. So, sitting at my desk in the BBC's Baghdad office, I sent him another email:

> Oh, shut up Alistair and stop quoting from your book. I'll
> get it out of the library when it comes out.

Somehow, that did the trick. After that, the remaining emails in the conversation were spiky but amusing. It was a strange end to a savage episode.

§

I've been careful all my professional life not to get too close to any political party, in Britain or anywhere else. For a start, I don't believe that any single party can possibly embody the only road to truth. And anyway, a lifetime of watching politicians and reporting on their doings has shown me that they are no different, and certainly no better, than the rest of us. In other words, they need to be watched and to be called to account from time to time.

In the past, though, I would have said that there was one political party that I preferred to many of the rest. I had followed the fortunes of the African National Congress in South Africa and in exile for nearly forty years. There were plenty of things that it had done that were wrong. But its principles were better than those of many other political parties around the world, and when it counted most – during the handover of power from white rule to majority rule in South Africa in 1994 – the ANC under Nelson Mandela behaved superbly.

Oddly enough, my experiences at that time led me back to the Church of England. The peaceful changes that took place in South Africa were very much an Anglican miracle, with Archbishop Desmond Tutu leading the way. I caught frequent glimpses of this miracle as it unfolded. The violence was not between supporters of the white parties and supporters of the ANC, but between the ANC and the Inkatha Party, which was mostly Zulu, and was led by Mangosuthu Buthelezi. I had known Buthelezi ever since the 1970s, and had a considerable liking for him. At the same time, it was hard to ignore the fact that he gave his supporters all the support they needed to attack the ANC, and the ANC was hitting back hard. Civil war seemed a very real possibility.

And then I went to report on a vast rally which Inkatha gave in Durban. The expectation was that Buthelezi would announce a final break with the ANC, and the war would come out into the open; but when Buthelezi came to speak, he didn't say anything of the sort. His fiercer supporters were heartbroken; the rest, it seemed to me, were distinctly relieved.

As the rally broke up, the cameraman and I rushed up to the directors' box at the rugby ground where the rally had been held. We just managed to catch Buthelezi, and I recorded a quick interview with him, in which he denied any thought of breaking off relations with the ANC. Then, when it was over, I asked him what had really happened. He looked at me quizzically for a moment, as though he was weighing up how much to tell me.

Then he said he had left a meeting with the ANC in great anger, and had boarded his private plane to bring him back to his stronghold of KwaZulu-Natal. But as the plane was about half an hour into its flight, he suddenly knew he had to turn back. He ordered the pilot to return to Johannesburg, and went straight back to the meeting place. There he told the ANC that he would join with them in the new administration after all. There would be no civil war.

'Why did you turn back?' I was genuinely interested.

'God told me to,' Buthelezi said simply.

When I went to St George's Cathedral in Cape Town a few weeks later and heard Archbishop Tutu give thanks for the totally unexpected peaceful outcome of the election, I understood something of what he was talking about when he said it was a miracle. It was one of the most important moments of my life: a turning-point, just as it had been for Buthelezi.

So South Africa and its politics have been something of a guiding principle for me. I watched as the ANC made mistakes, and did things it shouldn't have done. I could see the corruption growing. Yet I felt, and still feel, that South Africa and the ANC can teach the rest of us a great deal about decency and forgiveness.

In February 2007 I went back there with Oggy and Nick, intending to make a film about the political succession in the ANC. Thabo Mbeki's presidency was coming to an end, and the succession was difficult to predict. But none of the politicians who might take his place wanted to talk to us. In the ANC, the political tradition is to show reluctance, not ambition, if you want to progress. Announcing your candidacy and explaining that you are the best man for the job doesn't work: people will think you're pushy and arrogant. So, like the Speaker of the House of Commons, you have to be dragged with apparent unwillingness to take over the post. No wonder none of the big figures wanted to talk to us: it would look like overweening presumption on their part.

So we needed something else to report on. It wasn't difficult to think what that might be. The issue that obsessed everyone, from the passengers I spoke to on the plane, black and white, to the woman who changed my money at the airport counter, was crime. I picked up a copy of the *Johannesburg Sunday Times*, and saw that the entire front page was given over to the murder of a famous historian, David Rattray – a man who had been at Nature's Valley with us a few weeks earlier. The rest of the paper was full of stories of murder, rape, and robbery.

We were met at the airport by a slightly built man in his thirties, for whom I came to have great affection and admiration. Mbuso Mwele was a freelance journalist who worked as a producer and fixer for the BBC's bureau in Johannesburg. If you are lucky, you meet people like Mbuso occasionally in journalism. They know a lot, but they aren't dogmatic about it; they are quiet and gentle, but when you find yourself in a difficult spot, they stay calm and stand shoulder to shoulder with you, and you can stake your reputation on their political judgement. Dragan Petrovic from Belgrade is like this, and I could name four or five other people I've worked with in different parts of the world who are the same. Perhaps, in Mbuso's case, it was something to do with his being a Zulu. Fixers like these are a very special breed; Mbuso was to prove one of the best.

As we drove to our hotel from the airport it became clear that he agreed with us fully about the problem of crime, and would be able to set up a range of interviewees, from academics to business-men in Soweto and people who had themselves suffered from crime. Poor Mbuso – he was to find out for himself how bad crime was in South Africa. A few weeks after he had worked with us, he and his family lost everything they owned when burglars came and stripped his house bare. If he or his wife or son had been at home, there is a good chance they would have been murdered.

South Africa is, I think, my favourite country on earth, yet there is no doubt that it is one of the most violent countries on earth as well. In 2006, only Iraq and Colombia were more violent, and on some days there were more murders in South Africa than there were in either of them. On average, fifty people are killed there every day. The number of robberies and rapes is appallingly high. Every South African you speak to, black or white, has either suffered violence themselves or has someone in their close family who has been robbed, raped or murdered. When I rang one friend of mine in Johannesburg, soon after we landed, he told me he had lost four friends, all murdered, in the previous five days.

He happens to be white, but it is a great mistake to think that the crime is mainly directed by black people against whites. There is no such pattern to it, beyond the fact that poor people are attacking those wealthier than themselves. Not necessarily that much wealthier, either. A couple of weeks after we started working in Johannesburg, an Irish priest who had started a hospice for black people dying of AIDS was lucky to survive being stabbed by a robber.

'I told him, you'll find nothing of interest to you here,' he said, 'for I'm just as poor as you are yourself. But I suppose he didn't believe me.'

South Africa, which has been a model to the rest of the world in terms of calming civil strife, is a nation at war with itself. Sitting in an excellent restaurant in the wealthy suburb of Sandton that evening, I suggested to Oggy and Nick that they should look round them at the other diners: black, Asian, English, Afrikaners. They all seemed to be enjoying themselves, yet when it got late and they had to go home, not one of them could be sure they would survive the moment of maximum danger, when they had to sit in their cars in the roadway, waiting for their security gates to open. After 2003, politicians, journalists and academics had spent a good deal of time debating whether or not the situation in Iraq constituted a civil war. No one would suggest such a thing in South Africa, yet the waste of life and the daily destruction were just as great.

Human life seemed to count for nothing. One of the country's best brain surgeons slipped out for a bite to eat at lunchtime and was shot dead just yards from his hospital. A Nigerian woman and her two-year-old son were asleep in her tiny flat in Johannesburg when a man broke in and took the few small things of value she had. As he left, he casually pointed his gun at the little boy and blew his brains out. A woman sitting in her car was approached by a man as she was stopped at a traffic light. He pushed his gun against her head and forced her out of the car, and she gave him everything she had – money, credit cards, watch, car keys. He ordered her to kneel down as he got into her seat, and he shot her as he drove away. One late afternoon a woman I know was attacked when, like the people I pointed out at the restaurant, she waited for her electronic gates to open. Her two little children were in the back seat. She too gave the robbers everything she had, but they were plainly going to kill her and the children. She went down on her knees in front of them, and prayed for their lives. Perhaps something in the prayer touched them, because the robber with the gun lowered it and let her and her children live.

Nowadays the methods have changed. Gangs of two or three people spot someone in a supermarket or a shopping mall and follow them home. Then they force their way into the house and threaten or torture them into giving them everything. Sometimes they kill them, sometimes they don't. Many of the robbers are monsters, but not all. A white couple I know woke up to find two men standing over their bed with guns. They were made to lie on the floor, and the mattress was laid on top of them. Both the man and his wife were certain they were going to die, but the robbers apologized to them, and although they stole everything of value, they called them 'sir' and 'madam' throughout, and thanked them as they climbed out of the window they had come in by.

Anything can happen. Because attacks like these occur hundreds of times every single day throughout South Africa, the permutations are endless. The only certainty is that the great majority of the victims of robberies and murders like these are black people; and black women are the overwhelming majority of rape victims.

If you ask people in Johannesburg, whether black or white, where the offenders mostly come from, they will tell you that it is the central area of Hillbrow. So at our regular morning meeting over breakfast in our hotel, Oggy asked Mbuso to fix up a filming trip for us there. He was mildly reluctant, not for himself but for us. Nevertheless he told us he knew a security company there which would help us, and we decided to go there that evening.

When I was the BBC correspondent in Johannesburg, from 1977 to 1978, Hillbrow was my favourite area. It was changing fast, even in those days. The old central Europeans who sat playing chess for hours on end in the cafés with a glass of coffee and a piece of poppy-seed cake beside them were beginning to drift away to other parts of the city. In their place were increasing numbers of couples who were living together in defiance of the Immorality Act, which forbade sexual relations between people of different races, and the Group Areas Act, which stated that Hillbrow was a whites-only suburb. To me, simply walking up and down its steep streets was refreshing. The police, increasingly overstretched, seemed to turn a blind eye to what went on there. In Hillbrow you could see white girls and black men holding hands in the street. You could, if you knew where to go, buy books by banned authors. And you felt you could breathe here, away from the vicious nonsense of apartheid.

But thirty years of that kind of continuing change altered the entire face of Hillbrow. By the mid-1990s, most white people had left the area. Their places were taken by immigrants from other parts of Africa: Nigeria and Zimbabwe in particular. Nigerians were accused of running the drugs and smuggling rackets which started to plague South Africa. The Zimbabweans took refuge there when their own country, under the increasingly brutal regime of Robert Mugabe, could no longer support them and declined into cruelty and famine.

Hillbrow was now the main centre for crime and criminals in Johannesburg. It was only a short drive from our hotel that evening, but it seemed like a different world. Sandton was the area where the old centre of Johannesburg had shifted in the 1980s and 90s, in order to escape the growing dirt and crime. It was a delightful garden suburb, with flame trees and jacarandas, beautifully kept houses, well-mown lawns, busy shopping centres full of expensive goods. Plenty of wealthy black people lived in Sandton now, but it still had something of the air of English suburbia.

Hillbrow, by comparison, was rigorously urban, and always had been. But now the narrow canyon-like streets between the high-rise flats had been thoroughly Africanized. Great waves of people thronged the streets, buying and selling their wares. The shops were rougher, more basic than any I had seen here in the past. Beggars lay on the street corners, and the shops were often boarded up or barred against robbers. The red earth of Africa forced its way between the paving stones. The streets were pitted and broken, and the cars were rusting, old, full of noise. There was the frequent squealing of police and ambulance sirens.

Yet something in Hillbrow appealed to me, as it never quite had in Sandton. I might feel more at home in Sandton, but Hillbrow was exciting and vibrant and exhilarating. I caught the smell of meat cooking on the street corners, and heard the sounds of drums and whistles. It was dangerous and dirty, but it was thrilling to be back here. Back in the real Africa.

Mbuso drove us up and down the grid-pattern streets, now with the grain, now across it, now against it. The streets themselves were just how I remembered them, steeply cambered against the frequent rain, with the red-brown stains of the earth against the feet of the walls. 'Once you have lived in Africa,' an old friend of mine, now long dead, once said to me, 'you can never entirely get it out of your system. Not even if you go back and live in the First World for decades. It's there, and it grabs you the moment you see it again.' I was seeing it again now.

'It's here,' Mbuso said, and found a place to park.

I saw the sign he was pointing at: BAD BOYZ SECURITY.

'They're going to be guarding us?'

'They're the best.'

And he was right. We waited in a small, poverty-stricken supermarket on the corner of the street for a while, with the shoppers staring at this odd group of white faces, and then three or four young black men and an older one appeared. Oggy and Mbuso explained to them what we required: the camera would need to be set up on the first-floor balcony, and I would be in the crowd, walking along the street and talking to the camera on a radio mike. I would then come to a halt and talk a little longer. I would probably need to do it several times, they said; these long walking-and-talking sessions are hard to get right the first time. They looked at us: these were all new concepts to them, and they had no idea whether it would be easy or difficult.

I headed out, leaving the others on the balcony with Nick. Beside me walked the older man, hefting a sizeable stick in his hand. The head of it, I noticed, was made of iron. He had an enthusiastic look, as though he hadn't been able to use the stick for a while, and saw the chance of using it now. Three other members of Bad Boyz Security came with me. They all looked handy, and I was glad they were on my side.

It took me five goes before I got it right. I can't deny I was mildly nervous, which inclined me to trip over my words; though if I had been able to see what Oggy, Nick and Mbuso saw from the balcony, I would never have worried. My guards played their part as though they had done this all their lives. They stayed at a short distance from me, just out of camera shot, but whenever someone seemed to be taking too much of an interest in me they would move in quietly and ease him away. Only once did the older man get to use his knobkerrie, but from the look on his face afterwards I think he must have enjoyed himself.

After we had finished filming the piece to camera, we started on the really interesting part. Hillbrow, you should remember, was the place that many Jo'burgers regard as the criminal heart of the city, yet when I stood on the corner with Nick filming, and asked people what they thought about crime, they crowded round in their dozens, pushing forward and shouting out to attract my attention and tell me how bad things were, in the articulate way of black South Africans.

'People are being killed almost every minute and every hour around here,' one man told me. 'It's amazing. I think it's worsening. For me, the crime is worsening.'

Another man pulled up his shirt and showed me his knife-wounds, acquired just across the street a few weeks earlier. Would he give me his name? No, he said – they might come back and kill him next time.

At one stage the crowd grew so large and tempestuous that even our Bad Boyz told Oggy urgently that he should pull Nick and me out and get us to safety. But when Oggy pushed his way through the crowd to tell me that, I decided we should stay where we were. From my vantage point at the centre of the crowd I could see what the others on the edge couldn't: that the passion wasn't in any way directed against us. On the contrary, everyone there seemed to realize that we represented a way for them to express their anger and their fear about the high levels of crime they themselves suffered.

'What about the government? What does it do to help the situation?'

'The government? The government doesn't do nothing. They don't care about us.'

Eventually we extricated ourselves, said our goodbyes to the crowd and shook hands with our minders. They refused to accept any money for the work they'd done. Two nights later, on the exact spot where we had been filming, a man was stabbed to death.

And what was the government doing about it all? It seemed to most people – not just an ad hoc crowd in Hillbrow, but newspaper editors, senior policemen, businessmen in Soweto and virtually everyone else we spoke to while we were in Johannesburg – that the government didn't even accept that there was a problem. A government minister, assuming (wrongly, as we had seen) that only white people were complaining about crime, said they should leave the country if they don't like it. The chief of police, in charge of fighting crime, had been linked to an alleged crime boss, yet he hadn't been suspended.

A short time before we arrived, President Thabo Mbeki was interviewed by one of the best television commentators in South Africa, and asked, among other things, about the high levels of crime.

> I haven't come across anybody anywhere – these are ordinary
> people who live in the townships, in the rural areas and so on
> – who will actually stand up and say 'President, crime is out of
> control'. Nobody can show that it is. Nobody can, because it
> isn't true.

Thabo Mbeki was a complex and highly intelligent man. I have seen him charm small groups of people, and make them roar with laughter at his wit. But there was a fastidious and private side to him which made him shy away from any kind of personal publicity, and even from any kind of public defence of himself. It was as if he were saying, 'I have taken my position, and nothing you or anyone else can say will make me change.' He had no ability to make himself popular, and no interest in doing so. He rarely seemed to appear in public, and he was reluctant even to go on television at times of difficulty to keep up the national morale.

For several years he seemed to deny that AIDS was a problem in South Africa, and supported his health minister after she had told an international conference of AIDS experts that eating raw vegetables could control the disease. Telling a nation where the overwhelming complaint was that nothing was being done about crime that no one thought crime was out of control was scarcely a very popular thing to do.

We asked the government to put up someone to talk to us about crime, and we asked the police for the same thing. At first the country's most senior policeman agreed to be interviewed by us; then we were told the next day that it wouldn't be possible.

In the meantime, a doctor friend of mine told me I had been wrong to assume that Hillbrow had become an entirely black suburb. One of his patients, he told me, a Jewish lady of eighty-three, still lived there. He rang her to see if she would agree to see us, and she did.

We had to leave our vehicle in the parking lot in the basement of her block of flats; to leave it out in the street was to offer it up to the car thieves. The block had once been rather smart and expensive, but now it was in a sad state. Groups of noisy children were clamouring in the lobby, and the lift smelled.

On the eleventh floor it was obvious which was Mrs Joy Judes' flat; there were plants growing all round the door.

Inside, the flat was decorated in a heavy, old-fashioned but attractive way, with paintings on every wall and large, rather good furniture. She lived there alone. Her son was in Israel, her daughter in Cape Town.

'A little heaven in the hell of Hillbrow,' she announced proudly; not, I suspected, for the first time.

Mrs Judes was remarkably attractive and well turned-out, though fragile. She was trapped here in an inescapable cage of economics. Twelve years earlier she had sold her house in the up-and-coming suburb of Norwood – most places in Johannesburg sound as though they have been transplanted from Outer London –

and had been persuaded to buy this flat. It was still quite expensive then. Now, the value of property in Hillbrow had collapsed, while houses in the outer suburbs had sky-rocketed.

Yet, strangely, she felt safer in Hillbrow than she did when she visited her friends in the surrounding areas. She had a driver, a charming old servant who lived locally and looked after her every day, and she would go out and see her friends. And then, before it got dark, he would bring her back to her flat and make sure she was properly locked in.

'Crime here is violent and brutal,' she said. 'They're not just stealing something from you. No, it's very brutal. They want to hurt you. But I feel safe here.'

White South Africans of her generation are rarely enthusiastic about the political changes which have come over South Africa, and most would probably have been much happier if apartheid had continued unchanged. Mrs Judes didn't temper her opinions about black people simply because Mbusa was with us. He was charming to her, though, and treated her with the politeness due to her age. And she responded.

'I didn't catch his name,' she said after the others had left, 'but he seemed very nice. You're lucky.'

I agreed that I was.

Slowly, as the days passed and we talked to more and more people, I began to realize what the problem was, and what needed to be done about it. It wasn't necessarily obvious at all. Thabo Mbeki finally made a brief reference to crime in his annual message to the nation, and announced that he was increasing the number of policemen. Yet as one academic, Professor Barney Pitayana, the vice-chancellor of the University of South Africa, immediately pointed out to us, the present police force was under-trained and under-paid, and therefore liable to be ineffectual and corrupt; so putting tens of thousands more of the same sort of people into police uniform was certainly not going to put an end to crime. It might even increase it.

Professor Pitayana had been a friend and political ally of Steve Biko, the Black Consciousness leader whose murder by the security police in 1977 had been the most important and terrible news story of my time as a correspondent in South Africa. Professor Pitayana had escaped to Britain, where he had been ordained in the Church of England and spent many years as vicar of a parish there. It was natural, he said, for people to blame South Africa's breakdown in societal values on apartheid, but that was the easy way out, and it solved nothing.

'We need to know that dealing with crime isn't just a matter for the government,' he said. 'Each one of us must take responsibility for it. At the end of the day, we each have a duty to ask ourselves, what are we actually going to do to stop it? This is something we have to change as individuals, and as a society.'

We went to Soweto to interview a friend of Mbuso's. He was a businessman, who had set up what was fast becoming a chain of pubs and cafés. A big bear of a man with a loud laugh, he put his arm round my shoulders and sat me down for a beer outside his first and best pub, in a part of Soweto which had once been ugly and dangerous and had now changed its entire character for the better. He had, he said, built his business round three basic principles: never hire anyone whose background you can't be sure of, never buy any goods you think have been stolen, no matter how cheap they might be, and always try to raise the standard of living and the expectations of your employees.

I wasn't sure afterwards whether this wasn't a little too good to be true, but it occurred to me that, even if he didn't manage to live up to his own principles, they were probably good ones to follow. The great thing about South Africa is that, as events there have shown, it is capable of doing the right thing and changing itself accordingly.

It is possible for countries to change. Britain, in the middle of the eighteenth century, was a corrupt and crime-ridden society, where everything from justice to political power could be bought and where a walk through Covent Garden or a ride along the Great North Road could easily cost you your life. Slowly, though, new principles came to the fore. By the end of the century it was no longer fashionable to pay bribes, and crime was fading. By the time Queen Victoria came to the throne in 1837, crime had noticeably lessened, and there was intense disapproval of any kind of open corruption. The rest of the century might have been marked by considerable hypocrisy, but Britain became the most honest and upright society in the developed world: by no means perfect, but certainly not the dangerous, unprincipled place it had once been.

It wasn't done by putting more policemen on the beat, though the creation of a decent, well-paid police force helped greatly, and it wasn't done simply by exposing corruption, though that helped too. It happened because society as a whole began to demand better government and crime-free streets, and to regard those things as the norm. Decency and uprightness can't be imposed on a country; they come about because people won't accept anything less.

In our report, a three-minute version for the main news bulletins and a twelve-minute one for *Newsnight*, we didn't pull any punches. We mentioned that South Africa was one of the most violent countries on earth, and that even people in Hillbrow were clamouring for the government to deal with crime. We showed President Mbeki's condescending answer, that no one thought crime was getting worse. I explained that no one in the government or the police would even talk to us about the problem. And I revealed that the head of the police had been accused publicly of links to organized crime, but hadn't even been suspended from his job.

The ANC was outraged. A long and detailed rejoinder appeared on its website. It didn't challenge any of these accusations, but accused the BBC (i.e. me) of being racist and imperialist and suggested that we had made our report only in order to distract attention from Britain's own growing crime problem. Our purpose, the ANC said, was to damage South Africa. At no point did the statement suggest that anything about the reports was factually incorrect.

For my part, I was depressed that a political party I had always liked and often admired could either be so arrogant, or so lacking in self-confidence (I couldn't quite work out which) that it should have taken this wholly negative line. To criticize the ANC's handling of crime and corruption was, it seemed, to be racist – even though the proudest boast of the ANC, and its finest quality, was that it didn't represent any one race, and drew its Cabinet ministers from a whole range of ethnic groups.

But the ANC's reply gave us quite a problem now. We had offered BBC World a half-hour version of our film, using many more of the interviews we had recorded. This was partly because there had been such an outflow of support in South Africa for what we had said. When a reporter from a Johannesburg newspaper interviewed me about the controversy, I told him the date on which the full version of the documentary would be aired.

That locked us into broadcasting it. Ever since the Hutton Report, it has been even more necessary for the BBC to show that it won't yield to unreasonable pressure, especially from governments – British or foreign. If BBC World had dropped our documentary, it would have caused a scandal in South Africa and elsewhere, and our reputation would have taken a real knock. It didn't help that BBC World had just signed a lucrative deal with the South African tourist board for a series of advertisements which included appearances not just by Nelson Mandela (who had shown he understood the widespread complaints about crime) but also Thabo Mbeki himself. Would the tourist board pull the advertisements? Might the ANC's militants (as someone suggested) attack the BBC office in Johannesburg, or the BBC staff there?

That settled it. Of course you have to think about these things carefully, and bear in mind the safety of your staff, but to run your broadcasting schedule according to the likes and dislikes of governments, and to back away from reporting something because of a suggestion that there might be violent consequences, would be a complete betrayal of the principles the BBC claims to stand for. I would certainly have resigned if it had happened.

But it didn't. The possibility was never considered. Another long rant against us was posted on the ANC website, but that was that. Thabo Mbeki appeared on the South African tourist board advertisements, and there certainly weren't any attacks on the BBC bureau or its staff. I never thought there might be; South Africa isn't Zimbabwe, it's a country where the rule of law applies. And the ANC isn't Robert Mugabe's ZANU-PF, it's a decent and upright institution. Long may it stay that way.

As we were coming to the end of our filming, we drove through Soweto so that I could record a piece to camera there. Suddenly I realized we had reached the area known as Dube, which had been a pretty dangerous part of Soweto, virtually a no-go area, when I used to come here. Now the houses were nicely painted and the roads were paved. Dube isn't wealthy, but it had a new pride in its appearance: a big change from the bad old days. I spotted a small primary school as we drove past, and asked Mbuso to stop. We had wanted to film in a school, in order to get the material for the end of our report.

Mbuso jumped out and went to find someone he could ask for permission to go inside. I was pessimistic. It's one of the legacies of the past that government institutions like schools often prefer to duck the responsibility of letting a camera crew onto the premises. We didn't have any kind of permission from the Ministry of Education to film there, because it wasn't technically necessary.

Mbuso came back.

'Yeah, she says no problem.'

'She' was small but formidable: not, I could see the moment I met her, the kind of headmistress who required someone else's permission to do anything at her school.

'Welcome to Hoernle Primary School. What are you going to ask me?'

I explained we were making a film about crime, and after a good five minutes of being told how much crime there was in South Africa nowadays, and how little was being done about it, I managed to explain to her that I wanted to ask her and her pupils what they thought.

She nodded. She would make a good television producer herself, I thought. Also a good army general.

We went into a classroom. Most of the boys and girls, she explained, were AIDS orphans. They were aged about eleven, and they sat at their desks, bright and intent, in the neatest of uniforms: dark blue blazers, clean white shirts, straightened ties.

'Give me an example of an adjective,' the teacher called out, anxious to show them at their best.

She was the physical opposite of the headmistress, tall and angular. The pupil she had pointed at stood up.

'Today I was sad.'

'Good, yes. But why are you sad?'

The girl said nothing, and hung her head. Grammar had suddenly intruded into real life.

I looked around. Things were a great deal better than they had been thirty years before, when I filmed in Soweto schoolrooms. These children had schoolbooks, which were supplied to them free.

In the bad old days of apartheid, black children had to pay for their books; they were free for white children. The blackboard was a proper one; in the past, any old bit of wood or cardboard had to suffice. Now the windows had glass in them, and the room was properly painted.

The shabbiness and discomfort of schools in Soweto used to be infamous. It was, I used to think, the sheer meanness of the apartheid system that offended me, almost as much as its moral bankruptcy. That was all finished now. Hoernle School was pretty basic, but it was clean and comfortable, and people cared about it.

For many of these children, brought up by elderly grandparents who no longer earned any money at all, the only food they got was their midday meal here at Hoernle. But I couldn't get over how neat they all were: not a single scruffy child in the class. They were crisp and polite and, at least here in school, happy.

'It doesn't mean,' said the tall teacher, 'that if you see them being neat, they have everything, no. But they try. We emphasize trying to look neat. It peps you up. If you are not neat, it tells that you are not happy.'

The children filed out into the little playground so we could interview them.

They all knew about the high levels of crime, and they were all afraid of it.

'When you get older, are you going to commit crimes?'

'No,' said the boy I spoke to, 'because I have a shelter, food, and clothes.'

'And you?' I asked a quiet boy with curly hair, who reminded me suddenly of Rafe.

'I will not cause any crimes, because I'm a good boy.'

I'm increasingly sentimental nowadays, of course – it comes with advancing age – so I didn't trust my voice to ask another question, and I just pointed the microphone at one of the girls.

'I think we must stop doing crime. We must think of one another.'

This was what the vice-chancellor of UNISA, the former Church of England vicar, meant when he talked about needing a holistic approach to crime. It wasn't clear to me whether these children, so neatly turned out and polite, and with such exemplary opinions, would turn into criminals within four or five years, but I found it hard to believe. Of course, Hoernle was just one school; maybe if I'd spotted another one and we'd filmed there, I might have had a very different set of examples.

But at the very least Hoernle showed what one teacher and her headmistress could achieve.

'We have a song we always sing,' said the angular teacher. 'Can we sing it for you now?'

I nodded.

'Thank you!' sang these AIDS orphans who were often lucky to get one meal a day, and they clapped their hands enthusiastically twice.

'Very much!' [clap-clap]

'Keep it up!' [clap-clap]

'Sh-i-i-i-ine!'

§

The BBC bureau in Baghdad is small, old-fashioned and untidy. There are cracks in the walls, and ants sometimes march across the kitchen floor. Feral cats roam around it, fighting for rubbish. We're always meaning to do something about it, but everybody is too busy.

The people who keep it going are the local staff. It's not a good idea to give a precise indication of their numbers or their names, but they are remarkably dedicated. As well as drivers and security men and translators, we had two local producers, a Sunni and a Shi'ite. The Sunni, whose name was Samir, played an important part in the first year after the invasion in interpreting to the British people who worked there what was really going on. It was from Samir that I first understood how angry Sunnis were becoming with the Americans, who had smashed their political power and were taking their lives every day. He was a former office in Saddam's army, always well turned out with prematurely grey hair and a neatly clipped moustache.

Once, towards the end of 2003, I asked him to show me what he meant about the way the Americans treated the Sunnis. He took me to an American checkpoint, and we watched as an old man with a car filled with his female relatives drove up. He managed to get into the wrong lane. There was a sign telling him to stop, but it was only in English. An American soldier screamed at him. Then he raised his rifle to shoot.

'Jesus Christ!' I shouted, but the old man in his terror jerked his foot on the clutch and the engine stalled.

It probably saved his life; if he had driven another five yards, he and the women could well have been killed.

'These Americans don't use their brains,' Samir said, as the soldier continued to scream at the old man in a language he couldn't possibly understand. 'Now you see why people are starting to hate them.'

Later, Samir came to London for a technical course and ended up applying for political asylum. The death squads had found out he was working for us.

Laith was his Shi'ite counterpart. He stayed behind. He was a big man, sincerely religious, with a smile as permanent as his stubble and a willingness to take considerable risks. Sometimes I used to worry that he was more afraid of saying no to us than he was of heading off into some impossible danger, but he and we always seemed to survive. Everything of any value which I did in Baghdad during 2006 and 2007 was the direct result of his contacts and his hard work.

To mark the fourth anniversary of President George W. Bush's invasion of Iraq, Oggy Boytchev, Nick Woolley and I planned several strong reports. The Americans had supposedly taken control of the huge, poverty-stricken Shi'ite suburb of Sadr City. But our information was that the main Shi'ite militia, the Mehdi Army, was just keeping its head down and was continuing to run things rather more quietly. Laith had got Oggy and me into Sadr City to film the Mehdi Army the previous November; now we asked him to do it again. It would be a good deal more dangerous this time, because we would have to look out for the Americans as well, but Laith went ahead of us in his little car, made contact with the Mehdi people, and got us in. If things had gone wrong, they would have murdered Laith and taken us hostage; but things didn't go wrong.

After that we asked him to do something simpler: to find us the family of someone who had been kidnapped. It happens every day in Baghdad; but there is a spiteful twist. In about a third of the cases the family scrape together the ransom only to find that their relative has been murdered anyway. I had come across various cases like this over the years, but it took Laith to find the case which summed it all up. As always, he did the hard work.

It was felt to be too dangerous for us to go to the area of Baghdad where the family lived, since it would have meant driving through two Sunni no-go areas where we might well have been spotted and kidnapped ourselves. The risk for Laith was a real one, too: he had to drive through the two areas both coming and going, and there was certainly a danger that he might have been caught. Instead, he picked up four members of the family in his little car and brought them to our street.

Television news reports take a certain amount of planning. When Oggy and I talked it over with Nick beforehand, it was obvious that we needed pictures of people who had been kidnapped and murdered. That meant going to a hospital. Once again, Laith had to fix it up for us. So, early the following morning, we went to the Yarmuk Hospital, in a Shi'ite area not far from the Green Zone. There were men in orange boiler-suits standing round the hospital entrance, and a stack of stretchers. Not all the blood had been washed off the stretchers from the previous day's work, but there is little room for fastidiousness in today's Iraq.

We had hung around for half an hour, getting increasingly nervous (this was a disturbingly conspicuous place to spend so much time, but we had to have the pictures), when we heard the sound of sirens.

'They are bringing in the bodies,' murmured Laith.

The police car was escorting a pick-up truck. There were two bodies lying in the back, with several weeping relatives hanging onto the sides. I've seen too many bodies in my life to be at all squeamish, and Nick seems to have been born without any trace of squeamishness at all, but a BBC cameraman has to use the utmost care to avoid anything which the long pages of guidelines back at Television Centre might think was upsetting or contravened good taste.

Sometimes, of course, you wish that the framers of the guidelines could come and see these things for themselves, yet in your heart you know they're right. Why show a man's shattered skull or his exposed intestines when it will simply make large numbers of viewers switch to another channel?

Nick, by artfully concentrating on a flopping arm or a bloodless hand, showed everything that needed to be shown without breaching the guidelines. But the full, uncensored sight wasn't a pleasant one. As more flatbed trucks came in with bodies on them, you could see the signs that these people had been tortured before they died. Electric drills and saws had been used. It was disgusting.

Yet the faces mostly seemed calm in death, as though they had realized at the end that none of these things mattered very much. I found myself looking at the shoes or the shirts, and thinking that when the owners bought them or put them on, they can never have dreamt that these things would be seen, thanks to the BBC, by hundreds of millions of people around the globe.

Now we had the opening to our report on kidnapping. This was how we worked it into the report.

> Every morning at the Yarmuk Hospital in Baghdad, as regular as
> clockwork, the police vans bring in the night's crop of murder
> victims. It can be a pretty gruesome sight: many of these people
> have been tortured before being killed. All of them were kidnapped
> because they were in the wrong place at the wrong time, and were
> from the wrong religion. This is the story of one kidnap victim.

Laith found us a photograph of the man whose case we were going to focus on. His name was Farid Younis Khashai, and he was in his late thirties, a big, friendly looking man with a faint likeness to Laith. He, too, was a Shi'ite, and had a good job as a driver for the Ministry of Housing. It brought with it a small house, in which the whole of his close family lived.

But being a ministry driver in present-day Baghdad is a dangerous job. Shi'ite drivers must go into Sunni areas, and Sunni drivers into Shi'ite ones. Farid could have refused to go to places he thought were dangerous, but he would probably have been sacked. Jobs were hard to come by in Iraq, and a job which provided a house as well was immensely valuable. Farid kept quiet, and hoped that nothing would happen to him.

But one day he had to pick up a couple of people in north-east Baghdad and take them to the ministry. That meant driving along the edge of the hardline Sunni stronghold of Adhamiya. A group of armed men had set up an impromptu road-block, and they stopped Farid's car. He tried to talk his way out of trouble, but Iraqis are as attuned to identifying each other's religion or ethnic background as Bosnians or the Northern Irish are.

When we planned our film, we decided we would have to film on the road where this happened. It wasn't the safest thing I've ever done. A couple of our local people drove a car ahead of us, and an Iraqi and a British security man were in the one behind. We drove in our usual unremarkable vehicle, with an Iraqi driver and Laith in front. Craig Summers, our ex-Marine security adviser, sat with us, a Kalashnikov on his knees and a revolver in the waistband of his trousers. As we reached the place where Farid had been captured, I sat in the semi-darkness of our vehicle and I recorded a piece to camera.

> They drove into this area, the hardline Sunni stronghold of
> Adhamiya, just here. It's extremely dangerous for a Shi'ite Muslim
> to be here at all, just as it is for Westerners, but the fact was it was
> his job – he couldn't do anything else. Just around here somewhere
> a group of armed men stopped the car, realized he was a Shi'ite,
> and took him away.

Then we drove back to the safety of our bureau. Farid's family were waiting for us there, and we took them into the large hallway of the BBC house where we were staying. There were four of them: Farid's elder brother Zuhail, their mother, whom we just knew as Um Zuhail ('mother of Zuhail'), a younger boy, and Farid's little daughter Zahra. You only had to see them to realize how poor they were. Um Zuhail wore a black hijab which covered her head and body entirely, but not her face. Zuhail was dressed in a cheap shirt and a cheap pair of dark trousers. He was quiet and seemed nervous, with no hint of the jollity I thought I could detect in his brother's photograph.

These were just ordinary working-class Iraqis, the kind of people you see in the streets everywhere you go. They had nothing very much, and even our decaying house seemed to impress them.

When Zuhail heard that his brother had been taken at the road-block, he rang his mobile number. It rang for a long time, and then an unfamiliar voice answered.

'Yes?'

'My name is Zuhail. I'm trying to get hold of my brother Farid.'

There was a confused noise in the background.

'We are questioning him at the moment.'

He probably meant they were torturing him.

'Can I speak to him? Is he all right? What's going on.'

'You'll be told what to do.'

The phone went dead.

A day or so later, Zuhail's phone rang.

'Bring five thousand dollars. Drive to the outskirts of Adhamiya, on the turn-off to the big mosque. Someone will be waiting by the side of the road. You've got until Thursday.'

This was Monday. Five thousand dollars, to a working-class Iraqi getting by on perhaps ten dollars a day, is a very large amount of money. The equivalent for someone in Britain would be around fifty thousand pounds: a huge sum, but just conceivably possible to raise if you were prepared to sell everything you had and borrow to the hilt.

Zuhail was prepared to do these things. He sold all their furniture, all his clothes, even his mobile phone – though he had to keep it for a while in case of further calls. It wasn't nearly enough, of course, and he had to borrow the rest – probably around three thousand dollars – from friends, and from a money-lender. Money-lenders in Iraq are as unsympathetic as they are anywhere else, and with so many gunmen prepared to kill people for ten dollars or less it is unwise to leave them unpaid.

But Zuhail had no alternative.

He managed to get the money together by Thursday morning. A friend agreed to take it to the appointed place. A man was waiting by the side of the road, and took the bag without a word.

The family then waited to hear when Farid would be released. It was a long wait. Two days later, there was a call. The kidnappers wanted five hundred dollars more.

This time there was nothing left to sell. It would all have to be borrowed. Somehow, Zuhail managed to do it. The same friend drove back and handed over the money.

Days passed, and the family went from hope to despair. A long delay in handing over a kidnap victim after the ransom had been paid usually meant only one thing: the person was dead.

Zuhail went with a friend to the city mortuary. They had to look at a great many bodies – more than a hundred. In the end they recognized Farid's. There was a bullet through the side of his head. He had been tortured, and it looked as though he had probably been killed some days before, soon after the first ransom had been paid, perhaps. Or maybe even earlier. The kidnappers might have killed him as soon as they had finished torturing him. Demanding the money from the family was just a vicious trick.

Now the family was devastated, and completely penniless. Worse, Zuhail owed a huge amount of money, and had very little hope of paying any of it back. The Ministry of Housing had contacted them to say that Farid's house was required for the driver who had been hired to replace him. The family had six months to get out.

I sat there listening to this terrible story, unable even to ask another question. In the silence, Farid's little daughter slid off the sofa and went to sit on Zuhail's lap. He looked down at her, and stroked her head.

'We had to tell Zahra her father had gone to heaven. Then she asked me, "Will you be my father until he comes back?" So I said "Yes, of course."'

I looked across at Um Zuhail, Farid's mother. She was a woman of about sixty, big-boned and strong featured. These were just ordinary people; there was nothing special about them, and now they were penniless.

'Can you forgive the people who did this?' I asked.

She looked briefly at me for the first time, then down at the ground.

'Only God can forgive. I can't.'

She didn't look like a woman who would cry easily, but now tears running down her cheeks fell unchecked on her big coarse hands.

Zahra, Farid's little daughter, went over to her. She stood on tiptoe and wiped the tears away with a handkerchief, crooning something quietly to her.

These were poor people, unimportant, not clever or beautiful or even particularly interesting. Now they were ruined, and they might well slip down into the worst and most abject poverty. In the newly democratic Iraq it was perfectly possible they could starve to death, and all because they had sacrificed everything to save Farid's life – a life which had been already snuffed out in the cruellest way.

We gave them money and promises of help, and Laith put them in his car to drive the dangerous route to their home, through the most vicious city on earth.

That evening, as the three of us sat editing our pictures, I couldn't think of anything to say over the image of the little girl reaching up to wipe the tears from her grandmother's eyes. Any words of mine were bound to be banal. Worse, they might seem deliberately manipulative, the kind of thing television reporters say over scenes of suffering, trying to wring a little extra sympathy out of the people back home.

In the end, I decided to say something as neutral as I could. And the important thing wasn't to build up the suffering of Farid's family; it was to show how unexceptional it was.

'It's destroyed their lives completely,' I said. 'But there's nothing unusual about all this. It happens here virtually every day.'

14

RECIPES FOR DISASTER

Early on in my travelling days, with uncharacteristic decision and foresight, I decided that, wherever I was in the world, I would eat the food and drink the water. So for years and years I have bolted down the most revolting stuff, and thrived on it. Until very recently, indeed, I was able to boast that I hadn't been sick since 1978; but then, in the last couple of days of Dee's pregnancy with Rafe, when she was spending most of her time in bed, I rootled round in the fridge, which Dee hadn't been able to attend to for some time, and made myself an omelette. Afterwards it turned out that the eggs must have been several weeks old. As a result I passed a rather rough night with a mild case of salmonella poisoning, and welcomed Rafe's arrival twenty-four hours later with a stomach that was distinctly queasy.

But the principle of eating and drinking what is set before you is a good one. If you are always worrying about the things you eat and drink, and equip yourself with bottled water, which, we are now told, can be less pure than good tap water, and with pre-prepared food, which usually contains all sorts of preservatives and salts, you will no doubt survive perfectly well. But what happens when the food and water run out? You and your stomach will be on their own then. You will be exposed to everything the local germs throw at you.

If, on the other hand, your stomach has accustomed itself over the years to strange and sometimes worrying content, and your water has been drawn from God knows which questionable source, then you have been able to build up a little immunity. That, at any rate, is my theory, and it has served me well.

Nowadays, travelling with Oggy Boytchev, I have taken on some of his ways, as he has taken on some of mine. And being

Bulgarian, he has a good deal of faith in the healing powers of vodka. So when we have eaten something questionable, he is inclined to order a glass of it, and I do too. That appears to settle the stomach and counteracts the poisons; or maybe it just means you don't care and don't notice the consequences. My instinct is to down a glass of vodka anyway, just in case there might be something wrong with the food.

Although brought up as a communist, Oggy has a devoutly Orthodox mother, and whenever we go to Jerusalem we have to buy little crosses and other mementoes for her. At the same time, he has taught me one or two Orthodox habits, which I have taken up not so much as a superstition, because a lifetime of having strange and sometimes frightening things happening to me has ensured that I am not at all superstitious, but as a pleasant minor ritual. If I can, I sit on my luggage for a moment before I leave, and say the word *Sbogom*, which literally means 'to God' in Russian, but has the sense 'I, or we, are in God's hands'.

I am no more certain that there really *is* a God than many of my fellow Anglicans seem to be, but the thought that there might be one makes my life a little calmer and better and more ordered. It is, I suppose, a form of contemplation; though I would put it rather higher than that. And as a rule for living, I'm not sure that 'Forgive us our trespasses, as we forgive those who trespass against us' has ever been improved upon. There are people who want to force their religious views on you, and people who want to force their anti-religious views on you; and I find both types rather boring. But as Tristram Shandy says,

> so long as a man rides his HOBBY-HORSE peaceably and quietly along the King's highway, and neither compels you or me to get up behind him,—pray, Sir, what have either you or I to do with it?

Which has taken me rather a long way away from eating and drinking, though not from travelling. What I really want to do is to describe to you some of the stranger, more outlandish, more alarming or sometimes merely pleasant meals I have had in different places around the world. If I had the ability, I would describe the flavours and the methods of cooking. But I have never got the hang of describing tastes in terms of other, more unlikely flavours ('peaches, strawberries and roast beef with a background of wet paint and a faint suggestion of dog pee'). Nor am I any good as a cook, beyond making the kind of omelette that poisoned me a couple of nights before Rafe was born. So this is about eating as a social activity, and although I have called this chapter 'Recipes for Disaster', most of them have perfectly happy endings. It just shows you can never entirely believe what you read on the label.

§

Dee and I were in Los Angeles, after driving slowly and pleasantly down the coast from San Francisco. We had interviewed Condoleezza Rice at Stanford University for *Simpson's World*, with the splendid Nigel Bateson as the cameraman. Before that, the three of us had been on a desert island in the Pacific, the most isolated place I have ever set foot on, in order to watch the first sun's rays of the new millennium, or, more accurately, the year 2000, touch the earth.

We said a sad goodbye to Nigel in San Francisco, watching his great red bristly beard and massive frame disappear into a limousine which had seemed enormous until Nigel got into it, and headed off on our own. As we drove south along Highway One with the Pacific Ocean on our right, the car radio, which normally told us nothing except what crimes had been committed in that part of California and how hot it was going to be tomorrow, suddenly announced that the Serbian warlord Arkan, a particularly nasty piece of work whom both Dee and I had known and been threatened by, had been shot to death in the lobby of the InterContinental Hotel in Belgrade.

We drove on rather silently for a mile or two after hearing the news. It seemed almost like a personal message directed specifically at the two of us, since I doubt whether one Californian in a million would even have heard of Arkan. The reminder of our days in Belgrade shocked us rather more than the news of the death of a murderous ethnic cleanser.

We were heading eventually for Los Angeles, and were staying at some large and entirely featureless though fiercely expensive hotel, about which I can remember only that it stood beside the intersection of two seething motorways, and you couldn't walk anywhere from it. But we thought instead that we should go and have lunch at the Beverly Hills Hotel in Hollywood, so we drove there in our rather smart hired BMW.

The Beverly Hills Hotel, like the Royal Hawaiian Hotel in Honolulu, was done up entirely in pink: the precise shade, it seemed to me, of the Casa Rosada in Buenos Aires, which is where the Argentine president lives. The weather was beautiful, and we had had the foresight to get there well before twelve. Americans tend to eat their lunch absurdly early, but we had taken that into account too.

We didn't have a reservation, and my name and even that of the organization I worked for would be utterly unknown to the people at the desk with their ledgers and their forbidding looks, which showed that they didn't want any unknowns here. (Nowadays, I'm glad to say, the BBC's name probably would get us straight to a table, but this was in the ancient world of 2000.) But we were early, the restaurant was almost empty except for a very attractive older woman who was with a couple of friends, and Dee looked her best.

They sat us down in the courtyard, at a table for two. We ate a certain amount of salad and drank rather a lot of good Californian rosé, while the tables around us filled up with people who looked to me as though I ought to recognize them. The rosé helped with that effect a good deal. I found myself smiling at them, and encouraging Dee to smile at them as well. Dee even persuaded me to send the attractive older lady a bottle of champagne, which she acknowledged by kissing her black-gloved hand in my direction. It was, she told us later, her sixtieth birthday. I believed her, of course, and the rosé helped.

The table immediately behind us had stayed empty. I could see it, but Dee, sitting opposite me, had her back to it. At some point during the third bottle of rosé, two quite large youngish women dressed in blue were shown over and sat there. Probably I should have recognized them too. They sat side by side with their backs to us, but close to Dee. Even at that stage, neither of them seemed to think very much of me.

Our meal was drawing to a close.

'Why don't you smoke a cigar?' Dee asked me.

As it happened, I had brought a case of three rather good Cuban cigars with me. They were illegal in America, of course, which added to the flavour. I would have loved to smoke one. The meal had been good, and the large open courtyard, the blossoms and the occasional humming birds seemed to encourage the whole idea. But I was too nervous.

'They're bound to have banned smoking here,' I said feebly.

'Not out in the open, for God's sake.'

I wouldn't have been prepared to bet on that; the state of California seemed like the kind of place that would make it illegal even to think about smoking.

'Well, give it to me.'

She reached across, grabbed one of my best Upmann Number 2s, hacked the pointed end off and lit it. For a while, nothing happened. The day was perfect, and the smoke just rose upwards.

Yet I've noticed a similarity between cigars and cats. Just as a cat seems to spot a cat-hater, and insists on jumping onto his or her lap, so the smoke from a cigar always seems to gravitate towards the people who dislike it most. In this case, it was the two women with their backs to us. The delicate pale blue smoke, which is the finest thing about any cigar, rose up a little way into the clear sky, then seemed to be wafted by the faintest of breezes so that it settled around their heads. It seemed to me that every puff Dee took added to their own personal cloud.

She didn't realize it, and they didn't know who it was coming from. For a time they seethed, and tried to wave the smoke away, and spoke to each other in an angry undertone.

'Don't you think you should put it out?' I asked weakly.

'I'm just starting to enjoy it,' said Dee, a non-smoker, in a don't-be-so-bloody-wet kind of voice.

'I just think those two—'

But at that point I heard one of them say 'Men!' in a ferocious way, and the larger of the two reared up, hands on the table, through the delicate smoke. A fierce face glared round at me; then the ferocity faded a little when she saw I wasn't smoking. The angry eyes moved round to Dee, who was sporting one of Castro's finest; she also had on a rather fetching Panama hat.

'Hrrumph,' said the big woman, and she sat down again. There was some whispering.

'I don't believe it,' said the other one, and stood up too.

But it was true.

Dee knew none of this, but when I told her she took a couple of extra puffs, for the sake of it, and laid the cigar down in the ashtray.

That was it. We left soon afterwards, and had a word with the attractive older lady. But Dee got a look at the two women. One of them hissed, for her to hear:

'Disgusting!'

§

The streets were dark, the houses shielded by bushes. Our driver peered at them, and finally grunted. He could see several cars like ours ahead of us, the drivers leaning against them and smoking as they talked.

'I'll see you later,' I said.

Damascus had become a much calmer and less threatening place since the old dictator had died and his son, the ophthalmologist from London, had taken over. I loved coming here now. It was the best-preserved Arabic capital I had visited, and Syria as a whole was a revelation to me. But this time I was here in order to get an interview with the young President Asad, and I didn't want to put a foot wrong.

'Good evening, good evening, good evening,' said the minister jovially, opening his front door as wide as possible. An agreeable buzz of conversation floated out towards us on a cloud of blue cigarette smoke. Over his shoulder I could see a group of jovial old boys, each with a glass in his hand.

It was the minister's birthday, and I had bought him something expensive and unsuitable in the hotel gift shop, the rest of the city being closed at the key moment. He thanked me gracefully, and didn't open it; which was probably the kindest way. Then he led us into the sitting room.

A dozen men of a certain age and type were there: middle-to-late sixties, which made them a different generation from me, at sixty-two. The world over, something happened to people born in 1944 and after; so that men of sixty-two and sixty-six feel very different from one another. And they were all secular Arabs, fond of a glass of whisky and interested in their Islamic past only at certain times of the year. This, too, is the behaviour of an entirely different era.

'Let me introduce you,' said the minister. It was typical of him to invite a stray foreigner round to his birthday party on the spur of the moment.

He murmured names. I sometimes recognized them and sometimes didn't, as I shook the proffered hands. The face and name of one of them were both particularly familiar. He held out his left hand to me, his right being a strangely unconvincing prosthetic, a bit like the hand on an old-fashioned tailor's mannequin. It was the dull yellow colour of a hospital ward, and the fingers were fused. One of his eyes was false, too. It looked at me balefully, even when the other one was involved in smiling at some new guest.

I did a lot of ersatz laughing. The bomb-induced deafness in my left ear makes it hard for me to hear what is said to me in any kind of accent when there is a lot of background noise, but I try my best and sometimes, I can see, give some very weird answers. I remembered the names and faces as best I could. Raising my glass for the fourth or fifth time, I drank its contents down. I was starting to feel very encouraged.

Someone who seemed to be another minister came and sat beside me, speaking confidentially into my good ear.

'You see, what you people in the West don't realize is that everything in Syria has changed. You think we're all terrorists. We're not terrorists at all. We want a good peaceful outcome to the various regional problems here.'

I nodded enthusiastically. I wanted the interview with Asad, and would have agreed to any proposition as long as it didn't compromise me.

'And we never were terrorists, anyway,' the minister continued, letting out a cloud of cigar smoke. 'That was just something put about by our enemies.'

I moved my head in a way he might think was a continuation of the previous nod.

'What is more—'

But I never found out what was more, because it was time for dinner. It was a *meze*, with fifty dishes spread out over the table. In

the centre were large pots, with lamb and chicken stewing in them.
I chose a piece of hot white Syrian bread the size of a large beret,
and filled my plate with chicken cooked with, I think, plums or
maybe peaches. Then I looked round for somewhere I could sit and
enjoy it without being told what today's Syria wasn't.

Three older men were sitting side by side on a couch. One of
them in particular had a pleasant face and smiled at me and nodded,
as though he knew me. I smiled back. Fortunately, though, the three
of them were too busy talking to want to speak to me. They were
reminiscing about old times. Down here, at the end of the room,
I was safe for a while. I looked at the three old boys, and at the
others in the room. They were all getting on too well to notice me;
which suited me.

The chicken was excellent, but the lamb, which had a faint
flavour of lemon, was even better. We ate slices of succulent melon,
and then the host went round with a bottle of *raki*. The first
mouthful exploded inside my head, but it quickly became mellower
and easier to take.

'. . . terrorism,' mumbled another minister, into my deaf ear.

I assumed this was a variation on the Syria-has-changed-but-we-
haven't-been-given-credit-for-it theme, and nodded.

'Oh, so you agree with them.'

It took me a moment or two to get out of that. There was
music: mournful chords, a wheedling pipe. I had had enough *raki*
to like it. A minister was starting to sing.

'I think I'd better be off,' I said. 'Driver waiting. Early start.
You know.'

No one seemed heartbroken. I found my driver, and went back
to the hotel.

The next morning I discussed my evening with one of the
resident experts.

'They kept on about how the old terrorism days were over.'

'So describe who was there.'

I described them.

'The one with the funny hand is a senior Palestinian leader' – he
named him – 'who was blown up by an Israeli letter bomb and
never stopped planning his revenge.

'And the three who were sitting side by side were all former heads of Syrian intelligence in the old days. The amount of blood they've got on their hands is extraordinary, even for this country.'

'But there was one of them who had a really nice face. He kept helping me to food.'

'I know exactly who you mean.' He named him. 'There was a very strong suspicion that he was the mastermind behind the Lockerbie bombing.'

'But that was Libya, surely.'

He gave me the same look that one of the ministers had given me the previous night.

'Libya is who the British and Americans said it was, because they couldn't take on Syria and Iran, who actually did it. Iran asked its friends in Syria to put the bomb on the plane, because they wanted revenge for the shooting down of their Airbus by the Americans. The Syrians got some idiotic Libyan to put the actual bomb on board.'

'So in spite of everything they were saying, it was a terrorist get-together.'

'Welcome to the Middle East.'

§

I think it's my favourite restaurant in Paris, apart from the little one on the corner of the street where we have our flat. It is highly fashionable, yet I've never seen it in a list of the best restaurants. It can be hideously expensive, though if you choose carefully you can avoid spending absurd amounts of money. It is always full for lunch and dinner, yet they always let you in and eventually you will get a meal. The waiters are simultaneously assiduous and offhand, but they are good waiters, as good as any I have come across.

La Maison du Caviare is in rue Vernet, just off the Champs Elyseés, but the prices aren't high because of the tourist trade. In fact very few tourists visit it. The clientele is mostly Parisian. I've seen Alain Prost there, and Karl Lagerfeld, and various film stars and starlets, and once – only once – a French celebrity I actually knew: she was a famous newsreader, and the only reason I didn't go over and give her a kiss was because it looked to me as though she was negotiating her next contract with her boss.

The place has a charming 1950s feel to it, as though Jean Gabin might come in at any moment. A uniformed car-parker looks at you mildly disapprovingly because you have come on foot. You push your way through some heavy curtains, and a man who looks like the chairman of the board but is really just a waiter smiles. You tell him you want a table, and establish that you haven't booked. Instead of trying to humiliate you, he tells you it may take fifteen minutes before a table is free, but suggests that you sit at the bar. Sitting at the bar is so pleasant that sometimes you just stay there even when your table is ready. Dee and I always seem to do rather well there, because the French have a particular weakness for old chaps with attractive younger women. Caviar is the speciality of the house, of course, but I don't eat it nowadays, and not only because of the price; I've seen how they kill the sturgeon. I prefer the *borscht* and a lobster omelette and the Russian *zakuskis*. There is an excellent choice of vodkas, ice-cold. The great pleasure about coming here, though, is to look at the other people.

Fantastically dressed women, elegant men, wealthy older people, youngsters who eat here because their parents are paying. Once a local gangster sent his major-domo to buy a block of caviar – there is a kind of upmarket takeaway near the door – and a couple of heavies came with him to make sure no one stole the money he had brought. They guarded the door while a very large Mercedes waited outside, its engine running all the time. Then the elderly lady who runs the takeaway handed over the caviar, as large as a brick, and they moved out. The last of the bodyguards backed out through the door.

Sometimes entire wealthy families turn up there, quite late at night, with their badly behaved small children. More often you see women in amazing fur coats sweep in, sit down and allow their little dogs to poke their noses out from among the fur. And you get plenty of couples who are there so the man can show the woman how much he's prepared to spend on her. The head waiter, a delightful man from somewhere in the Caucasus, oversees it all from behind the bar. He has seen it all: the gangsters, the rich loners, the little dogs, the lovers. He greets the unknown among them as fulsomely as he treats the famous, and the famous as though they are merely first among equals. They in return treat him as a man of real importance, which he is. Once I asked him if I could come there and record an episode of my programme for BBC World. He considered it, and saw no reason why I shouldn't.

'Of course,' he said, 'not everyone may want their faces to be shown.'

He looked across at a table where a man of about my age was holding the hand of a girl who was much younger.

'We don't need to focus on them,' I said, though I'm not entirely sure what I meant.

I've never got round to doing the programme there, though. Maybe it's because, on television, the magic might not work. It might just look like another restaurant, a bit too crowded, a bit too full of people with more money than sense, a bit too *voulu*, as my director of studies at university, Arthur Sale, would have said: meaning, I suppose, that I would be trying too hard, that I was too keen on making some kind of impression.

Mostly, though, I can't think how the waiters would be able to push their way between the little tables if we were standing there filming. So I've never done it. It remains a film in the head, that's all; and La Maison du Caviare, unseen by a wider audience, remains my ideal of what an expensive restaurant should be like.

§

We called it Uncle Charlie's Roadhouse, though that might not have been its correct name. Since 1977 it has gone through as much of a change as the rest of South Africa has, and I scarcely think I'd want to go there now. But then it was a little paradise.

The Soweto uprising, which had started the year before, was continuing, though the police and army and government were starting to hope that it was gradually dying down. That degree of intensity could not be sustained for very long.

It was a frightening business. Groups of teenagers would suddenly gather, perhaps to mark some particular occasion or grievance, perhaps just by chance. They would attack the police with rocks and improvised weapons of different kinds, and the police would fire tear gas at them. If they didn't disperse, they would use live rounds. There were always injuries, and some deaths.

For us, it was also a dangerous business. The police regarded us as enemies, and were often pleased to be in a position where they could attack us under the pretext that they didn't know who we were. The teenagers were usually friendly, but when their blood was up they would attack any white face. The first death when the uprising began, the previous June, had been that of a white social worker, much loved in the township.

I was always nervous when we went to Soweto. There were usually four of us. I worked for radio at that time, so there would be a television correspondent, either Mike Sullivan or Brian Barron, and the BBC's Johannesburg crew, François Marais and his sound recordist, Carol Clarke. It wasn't always a good idea to have a woman with us, especially a tall, eye-catching blonde, but in those days you couldn't operate the equipment without having a sound recordist, and anyway Carol insisted on coming.

We would drive together in the same car, passing Uncle Charlie's just before we reached the turn-off to Soweto. Since Soweto, in the weird ideology of apartheid, didn't officially exist, it wasn't marked on the signposts, so unless you knew where the turn-off was, you wouldn't spot it. Soweto was said to be the biggest city in Africa, but because it didn't exist in ideological terms, it didn't exist in cartographical terms either. Apartheid was as ridiculous as it was disgusting.

I always looked at Uncle Charlie's with a particular longing as we drove past. This was where we would end up, assuming everything went well, so it represented everything I wanted: the calm after the storm, success, good company, and palatable if greasy food. But then we would drive on, and a dangerous afternoon lay before us.

On one occasion we filmed in Dube, where, thirty years later, I would return and interview the teachers and children at the Hoernle School. A crowd was starting to disperse there and the police had left, but tear gas still hung in the air, making our throats rasp and our eyes fill with tears. Brian, François and Carol got the shots they needed, while I roamed more freely, speaking to people and finding out what had happened. In that way, radio is a much better medium to work in. There had been shooting, apparently, and two school-kids had been badly injured. Then someone told us that there was another confrontation not far away.

We jammed into the car, and because Brian wanted François

to get some shots of him as we went along, I drove. We had to be quick, and I put my foot down. But as we headed out of Dube and towards an open area of marshland, we ran into an ambush.

As we came round a blind corner I saw twenty or thirty kids standing on either side of the road with rocks in their hands. They were too close for me to be able to stop and reverse away. The only thing to do was to put our heads down and drive fast. The kids scattered, but we must have taken a good ten hits from the fist-sized stones they were armed with. There was no sound from any of us; we just hunched down to present as small a target as possible, and didn't waste our breath. I thought we were through, when one of the last kids in the group leaned out and put a rock the size of a half-brick through the windscreen, right in front of my face.

I had a split second to move my head to one side, but the rock came through the glass and smashed against my shoulder. Then it spun off and landed between the two in the back seat. I was doing sixty miles an hour now, determined to get as far away from the crowd as possible. But gradually I realized that in all the noise of the air rushing through the windscreen and through the broken windows, Brian was shouting at me.

'Slow down, John, slow down!'

Eventually, I did.

'We need to stop and film this. Stop as quick as you can.'

My thinking was radio, Brian's was television. He needed pictures – of the crowd of kids, who were still clearly visible back down the road, of the car, of what damage had been done. I didn't need any of these things, because it would be enough to report what had happened. If I even did report it; after all, no one had been badly hurt, and a car being stoned was scarcely news.

But the pictures would make good, immediate television: the angry crowd, still shaking their fists at us in the distance; the hole through the windscreen; the glass which was all over us, and had cut our hands and faces slightly; the car itself, dented all over by rocks. At that stage I did very little television, but I was keen to do more and wanted to know the kind of shots you needed.

When François was finished, we got back in the car and limped out of Soweto. My shoulder ached abominably, though nothing was broken, and we needed to clean up the little flecks of blood on the windows and get the car windscreen mended. We turned out of Soweto onto the main road, and saw Uncle Charlie's ahead of us. We had planned to head back to Jo'burg, but somehow the attraction of a good roadhouse was just too strong.

And so we sat there, talking over what had happened to us and winding down, while the waitress brought us more and more coffee. I ordered what I always did: an open-faced steak sandwich with two fried eggs on top. Somehow they always got the steak the precise pinkish shade I liked, without my asking, and they turned the eggs over and got those crinkly brown edges to the whites. It wasn't healthy, of course, but in 1977 we didn't know that.

It was cool inside, with big overhead fans shifting and stirring the heavy atmosphere, and the noise from groups of truck drivers around us. And although Uncle Charlie's didn't have a special licence to allow black people to use it, they did anyway. No one ever seemed to complain. At that stage there were only two restaurants in the whole of Johannesburg which could legally accept blacks; one was in the centre of town, in the Carlton Hotel (now long since mothballed and empty), and the other at the Holiday Inn at what was then called Jan Smuts Airport. I took three guests to the Holiday Inn at different times, but I loathed the feeling it induced, and gave it up after that.

That afternoon, we talked over our ambush for the tenth time, and savoured the pleasure of eating and drinking when we might have been lying by the side of the road, injured or dead. Not for the last time in my life, I reflected on the narrowness of the margin between a near miss and a savage death. And the more I thought about that, and laughed about the whole experience with the others, and enjoyed my steak and fried eggs, the better and better life seemed.

§

Going to Peru to follow the Shining Path was, I knew right from the start, going to be an extraordinarily dangerous assignment. The Shining Path was a Maoist organization headed by a near-mythical figure called Abimael Guzman. It had grown and grown in strength through actions of the greatest cruelty. Its followers regularly skinned the faces and heads of their captives and left them to die. Once, it invited a beautiful journalist to an interview in order to give her a message of the greatest importance. They cut her tongue out. That was the message.

Despite such atrocities, legitimate government in Peru was riddled with corruption and seemed likely to fail, and many people felt that the Shining Path was the only organization capable of taking over. Together with a couple of friends, Rosalind Bain, a freelance television producer who specialized in working in Spain and Latin America, and Eamonn Matthews, who had been my producer during the first Gulf War, I wanted to go to Peru and interview the leader of the Shining Path, the heavy-set, bearded Guzman. He had never been filmed for television before.

Quietly, we made contact with Guzman's representative in London, and fixed up a meeting over lunch. It was to be the first of three meals which later seemed to define our entire trip, and it was on my own home ground.

The Chelsea Arts Club is a wonderful institution: unconventional, extremely lively, plentifully inhabited by women of all ages, and with a constant inflow of young art students to counterbalance the outflow from the far end of the age scale. Over meals there I have met some of my closest friends, shared some pretty significant confidences, been sacked by my old publishers and been begged, rather satisfyingly, to return to them. And I met, among other weird and wonderful people, the representative of possibly the nastiest guerrilla movement in the world.

Rosalind, Eamonn and I were having a drink at the bar when he came in. Neither he nor his bodyguard/girlfriend seemed entirely out of place in the Chelsea Arts Club, which was why I had invited them here. He was silver-haired, about an inch taller than me, which made him six feet four, and his halo of grey hair and curly grey beard, hanging over a loose green sweater, gave him the air of a particularly dissolute Roman emperor. He wore little round glasses with gold frames, and he looked quite magnificent.

His minder was in her twenties, which made her nearly thirty years younger than he was. She had pronounced Inca features, and was short and dark. Over a t-shirt she wore a leather jerkin. She clumped around in a pair of heavy black army boots.

In the dark, cool dining room we sat under the quizzical portrait of one of the club's founders, James McNeil Whistler. We ordered: the girl frugally, the representative with a certain gusto. He liked the wine I chose. The girl said nothing for the rest of the meal, but he spoke a good deal. His Peruvian accent came through quite strongly; but his grasp of English was magnificent. He called Margaret Thatcher 'the Boadicea of our times', and complained about 'all these intellectuals and their lucubrations'. I had read that word in nineteenth-century novels, but had never in my life heard it used; I wouldn't even have been sure how to pronounce it.

We had both ordered the fillets of John Dory, a club speciality, and we got down to business.

'I am glad to be able to tell you,' he said, 'that the people I have spoken to believe that you may get an interview with the Chairman. Apparently he wants to speak to the world.'

He beamed with pleasure, and even the girl cracked a sour smile. We moved on to the cheese, and a glass of brandy. I felt we'd all deserved it.

The second meal came a month later. Everything had changed. We were in Lima, and had been daily expecting to interview Abimael Guzman. It was an extremely difficult business; although the government and most of the civil service were hopelessly demoralized, one section of the police had kept their nerve, and was continuing to hunt Guzman down. On the very evening we were expecting to go and interview him, the news came through that he had been arrested. The special police unit had asked shopkeepers to watch out for anyone who seemed to be buying more groceries than usual, and they followed a woman who had started doing exactly that. Guzman and his ferocious girlfriend were living on the premises.

We had invested weeks of effort and filming, and had promised the BBC and several other broadcasting organizations that we would give them a world-class story about Peru. Now we had nothing. We held a long meeting, and decided that we should make our film about the deep, institutionalized corruption which linked the government, the military, the Shining Path and the cocaine trade. This was no less dangerous than trying to get an interview with the leader of the Shining Path, and it would mean burying ourselves in the Amazonian jungle, where the coca was grown and flown out of the country. We would be at the mercy of the army there, and wouldn't be able to spend two nights in the same place, or announce our plans to anyone in advance.

The night before we left Lima for the forest, we decided to have one last jolly meal. Our two local advisers, Cecilia and Gilberto, drove us to the most attractive restaurant in the city – one of the most attractive anywhere, I later decided. Lima isn't a very beautiful place, and in those days its poverty was shocking. But the ocean front was gorgeous, especially at night. Then you couldn't see the derelict cars and the hills of rubbish which had been left on the beaches, or the beggars sleeping rough, or the bodies which turned up there every night. Instead, the lights glittered magically along the coast, and the sound of the Pacific surf breaking onto the sand was hypnotically beautiful.

We drove down through a gap in the cliffs to the coast road, and saw it ahead of us: a pier, exactly like something from the south coast of England, stuck out into the water, a Victorian cast-iron creation of struts and curlicues. The restaurant lay at the end, brilliantly lit by coloured bulbs.

'La Rosa Nautica,' Cecilia announced proudly: the sea-rose.

There was a car park, with half a dozen heavies hanging round in it, smoking and talking. Even in the dark you could see the guns which broke the line of their ill-fitting black suits. La Rosa Nautica was a favourite place for politicians to come and eat, and kidnappings and political murders were frequent in Lima.

They watched us carefully, commenting to each other, as we walked down the pier, with the Pacific waves breaking against the cast-iron pillars below our feet. The lights along the coastline were getting brighter as the evening became darker and night descended.

The restaurant was almost empty. Peru was going through a savage deflation, and only politicians, gangsters and people who earned their money in US dollars could afford to come out to eat. This evening the restaurant was entirely empty except for three politicians, bulging out of their clothes and plotting some unsavoury coup in Parliament. It was their bodyguards we had seen in the car park.

The politicians turned to look at us, and especially at the women in our group. Then they turned back, just as their heavies had, passed some muttered judgement and forgot all about us. We were shown to a big circular cast-iron table in the middle of the restaurant, from which we could see the sea in three directions.

Over the *ceviche* we were still quiet, thinking about the dangers that lay ahead of us. But a few pisco sours soon sorted that out. We enjoyed each other's company, and the setting couldn't have been lovelier. Eventually the politicians left, but we scarcely noticed. We were telling stories in a mixture of Spanish and English, mocking the villains and thugs we had come across, and imagining what the crooked president, Alberto Fujimori, would say when he heard what we were doing. We had interviewed him a couple of days before, and found him to be a considerable slime-ball.

As the last light faded outside, we were starting our marvellous fish course (I never found out what it was, but the taste of lime juice on the white flesh was unforgettable). I glanced up and saw a flight of pelicans outlined against the last faint redness in the sky, catching the light from the restaurant as they passed us, heading down to skid across the face of the luminous ocean. Then it became impossible to work out which was sky and which was water, and the waves built up and crashed against the pillars which supported us. By now we were thoroughly happy, and the waiters gathered round us to listen, occasionally joining in the conversation and the laughter. The next morning could take care of itself. For now, we were content.

Our trip to the Huallaga valley, the centre of Peru's cocaine trade and scene of its worst human rights abuses, proved to be every bit as dangerous as we had expected. We confronted two different commanders at military camps in these nasty little drug towns, and after we had managed to escape with all our material, even the government of Alberto Fujimori had to take action against the two officers. They weren't arrested, they were merely moved to other postings; but since they were out in the desert, where they no longer had any connection with the hugely profitable drugs trade, that was a fairly effective punishment in its own right.

We eventually broke our rule about staying on the move the whole time. Tingo Maria was the biggest town in the area, and the hotel there seemed friendly and likely to take notice if the army came and arrested all six of us. There was even a frightened little newspaper in the town, which might summon up its courage to report our disappearance. So we spent two nights in Tingo, going out in the daytime to pay a sudden visit to an army camp, or interview the widows or parents of people whom the soldiers had murdered. In the Huallaga valley you could hire the army to wipe out your enemies, or get rid of your husband or wife, or the landowner you envied, or the worker who refused to take a cut in pay.

It was a charming hotel, with a creaking wooden verandah floored with split cane, a good kitchen, and a reasonably good swimming-pool, though the water was unfiltered and dirty. As a result, our eyes were swollen and inflamed as we drank our pisco sours, but the pool's coolness after the savage jungle heat of the day made it worthwhile. Around us, frogs and crickets gulped and chirruped, and fireflies flashed above our heads, small golden arcs of light in the darkness.

As we ate dinner, a splendid dorado in a sharp, acidic sauce, with sweet potatoes and some green leaf vegetable which might have been a local version of cabbage, we planned our next move. We wanted to go to the nastiest place of all, Aucayacu, where the level of killings had been appalling. There was someone there who was prepared to speak to us on camera, but the hardest thing was to get to the town without being spotted. The Shining Path infested the roads, and the army did nothing to get in their way. We found out later that part of the army's income came from the Shining Path here.

A driver came to see us, but he was a weaselly man who kept on asking for more money because of the danger. He had once been a policeman, and had the scars of plenty of shoot-outs on him, but he claimed that his wife was frightened and wouldn't let him go. In the end, we managed to rent an entire bus, one of those beautiful South American things with painting all over the bodywork. It came with its own driver.

The company which owned it was called the Company of the Marginal, the Marginal being the area along the Amazonian forest, but 'company' translated as 'empresa', so we called our bus *Empress of the Marginal*. She provided the perfect cover for our journey: one or two people tried to get us to stop and let them board, but no one else even glanced at us, either on the way there or back.

At the hotel back in Tingo Maria, our mission triumphantly accomplished, we sat down to dinner. Two men came and sat at a table a little bit too close to us. They were large and unpleasant looking.

'*Milicos*,' whispered Cecilia; an insulting word for soldiers.

One had a flat, open, Indian face; the other wore dark glasses even though it was night-time, had abysmal table manners, and laughed in a braying, spluttering way with his mouth full. We speculated among ourselves what the joke might have been; Eamonn suggested it was 'You should have seen his face when I cut his leg off.'

It wasn't clear whether they were there to spy on us, to frighten us, or to pick a fight with us and call in reinforcements. They proceeded to get very drunk on expenses.

Then the singing started: '. . . *de mi patria . . . la fortuna . . . alegría del corazón . . .*'

'Why don't we go over to them,' Steve the cameraman suggested, 'and say we're doing a feature on folk music?'

'You could say we were talent spotters,' said Matt, the sound recordist.

'Opportunity Knocks!' shouted Eamonn. 'And all the way from Tingo Maria, Peru, we have . . .'

The two men were getting potentially quarrelsome.

'Maybe you should go over and sing them one of your national songs,' I said to Matt, who was a Scot.

'I could always sing them "The Northern Lights of Old Aberdeen Are Home, Sweet Home to Me",' said Matt.

'Go on.'

'Will I?'

'Just softly.'

'You don't sing "The Northern Lights of Old Aberdeen" softly,' Matt objected.

'All right, slur it.'

He started to slur it, but it was wasted on the *milicos*.

'Hey, little girl, why are you looking at me?' the one with dark glasses sang drunkenly to Rosalind.

She stared at him, then looked away in contempt, but he was too far gone to notice. Soon they lumbered away, and one of them was sick in the driveway. They hadn't made a very good job of checking us out.

§

The thing I like most about working for television is the companionship. Meeting up with Nick and Oggy at the airport at the start of a new trip, shaking hands, exchanging greetings, then getting down to the business of checking in the gear and buying a few last-minute things, having a quick and entirely unnecessary snack in the lounge, and catching up with each other's news after a couple of weeks or so, is a quiet pleasure. Especially before we go to Baghdad or Kabul, and have to do some work which is likely to be particularly dodgy. But sufficient unto the day, as I have long had occasion to tell myself, is the evil thereof; and for the moment the pleasure of listening to Nick's account of his skiing trip to Bulgaria with his son, or Oggy's time in California, or their latest experience of BBC politics and machinations, and knowing that there is a six-hour flight ahead of me with nothing to do except watch a film or read a book, is a complete antidote to all the anxieties about the next couple of weeks.

It wasn't always like this. When I worked for radio as a foreign correspondent, I was on my own. No one to meet up with, no one's advice to listen to, no one's company to make the time go quicker, no one I had to be positive and jolly with, pretending that I was perfectly easy in my mind about the work that lay ahead of us. No one to share the experiences with afterwards, joking about what had happened, or trying to get reassurance about some foul-up. And not much fun. Nowadays Nick, Oggy and I play a game where we have to spot likenesses among the people we see around us, with extra points if the likeness is across an ethnic or gender boundary, and special points if it crosses the species boundary: someone who looks like a toad, say, or an antelope. It passes the time.

Once, when I was the radio correspondent in Johannesburg, I had to travel to Zambia to cover the latest stage in the talks to solve the Rhodesia/Zimbabwe crisis. I interviewed the president, Kenneth Kaunda, a charming and gentle man with a particular and rather

predictable line in warning the British government about the blood-
bath that lay ahead if it didn't sort things out in a way which
would, incidentally, suit Zambia's interests with some precision.

'You know, John,' he said, knowing how flattering journalists
found it when the great ones of the earth remembered their names,
'Mugabe is coming here tonight.'

Robert Mugabe was the head of ZANU-PF, the main group
fighting the white regime headed by Ian Smith. At this stage I had
never met him, though I was to interview him again and again over
the years that followed. In his considerate way, Kaunda was giving
me a very useful tip-off. I always liked him, and later he taught his
fellow Africans a vital lesson in democracy by standing down when
he was defeated in an election. Mugabe, by contrast, would use
every available weapon to stay in power by force, and would ruin
his country as a result. Kaunda disliked him intensely, and soon we
would realize that Kaunda was right.

There was a sad and ineffectual buffet, with slabs of meat
congealing in a salty brown sauce, flavourless white mealie-meal
and some dispiriting boiled vegetables. Britain had brought the
English language to sub-Saharan Africa together with a certain,
usually unfulfilled, set of principles about government and very little
else. It certainly didn't export a tradition of good cooking. The only
decent food in this entire part of the world, from Uganda and
Tanzania to Zambia and the white-ruled republics of the south,
originated with the Dutch settlers and the Malays and others who
settled with them at the Cape. A little of this filtered northward, but
that was all. The cooking of the British colonials was as bland as
their rule and, like their rule, you were always told it was good for
you but it was never really very palatable.

I was reflecting on all this as I sat eating, an unread book
propped up on the table. And then someone was standing in front
of me, blocking the light.

'Comrade Mugabe would like to see you,' the figure looming
above me said.

'Well, it'll take me about ten more—'

'He will see you now.'

Over the years to come, I learned to dislike Mugabe greatly, but
not to fear him. It was his sidekicks who added the menace; Mugabe

merely introduced the element of impatience. He was never a racist, even though a lot of white people suffered directly as a result of what he was to do to them. Racism is stupidity, and Mugabe was never stupid, whatever else he might be.

He was sitting at the head of a table in a small private room nearby. The same inch-thick sections of meat lay in front of him, moistened a little by the same gravy with its texture of salted chocolate. Mugabe was a fastidious man, and as I came in he was in the act of pushing his meal aside uneaten.

'I see you didn't like the food here either,' I said as I came up to him. Just because he had summoned me away from my meal didn't mean I was going to allow him to lord it over me.

He looked back at me with empty eyes. Joking wasn't something he understood. He could be savagely witty, but it was always for a purpose: to humiliate, to destroy an opponent's point, to swing a group of people round to his view. Humour had no value in his eyes when it was simply introduced for its own sake.

'I heard you wanted to interview me.'

That was Kaunda again, I thought: he really is a kind man.

'Now?'

'Why not?'

I went and got my tape recorder.

To be honest, I've lost all memory of what I asked him, and of what he answered. The recording must exist somewhere in the vast archives of the BBC, but it wasn't particularly enlightening as far as Mugabe's negotiating position was concerned, and the report I based on it was one of those Newzak pieces that you listen to and forget about immediately afterwards.

But as an introduction to the man himself, it was excellent. He sat there, sinewy and mobile, moving his arms together in parallel in a way I found very camp, his elbows planted on the table-cloth among the little plates and the unused knives and forks. Once or twice he picked up a fork and jabbed its tines into the cloth to emphasize a point. He drank occasionally from a glass of water; alcohol wasn't really his thing at all.

He treated my questions with contempt. There was nothing personal about this; right from the start of the interview, he had seen that I wasn't his intellectual match and had decided that I didn't count. Again, this wasn't racist. He treated the people around him in exactly the same acidic fashion. None of his associates was up to his mental level, and he wasn't prepared to hide the fact that he realized it.

The white regime headed by Ian Smith was full of dunderheads, and Mugabe behaved towards them accordingly. There were just two or three people in the British Foreign Office delegation whose level of intellect matched his own, and he treated them with a kind of surprised equality. To everyone else he was absurdly overbearing. Mugabe would, I think, be amazed to be told this was arrogance; he would have seen it as an exercise in recognizing self-evident fact.

His cold establishment as president, his slaughter of tens of thousands of possible opponents in Matabeleland and his determined emasculation of the powers of his junior partner, the volcanic Joshua Nkomo, all followed. (Nkomo, who was his rival for the presidency at one time, might well have been even worse than Mugabe. He once gave a press conference in London, and a BBC friend of mine, who was coincidentally called Ian Smith, asked him a difficult question. Bullyingly, Nkomo asked him to state his name. When he did, Nkomo assumed he was being made fun of, and his rage almost gave him an infarction. His aides had to spend some time calming him down.)

From the start, Mugabe was heavily influenced by Stalin and Mao Zedong; not quite the political models you would hope your leaders might follow. As a result, when he came under pressure from elements in his own ZANU-PF, in 1999 and 2000, he replied by turning them into the servants of an enemy against whom he could direct his party's anger. This enemy was a combination of Britain, the United States and the white farmers whose efficiency largely kept the Zimbabwean economy going. The results, as happened when Stalin and Mao tried the same tactics, were utterly disastrous for the country as a whole; but they were successful in silencing Mugabe's political challengers inside ZANU-PF.

By 2007, inflation was over 2,000 per cent a year, and a single brick cost what an entire three-bedroomed house with a swimming-pool had cost twenty years earlier. Bread prices would triple between morning and late afternoon, and directly you were paid you had to start buying things with the money if you were not to lose it completely. Eighty per cent of people were out of work, and at least two million fled the country to South Africa, in order to be able to send back money to their families.

I met Mugabe on various occasions during the following years. His vanity, which made him dress foppishly and encourage him to give his much younger wife almost unrestricted use of his enormous and largely illegal bank account in order to buy clothes in Paris and elsewhere, also made it impossible for him to ignore a microphone. He loved the sound of his own voice, and the almost effeminately acid phrases rolled easily onto tape. At a conference in Libya, I once asked him about the growing pressure from America and the EU for better governance and more transparency in Africa.

'These people have no understanding of the things whereof they speak,' he said, and I could see he included me in that. 'What do they know of Africa? Do they come here to see our ways of government for themselves? No. Do they know anything other than their own colonial version of our history? No. Do they have the interests of Africans at heart? Of course not, otherwise they wouldn't behave towards us in the way they do.

'Let them come here. Let them understand our problems. Let them change their policies in ways which might help the people of Africa. And then let them suggest how they might assist the governance of Africa. Until then, I suggest that they shut up and mind their own business.'

It was highly entertaining stuff, but there was a problem. Like most Third World leaders with tame newspapers and television stations used to reporting their every word, he talked at far too great a length. Imagine trying to edit down a seven-hour address by Kim Jung-Il, or a rant by Saddam Hussein: it can scarcely be done. The American television network NBC once interviewed Fidel Castro for four hours, and used nine seconds of it. The free media simply don't have room for immense speechifying by the great ones of the earth. As I recall it, all we could use of Mugabe's answer was this:

What do they know of Africa? Do they come here to see our ways of government for themselves? No. [Then an internal edit.] Let them suggest how they might assist the governance of Africa. Until then, I suggest that they shut up and mind their own business.'

Even so, it took about twenty seconds – a little too long by today's standards. A good sound-bite should never last beyond about twelve or thirteen seconds, otherwise your audience loses their sense of what you are trying to say. But Mugabe never understood any need to hold back, to ration his words, to moderate his arrogance, to keep his audience interested.

Nearly thirty years separated that interview from the moment when my meal in Lusaka was interrupted by one of Robert Mugabe's goons. In that time, while other African countries as well as more cynical ones like China looked on with approval, Mugabe slaughtered large numbers of his own people, and ruined one of the most productive countries in Africa. And it was all done with a sneer, and with the assurance that he was the cleverest man in the country.

§

I associate some of my most pleasant and interesting experiences with meals of different kinds and qualities. In the Paghman hills outside Kabul in the fierce cold of March 1989, for instance, I laboured up the steep mountainside with my friend and colleague Peter Jouvenal, and, led by a local guide, we reached the entrance to a cave where the local *mujaheddin* had their headquarters. We were expected; in fact they must have been watching our progress up the side of this incomparably beautiful snow-covered valley for the previous forty minutes.

They had prepared tea for our arrival. We pushed our way through the curtains that hung over the mouth of the cave and kept the warmth in, more or less, said our '*Alekum salaams*' to the dozen or so men inside, most of them elderly, and sank down with a certain relief onto the dark red cushions all round the edges of the cave. I never learned to draw my feet up underneath me – you have to do that from childhood, I think – but I stuck my legs out on the rich carpets which covered the floor of the cave, and watched as a young boy came in with a vast blue enamelled kettle almost as big as he was. The kettle was steaming and, using both hands, he poured the hot water into a second very large kettle: the tea-kettle, in fact.

The Afghans prefer green tea, which was a great relief to me.

We had spent the previous two weeks in Pakistan, where the taste, presumably influenced by the long British presence, is for milk in the tea. The Pakistanis have taken this literally, and the result is a tea which can almost be white with condensed milk or, even worse, goat's milk. They then add improbable quantities of sugar. The Afghans, instead, pour their tea into tall glasses, and can usually be stopped before they put too much sugar in. A cup of hot green tea after a lot of exertion on a very cold day can be a very pleasant thing indeed.

We began to talk to these twelve or so elders, who sat with their backs to the cave wall, their cunning eyes and bushy beards turned in our direction. Our hope was to persuade them to smuggle us into Kabul under the noses of the communists, who were running the city with characteristic savagery after the Soviet withdrawal three or four weeks earlier. Just as we were getting going, lunch arrived. A shiny plastic table-cloth was laid over the carpets on the floor, large amounts of flat, soft nan bread were carried in, hanging over someone's arm like a Dali clock, and someone else brought in a vast dish, three feet across, piled high with steaming brown rice dotted with raisins and thin strings of carrot. Another dish, equally vast, contained the meat. It seemed to be most of a sheep.

The custom is to reach into the rice dish, knead a little pyramid of rice with your fingers, then pop it in your mouth. After that you tear off a piece of bread, reach into the communal dish, and pick up a piece of meat with it. This you transfer to your mouth, and the louder the sucking noise you make, the greater the compliment you are paying to the food.

The mutton was very greasy, of course, and pretty tough; but the old boys were too concentrated on getting what they wanted to pay much attention to what I was doing. For a time, I couldn't remember where I had seen that particular look of animated anticipation before; but the next time I sat at the Members' Table at the Garrick Club and watched the main courses being handed out, I remembered. Old boys, whether turbaned and bearded and wearing long robes, or dressed in lounge suits with a pale green and salmon pink tie, are old boys the world over.

The meat took a certain amount of chewing, especially if, like our hosts, you have a good deal fewer than the normal ration of teeth. But at last everyone was finished, and the plastic cloth was taken away with the remains of the meal still on it. The tea-kettle came out again, and as I tried to get rid of the taste of my lunch twelve glittering pairs of eyes turned to me.

'Your country has chosen to publish a terrible slander against Islam. Why do the English hate the true religion with such vehemence?'

I hadn't expected this. There had been a certain amount of rioting while we had been in Peshawar, in Pakistan, after the news that Ayatollah Khomeini of Iran had condemned the publication of Salman Rushdie's book *The Satanic Verses*; but it hadn't occurred to me that I might have to defend it before we could get the help of these old men to get us to Kabul.

I explained the theory of the freedom of speech as best I could, and managed to link it with the valiant efforts of the *mujaheddin* in fighting the Russians. They had threatened our freedoms in Britain, I said glibly, just as they had threatened the freedoms of Afghanistan; and although many people in my country disliked *The Satanic Verses* (I was one of them, though I didn't say so; my objection was that it was boring as well as being probably intentionally offensive) we knew that we had to defend the right of people to say what they believed. I quoted Voltaire piously, and rested my case.

No one seemed at all convinced; but I soon realized that they had already decided to help us, and merely wanted to hear the argument in favour of publishing a libel on Islam. If I had said that this was just the start of a long period in hiding for Salman Rushdie, who would have to spend part of the next few years in the barracks of the Household Cavalry in London, in the company of people who came to loathe him for his superciliousness, the old men might have been a bit more enthusiastic. But I didn't find this out till later.

It was time for another glass of tea.

§

The hours of daylight were so short, here in the foothills of the Urals, that we had to set out at five in the morning to be sure we could start filming by ten. It was 1996, and Boris Yeltsin was fighting a presidential election which he was certain to win. We were in Yekaterinburg, which had been his power base in the past, and we wanted to drive to the village of Butka, where he was born.

The driver was surly, and said nothing to us. He merely took a plastic tool and opened a small hole in the ice on his windscreen, working at it until it was five inches long and one inch wide. This would be his only view of the world while we were driving. The road was immensely long and straight, which was something of a relief to us. When I got out, halfway to Butka, to have a pee by the side of the road, I fell flat on my face immediately. The road surface was entirely covered in ice, and if the driver had had to turn the steering wheel we would probably have crashed.

We reached Butka at nine-thirty, just as the sun was beginning to rise. It was as quiet as every other village in Russia, with wooden houses covered with snow, picket fences round each one to keep the hens and pigs in during the summer, and side roads filled with frozen mud. Russians like the winter, and celebrate the first fall of snow each year; but here in Butka it was a burden, trapping the inhabitants and preventing them from working for months on end.

Bob Prabhu was the cameraman. I loved working with Bob, for his cheerfulness and courage and endurance, and his habit of producing sweets at moments of tiredness or tension. For some reason the junior office-wallahs at the BBC, people who can wreck your life if you cross them, took against Bob and eventually stopped him travelling. But they didn't help the interests of the BBC.

We filmed up and down the streets for an hour or so. It was so cold that when I took my fur hat off to do a piece to camera, my jaw almost froze up and it was very difficult even to make basic sounds. Still, no matter how much discomfort you endure, the laughter which would greet your appearance on the screen in a fur hat would be much more damaging.

Fortunately, I managed to get my words out in one go, and saved us from having to wait in the open too long. The temperature, someone told us, was minus thirty degrees. By the time Bob had finished, it was nearly one o'clock and the sun was starting to descend towards the horizon.

There weren't any shops or cafés in Butka, but one or two of the houses offered cooked meals for a minimal price.

'What's on the menu?' I asked Bob.

'Some kind of cooked meat,' he said, which sounded encouraging. 'Sort of stew.'

That didn't sound so good.

We went in and sat down at the bare wooden table. The cook, a big woman with wattles on her upper arms, scarcely greeted us. Nor did the equally large policewoman in her bulging blue uniform, who came in while we were sitting there. She was going to have the pork stew as well.

But directly the cook plunged the ladle back into the pot, I could see we were in trouble. The liquid was thick and greyish, and full of disturbing shapes: bulbous white things, that turned on the ladle and slithered back into the fatty water. The pig's innards were there, and there was no concession to late-twentieth-century Western taste. The ladle went in and out again, and more shapes appeared.

Bob was magnificent. He attacked his bowl of soup with apparent gusto, sawing the objects in it into reasonably small pieces and swallowing them. He didn't even seem to mind the fat. I did. I couldn't take any of it, and the best I could do was to drink the tea. Even that tasted thick and fatty, as though the liquid from the pot had somehow got into the kettle.

The woman looked at me much as I had looked at the pot. She had every right; I had let myself down, as well as been rude to her. My principle was always to eat what I was offered, but in Butka I had allowed myself to be defeated. I looked at my watch, and at the snow-laden street outside. Three o'clock, and it was already getting dark.

§

Cuba is a wonderful place, but no matter how much you may sympathize with its past you can't altogether forget the fact that large numbers of its inhabitants are dissatisfied with the system.

Among them, the young women. Once, when I was there, all you heard older, educated, male Cubans talk about was the way the girls behaved. One night I had dinner with a well-known figure from Cuban television. A few nights earlier he had been driving home after the end of transmission, and had seen a rather attractive young woman standing under a lamp-post, waving him down.

He had stopped and was about to ask her where she would like to go when he realized to his horror that it was his own daughter. She had recognized him straight away, but was too shocked to say anything.

Over the next few days, sitting outside the bedroom where she was held prisoner, he interrogated her about her reasons for wanting to be a common prostitute. And slowly he came to understand. His daughter hadn't gone to the bad; she was merely bored. And the great ambition of her life was to get wealthy foreigners to take her out to dinner. If it became necessary to go to bed with them, then she would; she didn't mind, she said, as long as they had a bit of money and were clean. The Japanese were the nicest of all.

That decided me. I was in Havana with a woman producer and a woman director, and our local translator was a woman as well. This gave me a little confidence.

'Why don't we find a few girls like that, and take them to dinner somewhere and interview them?'

If I'd been with an all-male crew, I wouldn't have done it. But it seemed all right with our three women.

Finding the girls wasn't difficult. Every patch of lamplight seemed to have its own crop of them. Some spoke English, some didn't. But they were all happy to get a good meal with a little wine, air their grievances and go home without having to offer any sexual favours in return.

The stories they told were often sad and always innocent. Inevitably, because life is never as clear-cut or as pleasant as we would like it to be, growing up in Castro's Cuba was neither easy nor simple. One by one these girls told their stories of wanting a little excitement and glamour in their lives, but having to settle for something much more dreary and limited, and so they went out at night to get a little fun. Oddly, the authorities didn't seem to mind too much; none of the girls had been arrested, or even stopped by the police.

Except now. We had only just started on an excellent meal of lobster and brown rice, the dish the girls all agreed on, and the waiter had scarcely opened the first bottle of wine, when the police arrived. One of the staff must have rung them. There was shouting, and there were threats – many of them from our side of the table.

The police didn't touch our camera, and they didn't touch us, but they grabbed the girls and tried to frogmarch them away. There was a long negotiation which ended with everyone, both the girls and ourselves, being allowed to go free. No one, after all, had committed any offence. But the girls were in tears – until we told them we would take them somewhere else, if they were willing. They were, and brightened up immensely when the producer dug into her handbag and produced a ten-dollar bill for each of them.

We took the girls to a bar. It was dark and pleasant and not too noisy, and we filmed them some more. Then the police arrived again: a different group. More shouting, more threats, more man-handling, another eventual agreement. The girls were all in tears again, and only some more ten-dollar bills sorted the problem out.

But that was enough, for them and for us. Cuba had won. The girls had complained that they couldn't have fun, and now they weren't even allowed to tell anyone about it. The rest of the team went out to say goodbye to the girls, and to make sure they found taxis to take them home. I sat there, with the untasted glasses of rum and Coca-Cola, and daiquiris and mojitos in front of me on the table, just as the lobster and brown rice had sat untasted on the table in the restaurant. It all seemed so depressing. The state didn't object if nice girls prostituted themselves. It only got annoyed if they talked about it to outsiders.

I picked up my mojito and downed it in one. Then I signalled to the waiter for another.

'Shall I take these away?' he asked, gesturing to the other drinks.

I nodded. I didn't even want to speak to him, in case he was the one who had called the police.

§

Where eating is concerned, Buenos Aires is one of the finest cities I know. The range of cuisine isn't that great; once you've had one of the city's magnificent *bife de lomo* steaks, and eaten pasta at an Italian place and delicately grilled quid at a Spanish one, you've had pretty much the best the city can offer in the way of menus. But in Buenos Aires it isn't what you eat that counts, so much as the way you eat it.

At nine o'clock one pleasant autumn evening Nick Woolley,

Oggy Boytchev and I ambled out of the Plaza Hotel, once magnificent but now taken over by an American group and no longer quite what it was. We headed down Florida, the brash pedestrianized street where the leather shops compete noisily with one another by stationing barkers outside to encourage passers-by to enter, and where one of the world's great shoe-shiners, known only as Johnny, gives your footwear a glassy polish and tells you about his children.

We passed Harrods, in the past briefly associated with the store in London but now sadly empty and abandoned, and the Galería Pacífico, the finest shopping mall in Latin America. Then we turned right into a dark street with broken pavements and garish shops selling goods a quarter of the quality and a tenth of the price that you can get them in Florida.

I wanted to take the other two to the Palacio de la Patata Frita, the Palace of the Potato Chip. The food isn't fantastic, and the place certainly isn't grand, but the steaks are of a certain exceptional standard, the waiters are highly trained and traditional, and the clientele is almost exclusively Argentine. Oggy has a great dislike of places that are, as he says, 'touristicated', but we could be pretty certain of avoiding the tourists here.

The trouble was, Argentines eat late. Not just ordinarily late, but very late indeed, even by European standards. Even by Spanish standards. At nine-thirty, when we arrived and peered through the windows, the white-covered tables were almost all vacant. And so, at Nick's suggestion, we crossed the little street and headed into a bar. I trust Nick's sense about bars; he likes them, and on the very few occasions when we have finished work by nine o'clock at night and are not in too dangerous a place, he is inclined to go out for a drink.

This one was rough: the kind of place which should have had sawdust on the floor. Nine-thirty was still early evening here, and the two barmen had that kind of long-distance-runner look to them which meant they would be on their feet till at least three in the morning, and probably later. It wasn't at all like the kind of place that Raymond Chandler describes lovingly in *The Long Goodbye*, where everything is neat and tidy early on, and the first drink of the evening tastes sharp and good. All the same, the first drink here did taste superb. On the right as we came in, there were some elderly sandwiches and cakes from earlier on in the day, and a large, noisy, rather incontinent coffee machine that dribbled like an old man, even though no one was using it.

The action, such as it was at that time of night, was taking place on the left-hand side. The bar was long and rather chewed, as though generations of impatient drinkers had stood here, rubbing the wood with their empty glasses while they waited for the next round. Down the far end, a couple of middle-aged men, builders or plumbers perhaps, stood making two local beers last a longer time than seemed entirely reasonable.

There were two barmen. The one by the window was small and dark, and was mostly concerned with a customer as small and dark as himself, who was talking to him about football – the set was on above the bar, and Boca Juniors were, as usual, dismantling some lesser team – and nursing a villainous blackish drink of some kind.

The barman we aligned ourselves with was busy polishing glasses and staring absent-mindedly at the reflection opposite of the rows of bottles behind him: gins and whiskies with names you never see in Britain and tend to find only in the farther reaches of the world, names reminiscent of glens and bagpipes and tartans and stags, or else of the West End of London. It may be, I once thought, that these names aren't so much intended to differentiate one brand of whisky or gin from another as to alert you to which of the two drinks you have chosen. Perhaps, though, I have sampled too much of the output of Murree's distilleries in Pakistan, which produce whisky, gin and brandy indiscriminately, with only the label to tell them apart.

Our barman was tall, and wore a grubby white dress shirt with a made-up bow-tie on a piece of elastic. His nose was bottle-shaped, and he looked more like an old-fashioned Fleet Street hack than an Argentine barman.

'So what are we going to have?' Oggy asked.

Nick wanted a local beer, and Oggy himself ordered a vodka and tonic. But I remembered suddenly what the nasty-looking liquid the customer down the end of the bar was drinking. It was something which Argentines set great store by, as both an aperitif and a digestif.

'I'll have a Fernet Branca,' I said.

I regretted it, of course, and even after a local beer the acrid taste still followed me over to the Palacio de la Patata Frita when we finally decided it was time to make an appearance.

The eponymous chip is unforgettable. Somehow (it is a secret of the house) they manage to puff it up with air, so that it is more of a crisp, chip-flavoured bubble than the kind of thing we are used to. And the steaks are Argentine in size and flavour: vast, plate-filling, two inches thick, running with reddish juice. Raymond Chandler was still echoing in my head. I tried to adapt his line about the kind of blonde who would make a bishop kick a hole in a stained glass window, and make it fit a vegetarian. I was a vegetarian myself for some years, but a steak like that used to haunt my dreams, even so. In the Palace of the Potato Chip, cutting a steak was like cutting a rich, luscious cake, and to eat it was to taste the wood-smoke and breezes of the pampas.

But the best steak I have ever eaten was at an *asado*, a barbecue, somewhere on the pampas to the south-west of Buenos Aires, in the grounds of a charming nineteenth-century *estancia*; and it was cooked personally by the owner, while his attractive wife, dressed in white, played with their two blonde children. My colleagues and friends and I ate in companionable silence, too taken up with the flavour and texture of the food and the good Argentine red wine to want to talk much. Great eucalyptus trees cast their shade and their delicate scent over the tables where we sat, and I told my neighbour, who was also a rancher and a close friend of our host, how beautiful I thought the house was.

'You might not have thought so, ten years ago,' he said. 'It was completely decayed, and I told him he should pull it down and build something a bit more modern. But he was like a wild man in those days.'

I looked over to where our host was sitting, with a five-year-old girl on his knee and his arm affectionately on his wife's shoulder. He was wearing a rather well-cut English sports jacket, a pair of expensive jeans and Chelsea boots.

'I know,' said my neighbour, pouring me some more wine and following the direction of my glance, 'but you should have seen him before she came along. He was an orphan, you see, and after his parents died there was only an old housekeeper to look after him.

When he came back from school in Buenos Aires she let him run wild. He used to say that whenever the two of them needed anything to eat, he would just go out and kill it.

'He didn't have any friends, and certainly no girlfriends, and the place was going to rack and ruin because he didn't care about it. I think he was angry about being on his own like this, and he took it out on everyone around him. What's the English word? Morose? He was morose to the point where he never spoke to anyone.

'And then, one day, he had to go to Buenos Aires to buy something for the estate. And for some reason, maybe just because he was thirsty, he went to the bar at your hotel, the Plaza. He certainly wasn't looking for company. But Maria Elena was there, and maybe something about him, his wildness – you know, he never even combed his hair, and he always seemed to cut himself when he shaved – something, anyway, caught her attention. She went and sat down beside him, and started asking him questions. And he was so annoyed, he wouldn't even answer. But she carried on.

'Eventually he couldn't ignore her any longer. And when he started answering one or two of her questions, the whole thing came out and he couldn't stop talking to her, and telling her how miserable his life was. By the end, after just a couple of drinks, she said she thought he was the most wonderful and interesting man she had ever met.

'It took a long time for her to break him down, but in the end she managed it. You'd never guess now what a strange kind of wild monster he was, would you? She rescued him, like you might rescue some poor lost dog.'

I looked across at the four of them, the couple smiling at each other, their little blonde children playing around their feet, and knew I could never have guessed anything about them or their past.

An hour or so later, in order to get out of the sun, I went indoors. The furniture, the paintings, the carpets, all seemed to be marvellously from a single time, perhaps somewhere in the 1890s.

'I chose it all, you know,' said a voice behind me.

It was my host's wife. She looked extraordinarily beautiful, I thought, as she stood in the doorway, with the light behind her, shining in her golden hair.

'Look through this.'

She pointed to a seat, and pushed an old late-Victorian stereo-scope towards me. It was the kind which you load with glass photographic plates, peer through the eyepiece, then turn a handle and see each of them in 3-D. And as I looked, I exclaimed out loud.

'I know,' she said, and laughed with pleasure at my reaction. 'It took me ages to get everything exactly right.'

The photographs were of this very room, but taken a century earlier. In the foreground of most of them were two or three men of different ages, with tremendous whiskers, landowners from a long-dead era. And behind them were exactly the same pieces of furniture and paintings and carpets that I saw in front of me now. It was a precise reproduction in sepia.

'They're Enrico's great-grandfather and his brothers, photo-graphed just here in this room. Of course I had to cheat a little bit to make everything match. But it does look good, doesn't it?'

I nodded.

'And Enrico does love it so much.'

She looked out of the window, smiling at him as he stood pushing the children on swings, side by side, between the eucalyptus trees. I think I have never witnessed such a scene of family happiness.

A few years afterwards, I went back to Argentina, and bumped into someone I recognized from the *asado*.

'Any news of Enrico and Maria Elena?' I asked.

There was news. Not long after we had been there, she had been driving the two children to school when a big truck went out of control and killed all three of them.

It was a moment or two before I could ask the next question; my voice was a little husky.

'And Enrico?'

He still lived in the house. Since the funerals, he wouldn't see anyone at all. Apparently the place was falling apart. There was just one old man looking after him.

15

NOT THE END OF THE WORLD

Beneath the uncountable millions of silver birch trees along the side of the track as our train moved at a stately pace from Moscow to Yekaterinburg, there were a few patches of hard, resistant snow. It had fallen first in October, and was still clinging on in little folds and pockets at the beginning of May. Things don't change or give up quickly in Russia.

It was the spring of 2007, and I had come back to provincial Russia for the first time since Vladimir Putin had been elected president in 2000. When it became obvious that Russia was going to survive, and survive well, as a society and an economy, it dropped out of the headlines. And once that had happened it was difficult to persuade news editors to be interested in Russia again: even when dissidents were being murdered and independent voices silenced, and Russia itself seemed to be turning back into a secret police state.

The old controls over what you could say or do had been reimposed. There was a new Cold War between Russia on the one hand and Britain and America on the other, and the BBC's Russian-language service was no longer able to broadcast on FM from its headquarters in Moscow. According to the Russian authorities, this was for 'technical reasons'. Just like the bad old days.

Yet things had changed remarkably since I was here last. Yekaterinburg was just under 900 miles from Moscow, and a good ten years behind. When I visited it in 1996 there were no advertisements of any kind. The city's main hotel, the unreconstructed old Sverdlovsk, had refused to change its Soviet-era name (Sverdlov was the commissar who ordered the execution of the imperial family in the city in 1918) when the city became Yekaterinburg (named after Catherine the Great) once again. So although the spot where the tsar and his family were murdered is now marked by a new cathedral, the city's main hotel still carries the murderer's name.

Yet everything else was slowly changing. A gigantic billboard advertised the products of Mothercare. People drove round in little Italian, French and Japanese cars. The shops were well stocked and I saw half a dozen supermarkets. The main change, though, was in the way the people in the streets were dressed.

In 1978, when I first visited Moscow and travelled by Metro, the entire carriage would go quiet when a Westerner got on. Every eye was turned towards you, and they would examine your clothes with a kind of voluptuous care. Those were the days when Russians had the narrowest of choices in the clothes shops: dull grey windcheaters, badly cut dresses of cheap material, shoes made of imitation leather. In those days I was always followed around in the streets, but it wasn't only by the KGB. Often a black-market dealer in clothes would sidle up confidentially and make an offer for what I was wearing – though it was prudent, and probably often accurate, to assume that the man in the black leather jacket who spoke out of the corner of his mouth was an informer or an agent provocateur as well as a black marketeer.

Nowadays the sight of well-dressed people in colourful clothes, the women with decent make-up, their hair no longer frizzed and damaged by cheap second-rate products, is a real pleasure. The Russian people had suffered horribly throughout the twentieth century, and at the start of the twenty-first it looks as though they might stand a chance of leading decent, fulfilled lives at last.

Yet I can't resist a certain personal guilt when I see the way things have turned out. In the early 1990s I spent a good deal of time in Moscow, reporting on the savage changes that were taking place. Mikhail Gorbachev had relinquished the presidency in December 1991, never having recovered from his humiliation on live television after the attempted KGB coup against him four months earlier. In full view of the cameras Boris Yeltsin handed him a list of his personal assistants who had been part of the plot, and demanded that he should read it out to the nation.

So Yeltsin became president instead: the only man capable of taking over, even though his record contained plenty of dubious episodes. He was the man who, as the faithful Communist Party boss of Sverdlovsk in the 1970s, had ordered the demolition of the house where the imperial family had been murdered. And on the night of his greatest success, when he bravely climbed onto a tank outside his headquarters during the coup and defied the KGB, the former Soviet foreign minister Eduard Shevardnadze went to see him in his office, and found him lying dead drunk on the floor with three empty vodka bottles around him.

Yeltsin was reckless, and often didn't understand much about what he was doing; that was why being in Russia in the 1990s was like being on an express train hurtling down the track without a driver. Almost all Russians had been relatively poor; now many were reduced, literally, to beggary, while a very few became absurdly rich. The rest, who just managed to get by, were terrified. The most brazen crime flourished. Anyone who stood in the way of a deal, and sometimes of a divorce, could be wiped out by an assassin on a motorbike for ten dollars – little more than the price you had to pay for bullets in the West.

Yet a few dollars could mean genuine riches in Yeltsin's Russia. Wanting to seem generous, I gave an old beggarwoman twenty dollars when we filmed her in the street outside the old Intourist Hotel in Moscow, and arranged to meet her that night at the only place she could find shelter: Kazanskiy, one of the big railway stations. What I saw that night shocked me as I have never, I think, been shocked before. The entire station was full of homeless people, hundreds of them, pushing and shoving and fighting to get a place where they could sit and sleep. Lying down was virtually impossible: the floor was covered with great pools of water, which leaked in from the thawing snow outside. And yet some people, too exhausted to care, were lying there in the dirty, freezing water, fast asleep.

We didn't find the old woman, though we searched the entire place in the near darkness. Three days later, when we went back, another woman said she had been murdered for the twenty dollars I gave her.

That image of the dark, seething, stinking station, like a Gustave Doré drawing of hell, stayed with me and influenced my whole judgement of Yeltsin's Russia: quite wrongly, as it turned out. I felt it was impossible to destroy the fabric of a country like this, and expect that it could calmly remake itself afterwards. Even if the whole shaky financial structure of the new Russia didn't collapse around Yeltsin's ears, I couldn't think of another country which had gone through such a savage period of violent economic change and remained stable and normal. The unpleasant figures on the extreme right who were manoeuvring to win the next election and take power seemed certain to win, I thought.

In those days I used to work for the *Spectator*. The magazine didn't necessarily reflect my own politics, such as they were, but it was a forum for interesting ideas and good writing. A Canadian journalist, based in Moscow, had a regular column, and understandably disliked it when I went there and elbowed him aside for an issue or two. Slowly it became clear that we also had very different ideas about Russia's future. I felt certain the country was about to collapse; he thought it would pull through. Our articles clashed, as did we, but the *Spectator* didn't mind.

'History will judge,' said our editor, Dominic Lawson, calmly.

History found in favour of the Canadian. I, by contrast, got the whole thing very wrong indeed: culpably wrong. I think it's the most serious error of judgement I have made. Russia didn't collapse. Its society, which had endured so much in the past, proved able to endure this as well, just as the Canadian journalist thought it would. Russia in the 1990s wasn't, after all, Germany in the 1920s and 30s; it was itself. People gritted their teeth and carried on, and not because the secret police listened to them and followed them and punished anyone who spoke out against the government. On the contrary, this was one of the freest moments in Russian history, with the KGB temporarily disbanded and the newspapers, radio and television all free to say whatever they wanted about the situation and the government which had produced it.

In the end, after Yeltsin went, the Russian people got what they would probably have liked all along: strong government and economic freedom. The journalists were silenced: some were killed, some went quiet of their own accord. Slowly, very slowly, society found ways of looking after outcasts like the old woman whose death I had unwittingly caused by my small act of generosity. The economy began to show signs of improvement. There were plenty of ultra-rich people, of course – Moscow was home to more billionaires, sixteen of them, than any other city on earth – and the advertisements for luxury goods, and the yellow Porsches and red Ferraris in the main streets, most of which had been renamed since the old Soviet days, showed how the wealth was being spent.

Yet it also began to trickle down through more and more layers of Russia's population.

'It's only in Moscow that you see all this money,' people used to say. 'Out in the provinces, it's as though the communists are still in power.'

When I went to Yekaterinburg in 1996, that was certainly true. *Dzurnayas*, the nasty old busybodies of Soviet Russia, still sat at their desks on every floor of the utterly unreconstructed hotel, guarding the keys to everyone's rooms. After eight o'clock the streets were almost empty, except for groups of policemen. And in the daytime you could see how bare the shops were.

But when I returned eleven years later, everything was different. There was one street where every shop carried the latest imported goods. A great cathedral, with golden onion domes and remarkable statuary, now stood on the site of the house where Tsar Nicholas II and his family had been murdered in 1917. Most of the public buildings had been repainted. Even the buses looked new, and almost comfortable. And in the fifteen years since the huge deflation of Yeltsin's early period, a generation had grown up which scarcely remembered that there had been a communist state. Russia was a new country; it had rebuilt itself on slightly different principles, and it was prospering in a way that I had never thought possible.

What I had failed to take into account was the extraordinary resilience of human beings, their ability to endure suffering and then forget about it, or at least to put it in a different compartment of their minds. It's not just Russians who are capable of this kind of thing. Americans endured the awfulness of the Great Crash of 1929, and got through as best they could until the Second World War came along to make them rich again. The British and French thought their countries would be damaged irreparably by the dreadful losses of the First World War, yet by 1930 the memories were already fading, and the concept of the 'lost generation' of leaders, which was anyway largely false, existed only to provide an alibi for the weakness and cowardice of the late 1930s.

After the Second World War, the United States government

estimated that it would take a generation for the German and Japanese economies to reach pre-war levels; by 1955 they had both done so, and the arrogance of Nazism and Japanese militarism had vanished.

'Who in the 1930s would ever have thought,' the historian and philosopher Sir Isaiah Berlin once said to me, when I bumped into him on a staircase at a formal luncheon and stayed listening to him for an unforgettable half an hour, 'that the Japanese would become the world's great traders, while the Jews would be its best soldiers?'

Human beings are extraordinarily, unimaginably adaptable. We can endure the most dreadful experiences, and change everything about ourselves, and then, in a few years, we can forget everything that our nation or our world or we ourselves have been through. It is our greatest quality; and it is the greatest reason to be optimistic about our future.

§

Years ago, back in the 1970s, the magazine *Punch*, now no longer with us, ran a regular competition in which readers were invited to send in new captions for cartoons from editions long past. One of these showed a young couple in Edwardian dress, their arms round one another at the rail of a passenger liner, looking up at the full moon above them. A good friend and colleague of mine, Malcolm Downing, won that week's prize with the caption, 'Who do you think will get there first – the British or the Germans?'

We don't just forget the past, we find it impossible to envisage that the future will be any different from the present. And yet it always is. In the 1920s, even after Britain had bankrupted itself in order to win the First World War, people everywhere, from Europe to the imperial colonies around the world, found it impossible to think that the British Empire was on its way out. We are always slow to notice and acknowledge the changes that take place among the superpowers of our world.

The twentieth century belonged unquestionably and triumphantly to the United States. Yet for years America's position, like Britain's in the decades before 1914, has slowly been weakening. New forces – a united Europe, China, maybe even India – have been assembling themselves. A single, simple change would shift the

American economy from being the world's richest: pricing international oil supplies in euros rather than dollars. Saddam Hussein suggested as much at an OPEC meeting in 1998, and although he was ignored, other countries tucked the idea away in their minds. It probably won't happen, because any such change would send the international financial system into meltdown, but the possibility exists, and most governments recognize it.

We often think that American economic supremacy has been due to their management skills, their vast domestic market and their constant drive to work harder. All this is true. Yet it is also due to the fact that the oil which runs their cars and their businesses and their homes is paid for in their own currency, and doesn't count as an import to be bought with their foreign exchange reserves. Under President George W. Bush, America's trade deficit and its borrowings grew to frightening proportions. If it had to pay for its oil with its earnings from trade, the whole structure would collapse.

Yet it is also obvious, in 2007, that oil itself won't be the lifeblood of our economies for much longer. No one quite knows what will take its place, but something certainly will. And when that happens, everything will be different, and the American economy will probably be rescued as a result. Even so, it seems safe to assume that America will never again dominate the world as it did in the 1950s and 60s.

Change is happening faster than ever before in human history. Whatever did we do before we had mobile phones? Yet it was, relatively speaking, only the other day that we all started to carry them. I was equipped with one for the first time in order to cover Mrs Thatcher's election of 1987, and its battery was so heavy that I decided to leave it in my hotel for most of the day.

Soon, clearly, we will be able to take a daily pill to combat diseases which at present would kill us. We will have our faulty organs replaced by new ones which are genetically engineered. My son Rafe will, if he's lucky, live to 120 before his body wears out; old age will become the main killer. By that stage, the Second World War, when his father was born, will be as far in the past as the Crimean War is from us today.

Nothing except human nature will be the same. We will have robots to clean our streets and houses and protect them from thieves. And since they will be intelligent and perhaps sentient, they will integrate with our society and perhaps, as the science fiction writers often assume, dominate it. But because they will be programmed by us, they will share some of our characteristics too.

During my son's lifetime, the human race may have trashed the earth so comprehensively that we will have to move across the solar system like a band of wanderers, leaving our junk behind us and making everything ugly wherever we go. Or perhaps we will live under vast geodesic domes in the Sahara and the Australian Outback, safe and protected but always longing to visit the ruins of our once great cities, out in the unvisitable wastelands of Europe and Asia.

Or we may develop in altogether different directions. The fact is, we nearly always get our predictions about the future wrong. When Jules Verne wrote *Twenty Thousand Leagues Under The Sea*, he forecast the nuclear submarine with wonderful acuity. (Its inventor in Jules Verne's original, Captain Nemo, is an Indian nationalist who is seeking revenge for the subjection of his country to the British. Somehow, in the original English translation which is still in use today, this entire aspect of the book was edited out.) But no matter how clearly Verne foresaw the technological future, he got the social future entirely wrong. Often in his science fiction, trim housemaids enter the futuristic scene carrying a silver tray laden with tea things, and open the heavy velour curtains.

In other words, Verne didn't realize that in the future we wouldn't have trim housemaids any longer. He might have got the nuclear submarines and the rockets and the nuclear plants right, but he missed an entire, far-reaching social revolution: the fact that, after the First World War, people would no longer have servants, or want to be servants. In cities right through Europe and the United States, people had to sell up their big houses, with entire floors given over to servants' quarters, and settle for something much smaller. The first known conversion of a mews house, where previously a groom had lived with the horses he was in charge of, into a suitable dwelling for a wealthy young man about town was in 1919. The rather tame version issued in Britain of Cole Porter's song 'Anything Goes' (the one that starts 'In olden days a glimpse of stocking / Was looked on as something shocking') contains the words

> The duke who owns a moated castle
>   Takes lodgers and makes a parcel
> Because he knows
>   Anything goes.

Changes like this would have been entirely unthinkable, impossible, revolutionary, just a couple of decades earlier. They happened, of course, because of a war, which had thrown everything into the melting-pot. I don't imagine, though here I may turn out to be as wrong as Jules Verne, that we will ever again be embroiled in a war between fully developed countries.

The main achievement of the European Union has been to bring together countries which fought each other for a thousand years, and intertwine them so closely that nowadays they scarcely think of each other's citizens as foreign. And though China's political and military power is spreading fast throughout Africa, Asia and Latin America, it's hard to think it will take on the United States in any serious way; though of course I may live to see this anthologized as exactly one of the wrong predictions I have been talking about.

Nowadays, then, we scarcely seem to need wars to bring about faster social change. We have reached the point where it comes of its own accord, and brings more and more change with it. When I was a young man, I carried a rolled umbrella and wore a pin-striped suit to job interviews when I wanted to impress a potential employer, and I spoke a different kind of English from people who had been educated differently from me.

Such a thing simply doesn't happen any more, and thank God for it. I speak differently from the cut-glass way I used to (when I hear my recorded voice from the past, I always wince), and though I'm sorry in a way that one entire type of accent is slipping out of use in Britain, we are well rid of the social divisiveness it caused.

What doesn't really change is the quiet undercurrent of our attitudes. No matter how different the circumstances around us are, our ways of thought tend to stay the same. Recently I found an old collection of songs from the First World War, and glancing down the contents I spotted one called 'The Hymn of Hate', by a singer

called Tom Clare. There were one or two songs of an embarrassingly patriotic type, which seemed to have been written by official
propagandists, and I thought this might be one of them.

The Kaiser was said to have ordained (though it turned out
afterwards to have been an invention of Allied propaganda) that
German troops should spend a minute every morning expressing
their hatred for the British and French troops. Maybe, I thought,
this song was some British equivalent, insulting Germans to order.
But it wasn't. It turned out to be a joke, full of cracks about
aggressive mothers-in-law and girls who wouldn't return a kiss.

> Though I'm not a spiteful sort of chap,
> There are some people I would really like to scrap,
> In my hymn of hate,
> In my cheery little hymn of hate.
>
> I'd like to strafe the man I think
> Who stopped us standing pals a drink,
> And the wife who won't believe her hubby
> When he comes home late . . .

And so on.

There's something agelessly British about that. Throughout
history the response to some high-flown official hate campaign
about national glory and principle would always have been to
reduce it to the level of the pub and the ordinary chap and the
hallway of the terraced house at midnight, and to make fun of it.
You can find that kind of approach throughout Shakespeare and
Chaucer. There's even a faint hint of it (unless I am imagining
things) in Seamus Heaney's translation of *Beowulf*.

British people have always felt uncomfortable in the presence
of too much grandeur and formality. At the Battle of Hastings,
the Norman war-cry was 'God Is Our Help', but the Saxons just
chanted 'Out', because all they wanted was to get rid of the
invaders. Grand emotions, noble sentiments and pompous phrases
have always embarrassed and amused the Anglo-Saxon side of our
national make-up.

Of course, the same instinct exists in many countries. Jaroslav
Hasek's book *The Good Soldier Svejk* is a Czech example, and

there are plenty of others from France, Italy, the US and Germany. But there's something characteristically unexcitable, self-mocking and slightly subversive about the way people in Britain tend to respond to formality and grandeur, and anyone from these islands, especially the Irish, will immediately recognize it and identify with it.

If you listen to people in a factory or a school playground, or go to a theatre and listen to a stand-up comedian, you will hear the same ironic tone. It's something you imbibe instinctively from being in Britain and growing up British; whether your parents or grand-parents came from the Caribbean or from Africa or from the Indian subcontinent, or nowadays from Brazil or China. It's the default attitude of the people who inhabit our country, and over the centuries it has influenced the children of French and Dutch and German immigrants, Jews from Poland and Russia, West Indians, Indians and Pakistanis. They have imbibed it as they imbibe the accents of the areas they grow up in. 'You British Jews,' raved a famously extreme New York rabbi to a Jewish friend of mine, an editor, after he had run a report by someone else which was mildly critical of Israel, 'you are more like the self-hating Brits you live amongst than you are like real Jews.' By 'self-hating' he seems to have meant 'self-questioning'. But he was right; British Jews in Israel are almost always more moderate, more self-questioning than any others. It's a relief to be among them.

The deluded fools who set out to murder their fellow citizens on London's transport system in July 2005 spoke, for the most part, with the accents of Yorkshire and London. But we shouldn't necessarily believe all the stuff spoken by people who should know better about 'the clash of cultures' and the inevitable war between the West and Islam. No such thing exists, and the people who cry it up usually have other agendas.

In a few years the wars in Iraq and Afghanistan will be for-gotten, and the damage they have done will start to fade. After the complete failure of the enterprise in Iraq, neither the United States nor Britain will want to intervene in another Islamic country for some time to come. By the time my son Rafe leaves school, presumably around 2018, all this will be as ancient as the last days of the Cold War are today.

We move from one problem to the next very fast nowadays. From the 1970s to the 1990s there was a constant, underlying threat from Irish terrorism, and the people of the mainland were frightened and bitter about the bombings carried out by the IRA. During those years the BBC was often deluged with complaints about broadcasters with Irish accents – especially John Cole, the political editor, and Dennis Murray, the Northern Ireland correspondent. Now, some of the BBC's best and most popular broadcasters in news and entertainment are Irish, and according to a recent opinion poll, an Irish accent is second only to a Scottish one in the list of British listeners' and viewers' favourites.

We develop quicker than we realize, and we forget just as quickly. There will certainly be new problems, new worries; but I think it's reasonably safe to assume that in an open and relatively free society like Britain, British Islamists won't be a permanently alienated, embittered element in society. I know Norman Angell gave the impression just before the First World War that conflict between the great European powers was impossible, when what he really meant was that it was hard to imagine; and I don't want to find myself joining him in making the same sort of mistake. But that's what my instinct tells me, based on the experience of forty years.

§

The great moral, political and existential issue of our time has nothing to do with Iraq or the Middle East. It is the insanely wasteful way we as a species behave, destroying our own habitat and that of the creatures which have the misfortune to live alongside us. In my lifetime, which is the period of man's greatest wealth and greatest numbers, tens of thousands of species have vanished from the earth. During the 1940s, few would have objected even on moral grounds to anyone heading off to the Indian jungle to shoot a tiger. Since that time, the tiger population has fallen by something like 78 per cent, and three sub-species have become extinct.

Insects such as stag beetles, which I used to see every spring when I was a boy in the London suburbs, and used thoughtlessly to catch and keep in a little box until I set them free again, are now rarely seen. Virtually all types of butterfly are rarer than ever before.

The population of many species of bird suddenly drops without warning; even the once-common house sparrow is under threat. At both ends of the spectrum, the big creatures of distant, under-developed countries and the small, familiar ones in our own back gardens are being elbowed aside. Directly Rafe is old enough to remember the experience, I will take him to see tigers, jaguars, gorillas and polar bears in the wild, so that he can at least take the memory of them into the future.

Yet oddly, although we fear the future and think it will be ugly and empty, we don't necessarily feel that the same is true of the present. The present, for most of us, is just about manageable. Yet if you or I were suddenly transported to the 1940s, and we told the people there how barren the twenty-first century would be, they would be horrified. They, like the Victorians before them, or we now, thought their own time was the measure of how things should be.

The history of life, though, has also been the history of our coming to terms with the changes we have wrought. When I was a student at Cambridge I belonged to a small group at my college called the Kingsley Club, where we wrote and discussed papers about different matters of intellectual interest. (Mine, I remember with embarrassment to this day, was both stupid and boring.) The don in charge was my tutor, Dr Peter Grubb, a biologist with a wonderful Darwinian beard that merely grew bushier and more Darwinian over the years that followed. I still see him regularly at the college, and he is, if anything, more magnificent than ever. One evening he read us a paper about the damage we were inflicting on the natural world, and as I sat there, a cheerful, irreflective, more or less ignorant late adolescent, the tears ran down my cheeks when I heard his words.

That was in 1965. As the years have passed, more and more species have vanished, more and more forest has been destroyed, more and bigger cities have spread over the surrounding region. At such a rate we will kill everything else, and perhaps ourselves as well, by the end of this century.

But even now, at this appallingly late date, it still isn't by any means a certainty. Even among the items of grim ecological news there are often a few more positive ones. In the week or so in spring

2007 during which I have been writing this final chapter, I have gathered together some news items at random. Here they are:

The population of lowland gorillas in Rwanda has stabilized, and is actually increasing.

The largest and most magnificent of the world's big cats, the Amur tiger, has achieved its highest population figure for more than a century, coaxed back from almost certain extinction by Russian and Chinese scientists. Now, although some Russian experts believe that the reduction of their habitat will eventually kill off the Amur tiger, others think there is a reasonable chance that they may survive in the wild.

The blue whale, which is the world's largest mammal, and may be the largest animal ever to have lived on earth, was hunted to the brink of extinction until being protected in the mid-1960s. Now there are thought to be 2,300 in the seas of the southern hemisphere, and there is evidence that their numbers are growing by 7 per cent a year. Although there are no reliable estimates for their numbers in other parts of the world, there is some evidence that their numbers in the North Atlantic are increasing.

Cantor's giant soft-shelled turtle, which grows up to six feet in length and is close to extinction, has been discovered to be thriving in the areas formerly occupied by the Khmer Rouge.

Dedicated work by a British charity, International Animal Rescue, has been remarkably successful in helping to save the brahminy kite in Indonesia, a magnificent bird of prey which has been hunted almost to extinction by illegal traders. People buy them to keep in cages as pets. The charity has succeeded in buying many of them back, and allowing them to recover before releasing them back into the wild, where possible.

There are regular reports in the British press about animals and birds returning to areas they once inhabited. In June 2007 a small group of corn buntings was found in the Scottish Borders, where it had been thought they had more or less died out because of changes in traditional farming practices. Cranes have been nesting at Lakenheath in Suffolk for the first time in four hundred years, because a carrot field has been allowed to revert to fen and marsh.

I don't want to seem like an imitator of Russian state-run television, whose news programmes are now obliged to contain 50 per cent good news. ('News about things like the stock market going up,' a Russian official said, after being asked for an example and having to think for a moment.) The things I have listed are small gains, and some of them are questionable. But they show that the traffic doesn't have to be all one way. With a little care, we can nurse back some at any rate of the life our selfish ways have been choking out.

We will never get back to the way the world was during my childhood in the 1940s. Creatures like the orang-utan, whose numbers are now down to fewer than 30,000 in the wild, may soon survive only in zoos. Eventually, all the great apes could vanish from the wild; not, perhaps in our lifetime but in a hundred years or so.

Dr Richard Leakey, the Kenyan naturalist and anthropologist, believes there is a new threat to them from the effort to find an alternative to oil. Great swathes of forest are being destroyed in Asia and Latin America to make way for palm oil plantations. In Asia, as a result, the habitat of the great apes is being destroyed at a frightening rate. Yet his suggested solution is one which the European Union has employed to bring many species back from almost certain extinction: to pay farmers a competitive rate, rather than rewarding them for not cutting down the forests.

Experience shows that when mankind puts its mind to something, it usually achieves it – even though there are often other consequences which can be just as painful. And slowly people across the world are starting to realize that the natural world has a value. The lowland gorillas of Rwanda are being protected because the local people realize there is more money to be gained from acting as guides than from being poachers. All of the more positive examples I have just quoted are the result of concerted efforts by dedicated groups and individuals. The slide towards extinction is a very real one, but it isn't completely unstoppable.

It would be comforting to think that the same might be true of our planet as a whole. Some experts are moderately hopeful, and think that if governments can be persuaded of the need to act urgently, the situation by 2050 may not be seriously worse than it is at present. All the same, no one I have spoken to believes that the effect of rising sea levels can be avoided, with all that means for low-lying countries such as Bangladesh, or island groups including the Bahamas and the Philippines.

Other climatologists are even more pessimistic. In Australia, for instance – a country which has sided with President George W. Bush in resisting the Kyoto Protocol for reducing greenhouse emissions – a scientific report commissioned by the government of New South Wales suggests that by 2070 there will be a drop of 40 per cent in rainfall there, and temperatures on average five degrees centigrade hotter. Sydney, the report says, could resemble a desert town like Alice Springs.

Some of the worst predictions for the future of our world may well turn out to be wrong, but governments are always reluctant to do anything unpopular, and have to be forced into it by public opinion. Difficult choices lie ahead, yet as science and technology improve, so will our ability to halt, or even reverse, some of the terrible damage we have already done.

Take, for instance, the example of the Aral Sea: one of the worst ecological disasters of my lifetime. Stalin, without consulting his scientists, decreed that the Soviet republic of Uzbekistan should concentrate on growing cotton, which requires very large amounts of water. Long after Stalin was gone, the government of the Soviet Union continued to implement this policy.

In the late 1960s, as part of a drive to bring decision-making a little closer to the people (an idea much in vogue around the world), the entire government of the USSR held a plenary session in Tashkent, the Uzbek capital of Uzbekistan. During it, the deputy minister responsible for irrigation and water resources announced a new initiative to increase cotton production in Kazakhstan and Uzbekistan. The two main rivers of central Asia, the Amu Darya and the Syr Darya, would be diverted so that their waters would flow to the cotton-growing areas.

'But what will happen to the Aral Sea?' someone in the audience asked.

The Aral was the fourth biggest inland body of water in the world, and the two rivers were its major source.

The minister's response was chilling.

'The Aral will have to die off gracefully,' he said.

Its death was very far from graceful. By the 1990s, when I saw it, the Aral had shrunk to a quarter of its old size. The remains of rusting trawlers lay on their sides in the resulting desert, miles from any water. In the grey sand, camels grazed on the colourless grass. It was a vision from a new and dreadful world – the future, I felt, for our planet.

The old nearby port, Aralsk, was a sad place, bitter and resentful and dying, like a neglected patient in a cancer ward. More than half the population had left, and there were very few young people around. The fishermen had to drive or walk across the sands for miles to reach their boats, and there were fewer and fewer fish to catch. Someone had put up a sign which read, 'The sea may have left the harbour, but it hasn't left our hearts.'

And then things changed. The government of Kazakhstan decided, with international help, to reverse the damage. It constructed a dam to divert water back into the northern Aral Sea. Now the water has pushed the desert back, and 40 per cent of it is covered. A second dam is planned, which by 2010 should bring the shoreline right back to the port of Aralsk again.

It isn't the complete answer. The government of Uzbekistan, an unpleasant dictatorship closed to the outside world, has done nothing about its half of the Aral Sea, and there the water level continues to shrink. But the northern sea is a triumphant success. The fish are back in large numbers: flounder, carp, sturgeon. Fishermen are building houses, buying new cars, sending their children to better schools outside the glum little port.

Now there are big white cumulus clouds in the once hard blue empty sky. There is even the promise of occasional rain. It is, quite simply, a miracle of restitution.

§

I just wish Olga could have seen these things. She saw some of them, but not enough.

Olga was the producer and translator I always worked with

when I came to Moscow. She was tall and dark haired and indefinably elegant; not conventionally beautiful, perhaps, but very attractive. She had great presence. I used to call her 'Princess', which annoyed and pleased her in roughly equal measure. Her dark hair, slanting eyes and high cheekbones showed her Tartar ancestry.

Her family had once been landowners, members of the minor nobility. They had several houses in the countryside, and one in Moscow. When the Bolshevik Revolution came in 1917, they lost everything, and were lucky not to lose their lives as well. By the 1920s they were reduced to living in one room of the Moscow house they had once owned. They had to share a kitchen, bathroom and lavatory with seven other families.

Quietly, carefully, the family taught its children to conform outwardly to everything the Stalinist state demanded of them, but to think differently in their own minds. They were taught not to grab everything they could lay their hands on, not to lie and cheat, not to betray people for their own advancement. They had a hard time of it during the 1920s, when being bourgeois could mean a death sentence, and during the late 1930s, when hundreds of thousands were denounced as enemies of the people by their envious neighbours. In the Second World War, several family members were killed.

Olga was born in the late 1950s, when things were starting to improve. A solitary child by choice, she too was taught to think differently. At school, she stayed a little apart from the others. The authorities scarcely bothered to put pressure on her to join the communist youth groups, knowing that she was unpromising material and that she would refuse. There was little chance of getting into university, because for that you had to conform. But she could become a journalist. In Russia, as everywhere else, there are no class barriers, no hierarchies, in newspapers or television.

She met and married another outsider, a Jew. The two of them were dissidents and free-thinkers, and suffered further during the Brezhnev years. They had an only daughter, and then drifted apart. Olga met a visiting BBC journalist, who recommended her to other people. She was fanatical about succeeding in her work. If you asked her to set up an interview with the prime minister, as I did – it was Viktor Chernomyrdin – she would never accept the possibility that she might fail. Most, though not quite all, the Russians in the BBC office disliked her, and the feeling was mutual.

'They are all communists,' she would say dismissively – and wrongly, as it happened.

But she did have a couple of friends in the office, and they faithfully recommended her to every visiting crew from London.

By the time she and I worked together regularly, Olga was prospering. She was able to send her daughter, whom she worshipped, to an expensive private school, and she wore good though not showy clothes.

Sometimes she disapproved of me, with my brash Western ways. She hated it when I refused to take my winter coat off in offices and hotels, and even though she disliked officialdom and treated the jacks-in-office with disdain, she didn't like it when I started shouting at them. My Edwardian grandmother would have liked her, and would have called her a lady. And she was.

She was always an outsider still, and the Putin government didn't like her any more than the Yeltsin one had; yet both recognized her as a force of nature which couldn't be tamed. By now she was being hired by teams who made big-budget feature films, and she found it increasingly hard to get the time to work for television news. For me, though, she always made an exception.

I last saw her not in Moscow, but in Paris, when I was coming out of the Sephora cosmetics shop in the Champs Elysées with Dee. She had a group of six people with her, all close relatives, and had obviously paid for the family trip. She and Dee always got on very well, and it was a delightful meeting.

The following year I started to hear rumours that she was ill. Then someone told me she had died. I couldn't believe it; she was only forty-two. But the effort of living a life outside the system had been too much for a heart that was weakened by a hard life, bad food, and too little happiness.

Olga was as much a victim of Russia's painful past as anyone else. Working there, especially on your own, was immensely stressful. Just when it became acceptable to be an aristocrat again, her body had let her down. All those years of poverty and of fighting for a living had been too much for her.

Dear Olga: she always used to tell me that she would die young, but I thought she was just being melodramatic. She also told me that it was bad luck, or bad manners – for her the two were pretty much the same – to put the wrong number of flowers on her grave. So far I haven't been able to bring myself to visit it. But when I do, I will make sure to have the correct number of white lilies to lay on it. She won't rest properly if I get it wrong.

§

When you reduce things to headline form, they can look pretty fierce. My career, for instance.

I have been reporting for forty years, from the days of the Vietnam War and Watergate, of violence in Ireland and wage freezes and economic downturns and sudden rises in the price of oil, of weak government and strikes and ungovernability, to the rivalry of the superpowers, the Thatcherite revolution and the end of the old, comfortable, inefficient and ultimately ruinous ways of running national economies, and the sudden lack of stability which followed the collapse of the Soviet bloc and led to a number of vicious small wars, right through to the invasion of Iraq, the militant Islamism of today, and the overwhelming threat to our future posed by our grossly wasteful habits.

There, in just over a hundred words, is the story of our times. It's nothing remotely like the whole story, of course: that would have to take in the remarkable, thoroughgoing social revolution that we have undergone, so silent that no one in Britain speaks about it; the economic resurgence which has reshaped our lives; and the technological revolution that remakes our entire experience every couple of years, and leads us to wonder how on earth we could have existed without Wi-Fi, or iPods, or the mobile phone, or even the humble, superannuated fax machine.

By the time this book appears in paperback, there will probably be some new gadget that will define our times; and by the time the book ends up in the '5p to clear' box outside your local bookshop, if there are such things as bookshops and 5p's by then, all these things will have been eclipsed by inventions which will have taken us into a newer world altogether.

But the story of my career so far amounts to four pretty disturbed decades, and although it has kept me in a job – no one, as far as I can recall, has ever suggested that journalists might not be required in future because of a lack of work – I have sometimes wished I could turn to something quieter and more positive: arts reporting, perhaps, or archaeology, or religious affairs.

One of my earliest pieces of reporting, before I even joined the BBC, was about a new organization called Amnesty International. It had been in existence for only a couple of years when I, a skinny, rather innocent student at Cambridge University, went to its head-quarters in the magically named Turnagain Lane, near Blackfriars in the City of London, to write an article about it for an American newspaper in 1964.

It was a labour of love. Even as a teenager I had been profoundly affected by stories of people who stood up for their own and other people's rights, and suffered the consequences. Amnesty International existed to remember those people, and to campaign for their release. The people I interviewed showed me photographs of the hundreds of people on their books: victims of cruelty and brutality, whose ultimate fate might well depend on the fact that they weren't forgotten – that their names were spoken and passed on, and that free people chose to remember them with honour.

More than forty years later I was obliged to sever my formal links with Amnesty International and ask them to take my name off their literature. It was one of the sadder moments of my career, and it came about as a tiny part of the fall-out from the Hutton Report and the way the BBC had reported the British government's use of intelligence in the run-up to the invasion of Iraq. One of the recommendations resulting from an internal BBC inquiry was that no one who worked for the Corporation should be formally connected with any campaigning organization. I could see the point: there could easily be a clash of interests if I had to report on some controversy that Amnesty might be involved in. But it was a depressing event.

Since the day in 1964 when I went to Turnagain Lane and saw some of Amnesty's case files, the observance of human rights has changed quite remarkably throughout the world. Amnesty now has more names on its books than ever, but that is the result of a greater, deeper understanding of the many ways in which human rights are under assault. Under the cruder, more obvious practices of 1964, dozens of governments simply killed, imprisoned or tortured anyone who criticized them, and did it in silence.

This still happens, of course: in Zimbabwe, in Burma, in Russia, and plenty of other countries. But the world isn't what it was. Latin America and Africa are no longer the natural homes of military dictatorship. There are far more democracies and semi-democracies than there are autocracies. And most importantly, the argument for human rights has been well and truly won. Once, plenty of governments were fairly open about the fact that they were repressive. Nowadays they know this is something they have to hide.

In the mid-1960s there were dozens of wars around the globe: small-time affairs, mostly, which few of us had even heard about. Forty years later, there are very few wars, though we hear a lot about them. Countries which seemed likely to be shackled for ever against their will, like the nations of eastern Europe, the Baltic and the Balkans, are now part of the European Union. South Africa, once isolated from the rest of the world by its deliberately wrongful and cruel policies, is now a free, prosperous and multiracial society.

So we shouldn't necessarily be too depressed. The history of my time as a reporter is certainly the history of violence and suffering, but it is also the period when international agreements and the rule of law have come to dominate the behaviour of the vast majority of countries. In 1966 countries expected to take their own decisions and do what they wanted; nowadays they have to pay far more attention to the will of the international community. It was the determination of the government of President George W. Bush to go its own way, regardless of the opinion of much of the rest of the world, which created so much hostility in response to the invasion of Iraq.

'We are America,' said an article in the increasingly right-wing *Wall Street Journal* in 2002; 'we do what we believe to be right.' Yet as the disaster in Iraq unfolded, public opinion in the United States changed. By 2007 an opinion poll found that 82 per cent of Americans thought it would be a mistake to take action without international support.

How Groucho Marx would have loved President George W. Bush! In *Duck Soup*, the best of the Marx Brothers films, he plays Rufus T. Firefly, president of the nation of Freedonia. His long-suffering sidekick, played by Margaret Dumont ('Why,' he says elsewhere, 'you're one of the most beautiful women I've ever seen, and that's not saying much for you') asks him to outline his policy, and he sings:

> The last man nearly ruined this place,
>   He didn't know what to do with it,
> If you think this country's bad off now,
>   Just wait till I get through with it.

Groucho Marx would have loved Tony Blair's government, too, with its endless attempts to change bad social behaviour by legislating against it:

> No one's allowed to smoke,
> Or tell a dirty joke,
> And whistling is prohibited.

> If chewing-gun is chewed,
> The chewer is pursued,
> And in the hoosegow hidden.

> If any form of pleasure is exhibited,
> Report to me and it will be prohibited.

> I'll put my foot down, so shall it be.
> This is the land of the free.

At some stage quite soon, Zimbabwe and Burma and Tibet and Iraq and Iran and Sudan will cease to be the problems they are as I write these words, and the foreign correspondents who spent their time there will head off somewhere else. That is the lesson of South Africa and of Russia and elsewhere: today's problems will be obliterated by tomorrow's.

Rather, like H. G. Wells, I believe that science will provide us with solutions to the problems of global warming and of pandemic diseases. No doubt we will lose a great deal of what makes our lives colourful and interesting today. Yet the more colour and interest, by and large, the shorter the life. 'Globalization' is a depressing thing, if it means a Starbucks on every corner, everywhere. It's even more depressing if it means that some dreary American or Japanese or German or British businessman can both dictate our tastes, and make sure there is no alternative.

But globalization doesn't only mean that. It also means that countries are much less able to go their own arrogant way, smashing others in their path. The world requires a referee, an honest broker. What it has, of course, is the United Nations: not quite the same thing. Nowadays the UN seems feebler than ever, with the genial but hardly forceful figure of Ban Ki-moon as its Secretary-General. No one who was in Baghdad watching as Ban's press conference in the Green Zone was interrupted by a mortar bomb landing outside will easily forget the way he flinched and ducked. Poor Mr Ban: he seemed utterly out of place as a peacemaker. The Iraqi prime minister Nouri al-Maliki, who was standing beside him, scarcely blinked: Iraqis have become used to hearing loud bangs close by.

Nevertheless, the United Nations does have a validity which no other organization on earth has, and I doubt very much whether anything quite like the American and British invasion of Iraq will ever happen again. The lesson of George W. Bush's carelessness and rashness will lie quite heavily on this generation and the next. With luck, the world of the future will be, on balance, a more peaceable place. But if it is, it will certainly be a little duller.

§

On Christmas morning 2006, the weather on the southern coast of South Africa was overcast, but with that unspoken assurance that tells you it's going to be a really good day later on. We woke up early in the house we were renting from Jan Smuts' nephew in Nature's Valley. Rafe was already well awake, standing up in his cot beside our bed, grinning at us but not making the slightest noise. He is the most tactful of children. Still, there was no chance that I could lay him down in the middle of the bed between us so we could all get half an hour's extra sleep.

We got dressed instead, and I put him in his back-pack and hoisted him up behind me. In the garden, a couple of Hadeda ibises flew down with the harsh cry that gives them their name, and started rooting around with their long, curved bills. We walked through the woods towards the beach. Yellow butterflies played together, fluttering in and out of a patch of sunlight, and a beautiful dark one with brilliant stripes of electric blue landed near me, almost as big as my hand. Rafe made a hooning sound, pursing his lips with excitement and pleasure, making the kind of chimpanzee mouth which the newspaper cartoonist Steve Bell gave George W. Bush.

We were the only people on the beach: a mile of yellow sand, with the surf breaking languidly on it, and the mist rising off the lagoon at the far end. The three of us sat down, and Rafe crawled around in the sand, looking for unsuitable things to put in his mouth. Dee and I didn't speak much: it was too beautiful for that. And as we sat watching, a southern right whale rose majestically out of the sea and crashed back into the sea, throwing up water in great sheets.

Soon afterwards a school of dolphins passed through the bay, curving elegantly out of the surf again and again, as if they were showing off to anyone who might happen to be on shore watching. It was all too much for me: the whale, the dolphins, the mist, Dee beside me and the little, almost unhoped-for boy delving into the sand and making his crooning noises. Getting older has made me much more emotional, and having a young child has peeled off layer after layer of protective armour.

A couple of years ago I wrote a book about my childhood, which was immensely painful for me and dealt with the break-up of my parents' marriage and my decision, at just under seven, to stay with my father rather than my mother – a decision which did damage both to her and to me. Nearly sixty years later, with another young child to watch over, I'm still trying to sort it all out.

It's not easy. It's so complicated, for one thing, and for another these are matters as sensitive as a field of landmines. On the kitchen wall of the house where we are staying is a quotation from Carl Gustav Jung, Smuts' friend, which haunts me. There is a relevance to me and my life, I know, but I can't entirely grasp it. The meaning comes closer then moves away, like the yellow butterflies in the patch of sunlight:

> But what if I should discover that the very enemy himself is within me, that I myself am the enemy who must be loved – what then?

Somehow I can feel all these things coming together in my life, rearranging themselves, sorting themselves out. Perhaps I don't have to understand it all. Maybe I must just yield to it.

But what if – I sound like Jung now – the point of living isn't to be placid and happy and untouched by the world, but to be deeply, painfully sensitive to it, to see its cruelty and savagery for what they are, and accept all this as readily as we accept its beauty? To feel the force of everything we see around us? To be touched by it, moved by it, hurt by it even, but not be indifferent to it?

And its beauty is so wonderfully, extraordinarily moving on this December morning. The waves throw themselves onto the shore, as green as the lightest coloured jade, the white spume trailing off in the air, the droplets of water thrown skywards and falling again as the wave dies. And, as beautiful as that was, there is always another one to take its place immediately. The wave vanishes, but the tide continues.

The school of dolphins rises up again against the cool yellow sky, an albatross floats serenely above them, its great wings arched with a kind of easy purity. All of us in our different ways, the whale, the dolphins, the albatross and the three of us sitting close to each other on the windy beach, are endangered species now. But the very briefness of our time here adds to the beauty. Perhaps it isn't a handicap to have suffered, and to know for a certainty that you will suffer again; perhaps that's what makes it possible to get a glimpse of the magnificence surrounding us, and never forget it.

Rafe digs energetically in the sand, crooning to himself. A few days short of his first birthday, he takes no notice of the whale, the dolphins, the albatross. He knows nothing of their value and their rarity.

Will he be Aeneas to my Anchises, and carry me on his back in my old age, as I carry him now? What extraordinary sights will his merry eyes rest on during his lifetime?

He shifts, and I look significantly at Dee.

'He'll need a fresh nappy soon,' I say.

Index